Paul

Paul

The Theology of the Apostle in the Light
of Jewish Religious History

H.J. Schoeps

Translated by Harold Knight

James Clarke Co., Ltd.
Cambridge

Published by
James Clarke Co.
P.O. Box 60
Cambridge
CB1 2NT
England

e-mail: **publishing@jamesclarke.co.uk**
website: **http://www.jamesclarke.co.uk**

ISBN 0 227 17014 8 hardback
ISBN 0 227 17013 X paperback

British Library Cataloguing in Publication Data:
A catalogue record is available from the British Library.

Copyright ©1959 Hans Joachim Schoeps
Translation Copyright © 1961 The Lutterworth Press

First published 1961 by The Lutterworth Press
Reprinted 2002

Contents

Chapter 3

THE ESCHATOLOGY OF THE APOSTLE PAUL

Chapter 4

THE SOTERIOLOGY OF THE APOSTLE PAUL

CONTENTS

Abbreviations

AfZ	H. J. Schoeps, *Aus frühchristlicher Zeit*, Tübingen, 1950
Am	Amora, Amoraic
ARW	*Archiv für Religionswissenschaft*
ATAO	A. Jeremias, *Das Alte Testament im Lichte des alten Orients*
Billerbeck	*Kommentar zum NT aus Talmud und Midrasch I–IV*, ed. Strack-Billerbeck, Stuttgart, 1922
BZAW	*Beihefte der Zeitschrift für alttestamentliche Wissenschaft*
BZNW	*Beihefte der Zeitschrift für die neutestamentliche Wissenschaft*
CSEL	*Corpus scriptorum ecclesiasticorum latinorum*, Vienna, 1866 ff.
DG	*Dogmengeschichte*
DLZ	*Deutsche Literaturzeitung*
DSD	*Dead Sea Scrolls, Manual of Discipline*
DSH	*Dead Sea Scrolls, Habakkuk Commentary*
E(en). J(ud).	*Encyclopaedia Judaica*/Das Judentum in Geschichte und Gegenwart
GCS	*Griechische Christliche Schriftsteller*, herausgegeben von der Kirchenväterkommission der Preußischen Akademie der Wissenschaften zu Berlin
Hom	ʽΟμιλίαι, *Rezension des pseudoklementinischen Romans*
HThR	*Harvard Theological Review*, Cambridge, Mass.
HUCA	*Hebrew Union College Annual*, Cincinnati, 1924 ff.
JBL	*Journal of Biblical Literature*
J(ew). E(nc).	*Jewish Encyclopaedia*, London
JJ St	*Journal of Jewish Studies*, Cambridge
JQR	*Jewish Quarterly Review*, Philadelphia
JR	*Journal of Religion*, Chicago
Kittel *WB*	*Theologisches Wörterbuch zum Neuen Testament*, ed. G. Kittel, Stuttgart, 1933 ff.

MGWJ	*Monatsschrift für Geschichte und Wissenschaft des Judentums*
MPG	J. P. Migne, *Patrologiae cursus completus, series graeca*
MPL	J. P. Migne, *Patrologiae cursus completus, series latina*
NT Studies	*New Testament Studies*, Cambridge
NTT	*Norsk Teologisk Tidskrift*, Oslo
RB	*Revue Biblique*, Paris
Rec	*Recognitiones, Rezension des pseudoklementinischen Romans*
REJ	*Revue des Études juives*, Paris
RHPhR	*Revue d'Histoire et de Philosophie religieuses*, Strasbourg
RHR	*Revue de l'Histoire des Religions*, Paris
RLAChr	*Reallexikon für Antike und Christentum*, ed. Klauser
RThPh	*Revue de Théologie et de Philosophie*, Lausanne
SAB	*Sitzungsberichte der Preußischen Akademie der Wissenschaften Berlin*, Phil.-Hist. Klasse
SB	*Sitzungsberichte*
SEA	*Svensk Exegetisk Årsbok*, Uppsala
Tann	Tannaite
ThBl	*Theologische Blätter*
TheolJchr	H. J. Schoeps, *Theologie und Geschichte des Judenchristentums*, Tübingen, 1949
ThLZ	*Theologische Literaturzeitung*
ThR	*Theologische Rundschau*
Th. St. u. Kr.	*Theologische Studien und Kritiken*
ThZ	*Theologische Zeitschrift*, Basel
VT	*Vetus Testamentum*, Leiden
WZKM	*Wiener Zeitschrift zur Kunde des Morgenlandes*
ZAW	*Zeitschrift für alttestamentliche Wissenschaft*
ZKG	*Zeitschrift für Kirchengeschichte*
ZMR	*Zeitschrift für Missionskunde und Religionswissenschaft*
ZNW	*Zeitschrift für die neutestamentliche Wissenschaft*
ZRGG	*Zeitschrift für Religions- und Geistesgeschichte*, ed. H. J. Schoeps
ZSTh	*Zeitschrift für systematische Theologie*
ZThK	*Zeitschrift für Theologie und Kirche*
Z.wiss. Theol.	*Zeitschrift für wissenschaftliche Theologie*, ed. A. Hilgenfeld

Preface

COMPREHENSIVE studies of Paul have become rare indeed. The interest which, from the time of the first world war, the "History of Religion" school took in this fateful figure has been in the meantime transferred to other questions and problems, so that even in my student days I felt that despite Deissmann and Schweitzer there was here a disquieting gap. In consequence I began to plan the writing of this book on Paul, considered against the background of the history of the Jewish religion. The first draft of it was prepared twenty years ago. Then came my derivative investigations on the Ebionites, which prevented me from finally drafting my study on Paul, and my manuscript about him was perforce set aside. When I returned to the figure of this great opponent of the Judaists, I realized the necessity of rewriting the entire work, although I went back to my first draft and took over the arrangement of it almost without modification.

I find it an advantage to approach the study of Pauline theology as an impartial historian of religion, and as one who also wishes to do justice to the Judaism whence Paul sprang. Many matters are more clearly seen (especially in regard to the genesis of ideas) if one is not hindered by confessional allegiances from thinking through, to the end, dangerous trains of thought. Critics are not for the most part aware of the inner censorship under which their thoughts really stand. It must also be remembered, however, that the "History of Religion" approach with its emphasis on externals has its disadvantages as well, because it cannot enter fully into the inner faith of the apostle, since that rests on personal assent to the Christian religion. In this respect the Christian theologian is "engaged" in quite a different way, and is able to interpret the apostle's articulation of his faith on the basis of that Christian profession which he holds in common with him. The unbeliever, and the scholar who holds a different belief, remain dependent on sheer critical understanding. And to understand so great a man as the apostle Paul and the movements of his mind is a very considerable undertaking.

How far the present author has succeeded in doing so is a matter for the reader of this book to decide, and he on his part is asked, in the interests of truth, to overlook much that might be offensive and shocking to him. He is also asked to bear in mind that the historian of religion who tries to understand the apostle in the light of the special concerns of Jewish religious history will inevitably see misunderstandings where the Christian theologian sees evidence of divine guidance, even that by which Saul became Paul, and, according to the Christian faith, was really transformed into a new creation —a new man in Christ. These two views can never be adjusted to each other.

I would like to express here my thanks to my colleague W. G. Kümmel of Marburg, who undertook the labour of reading through my manuscript before it went to press, and who advised me on a number of special points, although he of course sees many things in a different light and assesses them differently from myself. I am also grateful to Dr. E. L. Ehrlich (Basle) for certain references. Dr. H. Pölcher once again has given me his kind assistance in the reading of proofs.

HANS JOACHIM SCHOEPS

Erlangen, January 1, 1959

I

PRESENT POSITION AND PROBLEMS INVOLVED IN PAULINE RESEARCH

Introduction

THE apostle Paul is a truly great figure. His greatness is shown in the very fact that he has found no congenial interpreter and probably never will. From Marcion to Karl Barth, from Augustine to Luther, Schweitzer or Bultmann, he has ever been misunderstood or partially understood, one aspect of his work being thrown into relief while others have been misunderstood and neglected. But if Paul offers so many possibilities of misunderstanding, is so capable of varied interpretations and modes of approach, the suspicion of ambiguity and confusion at once arises. This suspicion is not without foundation. For Paul, who sprang from the heart of Pharisaic Judaism and became the pioneer in propagating the Christian gospel among the heathen, had a self-contradictory nature, and by his background and course of mental and spiritual development was a product of diverse cultural *milieux*. Thrown by the pressures of his fate into a many-sided situation in life, in many respects aggressive, in others the victim of aggression, he finally became the first and the greatest Christian theologian. But his theology was that of a completely unique situation which will never recur. Compelled to be a theologian only by the exigencies of this historical situation, he has fallen into the.hands of the professional theologians of all times, who have thought to see and honour in him their ancestor and colleague. Nevertheless, the missionary apostle of Jesus Christ was no professor of theology—neither systematic nor exegetical—and there awaited him in the eventide of his life the very suitable and distinguished fate of martyrdom, just as the modern professor is rewarded with the distinction of the title "emeritus".

The generic difference between the existence of an apostle of Jesus Christ and that of a university professor has been acutely realized by the public consciousness since the time of Sören Kierkegaard's "insights" and implicitly delimits the scope of a professor's systems of thought. Within such limits, however, it is entirely his duty to make statements as to how Paul and his teaching may be most suitably understood. For not only the specialist exegete but every attentive reader of the Bible is constantly being provoked by the personality of Paul and the theology of his letters, and will always face them with a mind full of questionings. In the last hundred years erudite criticism and research into the origins of Christianity has contributed greatly to the task of enabling us to see Paul in truer perspective than was possible to earlier times. For, with a view to recognizing the "true shape of things", it has set out to reconstruct the historical situation of primitive Christianity, which is at least as multi-coloured, complex, self-contradictory, and confusing as is the political, cultural, and intellectual situation of our own times. Learned research is able to determine, and sees its appointed task in determining with approximate correctness, the position of the apostle Paul within the currents of cultural development characteristic of his age, within those situations of struggle into which he was cast by fate, in sketching an historically accurate picture of his doctrines and religious convictions, even though it has ever to bear in mind the dictum of Franz Overbeck: [1] "Nowadays no one has understood Paul if he still thinks he can agree with him. The opponents of this assertion involuntarily confirm it by the way in which they distort his words in order to wrest from them a satisfactory meaning."

Since Ferdinand Christian Baur's book on Paul (1866), which is still worth reading and which founded the "positive" criticism of the Tübingen school, a Hellenistic, a Judaic–Hellenistic, and a Rabbinical method of interpretation have appeared in turn. In consequence Paul has been understood and described as a chiliast, a mystic, a gnostic, an adept of the mystery religions, a Hellenist, and a Rabbi, and in the light of the numerous combinations which these make possible. Many of the differences between the critics, who have struggled fiercely with each other, have, however, been apparent differences only, since these conflicts have often arisen from the varying use of significant terms (Hellenism, gnosis, mysticism, eschatology, and so on). Much harm has been done in particular by unjust comparisons, by the fact that where genealogy failed or was difficult to establish, critics have shown a mania for collecting analogies, from which nothing can seriously be demonstrated. If, on the other hand,

[1] *Christentum und Kultur*, Basel, 1919, 54.

we take the point of view of life-history, and hence look to the apostle's background and course of life, then the three principal methods of approach just indicated are seen to have their inner justification because they refer to the main intellectual forces in the climate of his age, and come into question as possible sources or influential factors. Hence, with a view to elucidating the series of historical problems which beset this attempt to interpret the great apostle on the basis of the history of religion and civilization, let us sketch the bases and the main motives of the various ramifications of research, although for this purpose Albert Schweitzer's *Geschichte der paulinischen Forschung*, Tübingen, 1911 (E.T. *Paul and His Interpreters*) has not been referenced nor—what would be very desirable—continued,[1] neither do we at this stage propose to enter into the discussion of detailed problems and the controversies of investigators.

I. THE HELLENISTIC APPROACH TO THE INTERPRETATION OF PAUL

(a) *Being in the mystery religions*

The Hellenistic approach to the interpretation of Paul is a product of the so-called "History of Religion" school (Usener, Dieterich, Anrich, Bousset, Cumont, Reitzenstein, etc.) which could appeal to the fact that Paul, apart from the few years of his stay in Jerusalem, lived constantly in a purely heathen environment and must have been accessible to its influences. In particular, Richard Reitzenstein[2] wished to show systematically that in the work of Paul we are confronted by a consistent amalgamation of pagan Hellenistic mystery conceptions with a Judaic stock of ideas. It was suggested that with him the faith of the Hellenistic mystery religions was interwoven with the prophetic faith of ancient Israel to form quite a new product. Reitzenstein rightly saw the non-Jewish character of many a Pauline antithesis, such as πνεῦμα—ψυχή, πνεῦμα—σάρξ, ἔργα—πίστις etc., which, on the other hand, we do find in the sphere of gnosticism. He went on to point out further that Paul "imitates the technical use of the term γνῶσις, which is characteristic of Hellenism" (43) and accordingly he wished to "place him in this line of development, not as the first, but as the greatest of the gnostics" (56).

---

[1] A summary is given in ch. 2 of his later work: *Die Mystik des Apostels Paulus*, Tübingen, 1930, E.T. *The Mysticism of Paul the Apostle*. (Cited as Schweitzer: *Mystik*.)

[2] *Die hellenistischen Mysterienreligionen*, Leipzig, 1927; for Hellenistic elements in the cultural development of the apostle, cf. S. M. Gilmour, "Paul and the Primitive Church", *JR*, 1945, 119 ff.

He adduced conceptions of deification and rebirth proper to the Hellenistic mystery religions as providing analogies to Pauline soteriology, and as capable of illuminating even if not of explaining the latter. For Paul never speaks of rebirth or deification, but of resurrection and "life in Christ", by which he implies a Spirit-filled type of existence flowing from faith.

Further, Reitzenstein, rightly proceeding from the fact that there are to be found in the vocabulary of the apostle terms and concepts which demonstrably play a part in the language of mystery theology as well, has made impressive reference to the Hermetic writings in particular, which in many places bring together γνῶσις and φῶς just as Paul likewise speaks of the φωτισμὸς τῆς γνώσεως (2 Cor. 4:6). Hellenistic mystery religion understands stages of gnosis and illumination as implying transformation of being; the adept as a result of his initiation becomes a *renatus in aeternum*. The vision of the divine glory changes the beholder into the bearer of this glory. A mystery prayer of the *Corpus Hermeticum* (XIII, 19) runs: τὸ πᾶν ἀπὸ σοῦ καὶ ἐπὶ σὲ τό πᾶν τὸν νοῦν τὸν ἐν ἡμῖν σῶζε, ζωή, φώτιζε, φῶς τὴν ψυχήν... σῶζε ζωή πνεῦμα θεέ (Scott 252). Reitzenstein comments: "God, who is πνεῦμα, gives to the initiate pneumatic character by imparting ἀθανασία and γνῶσις" (120). But the hermetic mystery of rebirth is not the same thing as the Pauline mystery of resurrection; so much is clear, yet the latter stands close to the former.

For Reitzenstein, apocalyptic and rabbinical writings do not enter into the question. He feels that Oriental spirituality—the mystery religions, the hermetic literature, and Mandaeism offer closer points of contact. For him analogies from Greek and Oriental syncretism over a broad field furnish a means of explaining Pauline theology on the basis of the "History of Religion" school. He starts from the presupposition that Paul the "syncretist" had concerned himself with the literary documents of all these religions and cults when equipping himself for the task of preaching among the Hellenists. Schweitzer (*Mystik*, 29) is right when he scoffs at Reitzenstein's picture of Paul in the following terms: "This Paul who prepared himself by suitable reading for his vocation as a missionary has been so distorted into a professorial figure that he no longer bears any resemblance to the character who meets us in the letters." This witticism would have been still more appropriate if directed against Karl v. Hase, since the latter in his *Kirchengeschichte* (Leipzig, 1885) did in fact say of Paul: "He is a scholar like one of us, only more highly gifted" (152).

(b) *City and public mystery cults*

The question of the influence of the mystery religions on the apostle, which Reitzenstein supported simply as a fact, gains in plausibility when, looking at the life of the apostle, we ask the question what kind of mystery cult could have been known to him with homely familiarity in his youth. It is well known that Paul was born in the Cilician port of Tarsus in the south of modern Turkey, the "Athens of Asia Minor", which was not only a large emporium for trade and commerce but also a focal point for cultural influences, for religious and mystery cults of all kinds. According to Acts 7: 57 he first left Tarsus for Jerusalem as a νεανίας, probably when sixteen or seventeen years old. We have evidence that Tarsus was the centre of the cult of the vegetation deity Sandan, which resembled the mystery cults proper. Dio Chrysostom indicates that this city god was also venerated under the Greek name of Heracles. In honour of Sandan-Heracles there was celebrated every year in Tarsus a funeral pyre festival, at the climax of which the image of the god was burned. The dying of nature under the withering heat of the summer sun and its resurrection to new life was the content of this mystery, which at once suggests its kinship with the cults of the Syrian Adonis, the Phrygian Attis, the Egyptian Osiris, and the Babylonian Tammuz. For the dying and the rising again of vegetation gods was the essence of them all.

H. Böhlig,[1] to whom we owe an exhaustive monograph on Tarsus, thought it possible to prove the soteriological character of the feast, since numerous inscriptions refer to the θεοὶ σωτῆρες. That the young Saul had seen processions in honour of this deity in the market-place or the streets of Tarsus is something which, of course, cannot be demonstrated, but appears highly probable. He would have known them as to-day every citizen of Britain knows his Bank Holidays. It is certainly not possible to postulate that this *milieu* influenced with an "inner rigid necessity" the development of Paul's later Christo-centric soteriology,[2] but none the less many traits of his world of ideas are more easily understandable if we may assume the associative influence of the apostle's youthful memories, which

---

[1] *Die Geisteskultur von Tarsus im augusteischen Zeitalter mit Beurteilung der paulinischen Schriften*, Heidelberg, 1913; cf. further A. Steinmann, *Zum Werdegang des Paulus, die Jugendzeit in Tarsus*, Freiburg, 1928, and now W. C. van Unnik, *Tarsos of Jerusalem, de Stad van Paulus Jeugd*, Medel. d. Kon. Nederl. Akad. van Wetensch., Afd. Letterkunde N. R. Deel 15, 5, Amsterdam, 1952.

[2] E. Barnikol (*Die vorchristliche und frühchristliche Zeit des Paulus*, Kiel, 1929) had already protested against these exaggerations.

will have gained a new colouring from similar travel impressions received later.

Further, we may mention here the ancient imperial cult with its solemn apotheoses which was strictly observed in the whole Imperium Romanum, and therefore also in Tarsus.[1] It is in consequence of the traditional devotional material of the Orient that the *Divus Augustus* was also described as κύριος and σωτήρ. In Phil. 3: 20 Paul seems to have used the imperial titles of this official religion when he here describes Christ as the "emperor" of Christians awaited from above. According to Josephus at least (*Ant.* 12, 3, 1 f.) the Jews were officially exempted from compulsory participation in this cult. As a public institution it was, of course, known everywhere; but the veneration of the emperor did not exercise any greater influence either on Christian thought in general or on the formation of Paul's world of ideas in particular, and this consideration reduced many a bold hypothesis to its true proportions.[2]

(c) The "kyrios" cult

Wilhelm Bousset[3] proceeded more cautiously. In consequence of his uncommon knowledge of the history of religions, he approached the problem from a much more comprehensive point of view. He, too, was of the opinion that syncretistic influences were very strong in the formation of early Christianity and were responsible for the fact that, from the original and simple gospel of Jesus, there developed a religion of redemption centred in the mystery cult of the Christ. He saw the axis of this development in the Kyrios cult, which the early Christians coming from Hellenistic circles already brought with them. On the analogy of the many divine "lords" in the Orient, in Hellas and in Rome, the first Hellenistic Christian communities had in fact given their cult hero the title which was intended to describe the sovereign position of Jesus in the practice of divine worship. It was supposed that "the name above every name" of Phil. 2: 9, the holy cult-name of the Old Testament Yahweh, the almighty God, had been transferred to His chosen and anointed one.

---

[1] Cf. Art. "Herrscherkult", *PWK*, Suppl. IV, 826 ff.; E. Lohmeyer: *Christuskult und Kaiserkult*, Tübingen, 1919; H. Frankfort: *The Kingship and the Gods*, Chicago, 1948.

[2] According to St. Lösch: *Deitas Jesu und antike Apotheose*, Rottenburg, 1933 (65), the apotheosis of the early Roman emperors was a mere titular ceremonial, since there was no real belief in the divinity of the wearer of the crown.

[3] *Kyrios Christos, Geschichte des Christusglaubens von den Anfängen des Christentums bis Irenäus*, Göttingen, 1921.

Paul had been confronted by this fundamental conviction of the primitive Christian Hellenistic communities with regard to Jesus, the "cult hero, present to His church and revered by it as Kyrios" (90). This conviction had emerged "in the region of the unconscious, in the uncontrollable depths of the collective psyche of a community" (99). No doubt those central ideas of Pauline Christology, κύριος and υἱὸς θεοῦ, have points of contact with Judaism as well as with heathen religions, but it is simpler to understand Paulinism in the light of Hellenistic cult piety with its ideas of the θεῖος ἄνθρωπος (117 ff.).

The "Hellenization" of Christianity was prepared for by the sacramental cult of Jesus as Kyrios, a cult of which Paul was the leader. He then completed the process of Hellenization by his spread of the gospel from Palestinian to Hellenistic territory. Thus it was suggested that Paul introduced a cult of the Risen Christ, stemming from the mystery religions. Even if Paul himself avoided the use of a divine predicate for the Kyrios Christos, the massive faith of the community must, in short, have gone further (154).

Schweitzer (*Mystik* 31) has characterized Bousset's standpoint as follows:

> Paul is not so much the Hellenizer of Christianity as a purifying influence through which pass the waters of the Christian faith, muddied by Hellenization. Bousset's theory however is ruined by the fact that it is not really possible to prove the existence, in Hellenistic communities (e.g. that of Antioch) of a sacramental Kyrios cult, supposedly disclosing the roots of Pauline mysticism, alongside the faith in Christ the Messiah.

That there is no objective basis in Pauline thought for the problem of Hellenization or syncretization, was therefore the judgment of another interpreter of Paul[1] who, however, too lightly eluded the whole complex of problems facing us here.

In any event, what the investigations of the "History of Religion" school have made perfectly clear is the intellectual and religious climate in which Paul and his communities lived. And this climate was undeniably heavy with conceptions proper to the ancient mystery religions.[2] Thus the idea of a sacramental participation in the

---

[1] Ernst Lohmeyer, *Grundlagen paulinischer Theologie*, Tübingen, 1929, 231.

[2] Thus, for instance, Hans Windisch, *Paulus und das Judentum*, Stuttgart, 1935 (38) comes to the conclusion: "The question of Paul's relation to the mystery religions has by no means yet been settled and it is not yet certain that we should reject the idea of any connexion. What is indisputable is that Pauline religion, historically considered, shows the 'type' of a mystery religion."

death of a deity, which seems to us to-day so difficult to conceive, was thoroughly familiar to ancient ways of thought, and Paul had before him many analogies to his doctrines which, as we shall see, stem from other sources. As we have been told, Attis, Osiris, and Dionysos were also gods which died and rose again. Union with them, mediated by ritual acts, likewise secured σωτηρία against cruel fate or death, and often led to the deification of the initiate. But we know too little about the character of these mysteries[1] to be in a position to make a material comparison between them and the Christian ones. We realize, of course—and it is remarkable that Reitzenstein had no perception of this distinction—that the pagan mysteries were timeless, individualistic ways of salvation, whereas Paul, following the Jerusalem kerygma, understood the sharing in the death of Christ on the cross to be an historical event, and to imply a communal incorporation of believers in a saving body. Furthermore, the Jesus who came in the flesh (ἐν ὁμοιώματι σαρκός) was no mythical figure, no "projection of religious experience", while His resurrection was for faith much rather a fact of the quite recent past. The terms used by both parties in this connexion—for instance γνῶσις, σωτηρία, σοφία, μυστήριον, τέλειος—have on account of this difference quite another content for the mind of Paul than that which they possess in the mystery religions.

(d) Gnosis

Nevertheless, the terms just mentioned remain suspect, for they show plainly that here transitions become possible into the spiritual sphere of gnosis, whose doctrines of redemption had their place in the syncretism of declining antiquity. Rudolf Bultmann and his pupils have laid great stress on these points of contact and continuity. And in point of fact, gnostics penetrated into the Pauline communities; thus it was in Corinth, where they spiritualized the resurrection (1 Cor. 15) and preached a different Jesus from that of Paul (2 Cor. 11: 4), as also in Colossae, where misguided teachers held the veneration of the primal elements of the universe (στοιχεῖα τοῦ κόσμου) to be an integral part of the Christian faith.

Even as regards the apostle's own terminology gnostic mythological symbols have insidiously crept in, as when he speaks of

---

[1] The relevant material has been surveyed and discussed by Hepding, Baudissin, Cumont, Deissner, Leipoldt, Kern, etc. A review of these researches has been given by Joh. Leipoldt in the *Handbuch der Religionswissenschaft*, ed. G. Mensching, 1, 4, Berlin, 1948.

the daemonic world-rulers (ἄρχοντες τοῦ αἰῶνος τούτου) which brought the Kyrios to the cross (1 Cor. 2: 8), or of enslavement under the rule of στοιχεῖα (Gal. 4: 3, 9), or again in his discourse on the fall of creation (Rom. 8: 20 ff.), where there emerges the dualism between the ψυχικός and the πνευματικός (1 Cor. 2: 14 f.; 15: 44), and much else. He himself feels that he is a πνευματικός who has pierced the mysteries of divine wisdom, the βάθη τοῦ θεοῦ[1] (1 Cor. 2: 10). The God who created light has also made light to shine within his own life: the γνῶσις of the δόξα τοῦ θεοῦ in the face of Jesus Christ (2 Cor. 4: 6). It is undeniable that this gnosis, considered as irrational awareness, is very close to the cultic mystic consciousness of the mystery religions. "Vision effects a transformation of the soul."[2] It is certain that there are cross currents between the thought of Paul and the world of gnosis, for the specific soteriology of the apostle which clad the figure of Jesus of Nazareth in the garment of a cosmological redeemer myth must have had—as Bousset[3] rightly pointed out—a magnetic influence on gnostic circles. Nevertheless, Bousset (and in this matter he was more reserved than Bultmann) justly emphasized that the gnostic trends of thought in the mind of the apostle (or, as it would be better to say, those approximating to gnosis) remained in the background of his total outlook, and did not play a primary part.[4]

This state of affairs is not changed until we reach the Deutero-Pauline writings, and Käsemann and Schlier were able to show that the letters of this group—whoever their author might be—speak the language of specific gnostic circles. In particular, the use of the concept σῶμα Χριστοῦ which identifies the church with Christ—this, Schlier thinks, occurs only in the Deutero-Pauline, Käsemann in the great letters also—would seem to be of a highly gnostic character.[5] Motives in the Letter to the Ephesians, such as the

[1] Cf. R. Bultmann, *Theologie des Neuen Testaments*, Tübingen, 1948, 180. (E. T. *Theology of the New Testament*.)

[2] M. Dibelius, *Paulus und die Mystik*, Munich, 1941, 7 (now *Botschaft und Geschichte*, II, Tübingen, 1956, 142) interprets it thus: "This is felt to be a real event, not merely something practised in the cult as is the case with the mystery religions; it is an event taking place in the life of Paul. History instead of cultus (or instead of myth) as the locus of the mystical experience—it is a phenomenon typical of Paul's mysticism which we see here."

[3] Cf. *Kyrios Christos*, 191.

[4] R. McL. Wilson has well defined the relation in *The Gnostic Problem*, London, 1958, 76. "The whole distinction between Paul and the Gnostics is that he accepts the contemporary *Weltanschauung* but rejects the gnosticizing interpretation."

[5] H. Schlier, *Christus und die Kirche im Epheserbrief*, Tübingen, 1930; E. Käsemann: *Leib und Leib Christi*, Tübingen, 1932. Cf. also A. Schweitzer, *Mystik*, 117: "In the whole literature of mysticism there is no riddle comparable with that of the mystical body of Christ."

Redeemer's journey through earth and heaven (4: 7–11), the heavenly wall (φραγμός) which divides souls imprisoned in the underworld from the world of light (2: 14–18) the *syzygy* in heaven (5: 22–32) take us into the world of gnostic language and ideas, which also controls Mandaean literature. In fact, as Käsemann puts it (*op. cit.*, p. 155) Ephesians and Colossians are intelligible "only from a mode of interpretation which takes gnosticism fully into account".

(e) *Assessment*

The "History of Religion"[1] school, as exemplified by Reitzenstein and Bousset, was occupied with a truly legitimate concern, and therefore found a considerable following in Germany, France, and the Anglo-Saxon world, for it rightly perceived and demonstrated in the thought-world of Paul much that was non-Jewish. Accordingly, Alfred Loisy and Kirsopp Lake considered that under the influence of "Pauline mysticism" Christianity was transmuted into a mystery religion. Yet the researches of other scholars (cf. section 4) have arrived at quite other and perhaps more accurate explanations of the so-called Christ-mysticism of Paul. And it is difficult to explain away the point that Paul had no demonstrable contacts with Hellenistic paganism.[2]

The situation appears different if we take account of the fact that rabbinic Judaism, at least that of the Diaspora, had itself received the impress of Hellenistic mystery cults or at least made use of them for missionary purposes: "that Paul undoubtedly would therefore be open to their influence, and that many of the terms he used would have an undertone of meaning which would strengthen the appeal of the gospel to the Hellenistic world".[3] And Bousset himself has shown in his great and unsurpassed work *Die Religion des Judentums im hellenistischen Zeitalter* (3rd ed., H. Gressmann, Tübingen, 1926) that the Judaism of the New Testament period was not identical with that of the rabbinic schools of Palestine which were engaged in the codification of the Mishna, but that in this period there were many other unorthodox groups and circles, and especially in relation to the

---

[1] There is the dissertation of one of my pupils on this point: G. W. Ittel, *Urchristentum und Fremdreligionen im Urteil der religiongeschichtl. Schule*, Erlangen, 1956.

[2] Cf. W. D. Davies, *Paul and Rabbinic Judaism*, London, 1949, 93: "It cannot be overemphasized that while his direct contacts with Hellenistic paganism would be few, his relations with Hellenistic Judaism would be peculiarly close throughout his life."

[3] W. D. Davies, *op. cit.*, 98.

Hellenistic *koine*. This state of affairs, which was, of course, known before the time of Bousset, has led to various attempts to interpret Paul in the light of the Jewish Diaspora.

Essentially one must rather say—and this consideration qualifies all pagan-Hellenistic interpretations of Paul—that a considered assessment of the spiritual forces of his environment as possible sources or influential factors in his theology must exclude pure Hellenism, however certain it may be that he was directly acquainted with it as a reality of his age. The "Hellenistic" trait in his thought which undeniably exists is not to be explained by direct influence, was obviously not an independent formative factor stemming from his youth in Tarsus, but rather the result of a process of assimilation, since Hellenism had long before been penetrated by the spirit of the Jewish Diaspora.[1] For according to all the data which can be collected from Jewish history up to the modern period of emancipation, environmental influences have always been effective only in the form of a process of infiltration, whether it be a question of Parsee or Hellenistic, neoplatonist or gnostic, Aristotelian or mutazilitic influences. The heterogeneous elements of thought and teaching were every time assimilated, i.e., integrated to Judaism, and the evidences of this process were plainly perceptible in the face of the Judaism of the place and time in question.

Hence it is of the highest importance for the genealogy of Pauline thought to take into account information about the Hellenized Judaism of the Diaspora of his time, even though primary sources are lacking for the Jewish community of Tarsus in this critical epoch. Those monographs which bear on Pauline investigation must be considered. We must give broader scope to this debate on account of its fundamental importance. For if we succeeded in reconstructing the picture of the Judaism in which the young Saul of Damascus lived, then we should have in our hands an important clue to the understanding of Pauline theology. For after all, Paul by his origins was a Jew of Tarsus and not a Syrian, Persian, or Egyptian; a native of that great town, situated in the modern Gulf of Alexandretta, where the Syrian and Turkish coasts touch almost at right angles.

[1] Cf. on this also Rudolf Meyer, *Hellenistisches in der rabbinischen Anthropologie*, Stuttgart, 1937; S. Liebermann, *Greek in Jewish Palestine*, New York, 1942.

2. THE HELLENISTIC–JUDAISTIC INTERPRETATION OF PAUL

(a) *The problem of the Pharisaism of the Diaspora*

Paul, according to his own statement reproduced in Acts 23: 6, came of a family of Pharisees (ἐγὼ Φαρισαῖός εἰμι, υἱὸς Φαρισαίων). The family was doubtless of purely Jewish origin and derived from the tribe of Benjamin, for which reason Saul was named after the most famous Benjaminite. He repeatedly avows himself to be a "Jew of Tarsus" (Acts 21: 39; 22: 3) and declares that he belonged to Jewish orthodoxy, to the Pharisaic sect which expressed the most austere tendencies of his religious communion (Acts 26: 5). In Phil. 3: 5 he says with regard to his origins: "Circumcised on the eighth day, of the people of Israel, of the tribe of Benjamin, a Hebrew born of Hebrews; as to the law a Pharisee, as to zeal a persecutor of the church, as to righteousness under the law blameless." This self-characterization throws a flood of light on the conservative religious tendencies of his parents. We are faced here by strict observers of the law. The statement implies that Paul's father, like so many eminent and well-to-do people, belonged to the Diaspora of the Pharisaic party, as did perhaps his grandfather and great-grandfather.[1] The Pharisaic heritage and the connexion with Jerusalem are confirmed by the fact that a sister of Paul was married in Jerusalem and that the father considered it a matter of course to send his son to the rabbinic high school there.

The parents of Paul were members of the Jewish community of Tarsus, the capital of Cilicia. In this home therefore the Hebrew of the Bible, the colloquial Aramaic of the Jews, and the current Greek of the town must have been, if not spoken alternately, yet equally well understood. The families of the Pharisaic Diaspora were essentially polyglot, and especially the family of Paul, which enjoyed citizenship both of Tarsus and Rome—a privilege which protected from dishonouring punishments, and at any time conferred the right of appeal to Caesar.[2] Roman citizenship, which meant much at that time, and the chance of which had existed since

---

[1] Reports by Jerome (*De Viris Illustribus*, ch. 5, and *Comm. in Ep. ad Philemon*, 23), which through Origen go back to oral tradition, suggest that the family came from Giscala (modern el-Jish) in northern Galilee near the lake of Gennesareth, and perhaps left for Tarsus after the Roman conquest.

[2] Cf. Th. Mommsen, "Die Rechtsverhältnisse des Apostels Paulus", *ZNW*, 1901, 81 ff.; H. J. Cadbury in *The Beginnings of Christianity*, V, London, 1933, 312 ff.; M. Brücklmeier: *Beiträge zur rechtlichen Stellung der Juden im römischen Reich*, Diss. Munich, 1939, 23 ff.

the period of Augustus, greatly distinguished the young man as belonging to a middle-class home of substance from those poor Galileans who stood at the head of the first church. This combination: *civis Romanus* and Φαρισαῖος ἐκ Φαρισαίων, was no doubt a rare one in Palestine and confronts us with an extraordinary phenomenon of the Diaspora. It had its effects not only juridically but also, and above all, culturally. Nevertheless, such a home was able to bind Paul so indissolubly to his people that later on he was able to write of the great grief and pain in his heart at the thought of being separated from the Jews—those to whom belong the sonship and the glory, the covenants, the giving of the law, the worship, and the promises, etc. (Rom. 9: 2–5).

The obvious situation, that Paul was a Pharisee of the Diaspora, has led some investigators—at their head Claude G. Montefiore,[1] who was followed by James W. Parkes[2] and others (in part Puukko and Windisch)—to explain as features of the Pharisaic Diaspora those Pauline views which markedly deviate from the teaching of the Palestinian schools and cannot be shown to belong to these. It was Montefiore's opinion that before his conversion Paul must have known Judaism in a different form from that which it assumed in Palestinian rabbinics, for a whole series of difficult phenomena are otherwise not explainable. Montefiore supposed further that in Judaic Hellenism Paul knew an emotionally poorer, more austere, and also more pessimistic religion than that which Palestinian Judaism represented. Just as the loving and merciful Father-God of the rabbis disclosed in the Hellenistic Diaspora much paler features, the same was true also of the Messiah, who in this *milieu* assumed cosmic rather than human traits. Fundamentally this hypothesis has much to be said for it, and should not be hastily discarded.

Montefiore distinguished eight doctrines which Paul could not possibly have come by under the discipline of the Talmudic teachers: the deified Messiah; pessimism about sin and despair over the evil which reigns in the heart of man; his teaching about the law; his neglect of the certainty of the repentance and forgiveness of the Jews; his mystical doctrine of the Saviour; his strong interest in the mission to the heathen and the universalism of his doctrine of

---

[1] "Rabbinic Judaism and the Epistles of St. Paul", *JQR*, 1900–1, and *Judaism and St. Paul*, London, 1914. For Montefiore's exegetical feats, cf. G. Lindeskog: "Claude G. Montefiore, en judisk evangelieforskare", *SEA*, 1940, 295 ff.

[2] *Jesus, Paul and the Jews*, London, 1934.

salvation, offered equally to Jews and Gentiles; his antithesis of works
and faith; and the anthropological dualism implied in the contrast
between πνεῦμα and σάρξ. This enumeration is untenable for two
reasons: firstly, because it wrongly understands the so-called
"Rabbinism" as a unified whole, which it was not—some of the
positions here mentioned also found exponents in Palestinian schools
—and secondly, because the whole apocalyptic movement, which
flourished in Palestine also in the New Testament period, has been
excluded from "Rabbinism". What is still more serious is that the
procedure of Montefiore amounts to this: to replace one unknown
quantity—the theology of Saul—by another unknown quantity,
the theology of the Pharisaic Diaspora.[1] We know far too little about
the Hellenistic Halakha and Haggada, the so-called "Deuterosis",
since they were never codified in writing; but what we do know of
them does not justify us in concluding that there was an irrecon-
cilable opposition between Hellenistic and rabbinic Judaism.

Nevertheless, I think we should go forward in the direction outlined by Montefiore, provided the work proceeds by a correct
method: namely, first to investigate those actually extant testimonies to Hellenistic Judaism which are relevant for the reconstruction of the type of Judaism in which Saul, the Diaspora Pharisee,
grew up. Secondly, to make a careful study of all the Palestinian
sources of both apocalyptic and pseudepigraphic literature, so that
what remains unsolved may then be cautiously claimed for Judaistic
Hellenism. Our own researches will show that what remains over
is something quite different from the factors which Montefiore indicated: namely, decisive shifts of emphasis and curtailments in the
structure of the Jewish faith which must be laid at the door of the
Jewish Diaspora (including, obviously, the Pharisaic party). Something of this may already be indicated in this introductory survey of
the position and problems of Pauline research, if we go on to ask:
What do we know positively about the doctrinal deviations of
Hellenistic from Palestinian Judaism?

The chief sources which are in question are clearly the piety of
the Septuagint and the philosophy of Philo. But great caution is
advisable, for here we stand on extremely insecure ground. Is
Philo's philosophy typical beyond the circle of a certain group of
Alexandrian Jews? May we legitimately consider the piety of the
Septuagint to be representative of the Jewish Diaspora as a whole?
And may we with Adolf Deissmann[2] describe Paul as a "Septuagint

---

[1] Cf. also W. D. Davies' criticism, op. cit., 4–16.   [2] Paulus, Tübingen, 1925, 69.

Jew"? Because of the lack of sources for the religious life of the Jewish community in his native city we do not even know whether the Septuagint was known in Tarsus and read in the services of the synagogue there. The fluctuating character of the scriptural quotations in the letters of Paul does not enable us to decide with certainty whether he had in his hands the Alexandrian translation of the Bible.[1] But let us look more closely at these two witnesses to Hellenistic Judaism, viz., the piety of the Septuagint and the individual case of the professional philosopher Philo, in so far as they are at all relevant to the concerns of Pauline research.

(b) *The piety of the Septuagint*

It is instructive to cast a glance at the piety of the Septuagint considered as a "Greek Targum of Hellenistic Judaism", because it was at least one work emanating from the orthodox Diaspora, however many-sided the latter may have been. And to be sure, its influence in the ancient world went far beyond that of the translation of the Bible by Mendelssohn, Zunz or Buber-Rosenzweig, in the world of German Judaism, whose piety a later researcher could hardly deduce solely from the knowledge of this "German Targum".

In his significant monograph on Paul, Adolf Deissmann has justly called the LXX an "East–West" book. By this he meant "an adjustment of the eastern faith to the western world" (69) as a result of which an effective missionary propaganda of Jewish monotheism became possible in the Greek-speaking world. But the investigation of the problem as to how far this translation also involved a material Hellenization of Judaism still remains in its infancy,[2] despite the

---

[1] The reformed theologian Capellus (1650) was the first who tried to show that Paul quoted from the LXX. Kautzsch (*De veteris Testamenti locis a Paulo Apostolo allegatis*, 1869), who counted 84 OT quotations in Paul and studied their text, thought this probable, but felt that on account of the many deviations—very bad in Job quotations—Paul was citing from memory. This view has often been repeated. Hatch, Vollmer, Weizsäcker, etc., thought there were Biblical anthologies, arranged according to the threefold division of the Canon; others again supposed the existence of Hebraic versions from which Paul translated freely (Zahn); another theory was that of the existence of an Aramaic Targum (Böhl), a legendary Proto-Theodotion, etc. Passages such as Rom. 4:25; 9:22; Gal. 3:17 seem to suggest his knowledge of the LXX, of which various local versions may have been current. Vital for these questions are: O. Michel, *Paulus und seine Bibel*, Gütersloh, 1929; E. E. Ellis, *Paul's Use of the Old Testament*, Edinburgh, 1957.

[2] The later rabbis regard the translation as so inauspicious that they look on the traditional day on which it was done, the 8th Tebeth, as an unfortunate day. In Tr. Soferim 1, 8 we read: "It was as unlucky a day for Israel as the day of the fabrication of the golden calf, because the Torah cannot be adequately translated." Cf. H. Bardtke, "Der Traktat der Schreiber", *Wiss. Zeitschr. der Karl Marx-Universität*, Leipzig, 1953/54, 15.

efforts of Deissmann, Bertram, Dodd, Marcus, Prijs, Seeligmann, and others. And in fact the question of its unity, whether the traces of the seventy different translators can be recognized, whether considerable doctrinal deviations between the twenty-four books can be established, is not answerable at all. Yet it seems to me that this is a comparatively lesser concern. Far more important is the problem of a special mode of thought in the LXX and of a characteristic piety. And this aspect of the matter is the one which has been least of all investigated by Pauline researchers, although on account of its consequences it might prove to be one of the most important.[1] In my opinion, with regard to the change of consciousness in the piety of Hellenistic Judaism as contrasted with that of the Palestinian schools we can now make certain general observations, based on adequate sources, as follows:

First to be mentioned is the missionary purpose of the LXX (cf. for example LXX Jer. 3: 19 as compared with the Massoretic Text: "I appoint you for the heathen", and many other texts[2]) and its universalistic position, which enables Paul (Rom. 10: 20) in the style of the LXX to apply Is. 65: 1 to the Gentile world. This missionary tendency of the LXX is in the very blood of Paul, who even pictures God as a missionary, as one who changes his methods of working in order to make the greater impression on men (1 Cor. 1: 21). Propaganda and the mission to the Gentiles appear in the LXX as a specific task incumbent on Jewish piety. For this end, texts such as Is. 18: 7; 55:5; 65: 1; Jer. 3: 19, etc., which rather give expression to Jewish national pride, are transformed by the LXX so as to convey a missionary idea, to some extent against the clear meaning of the text. Even prophetic declarations which properly afford no opening for this tendency, are at times made to yield such a meaning.[3] This universalistic "pathos" of the world mission which was the

---

[1] Most important apart from English studies are those of Georg Bertram, among which I cite, aside from his numerous contributions to Kittel's Wörterbuch, the following: "Umschrifttext und religionsgeschichtliche Erforschung der LXX", *BZAW*, 66 (1936); "Die religiöse Umdeutung altorientalischer Lebensweisheit in der griechischen Übersetzung des AT", *ZAW*, 1939; "Der Sprachschatz der LXX und das hebräische AT", *ZAW*, 1939; "Das Wesen der Septuagintafrömmigkeit", *Die Welt des Orients*, 1956; "Praeparatio evangelica in der Septuaginta", *VT*, 1957, 3.

[2] Cf. Rosen-Bertram, *Juden und Phönizier*, Tübingen, 1928, 36 ff.

[3] In order to illustrate the special LXX theology, I consider Is. 54: 15 in detail, with deliberate LXX modifications. MT runs: הן גור יגור אפס מאותי, מי־יגור אתך עליך יפול which can only be translated: If people conspire together, they are nothing apart from me; whosoever conspires against me, however, will fall. LXX translates: ἰδοὺ προσήλυτοι προσελεύσονταί σοι δι᾽ ἐμοῦ καὶ ἐπὶ σὲ καταφεύξονται, Proselytes will join themselves unto you for my sake, will seek refuge with you.

very soul of Septuagint Jewish circles—and we must remember the many expressions in the LXX referring to the whole, to "all"[1]— was alive also in the young Saul of Tarsus, who chose as his vocation the mission to the Gentiles.

Another important tendency of the LXX, which is reflected in a distorted form in Paul, is the following: the tendency to ethicize Judaism, to understand it as a moral law, disconnected and isolated from the controlling reality of the covenant. It is well known that the Old Testament idea of the "Torah" is best explained as instruction embracing both law and doctrine. In the LXX there takes place with the translation תורה —νόμος—a shift of emphasis towards legalism. And the Torah comes to imply a moral way of life prescribed by God. Hence Dodd[2] speaks of "a hard legalistic way". Thus, for instance, in the LXX translation of Prov. 14: 27, προστάγματα takes the place of יראת יי which twists the meaning of the whole sentence. Apart from the passages where he has allegorized in the manner of Philo, Paul implies such an understanding which is in harmony with the LXX rather than the original. Only so can he tirelessly insist on substituting for the Jewish law a new law, νόμος τοῦ πνεύματος (Rom. 8: 2). We shall see later (ch. 5) that the source of many Pauline misunderstandings with regard to the evaluation of the law and covenant is to be sought in the legalistic distortion of the perspective for which Hellenistic Judaism was responsible.

Similar to the relation of תורה and νόμος is the relation of צדקה and δικαιοσύνη which the LXX often similarly formalizes in a juristic sense. Even משפט in Is. 61: 8 and Mal 2: 17 can be translated by δικαιοσύνη. Likewise with Paul δικαιοῦν means not only "to make someone righteous", it is also a verbum causativum: "to secure vindication for someone", e.g., Rom. 4: 5: δικαιοῦν τὸν ἀσεβῆ. In the Hebraic basic outlook righteousness, grace, and mercy were included in צדקה, for which reason the LXX also translates Is. 56: 1 and Dan. 4: 27 by ἐλεημοσύνη. But ἐλεημοσύνη (mostly for חסד) and πίστις for אמת also undergo in the Septuagint usage a shift of meaning in the direction of the intellectual and abstract, which has repercussions on the Pauline world of ideas.

---

[1] Cf. πᾶς, in LXX, Kittel V, 889 ff.

[2] Cf. C. H. Dodd, *The Bible and the Greeks*, London, 1934 (4). At times the Torah may be indicated by images (e.g., LXX Prov. 13: 15 by חן); cf. J. L. Seeligmann in *Suppl. I to Vetus Test.*, Leiden, 1935, 179. The petrifaction of the Torah into legalistic formulae is most visible in ben Sira (*op. cit.*, 178).

Further, in the LXX the far richer Hebrew vocabulary for sin and evil is narrowed down to ἀδικία and in particular to ἀνομία, whence Dodd (*op. cit.*, 80) comments: "This is one more symptom of the growing legalism which we have noticed in other connections." Paul, who mostly uses ἁμαρτία and its derivatives, passes once more far beyond the legalistic conception of sin. On the other hand, his anthropocentric emphasis in the idea of sin springs from the LXX which is important for the assessment of Rom. 7. The LXX formulated the idea of sinfulness by contrast with concrete individual sins, and suggested the fundamental sin of man to be separation from God. For the LXX the act of sin is not so important as the rebellious and arrogant disposition.[1] The converse of this is that in the LXX the pious life often appears in such a light that it gives man a basis for asserting a claim towards God constituted by the righteousness of his works.[2] This would bring us into a *milieu* which is very familiar to us from the Pauline polemic against the self-glorying of the Jews. The point of view of the LXX is that of the pious man and his antitype, the overbearing and arrogant man. The popular ethic of the two ways as possibilities of human existence, which was so important for Hellenistic missionary propaganda, is linked with this whole outlook (most plainly in LXX Prov. 4: 27).

The researches of Dodd yield a further important result for Pauline theology, namely that in the LXX the cultic and central idea of atonement, כפר with its derivatives, is transferred by means of the word-group ἱλάσκεσθαι from the cultic to the ethical sphere, and so in many contexts the meaning has been shifted from expiation to forgiveness. The LXX Is. 27: 9 seems to be a very important text for the penetration of a deritualized doctrine of grace. Dodd (*op. cit.*, 93) comes to the important conclusion: "Thus Hellenistic Judaism, as represented by the LXX, does not regard the cultus as a means of pacifying the displeasure of the Deity, but as a means of delivering man from sin."

Finally, we must bear in mind the strikingly psychological–pedagogic outlook of the LXX, which regards law and prophecy from the standpoint of παιδεία—a tendency which has been investigated by G. Bertram.[3] It is obvious that this is of particular

---

[1] Cf. Kittel I, 290 (ἁμαρτάνω); for the LXX idea of sin as arrogance, see Bertram, *ZAW*, 1936, 167, also E. Jentsch: *Urchristliches Erziehungsdenken*, Gütersloh, 1951, esp. 88 ff.

[2] G. Bertram, *BZAW*, 66, 107.

[3] *The Idea of Culture in the Greek Bible, Imago Dei*, Festschrift für Gustav Krüger, Giessen, 1932.

importance for the presentation of νόμος as παιδαγωγὸς εἰς Χριστόν (Gal. 3: 24). Or again we should think of Rom. 15: 4: "For whatever was written in former days was written for our instruction." In Hellenistic Judaism the law was in fact the tutor of the pious Jew and of the Jewish community; it is the intention of God to educate His people by means of the law (LXX Hos. 5: 2); μισθὸς χαρίτων ἡ παιδεία τοῖς χρωμένοις (Prov. 17: 8 as distinct from the Mass. T.). We often meet in the LXX the idea of παιδεία as the content of God's self-revelation, as also its verbal form παιδεύειν. Often it is a translation of לקח and יצר where the double meaning, teaching as discipline and chastisement, plays a part. Alongside the special pedagogic term מוסר (moral–pedagogic books are called Musar literature in Judaism) the word סוד (secret) is also frequently translated by παιδεία. In Judaism the law became the basis of its culture, both in a spiritual and worldly sense. Hence the cultural pretension of Hellenistic Judaism had a universalist implication. The law, the Torah, as a comprehensive symbol for discipline and moral and spiritual education is to be the educative book for humanity as a whole. Ecclus. 24: 27 is translated in the LXX: "the law makes good culture to shine forth as the light". Paul also in Rom. 2: 20 puts forward the idea that the law is the embodiment of truth and knowledge.

This pedagogic concern is closely interwoven with the anthropocentric humanistic piety of Hellenistic Judaism. The focal point is the pious life of man, the human religious disposition. In the LXX Proverbs there even appear, together with a more friendly attitude towards Greek culture and thought, traces of influences stemming from the stoic conception of life.[1] Here lurk all the dangers of establishing a human claim over against God, and of replacing the Old Testament religion of grace by a human religion of virtuous works.[2] Paul's protest, already mentioned, against the Jewish righteousness of works and "self-glorying of the Jews" is thus—and this seems to me to be an important recognition—directed much less

---

[1] Cf. examples in G. Gerleman: "Religion och moral i Septuagintas Proverbia-Översättning", *Sv. Th. Kv.*, 1950, 229 ff. But J. W. Wevers (*ThR*, 1954, 187 ff.) had certain objections to his interpretation.

[2] For the way in which the LXX modifies I give two examples taken from Bertram. Proverbs MT. 16: 7 has: "When a man's ways please the Lord, He makes even his enemies to be at peace with him." LXX makes of this: "The ways of righteous men are pleasing to the Lord; because of them even their enemies become friends." In 12: 21 MT. says: "No ill befalls the pious." LXX makes of this: "Nothing unrighteous pleases the righteous." Such examples might easily be multiplied.

against the rabbinical than against the Hellenistic Judaism of his origins.

Finally, the peculiarity of the LXX must be characterized by saying that it represents a Hellenized form of Palestinian religion and culture. Ralph Marcus[1] has with justice pointed out that this process of Hellenization took place in the service of Jewish doctrine, of "Jewishness" as he says. Paul, who knew both the Massora and the Greek translation—whether in the form of the LXX or of a closely related version—mostly favours the Hellenistic interpretation wherever the sense of the text is disputable. And this, it seems to me, has fundamental importance for an assessment of his position.

(c) *The piety of Philo*

As far as Philo is concerned, a comparison with Paul on specific questions, as has often been made (by Siegfried, Vollmer, Michel, etc.) yields but barren results, because his thought has quite a different orientation. But more recent criticism (Heinemann, Belkin, Wolfson, etc.) has been able to show even in the case of Philo how strong are the Jewish elements in him, and over what a wide field he still agrees with the Palestinian Halakha. Nevertheless, he has a noteworthy tendency which reveals itself in the course of his allegorizing exegesis, and which, in relation to Paul, makes us pause to think: as Pascher, Goodenough, Knox, and others have noticed, he has assimilated to Judaism for apologetic and missionary purposes certain elements proper to a mystery cult. These influences have caused him to describe the history of the patriarchs, and especially that of Moses, as a deification mystery in the style of the Hellenistic mysticism of the soul's ascension. Abraham, Isaac, and Jacob, as also Moses, become for him figures symbolizing the way of the human soul and its ascension towards God. Probably it is going too far to deduce from this, as does Goodenough, that through Philo the mystery religions reached the Hellenistic synagogues. Philo himself is firmly convinced that the Jewish tradition contained these symbols originally. But it is undeniable that with him the patriarchs have become types of mystical perfection, while Moses, distinguished by his possession of the pre-existent logos, towers above them as a kind of mediator.

The transformations to which we refer are in any event fairly

[1] *Jewish and Greek Elements in Septuagint*, Louis Ginzberg Jubilee Volume, New York, 1945, 244.

considerable. Thus Philo explains (*De post.* C. 28 ff. par.) that when God commands Moses on Sinai: "Come here to me", it is an indication that God is imparting to him a share in His own divine nature. By this Philo means the possession of a share in the θεῖος λόγος. As an unchangeable quality this constituted Moses a σοφός. Like the patriarchs, the other σοφοί, he was from the beginning distinct from the rest of humanity, and together they formed a τρίτον γένος as the Pythagoreans would say. But did Philo think Moses to be truly divine? Goodenough[1] answers: yes and no. No, because Philo was and remained a monotheist, hence was bound to conceive all human being as forming a contrast and contradiction to the pure being of God. Yes, in so far as Moses became an ἄνθρωπος θεοῦ, and this fact for him denoted, in the sense of the mysteries, a metamorphosis of his whole nature. That is the reason why Philo can directly identify Moses respectively with the ὀρθὸς λόγος and νόμος ἔμψυχος. That Philo has described both the ascent of Moses to Sinai as also his dying as a transmutation of his nature into a supernatural substance (εἰς νοῦν ἡλιοειδίστατον)—hence as a process of deification (*Vita Mos.* II, 2 ff.—Mangey 135; II, 288 ff.—Mangey 179) is surely relevant for the Pauline Christ-soteriology, even though it is impossible to prove the influence on Paul which Goodenough claims. H. Windisch[2] has quite rightly perceived that "in this presentation of the deified and divine Moses there is a subtle penetration of the whole complex Greek doctrine of the θεῖος ἀνήρ".

(d) *Greek philosophy*

Although it is hardly possible to establish securely any influence on Paul of the neoplatonist philosophy, as Philo expounded or rather distorted it, we may here touch upon the question of the situation in regard to other tendencies in Greek philosophy. Only stoicism should come into the question, for at the academy of the philosophically very lively city of Tarsus, Paul's native place,[3] the stoic Athenodorus of Canana (74 B.C. to A.D. 7) taught after his return from Rome in 15 B.C.; a lengthy extract from his work on the rest of the soul is given by Seneca (*Dial.* IX 34 *ad Serenum*). The idea of the ἀγαθὴ συνείδησις

[1] *By Light Light, the Mystic Gospel of Hellenistic Judaism*, New Haven, 1935, 228. For a critique of the book, cf. H. A. Wolfson, *Philo*, Cambridge, 1948, I, 45 ff., etc.

[2] *Paulus und Christus, ein biblisch-religionsgeschichtlicher Vergleich*, Leipzig, 1931, 106.

[3] Cf. the information given by the geographer Strabo (*Geographia*, XIV, 9-15): "The zeal which the men of Tarsus show for philosophy and culture in general is so great that even Athens and Alexandria are surpassed."

in the sense of an inner court of judgment, lacking in Hebrew and Aramaic, which Paul is very fond of (it occurs twenty times) is met with here. Rom. 1: 19 ff. is often understood as a stoic proof of the existence of God from φύσις, implying the capacity to recognize essential attributes of the Deity from the works of creation. Likewise the opinion expressed in Rom. 2 to the effect that the heathen bear an unwritten law in their hearts may reflect such influence, although it would seem more obvious to understand their "reasonable service" of God in the light of typical trends of thought in Hellenistic Judaism, remote as it was from the Jerusalem cultus. Yet quite a few other expressions and terms, such as τὰ μὴ καθήκοντα (Rom. 1: 28), αὐτάρκης (Phil. 4: 11), etc., may appear suspect of stoicism. Many expressions and images, especially in the Corinthian letters (1 Cor. 9: 24 ff.—the comparison of moral striving with the runners in a race at the stadium; 11: 14—nature itself teaches us that the two sexes should wear their hair differently, and other such instances) seem to be an echo of stoic modes of expression, which Paul may have absorbed in his youth as a part of his Hellenistic culture.[1] But the most important terms in stoic ethics, such as ἀπάθεια, ἀταραξία, εὐδαιμονία, etc., are completely lacking. Thus the greatest expert in these matters, M. Pohlenz,[2] is probably right in saying with regard to this problem which at times has been so much discussed: "Paul received certain stimulations from stoic philosophy, but he completely transforms such material by his own spirit and outlook and his inner life remains scarcely touched."

Finally, in regard to other literature of Hellenistic Judaism which was influenced by stoic ideas (the Wisdom of Solomon, IV Maccabees, the Sibylline Oracles) there is only question of Paul having known the first mentioned, whose philosophy of history in the opinion of some—and among them modern critics—(e.g., Nock, Klausner) is supposed to have left traces on Rom. 9. It is more probable, however, that Wisdom and Paul—occasionally also Philo—depend on common older sources.[3]

[1] In the letters of the third missionary journey in particular, the rhetorical formulae of the cynic-stoic diatribe seem to increase. They have been studied in a well-known early work of R. Bultmann. But the point about them is the same as that made by O. Eger and W. Straub in their collection of images drawn from ancient law: acquaintance and use prove nothing other than that the writer belongs to the Hellenistic cultural *milieu*, where all this kind of thing is taken for granted.

[2] "Paulus und die Stoa", *ZNW*, 42 (1949), 80. Also A. J. Festugière, *L'idéal religieux des Grecs et l'Évangile*, Paris, 1932, 264 ff. Excursus D, *St. Paul et Marc-Aurèle*; and also H. Almquist, *Plutarch und das NT*, Uppsala, 1946.

[3] Cf. O. Michel, *op. cit.*, 111.

(c) *Assessment*

It is our conviction that Judaistic Hellenism represents an essential factor which is to be taken note of for the reconstruction of the doctrine and faith of Saul the Diaspora Pharisee. We must proceed on the assumption that it was just as complex as was Palestinian Judaism in this critical epoch. But this Diaspora Judaism, in which there were orthodox and latitudinarian, assimilatory and Zionistic tendencies, was a phenomenon *sui generis*. We do not know what form in particular it assumed in Tarsus or under what guise it entered into the cultural development of the young Saul, just as we do not know any details about his home and parents.[1] For the Septuagint and Philo afford information about Alexandrian Judaism only, with any certainty. We do not know whether Paul was acquainted with them or whether quite a different state of affairs obtained in Tarsus. The conclusions of historical research make the latter appear improbable; for every stream of culture normally has a unity springing from common basic convictions, by which it is sustained. For this reason it may be assumed that the Jewish community of Tarsus offered a similar form of Judaistic Hellenism, from the point of view of faith and doctrine, and the same kind of Diaspora situation as that of Alexandria. Probability speaks for this in the same degree as the spiritual structure of the Jewish communities of London, Amsterdam, Frankfurt, Leghorn, in the second half of the 17th century was similar through the combination of mysticism and orthodoxy—for the apostles of the Sabbatian movement confronted them with a Messianic situation, even a post-Messianic situation.[2]

Considered culturally and sociologically, the Judaism of Tarsus should be characterized by the same situation of tension and wealth in a politically, culturally, and religiously dualistic *milieu* as we find in the case of Alexandria and as is typical of any Diaspora community, which can never escape the process of assimilation unless it is artificially confined to a ghetto. Hence we may comfortably assume that Hellenistic elements of culture were also assimilated by the Judaism of Tarsus, which was likewise Hellenized. Certainly in this respect there will have been considerable differences, and it is probable that Paul was much less of a Hellenized Jew than the Jewish Philo, the highly learned citizen of Alexandria. In the

---

[1] It will hardly do to infer with Gottlieb Klein from Rom. 7: 9: "I was once alive apart from the law", that Paul's home was liberal in tendency (see *Studien über Paulus*, Stockholm, 1918, 29).

[2] Cf. in my book *Philosemitismus im Barock*, Tübingen, 1952, sources adduced for this.

orthodox family of Paul, which held fast to traditional customs, it is certain that Hebrew was understood and it is probable that Aramaic was also spoken, if we are to believe the statement of Jerome (see p. 24, n. 1), who reports that the family originated from Galilee; on the other hand, the Jewish philosopher of religion, Philo, hardly understood a word of either language.[1]

In Acts 21 : 40 Paul himself tells us that he addressed his opponents in Jerusalem τῇ Ἑβραΐδι διαλέκτῳ, hence in Aramaic. And it is so plain that Hebrew–Aramaic has coloured the Greek of his letters that, on account of its Semitic idiom, his language has often been described as Jewish–Greek. Typically Semitic constructions such as the accumulation of genitives, which often take the place even of the attribute, the plural translation of the Hebrew dual, etc., have always struck critics.[2] Paul could hardly have lapsed into such an idiom had Greek been his mother tongue.

The net result of these considerations is therefore that the Judaic–Hellenistic approach, indicated by the biography of the apostle, has its inner justification and must be taken into account in any attempt to understand his Christian theology. For it is the same human being who both before and after Damascus pondered the problems of God, the law, the Messiah, and salvation—an elementary truth which has been forgotten in many quarters. The exponents of this approach need not deny that in the long course of his travels Paul came directly into contact with pagan Hellenism and its many mystery cults. For it is clear that this was the alien, while Judaized Hellenism was the native and familiar, *milieu* of the apostle's youth. A type so extraverted as Paul must have been roused to a passionate reaction towards every situation and state of affairs which he encountered. How else could he have become a Greek to the Greeks? Eduard Schwartz[3] thinks that he had learned to do this in his youth. To that extent he will have had knowledge of all the spiritual and religious tendencies of the *koine*—at least in the proportion in which every moderately informed newspaper reader of to-day is *au fait* with the state of affairs in his continent.

---

[1] Cf. the arguments of I. Heinemann, *Philons griechische und jüdische Bildung*, Breslau, 1932, 524 ff.

[2] For the accumulation of genitives, I give as a crude example 2 Cor. 4: 4: τὸν φωτισμὸν τοῦ εὐαγγελίου τῆς δόξης τοῦ Χριστοῦ; for the dual in Greek: αἰῶνες—eternity, οὐρανοί —heaven, etc. Many other peculiar traits are noted in the grammars of Rademacher, Blass-Debrunner, etc. Also Eduard Norden has more often compared for Pauline texts the Semitic of the LXX than the stylistic forms of Hellenism.

[3] *Charakterköpfe aus der Antike*, Berlin, 1950, 217.

Since we have undertaken to survey the condition and problems of Pauline research from the point of view of Paul's life-history, we must now go further and inquire what influences emanating from the rabbinical and apocalyptic theology of the Jerusalem schools produced a demonstrable effect on the mind of Saul, the youthful Diaspora Pharisee, as a result of his migration thither.

3. THE PALESTINIAN–JUDAIC APPROACH

In Jerusalem, where his sister was already married (Acts 23: 16), Paul—if we may believe the Acts of the Apostles—became a pupil of (or "sat at the feet of") the Rabbi Gamaliel I, the elder Gamaliel who—likewise a Benjaminite—was the acknowledged leader of Pharisaic circles (22: 3).[1] We know that in his school the mild tolerance and friendliness towards proselytes typical of Hillel was considered the ideal, and that he himself in his expositions and "Halakha" decisions was no fanatical zealot, but a man of conciliatory disposition.[2] In some passages of the Pauline writings critics have seen allusions to the doctrines of his teacher,[3] and even parallels to the ideas of the son, Simon ben Gamaliel, are found.[4] Particular influences seem not to have been great, but so much the greater was the general influence of the climate of the school, the mode of rabbinical argument and exegetic method. Those critics like Delitzsch, Vollmer, Klein, Puukko, Michel, Bonsirven, Klausner, Davies, etc., who have investigated these influences, have been able to collect sufficient material to form a picture of the situation. The fact that Paul was a "rabbinist", that his religion is to be approached as a "radicalized Pharisaism" or "Pharisaism on a new

---

[1] W. C. van Unnik (*Studia Paulina in hon. J. de Zwaan* 233) thought even that Acts 22: 3 should be understood to imply that although Paul was born in Tarsus he grew up in Jerusalem, that Aramaic was therefore his mother tongue, and rabbinism his spiritual home; Hellenism he got to know only after his conversion.

[2] About Gamaliel I cf. Bacher, *Agada der Tannaiten* I, Strasburg, 1884, 12; Schürer, *Geschichte des jüd. Volkes* II, Leipzig, 1901, 428 ff. The assertion of Klausner, *Von Jesus zu Paulus*, Jerusalem, 1950, 296 ff. (E.T. *From Jesus To Paul*) that in Sabb. 30b Gamaliel meant to allude to Paul as the "certain pupil" seems to me not exactly probable.

[3] Thus it is supposed that the allegory about the leaven and the dough (1 Cor. 5: 6; Gal. 5: 9) goes back to a "Halakha" of Gamaliel about the leavening of dough in M. Orla 11, 12, that the statement of Rom. 7: 2 ff. about a woman being bound to her husband only during his lifetime rests on his decision intended to facilitate remarriage in M. Yebamoth XVI, 7.

[4] Thus it appears that a tenet very important for Paul about the expiration of legal validity at death reflects similar views held by his fellow-pupil, set down in Sabb. 151b; cf. below, ch. 5, 1.

basis" (Lohmeyer) may be accepted without further discussion. The only difficult question is to what extent the rabbinic interpretation is valid, and at what point we must revert to Judaic Hellenism, where the possible influence of the latter ends and the underivably "new" of Christian existence—a θαυμαστόν τι from the standpoint of Judaism—begins. We propose to discuss therefore the present position of the problems which arise from that stage in the apostle's life when he passed within the spiritual sphere of Palestinian Judaism.

(a) *Rabbinical exegesis*

For Saul, throughout his life, scripture remained the supreme norm of all thought and action. Thus even Paul the Christian adduces no argument to which he does not try to give a Biblical basis, and this applies also to the Messianic character and the soteriological role of Jesus. Even the abolition of the law must be proved from the law, and this is done by means of a principle of the rabbinic law of inheritance. Hence Paul has rightly been called an "Old Testament Biblicist".[1] Without a detailed knowledge of the Old Testament and its exegesis whole passages of the major Pauline letters remain almost unintelligible. For this reason I agree with the summing-up of Vilhelm Grönbech:[2] "The attempt to understand the logic and argumentation of Paul must give a Greek a headache. For a Jew he is a theologian who is a master of the correct technical method of scriptural exegesis but in consequence of some perversity applies it so falsely that he arrives at nonsensical results."

To consider more closely the peculiarity of his rabbinical exegesis: following rabbinical custom and judgment of value—we may think of the proems of many homilies—in Paul also quotations from the Torah precede in demonstrative power those from the Nebiim and Kethubim, though in this matter we may observe an unmistakable tendency of the apostle to combine quotations from the three different classes of scripture.[3] Paul is just as far removed as the rabbis from historical critical exegesis in the modern sense, and his comments are in no way motivated by the attempt to explain the

---

[1] Thus H. Windisch, *Paulus und das Judentum*, Stuttgart, 1935, 72.

[2] *Paulus, Jesu Christi Apostel*, Copenhagen, 1940, 18; cf. also the reference of E. Hirsch in *ZNW*, 1941, 229 ff.

[3] Cf. the early studies by H. Vollmer, *Die atl. Zitate bei Paulus*, Freiburg, 1895, 37 ff. and the early work of O. Michel, *Paulus und seine Bibel*, Gütersloh, 1929, 83 ff.; both of whom give examples of such links. Apart from the Torah Paul most frequently cites the Psalms.

text in question in the light of its intrinsic meaning and context. Rather he tries with the resources of traditional rabbinic logic to gain from the text new meanings by a process of inference and combination with other texts. The methods of proof characteristic of his writings make it clear that he had learnt in the schools the seven hermeneutical rules of Hillel for the Halakha.[1] Since, however, he considers the law to be superseded, he is no longer like the rabbis interested in applying it by means of a process of logical inference to the countless cases occurring in everyday life, although there may be echoes of the "Halakha" casuistry in his doctrine of justification (considered as objective satisfaction). His background of Diaspora Pharisaism and the peculiarities of Judaic Hellenism may be connected with the fact that instead he uses so much the more extravagantly the midrashic exegesis and the allegoric Haggada, which embroider the historical and narrative parts of the Bible, and often also distort them. Of course the midrash and the Haggada never attained authoritative status in rigorous Judaism, but as an allegorizing midrashist Paul became great among his contemporary rabbis.

Haggada traditions are frequently met with among the Pauline letters. I will confine myself to a few well-known examples: the unusual midrash about the wandering in the wilderness (1 Cor. 10) with the rock which followed and which was Christ (v. 4); the old (cf. LXX to Deut. 33: 2) Haggada addition of the presence of angels at the giving of the law on Sinai which in Gal. 3: 19 Paul applies in a hostile sense against the saving role of the law; or the remark (with sexual implication) in 2 Cor. 11: 3 that Eve was deceived by the serpent, covered by the midrash on Gen. Par. 18. Further, the daemonological basis for the covering of a woman's head in prayer, suggesting that this "power on the head" is meant to ward off and banish the attacks of evil spirits (1 Cor. 11: 2–16); for which Gerhard Kittel[2] has adduced parallels from rabbinic literature and the history of religion. Again and again in his scriptural exegesis Paul bears in mind the traditions and speculations of the Haggada tradition, which are somewhat difficult for us to fathom to-day. Certain doctrinal tenets expounded in the Palestinian schools of the time, such as the זכות אבת (merits of the fathers), the pessimistic judgment of the יצר הרע (evil impulse), the increase of wickedness in

[1] Cf. A. F. Puukko, *Paulus und das Judentum*, Studia Orientalia II, Helsingfors, 1928, 64 ff.
[2] *Rabbinica, Arbeiten zur Religionsgeschichte des Urchristentums*, Vol. I, section 3, Leipzig; also L. M. Epstein, *Sex Laws and Customs in Judaism*, New York, 1948, 31 ff.

the outbreak of the Messianic age, the typology of Adam and Messiah, the praise of אמנה, and certain Messianic speculations occupy a large place in Paul's thought, and we shall meet them later. That not only in the cast of his thought but also in the material content of doctrinal convictions we are moving fully in the rabbinic sphere, is made plain by any precise study of his arguments (quite apart frcm certain specific exegetic points), especially when we consider that the letters are addressed to communities which count among their members many native Jews.

Rabbinic connexions and parallels[1] may be discovered for most of Paul's doctrines and expressions of faith, without its being necessary to exploit in a prejudiced way the criterion of "Hellenistic Judaism". It goes without saying that we are not thus giving preference to simplicity as if everything were to be explained from one point of view, and now for a change from the point of view of rabbinism. It must be shown by the very means of the precise delimitation of the various possibilities of Judaic derivation, including apocalyptic and Judaic Hellenism, at what point Pauline theology transcends those possibilities, of whatever complexion, existing within the framework of Judaism. But every explanation proceeding from rabbinism deserves *a limine* preference over all other explanations, in so far as it can be demonstrated sufficiently clearly and with an adequate basis of proof. Nevertheless, all these are only materials which Paul has used—thoughts from the stock of ideas belonging to the tenets and faith of his past—and by means of which he now wishes to give expression to something quite new. This new element has dawned for him through his encounter with the risen Messiah, convincing him that the new aeon has already supervened. For this reason apocalyptic thought gains a special significance for the Palestinian Judaic interpretation of the apostle, for he has drawn certain consequences from it, without which his basic conviction is unintelligible.

(b) *Apocalyptic*

Without anticipating what we have to say in our special chapter on the question of eschatology in Paul, we have here merely to determine the place of apocalyptic in Palestinian Judaism, and to suggest its value as a means of assessing Pauline theology. The

[1] Among the Jewish contributions on this point I find the most important to be the small work *Studien über Paulus*, which was published in 1918 from the literary remains of the Chief Rabbi of Stockholm, G. Klein. Unfortunately little attention was paid to it.

opinion of A. Schweitzer[1] in 1911 that apocalyptic represents a "special and isolated phenomenon in Judaism" or of G. F. Moore[2] that apocalyptic interests lie quite outside the sphere of rabbinism, and thus are not normative for Judaism, is recognized by modern critics to be a judgment influenced by the later course of develop- ment—which declared the apocalyptic writings to be uncanonical —and hence a perverse view of the Palestinian situation. Apocalyptic is rather, as Goguel[3] has well expressed it, a special form of the eschatological hope, and one which existed since the 2nd century B.C. It may have developed from cultural contacts with Persia.[4] Thus Bonsirven found,[5] in examining the contents of faith and doctrine, that there was no great contrast between apocalyptic and Palestinian–rabbinic writings of the time—not even as regards the status of the law. Apocalyptic is to be found even in the Talmud,[6] while in apocalyptic "Halakha" is also to be found,[7] even though shifts of emphasis are obvious.

Nevertheless, this type of literature can no longer be said seriously to be sectarian in tendency, although it might have been read in certain conventicles in particular. But the entire Tannaitic epoch was penetrated with eschatological expectations; one might even say that from the time of the apocalypse of Daniel, written under the impact made by Antiochus Epiphanes' desecration of the temple (168–164 B.C.), up to the collapse of the Messianic movement under Bar Kokhba (A.D. 135), there was a period of uninterrupted eschato- logical tension. In these 300 years the most varied forms and ex- pressions of chiliasm were confusedly interwoven. Because this is so, there is only limited truth in the many learned attempts at classifica- tion of this material, at noting oppositions between the varied forms

---

[1] *Geschichte der paulinischen Forschung*, Tübingen, 1911, 188. (E.T. *Paul and His Interpreters*.)

[2] *Judaism in the first centuries of the Christian Era*, I, Oxford, 1927, 127 ff.

[3] "Eschatologie et apocalyptique dans le christianisme primitif", *RHPhR*, 1932, 381 ff.

[4] A view expressed in the many works of G. Widengren, e.g. recently in the study "Juifs et Iraniens à l'époque des Parthes", Supplements to *Vetus Testamentum*, IV, Leiden, 1957, 197–240.

[5] *Le Judaïsme Palestinien au temps de Jésus-Christ*, I, Paris, 1934, XXII. But already before Moore, C. C. Torrey (*Jew. Enc.*, I, 673) had arrived at a similar conclusion: "The Jewish apocalyptic writings were not the property of any sect or school. Their point of view was that of Palestinian orthodoxy of which the Pharisees were the best representatives."

[6] I refer only to the studies by N. N. Glatzer, *Die Geschichtslehre der Tannaiten*, Berlin, 1933, which of course shows the shift of emphasis within apocalyptic itself.

[7] Cf. the collection of material in P. Volz, *Die Eschatologie der jüdischen Gemeinde im ntl. Zeitalter*, Tübingen, 1934; further also H. H. Rowley, *The Relevance of Apocalyptic*, London, 1947. In particular, "Jubilees" according to the studies by Albeck, Büchler, Zeitlin, Morgenstern, Dupont-Sommer, etc., is of interest from the "halakha" point of view.

of the expectation. Of course it may be shown from the very specific eschatological ideas of Paul—as also of Jesus—on what particular elements in the expectation they were based. Albert Schweitzer has above all the special merit of having selected and applied those literary documents of Jewish eschatology which were of special significance for Paul. In this connexion the twofold eschatology of the apocalypses of Baruch and Ezra is important, with their separation of the advent of the Messiah from the general resurrection of the dead by an intervening Messianic period, such as corresponded to the character of the Christian situation in which Paul believed himself to be living. Paul then found himself forced to change the time programme of the end-events which he had taken over from Baruch, IV Ezra, and the ten-week apocalypse of the Book of Enoch (91: 12–17; 93: 1–10), for as a result of the unexpected dying and rising again of the Messiah it had become necessary to assume a second parousia, while, for the interim generation of the Messianic kingdom, participation in the resurrection had to be explained by a non-Jewish sacramental mysticism. Hence Schweitzer presented the apostle's work in the guise of what I might call a "theology of the post-messianic situation". (Cf. for details the next section.)

Obviously apocalyptic writings, as W. D. Davies has also shown, have contributed many other ideas to Pauline theology. Thus he derives from that source his theory of aeons, which lies behind his typological exegesis.[1] Its limits as marked out by the rabbis[2] were often overstepped by Paul. Thus for him Adam became the type of Christ (Rom. 5: 12–21; 1 Cor. 15: 45–49) as also Isaac (cf. ch. 5, section 4); the beginning of time became the type of the end (2 Cor. 4: 6; 5: 17) and the period of Moses the type of his own day (2 Cor. 3: 7–18). All this is possible because the aeon of the Torah is dissolved by that of the Christ, and the Torah was transferred to Christ.[3] Apart from this theology of the aeons, stemming from apocalyptic, Paul came under the influence of the conception, specially elaborated in IV Ezra, that the law was a divine gift to Israel (3: 19 ff.; 9: 31 ff.) but could not justify sinners (9: 36); also of a strongly marked pessimism with regard to sin (e.g., 7 : 116–131) and of suggestions concerning a dual doctrine of predestina-

---

[1] Cf. R. Bultmann, "Ursprung und Sinn der Typologie als hermeneutischer Methode", *ThLZ*, 1950, 206 ff.

[2] Sabb. 63a: אין מקרא יוצא מידי פשוטו (no verse of scripture can ever lose its original meaning).

[3] Cf. C. A. Bugge, "Das Gesetz und Christus", *ZNW*, 1903, 105 ff.; Lohmeyer, *op. cit.*, 141 ff. W. Schmauch, *In Christus*, Gütersloh, 1935, 165 ff.

tion—which Montefiore had reserved for his idea of Judaistic Hellenism. Since, however, similar isolated opinions had been voiced in the school debates preserved by the Talmud, while never becoming generally acceptable, parallels can be referred to, but no sure genealogies of such Pauline doctrines can be established. In so far as eschatological expectations were the sustaining basis of his Christian attitude, the contacts of his theology with apocalyptic material were especially close, and some knowledge of its literature or at least of its traditional stock of ideas must be assumed.[1] For Paul produced a final clarification of its realistic consequences by applying it to a situation which he considered Messianic in the apocalyptic sense, and so himself—*sit venia verbo*—reared the structure of a post-apocalyptic theology.

4. THE ESCHATOLOGICAL APPROACH TO PAUL

That the doctrine of the last things forms the "greatest block of Jewish material in the thought-world of Paul"[2] is clear beyond a doubt. Eschatological expectation: the personal Messiah, the coming Day of Judgment, and the doctrine of the two aeons remained unknown and unappreciated in the Hellenistic Mediterranean world of the time, as is plain from the lasting misunderstanding of the apostle among the Greek Christians in Salonica (1 Thess. 4: 13 ff.; 2 Thess. 3: 6 ff.) and Corinth (1 Cor. 15). Consequently, the eschatological approach to Paul is fully legitimate in the light of exegetical data. It began as a reaction to the excessive emphasis on his Hellenism in that Kabisch, Brückner, and most insistently W. Wrede pointed out that the event of his call on the Damascus road could not have been without presuppositions, for Paul clearly believed in the Christ before receiving the vision of the risen Jesus. The situation was rather that he applied to the latter all those ideas which he entertained concerning the apocalyptic heavenly being. This heavenly being, or the Son of Man of apocalyptic, and the expectation of redemption understood as a material change in the objective world on the advent of the Messiah, were, in

---

[1] Origen already (*Comm. ad Mt. 27: 9*, Lomm. V, 29) was struck by the fact that in the formula καθὼς γέγραπται (1 Cor. 2: 9) Paul once cited a text which is not to be found in the Bible but in the Apocalypse of Elijah, which we know only from a late fragmentary form.

[2] Thus J. Leipoldt, *Jesus und Paulus—Jesus oder Paulus?* Leipzig, 1936, 70, who interprets Paul hellenistically and supposes as regards eschatology that his churches compelled him to think things out in a new way (74).

the opinion of these critics, a faith-certitude cherished by Saul, the Pharisaic theologian.

Albert Schweitzer took over this insight and elaborated it in the spirit of the positive criticism of F. C. Baur,[1] to whom he refers as the "master" just when he is endeavouring to demonstrate the superiority of his own thesis and therewith to eliminate all other explanations. In fact, Schweitzer's "consistent eschatology" has high significance for modern Pauline research, because in spite of some excesses and some violence[2] he built his thesis on the right foundations. In the programme sketched as early as 1911 he avowed his purpose "of attempting the one-sidedness of wishing to understand the doctrine of the apostle to the Gentiles solely from the standpoint of the primitive Jewish Christian community" (187). On the basis of eschatology he then fulfilled this intention in his great work, *The Mysticism of Paul the Apostle* (1930).[3] Schweitzer gave an impressive explanation of this procedure:

> While they [the other critics] pulled at the first best thread, they entangled the skein to start off with, and condemned themselves to have to give an unintelligible chaos of thoughts as Pauline doctrine. The only objective procedure consists in this, viz. to begin with the simple factor which Paul has completely in common with the first church, and to see how his doctrine grows from this root. Until he is explained in this way he is not explained at all. This simple factor is the messianic expectation. This he put forward when in his missionary work he went from place to place. He harks back to it in his letters. Hence with this any account of Pauline teaching must logically begin (41, German edition).

Schweitzer thinks that from this standpoint redemption-mysticism, the teaching about the law and sacraments cohere in the common forms of expression of an "inner logic". Paul's theology, Schweitzer thinks, is to be understood solely in the light of the primitive situation, of the new position of the world which arose as a cosmic event between the death and resurrection of Jesus and which looked forward to His parousia. Two aeons clash; the supernatural status of the world has begun with the resurrection of Jesus from the dead, and through the eschatological sacraments of baptism and the Lord's

[1] *Geschichte der paulinischen Forschung*, Tübingen, 1911, 194.
[2] Cf. the arguments of J. Héring, "St. Paul a-t-il enseigné deux résurrections?", *RHPhR*, 1932, 300 ff.; E. B. Allo in *RB*, 1932, 187 ff.
[3] Cf. the repeated appreciations of M. Werner in the last thirty-five years and the monograph of H. Babel, *La pensée d'Albert Schweitzer*, Neuchâtel, 1954.

Supper, which confer Messianic blessedness, a dying and rising with Christ, a "being in Christ" as a new form of existence has become possible to believers, for the powers of the last times are already efficacious through the Spirit and the response of faith. The present time is post-messianic; already there reigns an "objective mysticism of facts" (100).

Schweitzer considered that Paul represented the speculations of Baruch, IV Ezra and certain Tannaites with regard to the aeons, the thought that the end of the age had really begun with the death of the Messiah, and that the interim Messianic kingdom considered as the final year-week of world time would shortly close with the general resurrection of the dead distinctive of the coming aeon. The surviving elect of this last generation would participate in this event, and even for those who had died beforehand, participation would be possible through their baptism into the death of Christ. In distinction to this twofold order of the last events עולם הבא—ימות המשיח the Jewish-Christian first church held fast to the simple conception of the last things, according to which the course of eschatological events was expected to begin only after the advent of the imminent parousia, and thus it did not co-operate in this post-messianic theology. This difference in eschatological outlook between Paul and the first church was supposed to be the reason for the controversy about the continued validity of the law, which, Schweitzer thought, was utterly dependent on the views of the early Christians with regard to the last things.

Pupils and compatriots of Schweitzer, such as M. Werner, F. Buri, H. Babel, U. Neuenschwander, etc., have been keenly sensitive to the historical force of this view of Paul. Werner[1] exploited it for a quite new presentation of the history of the early church and its dogmas, suggesting the revolutionary consequences which flowed from the undeniable fact of the indefinite delay in the appearance of the parousia; a thesis which has also met with much opposition.

Objections to the Schweitzer–Werner thesis are that the old Tübingen emphasis on the differences in the primitive church has misled them into overlooking the common element which exists, despite the peculiarities of Pauline thought, in all forms of the

[1] Cf. his important work *Die Entstehung des christlichen Dogmas*, Berne, 1941 (1954). Werner already announced this intention when he took from Schweitzer the "fundamental insight" that the "non-appearance of the parousia in the 1st post-Christian century implies a fact which makes it impossible even for the most orthodox Christian dogmatist to take seriously, without more ado, true Paulinism" (*Weltanschauliche Probleme bei K. Barth und A. Schweitzer*, Munich, 1924, 9).

45

primitive Christian kerygma (Goguel); that the whole of primitive Christianity was marked by the co-existence of hope for the future and certitude in the present, with the result that redemption was awaited not merely from the future (Kümmel, Manson, Cullmann), and that the doctrine of a twofold resurrection was unknown among the Jews and can be proved from the Pauline writings only by doing violence to the text (Héring). That "consistent eschatology" has drawn a distorted sketch of Jesus seems to me to have been proved by criticism which has seldom been so unanimous in speaking from different points of view. But as far as Paul is concerned, this school seems to be right to a large extent. For it is undeniable that Paul, with the whole of primitive Christianity, erred about the imminently expected parousia. And that considerable parts of his doctrine so quickly became unintelligible is a fact which favours Schweitzer's thesis of a unified composition most closely bound up with a certain situation.

Although Schweitzer has introduced much confusion into this subject by his idea of mysticism[1] and by the consequences of his doctrine of resurrection, and although his complete rejection of Hellenistic thought-forms for soteriology and the doctrine of the sacraments is in my opinion untenable, he has none the less shown the fruitfulness of the eschatological approach. For the latter is able to clarify the Jewish faith-presuppositions from which the apostle of Jesus Christ, placed in a new and unforeseeable situation, namely, the post-messianic, developed something original and really new: that is, Christian theology. Thus it is in the light of this approach that the originality of Paul's genius is first fully realized, for it is then appreciated that he was not merely the inevitable end-product of specific premises. Although I am not able to see Paul—as Schweitzer does—as a logical systematic thinker in one cast of ideas, and prefer to see and think of him as dynamic, ecstatic, and exalted, in the whole mode of his personality, the truth will probably lie somewhere between these extremes—between Adolf Deissmann, who almost absurdly exaggerates these latter elements, and Albert Schweitzer, who over-emphasizes the logical consistency of the apostle.

[1] R. Bultmann (*DLZ*, 1931, 1153 ff.) emphasized in his critique of Schweitzer's work that in many places the author says "eschatological mysticism" when he really means or should mean "gnosis". How problematic is the term mysticism in connexion with Paul, and how limited should be the use made of it, has been shown by Dibelius in his short study *Paulus und die Mystik* (Munich, 1941); reprinted in *Botschaft und Geschichte*, II, Tübingen, 1956, 134 ff.

5. NET RESULTS FOR A JUST AND OBJECTIVE APPROACH TO PAUL

In this attempt to sketch a map of the present position and problems of Pauline research we have explained the various chief types of
approach, as represented and variously combined in the last fifty
years. In this we have proceeded with reference to Paul's biography,
and have surveyed the spiritual forces of his environment up to the
time of his Damascus experience, and we have asked how far they
might be considered as possible sources or influential factors. Our
retrospect of the history of Pauline research has already taught us
that this basic problem is uncommonly difficult to solve; that the
picture given of Paul is determined by the point of view which each
critic adopts. Whoever wishes to understand the spiritual stature of
Paul, his life's destiny, his theology, and lastly his influence must
reckon with an integrated but composite cultural *milieu* such as his
origins suggest—hence with the three spiritual and cultural forces of
his youth, whose effective influence on his thought is so difficult to
determine. My opinion is that all the attempts at interpretation
which we have studied are relatively right. The problem is only to
decide correctly on their limits, to decide where and how they over-
lap. I have already suggested the most important demarcations.

In fact, Paul must be interpreted on the basis of his Hellenistic
Diaspora background, although here it is only a question of Judaic
Hellenism, to which pagan Hellenism with its mystery cults had
percolated. Of course, he may have had a direct encounter with the
latter. Especially in the central soteriology of the apostle and his
"sacramental mysticism" the influence of these cults is unmistakable,
at least in so far as they supplied a model, as we shall plainly see in
our treatment of this theme in ch. 4; particularly when the theme is
dealt with on the basis of Judaic premises. In the first place, however, Paul must be assessed as a rabbinical exegete; for his doctrine
of sin and the law, and much else, would be incomprehensible apart
from the debates of the Palestinian schools (details in ch. 5). Presumably the latter guided his eschatological thought into the field of
apocalyptic and its special literature which was obviously known to
Paul, and after Damascus this led Paul to interpret his present as a
post-messianic situation (details ch. 3), just as it furthered his whole
new and pregnant conception of saving history (ch. 6). The eschatological relevance of the situation stands throughout behind all his
statements; a fact which Jewish scholars have for the most part failed
to recognize, preferring like J. Klausner to expound an extreme and

long-out-of-date liberal attitude. But this whole delimination of spheres of influence is never meant to suggest sharp lines of separation, but rather main tendencies, beneath which there may have been constantly at work currents of a different kind. In particular, schemes of thought stemming from the Hellenistic mystery cults may often be latent behind his expositions, especially when he is addressing communities containing Greek Christians. The talk of Paul's acute Hellenization of Christianity which has sprung up in consequence of the Tübingen school must, however, be rejected, for this phenomenon is post-Pauline only, and its first signs are to be found in the Deutero–Pauline writings.

What seems to me most doubtful in this attempt at analysis is the possibility that it might give rise to a sort of arithmetical misunderstanding, as though the critic might, at least approximately, reckon up the theology of the apostle as the sum of its various component parts. But it is just this which is not possible or—to retain the metaphor—only when one first finds the new denominator: the personality of Paul himself. This, however, can be found only if we recognize the utter newness and uniqueness of his existence, which is not derivable from some hypothetical special tradition of early Hellenistic communities, but solely from the event of Damascus. And the latter was necessary neither as thought nor as event; even Wrede, who was most inclined to such an idea, never asserted so much.[1] The new and effective element in his theology is what is most properly Pauline.[2] It has entered so deeply into the essence of Christianity, and entwined itself so closely with Christian existence, that a deliverance of Christianity from its Pauline elements has become for ever impossible. This was decided by the defeat and elimination of the Ebionites. It is not they but Paul, and his followers, who paradoxically have become the representatives of the Judaic element in Christianity.

As we have just been speaking of the new and special features in Paul, a word in conclusion may be necessary about the peculiarities of his mode of thought. Hans Leisegang[3] once said that Paul does not think with progressive continuity but in circular fashion. For this reason his ideas are so often intertwined (e.g., Rom. 5: 18;

[1] As W. G. Kümmel informed me by letter, C. Holsten should be excepted: cf. below, p. 54.
[2] The systematic accounts of Pauline theology have with good reason considered this characteristic; cf. that of E. Lohmeyer or Bultmann's existential–anthropological interpretation.
[3] *Paulus als Denker*, Leipzig, 1923, 37.

1 Cor. 15: 20 ff.). From the idea of life springs that of death, from death he passes again to life. This is because Paul's style of thinking is dialectic. In thinking of "a" he thinks at once of "non-a". If he says "life", he thinks immediately "not death". With this remarkable form of thought by contrasts, he proceeds from flesh to spirit, from the natural man to the spiritual man, etc. Such a peculiar associative and contrasting type of thought may strike anyone as strange who comes to Paul from the writings of the ancient philosophers. But in Hellenistic Judaism, as in Orphic circles, this type of thought, as Leisegang thinks, may be rooted. Another integral feature of it is that series of logical implications may cancel each other out. Also there corresponds to this discontinuous mode of thought a striking emotional excitement, a swift change of mood and feeling, and with Paul feelings are expressed not in succession but in conjunction. In reading his letters we often come across this,[1] and he appears at times as one possessed, always in pursuit, always pursued. His destiny of suffering as an apostle of Jesus Christ he has most vividly depicted in 2 Cor. 11: 23–30.

Paul was a dynamic personality, on whom thoughts rained so that he was driven ceaselessly from the one to the other. Moreover, his thought was penetrating, leading us to well-nigh unfathomable depths. Often he merely suggests and instead of a whole chain of thought will give us flashes of ideas. Further, he does not always discipline linguistically these thoughts which tumble over each other. The mentality of Paul was that of an intellectual living in the environment of a large city, of one who draws his imagery from the life of the state and is adapted to the world of affairs. It is not without significance that we constantly meet, in the apostle's work, images derived from trade and craft, building, seafaring, courts of justice, the theatre, etc., but hardly ever from the world of nature, the land, or agriculture. Apart from his self-contradictions, a further difficulty lies in the fact that he is rooted in traditions which we cannot completely grasp. All this makes it sometimes most difficult to follow the sequences of his thought and to seize the connecting links, yet there speaks in his letters "an individual stamped by a peculiar subjectivity, and by an originality which shatters all traditional forms".[2]

---

[1] Martin Dibelius therefore concluded in his little book on Paul that organic unity, harmony, and integration were lacking in the apostle. In fact, he says "any sort of humanism" was lacking in the apostle.

[2] Thus Eduard Schwartz, *Charakterköpfe der Antike*, Berlin, 1950, 207.

We wish now to attempt, on the basis of these recognitions, to present the "true" picture of Paul and of Pauline theology, as it is made possible after many decades of scholarly effort and exact methods of research. We agree with the demand of F. C. Baur—despite his most recent critic (Joh. Munck)—that after a truly "positive criticism" of the situation and its general features, we should attain a view of the whole picture and see the true significance of Paul within primitive Christianity and within the realities of the first generation of Christians. For this reason our second chapter will maintain the biographical point of view, and will discuss the position of the apostle within the first church, as it may be reconstructed from his hard struggles with his Christian opponents, before we pass to the more systematic presentation of his main doctrines.

The great touchstone for this presentation will be the question how far it is objectively adequate and exegetically tenable, how far, in cases where it shifts the emphasis, it does so convincingly, whether it attains a view which is nearer to reality, or whether it succumbs to the dangers of an eclecticism stemming from the "History of Religion" method. The author feels it to be an advantage that as an independent historian of religion he is not limited in his views by confessional prejudice, as are many professional theologians who approach Paul from the standpoint of their confessional faith, which they involuntarily read into him. But he realizes too his own limitations, that he too does not have an equally open mind on all points, that he is lacking in the knowledge and experience of the professional exegete, that he has not sufficiently mastered the enormous literature on the subject, and perhaps not all the relevant questions. The author has tried to give of his best, and finally is comforted by the reflection that in our day the ideal interpreters of Paul, who were so much at home in three worlds at once that they were really competent to grapple with their hero's thought, are no longer living. That they all fail to do justice to the towering stature of Paul must not, however, be considered any discredit to them.

2

THE POSITION OF THE APOSTLE PAUL
IN PRIMITIVE CHRISTIANITY

Introduction: The Question of Sources

BEFORE going into detail, we must say briefly a word about sources, and the question as to which documents might form a sound basis for our knowledge of the person and teaching of Paul. First we ask which writings may be considered valid sources for his teaching.

F. C. Baur and the Tübingen school, with which modern exact research about Paul begins, recognized as genuine only the four major letters (Romans, 1 and 2 Corinthians, and Galatians). The whole account put forward in the Acts of the Apostles, which of course every non-Pauline mission—doubtless contrary to historical truth—discards, they rejected as tendentious and incompatible with the genuine picture of Paul conveyed by the letters. This Tübingen standpoint has been on the whole maintained, but corrected and toned down in the meantime. The modern viewpoint is rather as follows: the speeches of Paul as given in Acts may possibly go back to the traditions of speeches which he really delivered. But in the form in which they are now extant they are doubtless the work of the author of the document, and have been adjusted to the tendency of his writing as a whole. As authentic testimony to the teaching of Paul—and the Tübingen school was correct in this—they do not enter into the question. Nevertheless, for the reconstruction of Paul's life story they are indispensable.

Tübingen doubts have not been maintained in regard to 1 Thessalonians, Philippians and Philemon. These letters too are now felt to be authentic. But most modern New Testament commentators still reject the letters to Timothy and Titus, while opinions as regards 2 Thessalonians are much divided, for, apart from the dubious language, it has given up the expectation of an imminent parousia. The letters to Timothy and Titus, usually termed "pastoral letters",

51

offer us Pauline ideas only in common expressions and are mostly dated at the end of the 1st century. Colossians and Ephesians present a very difficult problem. More recent research, especially that indebted to Bultmann, has stressed their gnostic character, reflected both in style and in essential sequences of thought. It is probable that they were written in the post-Pauline militant situation governed by gnosticism, though the composition is in the Pauline spirit. Hence they have been called Deutero-Pauline, for as an account of Pauline theology they can rank only as secondary sources. Thus the best course is to proceed from the seven certainly genuine letters (Romans, 1 and 2 Corinthians, Galatians, Philippians, 1 Thessalonians, Philemon) which were written between 49 and 63, and to classify as sources of secondary importance the ideas of the others, as of the speeches in Acts wherever relevant.

Primary sources for Paul outside the New Testament are not extant. Some secondary or rather tertiary sources, which prolong reflections of his life and work and may have a certain relevance for problems of detail, must briefly be mentioned:

1. The apocryphal Acts of Paul (*Acta Pauli et Theclae*) give more than a hundred years later a quite vivid description of his appearance. We there read: "I saw Paul coming, a man of small stature with a big bold head and crooked legs, but of noble bearing, eyebrows grown together and rather prominent nose; a man breathing friendliness." The suspicion cannot be avoided that here the features of Socrates have been transferred to Paul.[1] In iconography likewise, from the 4th century onwards, a certain cast of countenance has fairly constantly been attributed to him.[2] 2. The Talmud has preserved no notice which can be certainly referred to Paul. Gerhard Kittel[3] has proposed to see an allusion to him in the Mishna handed down in the name of Rabbi Eliezer of Modaim: "He who violates the Sabbath, breaks fasts, and scandalizes his neighbour, annuls the covenant of our father Abraham, and twists the meaning of the law— even though he has a knowledge of the law and can point to good works—will have no part in the world to come." One can only say that such a Mishna attacking antinomists includes from the Jewish point of view even men of the stature of Paul. Suspect also is the remark in Ruth Rabba III about the man who "made himself peculiar with regard to circumcision and the law" (gloss on Prov.

---

[1] Cf. L. Baeck: "The Faith of Paul", *JJSt*, 1952, Nr. 3, 99.
[2] Cf. Jos. Wilpert, *Die Malereien der Katakomben Roms* (Freiburg, 1903), pp. 112 ff.
[3] *Rabbinica*, Leipzig, 1920.

21: 8). We find perhaps a pseudonymous allusion under the name Gehazi, the faithless servant of the prophet Elisha, in the Talmud (Sanh. 107b; Sota 47a). Here Rabbi Jochanan says: "Of Gehazi it is said that he was incapable of penance, because he sinned and led others astray into sinning. Moreover Gehazi became leprous." Is this perhaps the "thorn in the flesh"? But all these are doubtful allusions.[1]

In the Jewish–Christian pseudo-Clementine writings we have a clearly identifiable polemic against Paul, who is alluded to under the name "homo quidam inimicus", as also under that of Simon. He is here viewed in hostile guise as the ἀντικείμενος καὶ ἐχθρός and his teaching is travestied. In particular these writings are marked by a polemic against his apostolate, which he is said to have stolen by visions and hallucinations. Such views are not without their value for the reconstruction of the opinions of his Jewish opponents in the field of missionary work. Later (section 5 of this chapter) we shall go into these matters in detail.

But on the whole it must be confessed that these sources are very vague and of little value. For the real knowledge of the life and teaching of Paul is obtainable only from his writings themselves. In this respect we need not be disturbed by the *silentium saeculi*. Paul was neither a man of letters nor a socially-minded person; he was not likely to have struck his contemporaries either by his works or his appearance among men. Contemporary historians have mentioned him as little as to-day a daily newspaper would mention a wandering adventist preacher and his meetings, unless he happened to occasion something sensational. The statement of his enemies in 2 Cor. 6: 9 that he was "unknown", by which it was probably meant to indicate that he was not known in the circle of the original Jerusalem apostles, contains, with regard to the whole position of Paul in the world of his time, a deep truth. We now turn to the proper subject of this chapter.

I. PAUL AND JESUS

(a) *The event of Damascus*

The much-discussed question as to the relation of Paul to Jesus Christ Himself depends largely on the orientation with which the individual exegete approaches the interpretation of the apostle. Those who think that Paul had fixed preconceived views of the

---

[1] Still more uncertain in H. Hirschberg, "Allusions to the Apostle Paul in the Talmud", *JBL*, 1943, 73 ff.

Christ already moulded by Hellenism, rabbinism, apocalyptic and other sources, must accordingly reduce the significance of the Damascus vision for the life story of the apostle, and grant relatively little importance to the influence of the teaching of Jesus Himself on his thought. Others, who stress the unity of the apostolic kerygma in early Christianity, think that Paul was largely dependent on the summons of Jesus, and see in the Damascus event the incalculable miracle of grace which determined both the life destiny of Paul and also the history of early Christianity.[1] It will be best to proceed from the accounts themselves.

As is known, we have two sources for the Damascus event: the indications of the apostle in his letters and the three reports in Acts (9: 1 ff.; 22: 3 f.; 26: 10 ff.)—which are inconsistent in detail—and which in essentials may well rest on Paul's own story.[2] In his letters, Paul had understood the event of his call as a genuine theophany, as may be seen from the similarity of his language with that used by the LXX for theophanies. 1 Cor. 15: 8; ὤφθη κἀμοί. In his letter to the Galatians he speaks of a revelation within himself (1: 16: ἀποκαλύψαι τὸν υἱὸν αὐτοῦ ἐν ἐμοί). And in a further place, which is probably also to be connected with the Damascus experience, he speaks of the light which springs up out of darkness, and—in what is, moreover, a typically Judaic–Greek phrase construction—of the φωτισμὸς τῆς δόξης τοῦ θεοῦ ἐν προσώπῳ Χριστοῦ (2 Cor. 4: 6). This appeal to a vision of light is fully in agreement with the reports in Acts, according to which a light from heaven shone around him, when the risen Jesus appeared to him and called to His service one who had been His persecutor.[3]

Since C. Holsten ("Die Christusvision des Paulus", Z. wiss. Theol., 1861, 223–284) repeated attempts have been made to analyse this conversion experience on psychological lines, for other ecstatic experiences which he reports (his being caught up to the third heaven, 2 Cor. 12: 2–4; the speaking with tongues, 1 Cor. 14: 6 ff.) plainly invited such an approach.[4] Discussions have taken place

---

[1] On the whole subject cf. from the catholic point of view: E. Pfaff, *Die Bekehrung des Paulus in der Exegese des 20. Jahrhunderts*, Rome, 1942.

[2] Cf. now Ernst Benz, *Paulus als Visionär, eine vergleichende Untersuchung der Visionsberichte des Paulus in der Apostelgeschichte und in den paulinischen Briefen*, Akad. Wiss. Lit. Mainz, Geistes- und Sozialwiss. Kl. 1952, Nr. 2.

[3] Radiance of light is the most frequent accompaniment of visions; material from Jewish and Christian sources has been collected by E. L. Ehrlich, *Der Traum im AT*, Berlin, 1953, 39 ff.; also Davies, *op. cit.*, 184 ff.

[4] The most recent study on these lines, set out with some reserve, is the essay by Joh. Munck, "La vocation de l'Apôtre Paul", *Studia Theologica*, I, 1–2, Lund, 1948, 131 ff.

as to how far it was psychologically prepared, as to whether it sprang from an ecstatic visionary disposition, as to whether its objectivity is reliable, and so on. It is difficult to get anywhere in this way. If we adopt this approach and explain away the vision on a psychological basis, so that it becomes but the subjective vision of an ecstatic in a state of tension, then to be consistent we should have to adopt the same method of easy explanation—which is only an explaining away—for Moses' vision of God at the burning bush, while the divine voice to the patriarchs and prophets would have to be similarly explained as subjective and fanciful. If we wish to understand what happened at this point in the life of the apostle, and what were its consequences, then we must accept fully the real objectivity of the encounter as it is testified in the letters and in Acts. Certainly the "History of Religion" viewpoint is different from the theological. It is assumed of the theologian that in his own existence he becomes the contemporary of Paul, that with Paul he believes in Jesus as the manifested and risen Son of God. The historian of religion is expected to recognize the faith of Paul in the manifested Son of God to be the factual result of his encounter with the crucified and exalted Jesus of Nazareth. Hence he must accept the faith which inspired Paul. If he does not do so, if he fails to recognize the objective content of this encounter, then he can only stupidly fail to understand an event which made history; which, according to the Christian faith, is itself saving history.

But in this matter the relevant question for both historian and theologian is a different one, not psychological but objective: which aspects of his consciousness were so changed by his call that the zealot for the law could become its critic, the Jew a Christian? We shall constantly be meeting this question in the course of our work, and shall try to give an appropriate answer. As regards Paul's relation to the historical Jesus, there is a further dual problem to be considered: (1) What significance has the Jesus who walked on earth, and whose preaching is preserved particularly in the synoptic gospels, for Paul and his theology? (2) What place is occupied by the exalted Jesus in Pauline thought?

(b) *The significance of the historical Jesus for the apostle Paul*

As is well known, the earthly life of Jesus falls strikingly into the background in the letters of Paul. He mentions the following details: Jesus was born under the law as a Jew (Gal. 4: 4), was of Davidic descent (Rom. 1: 3), was betrayed (1 Cor. 11: 23), and was crucified by the ἄρχοντες τοῦ αἰῶνος τούτου (Gal. 3: 1; 1 Cor. 2: 2; Phil. 2: 8, etc.), was buried and rose again (1 Cor. 15: 4; Rom. 6: 4). The resurrection on the third day took place κατὰ τὰς γραφάς; hence, as was predicted of the Messiah. This is all, with regard to the dates and facts of the earthly life of Jesus. These allusions are of a parenetic character,[1] and in any event do not occupy a central place in Paul's teaching. They simply suggest that for Paul Jesus was no mythical figure, but a real historical fact. Logia of Jesus are very seldom expressly cited: the words of institution of the Eucharist, as handed down to him by common church instruction (1 Cor. 11: 23 ff.); a λόγος κυρίου about the fate of those who have fallen asleep and those who survive at the time of the parousia (1 Thess. 4: 15), as also two "Halakha" decisions of Jesus which are of small importance for the preaching of the apostle: burdensome decisions about divorce (1 Cor. 7: 10, παραγγέλω οὐκ ἐγὼ ἀλλὰ ὁ κύριος), and about the duty of the church to support its ministers (1 Cor. 9: 14). In addition, there may be echoes of the Lord's teaching not made known as such.[2]

These facts speak for themselves and can hardly be mended by the *argumentum ex silentio* which has often been tried, to the effect that Paul's teaching was oral and is only reflected in his letters, which are, after all, merely fragmentary (Deissmann) and that we know nothing of the rest, etc.[3] The observation of Schweitzer[4] is much more to the point: "Where possible he avoids quoting the teaching of

---

[1] If need be one might think of faint echoes such as the allusion to the gentleness of Christ in 2 Cor. 10: 1 ff., or His endurance of infamy, Rom. 15: 2 ff. But even so, it only increases the negative impression.

[2] The following are usually considered such: Rom. 12: 14 (Mt. 5: 44), 13: 9 (Mk. 12: 31), 16: 19 (Mt. 10: 16), 1 Cor. 13: 2 (Mk. 11: 23). Bultmann admits these (*Theol. NT*, 185). Kümmel ("Jesus und Paulus", *ThBl*, 1942, 212) adds Gal. 5: 14. Further possible allusions to the words of Jesus have been collected by H. J. Holtzmann: *Lehrbuch d. ntl. Theol.*, II, 1911, 232 ff.

[3] Those who hold these views must take refuge in probabilities, since they cannot get anywhere exegetically. As typical I quote K. Karner ("Die Stellung des Apostels Paulus im Urchristentum", *ZSTh*, 1937, 165): "The story of the inner development of early Christianity as worked out by historical critical methods is completely shattered by the fact that it rests on the assumed indifference of Paul to the preaching of Jesus and the traditions about Him. It is far more probable that Paul instructed his churches in the history of Jesus, as told in the gospels, to a far greater extent than is recognizable from his letters."

[4] Schweitzer simply follows here well-known insights of the "History of Religion" school, which made its deductions only from the meaninglessness of the earthly life of Jesus for Paul's view of Christ. Cf. the formulae in Brückner, *Die Entstehung der pln. Christologie*, Tübingen, 1903, 41 ff. and in *ZNW*, 1906, 114 ff.; also W. Wrede, *Paulus*, 1907, 53 ff. (E.T. *Paul*).

Jesus, in fact even mentioning it. If we had to rely on Paul, we should not know that Jesus taught in parables, had delivered the Sermon on the Mount, and had taught His disciples the 'Our Father'. Even where they are specially relevant, Paul passes over words of the Lord" (*Mystik* 171). Schweitzer gives a series of examples.

Hence other explanations must be given of this striking fact. Paul gives them himself: he explains in Galatians that his gospel does not go back to common church traditions but rests on a special ἀποκάλυψις Ἰησοῦ Χριστοῦ, Gal 1: 11–12: "For I would have you know, brethren, that the gospel which was preached by me is not man's gospel. For I did not receive it from man, nor was I taught it, but it came through a revelation of Jesus Christ." He can only maintain his insistence on his independence of the common tradition by giving to his Damascus experience a higher authority than that which he accords to the words and teaching of the earthly Jesus, to which the twelve in consequence of their personal intercourse with their Master can always appeal. It seems to me that this claim lies behind the words of 2 Cor. 5: 16, which can only be hypothetically translated: "even though we once regarded Christ from a human point of view, we regard him thus no longer." Since this contrast leads to a different idea of the apostolate, we shall discuss it in its proper connexion.

A further reason for the insignificant part which the earthly life and teaching of Jesus play in his thought, seems to me to lie in the following circumstance: the logia of Jesus for him recede behind the course of saving events; Jesus is risen but His kingdom has not yet come, and, in this situation only, the exalted Jesus who now has become κύριος Χριστός has meaning for His church. The fact is that Paul preaches "only" faith in Jesus, not the faith of Jesus!

To sum up: it should be clear that Paul never saw the historical Jesus[1] and was somewhat shy of the Palestinian traditions of the earthly life of Jesus.[2] In any case there can be no question of a significant influence of the earthly person of Jesus on the piety of the apostle. Kümmel (*op. cit.*, 213) explains quite truly: "Paul does not feel himself to be a disciple of the historical Jesus, but a man commissioned by the risen Lord. Hence it is not his mission to hand on the traditions he has received about the historical Jesus and His teaching, but to proclaim the Christ." And this is in harmony with

---

[1] This is often based on 1 Cor. 9: 1; cf. H. Windisch in *Th. St. u. Kr.*, 1934, 5, 437.

[2] Cf. R. Bultmann, *Theol. NT*, 185: "His letters show in fact little trace of the influence of the Palestinian tradition of the story of Jesus."

the exegetical finding that the gospel preached by him is at the crucial points of his letters constantly characterized as the proclamation of the crucified and risen Christ (e.g., 1 Cor. 1: 23; 15: 3 ff.; Gal. 3: 1, etc.). Consequently we must now, without anticipating the Christological and soteriological aspects to be dealt with later, sketch:

(c) *The place of the exalted Jesus in the thought of Paul*

This is to be measured by the judgment which Paul makes on the historical situation of his own day. The Messiah, who until the time of Jesus was awaited as still to come, has in fact come, the last age has dawned, and the times are now post-messianic. The Messiah or Christ—the Anointed of the Lord—has been exalted by the latter to be the *kyrios* over all earthly beings (Phil. 2: 11). Hence the death and resurrection of Jesus are for him cosmic events, for they have utterly transformed the very substance of the cosmos. The unambiguous sign of the new age is for him the experiential conviction that the resurrection of the dead has come to pass in that Jesus the "firstfruits of those who have fallen asleep" ($\dot{a}\pi a\rho\chi\grave{\eta}$ $\tau\tilde{\omega}\nu$ $\kappa\epsilon\kappa o\iota\mu\eta\mu\acute{\epsilon}\nu\omega\nu$) is risen from the dead (1 Cor. 15: 20). Schweitzer suggests that this consciousness of the age of salvation which marked the apostle implied an "interweaving of the natural and supernatural worlds".

> The resurrection of Jesus has made it clear that resurrectional powers, i.e. the powers of the supernatural world are already in operation in the creaturely world. With the resurrection of Jesus the supernatural world has already broken in, only it is not yet fully manifested. (*Mystik*, 99 ff.)

W. Bousset (*Kyrios Christos, op. cit.*, 105) understood the matter quite rightly when he observed:

> The picture which Paul really draws of the $\kappa\acute{\upsilon}\rho\iota o\varsigma$ ʼ$I\eta\sigma o\tilde{\upsilon}\varsigma$ is not taken from the earthly life and course of Jesus of Nazareth. The Jesus whom Paul knows is the pre-existent supernatural Christ, who was rich and for our sakes became poor, who was in the form of God and accepted the form of a servant, the Son of God whom the Father gave as a sacrifice, the Fulfiller of the prophecies and of the promises. It is into this portrait that those individual features are fitted which Paul here and there brings out: His humility, His obedience, His love, His truthfulness, His faithfulness to the point of His death on the cross. The subject of all these predicates is not the historical Jesus.

It seems to me that only in regard to His death on the cross should an exception be made to this: for he understood the death on the cross, as we shall see, as an atoning death, as a disposition of God for man's salvation, and this conception he held in common with the tradition of the church (1 Cor. 15: 3). Further, he combined it with a sacramental doctrine which Schweitzer misguidedly called "eschatological mysticism" but which in any event made possible a contact with Hellenistic syncretism.[1] ·The exalted Jesus was destined soon to become the Saviour and the Son of God of the Christian Church. Our later discussions (ch. 4) will seek to clarify to what an extent He had already become such for Paul.

That the earthly and the exalted Jesus may not be opposed to each other, but that in two modes of being the same Person embodies the saving action of God, was the faith and conviction of the whole of primitive Christianity, which developed from a historical fact behind faith and not from an unhistorical myth. Paul too in this regard, despite the mythical expression of his thoughts, especially in Philippians, should not be misunderstood in a gnostic sense. But let us now consider in what relation Paul stood to the kerygma of the church which he entered, in order that we may more precisely decide his position within that church.

2. PAUL'S DEPENDENCE ON THE THEOLOGY OF THE EARLY CHRISTIAN COMMUNITY

What doctrines and views of the faith prevailed in the first Christian community before Paul joined it, and thus formed the common theology of the primitive church? This question is a complex one, and in the state of our sources may probably never be answered in such a way as to exclude all doubt. No doubt it is certain that in the circle of the twelve there was no figure so richly endowed as that of the apostle to the Gentiles, and it is certain too that as a thinker and a spiritually significant personality he was far superior to the comparatively naïve personalities of the other apostles. But however highly we estimate the genius and originality of this apostle, we shall hardly suppose that his form of the Christian gospel represents something entirely new, and that he is not dependent in part on the teaching about the faith which, before his joining it, the first

[1] H. Windisch, *op. cit.*, 450 ff., spoke even of deliberate association. That the myth of the descent of the man from heaven—together with Judaic–Hellenist wisdom speculations—lies behind Phil. 2: 5–11, and that this myth, assimilated perhaps in Hellenistic Judaism, is of purely pagan origin can hardly be doubted. Details ch. 4, 4.

Christian church had for several years spread abroad; the more so as he himself repeatedly refers to this teaching. It will be expedient to take as our point of departure the common primitive apostolic faith, in so far as this can be compressed into a short survey.

According to the testimony of the Acts of the Apostles (3: 18 ff.) the emergence of the first Christian community began with the descent of the Holy Ghost at the first Pentecost, an event symbolized by a real speaking with other tongues. The first church considered this to be a sign that it was itself the church of the end of the ages, since Jewish expectation (e.g., Joel 2: 28) awaited such an outpouring of the Spirit as the mark of the end. This had been preceded by so-called resurrection experiences, epiphanies of Jesus to Simon Peter—to him first, as all the reports agree—to the twelve apostles, and according to Paul (1 Cor. 15: 6) to five hundred believers at once, as also lastly to James the Lord's brother. The accounts of these resurrection appearances—unnecessarily coupled with the tradition of the empty tomb—have often been treated as legendary elaboration. The scepticism of a Goguel who thinks that the first Christophany to Peter had a catching effect, and the psychologizing reconstruction of the supposedly oldest Marcan report of a Galilean appearance, which amounts to the same thing as Goguel's thesis, undermine any possibility of understanding how the cult of Jesus arose in the first community of Christians. If we do not accept the multiple theophanies in various places as reported in the texts, it is difficult to see how the Messianic débâcle, and the despair which accompanied it, could have given rise to the certainty that the story of Jesus and His mission was not sealed and settled with His death. An historical point of view requires absolutely a multiple testimony to the resurrection appearances. The community of this witness to the resurrection is one of the strongest links which bind Paul to the men of the Jerusalem church. He has derived his special teaching from the singularity of his experience of vocation—the last of the Christophanies in time.[1]

In his presentation of the gospel Paul uses many formal expressions, which he may have derived from the paradosis (קבלה) of the community; cf. 1 Cor. 15: 3 ff. Thus Bultmann (*op. cit.*, 47, 83)

---

[1] The idea of a special instruction of the disciples by the risen Christ is often claimed in the early church, but more frequently expressed in Christian gnostic circles. Cf. Carola Barth, *Die Interpretation des NT in der valentinianischen Gnosis*, TU 37, 3, Leipzig, 1911, 52 ff.; Walter Bauer, *Rechtgläubigkeit und Ketzerei im ältesten Christentum*, Tübingen, 1934, 207; A. Wikenhauser, *Die Belehrung der Apostel durch den Auferstandenen*, Festtchr. f. M. Meinertz, Münster, 1951 ff., 105 ff.

sees in Rom. 4: 25—on account of the style and syntactical parallel-ism *membrorum*—a quotation, a keyword of the new preaching formulated on the pattern of Is. 53. Of course it was Paul who first filled with a specific soteriological content the image of the servant of God known in the first church. In connexion with this the doctrine of the character of Jesus' death as a sacrificial atonement no doubt goes back to traditional church formulae, for the idea of the ransom of sinners as a word of the Lord was known to the church, which, in the opinion of many exegetes, put in the mouth of Jesus the Marcan word (10: 45) about the λύτρον ἀντὶ πολλῶν. Bultmann (*op. cit.*, 47) thinks also that ὑπὲρ τῶν ἁμαρτιῶν ἡμῶν is likewise derived from the community; perhaps also the images of the Paschal lamb (1 Cor. 5: 7) and the sacrifice of Christ (2 Cor. 5: 21) for sin. Likewise Paul found rooted in the primitive church, along with the thought of the new covenant, the idea of baptism as a rite of initia-tion and the κυριακὸν δεῖπνον as a memorial meal. I feel that it is impossible to decide whether the transformation of baptism, on the lines of Hellenistic cult mysteries, into a real dying together with Christ (Rom. 6: 3) was due to the creative thought of Paul or whether it was only the adoption of a custom already practised in Hellenistic communities (Bultmann). The same applies to the Pauline reinterpretation of the celebration of the Lord's Supper as a sacral communion of the participants with their Kyrios (1 Cor. 10: 16 ff.). It therefore seems advisable to be cautious about regarding the idea of a pre-Pauline Hellenistic community as an assured truth —an idea which Heitmüller and Bousset proclaimed in their day and which has been accepted by Bultmann. Such a factor is un-certain, it is quite unknown and therefore indefinable. I would rather be inclined to credit Paul as a Hellenistic Diaspora Jew with independent reinterpretations of teaching and practice which was already in existence in the non-Hellenistic Palestinian traditions.

But the important point for us to notice here is simply this: that baptism must have been institutionalized from the start as a rite of initiation, for Paul assumes that all the Christians in his churches are baptized (Rom. 6: 3; 1 Cor. 12: 13) and similarly the rite of breaking bread as a memorial of the Lord's Supper was practised in Jerusalem before Paul (Acts 2: 42–47). Finally, we know from the synoptic tradition that the works and the sufferings and death of Jesus were quite early viewed against the background of Old Testa-ment prophecy (*l'kayem ma shene' emar*) and that decisive value was assigned to the verification from scripture, to the fact that all had happened κατὰ τὰς γραφάς. Here again Paul is rooted in an older tradition, and many a scripture proof that he uses may depend on primitive traditions not known to us. Only in one well-known text, 1 Cor. 15: 3 ff., has Paul expressly referred to these, and from this passage we see that church theology[1] for its kerygma: "Jesus of Nazareth was crucified and rose again" must already have adduced proof from scripture regarding the necessity of the passion and death of Christ.

Hence we arrive at the conclusion that ideas of the faith cherished and taught by the Jerusalem church were taken over by the neophyte Paul and are reflected in his letters. In consequence, the belief of the first church that it was the church of the end of the age became the basic eschatological point of departure for the structure of his own theology. This corresponds to the state of affairs which we should expect; it is hardly possible to make more detailed specifications of his dependence, beyond those already established. I can see no reasonable grounds for assuming with Heitmüller and Bousset[2] (an assumption which lies behind Bultmann's *Theology of the New Testament*) that between Paul and the Palestinian first church a decisive link is supplied by Hellenistic churches on whose traditions Paul drew; such an assumption I can only describe as improbable.[3] What do we know of the special kerygma taught by the Hellenistic churches of Antioch, Tarsus, Damascus, etc.—churches first founded by those who fled as a result of the persecution of Stephen? Nothing at all! And what do we really know about the situation in the mother church? Heitmüller's (331) "admittedly good Hellenistic source" (Acts 6–8, 11) at most expresses a tendency within the original Palestinian church, and the τύπος τῆς διδαχῆς of the Roman church (Rom. 6: 17) which Bousset invokes—a church which in the opinion of both older and younger critics was a mixed church arising from the Jewish community in Rome—is still less to be interpreted as a specially Hellenistic kerygma. I think rather

---

[1] Of course that of the Palestinian and not "that of the Gentile Christian church of Antioch", as Bousset, *op. cit.*, p. 76, asserts without the shadow of a proof and in contradiction of his statement on p. 69. Cf. also J. Jeremias, *Die Abendmahlsworte Jesu*, Göttingen, 1949, 95 ff.

[2] Cf. W. Heitmüller, "Zum Problem Paulus und Jesus", *ZNW*, 1912, 330: "Paul was separated from Jesus not only by the primitive church, but also by a further step. The chain of development is: Jesus—primitive church—hellenistic Christianity—Paul." Similar formulae in W. Bousset, *op. cit.*, 75 ff.

[3] Now O. Cullmann too, *JBL*, 1955, 213 ff. has energetically championed the idea that the Hellenists were the special or central group in the early church. Cullmann too is very fanciful.

that the position which the sources indicate is in fact to be interpreted conversely: it was not Paul who was dependent on a special
Hellenistic tradition, but the latter which is to be derived from him,
inasmuch as he, the Jewish Christian, became the spokesman of the
Greek Christians, and by his own interpretations of the post-messianic situation has conveyed to us not only the catchwords of these
communities but also highly important descriptions of their position
in the critical age between the resurrection and the parousia. This,
however, leads us to consider his own notoriously polemic position,
both with regard to the original apostles and radical Judaizers.

3. PAUL AND THE FIRST CHURCH

Very difficult and still a controversial matter is the exact demarcation of the groups within primitive Christianity. We realize to-day,
in opposition to Baur and his older pupils, that the contrast which he
suggested between Paul and the college of the twelve, although containing some truth, was still even for the earliest period an over-
simplification. The groupings were obviously much more intricate.
It is fairly clear that on the apostolic council of Jerusalem[1] there was
a more tolerant middle group between the intransigent Judaizing
party and Paul. As we shall see, these two groups may still be distinguished in the first letter to the Corinthians. E. Lohmeyer has
also desired to recognize a special Galilean group existing alongside
those of Jerusalem. And W. Grundmann, partly catching at and
partly modifying these ideas, has reconstructed with quite Oriental
fantasy a Gentile Christian first church, which is supposed to find
expression in Acts 3–5. We know nothing of all this, for audacious
combinations such as have always been sketched out in order to
explain the contradictions in our sources can only be verified or not
verified by the latter themselves. Now all pre-Pauline groupings of
the first church remain unverified by our sources; only with the
appearance of Paul can anything be said about the divisions which
emerged by reaction to his teaching. This is to be sure no wonder,
for our sources are only the letters of the apostle and the semi-
Pauline Acts of the Apostles, which book, moreover, is plainly

[1] No doubt the same conference is depicted in Gal. 2: 1–10 and Acts 15: 6–30. But the
harmonizing tendency of Acts has turned the stormy sitting of Galatians, where the
historical Paul calls Peter a dissembler, into a friendly discussion, or, as C. Schneider says
(op. cit., I, p. 95) an innocuous meeting. Cf. the dissertation of Günter Strothotte, *Das
Apostelkonzil im Lichte der jüdischen Rechtsgeschichte*, Erlangen, 1955, which gives the present
state of research.

interested in minimizing divisions, in softening strife, and diluting the arguments on either side.

What, then, do we really know? We know that there was an opposition of parties in questions relating to the mission to the Gentiles and the practice to be adopted in admitting the latter, that these questions were discussed at the apostolic council, were reflected in the letter to the Galatians and had painful repercussions in Antioch. And we know something of a difference of opinion in regard to the conception of the apostolate, which was especially a controversial matter in Corinth, and appears to be connected with a variance of view in the idea of the church (thus Holl with keen insight) and further even with a difference in Christological outlook (thus Goguel). These divisions obviously did not exist from the beginning. Paul probably went his own way from the start; though, as his journey to Jerusalem shows, he probably sought a good understanding with the first church, and the Judaic Christians no doubt at first rejoiced in his proclamation of the gospel.[1] Paul's theology doubtless first ripened in the one and a half decades which (cf. Gal. 2: 1) passed between Damascus and his public activity. The experiment of his missionary work was necessary before a conflict of views after the first missionary journey (A.D. 48–49) became evident. We must now speak of this conflict.

(a) *Conflict of opinion as regards the mission to the Gentiles*

According to Gal. 1 : 16 Paul recognized already at the time of his Damascus experience that the mission to the Gentiles was his special charge in the service of Christ.[2] Hence he was at once confronted by the problem as to what mode of procedure should be adopted for the admission of Gentile converts. Already in the matter of the Jewish mission to the Gentile world the question had arisen as to the

[1] Cf. A. Hilgenfeld, *Einl. in das NT*, Leipzig, 1875, 225: "That Paul's mission to the Gentiles should lead to strife with Jewish Christianity was suspected neither by Paul nor by the primitive church at the outset. As apostle to the Gentiles Paul did not from the start and of set purpose fight against Judaic Christianity, nor did the latter originally adopt a hostile attitude towards him."

[2] Hence E. Barnikol, *Die vorchristliche und frühchristliche Zeit des Paulus*, Kiel, 1929, 18 ff., proposed to read out of Gal. 1 : 13–16 the idea that Saul had already worked as a missionary to the Gentiles, and in particular had been a Jewish preacher of circumcision. Although resting on an oversubtle exegesis, this possibility cannot be excluded in spite of the contradiction of Oepke (*Th. St. u. Kr.*, 1934, 387 ff.) and might render the quick decision of Damascus more intelligible as a persistence in the same vocation. Unfortunately we know just nothing about it.

extent to which the law of Moses should be made obligatory for proselytes. It had proved difficult of solution and had led to semi-solutions and compromises, after the pattern of which the Jewish–Christian first church proposed to proceed, by insisting on the *Berith Mila, Kashruth*, as also the *Tahara* ritual through the custom of baptism. This was a normal solution such as we would have expected Jewish Christians to adopt, and had it not been for the intervention of Paul it would never have become a subject of lengthy discussion.[1] As is well known, Paul's "abrupt repudiation of all claims of the law on the Gentiles"[2] in his missionary practice was based on a deliberate position with regard to the Mosaic law, an account of which will be given in its proper context in ch. 5.

The Galatian church had fallen into lively dispute and confusion over the question of circumcision, after the περιτεμνόμενοι (6: 13) —who were obviously Gentiles converted by Judaizers to the requirement of circumcision—had fanned the flames of a wild propaganda on the subject with all the fanaticism of the newly converted. Paul saw in this a real danger for his gospel, when he came to Jerusalem.[3] The debates about the propriety of applying this piece of Jewish ritual to the new Christian churches led to apostolic advices which issued in the formation of the groups visible in Acts 15.[4] We may take it as certain that Gal. 2: 1–10 is concerned with this same meeting in Jerusalem and that the information given in Acts 11: 27 ff. offers us a somewhat confused doublet; the assertion often made by literary critics to the effect that a redactor in Acts has interwoven and wrongly arranged two sources may here be passed over,[5] like all such theories. Since the actual contradictions of the two sources bid defiance to all exegetical insight, we confine our attention here to what, according to the report in Acts, is for us the

---

[1] Cf. G. Kittel, "Der geschichtliche Ort des Jakobusbriefes", *ZNW*, 1942, 101: "The prejudice that from the start Jewish Christianity did hardly anything else but quarrel about ritual questions, gives a completely false picture."

[2] Cf. H. Lietzmann, *Geschichte der alten Kirche*, I, Berlin, 1937, 129. (E.T. *The Beginnings of the Christian Church*.)

[3] It has often struck critics that the demand for the circumcision of Paul's companion, the Greek Titus, reported in Gal. 2: 3, does not appear in Acts 15; but this omission may be explained by the harmonizing tendency of the author of Acts.

[4] The patristic report on the later Jewish Christians clung for a long time to both parties of Acts 15. Where a difference in the handling of the missionary problem is seen, the suspicion arises that the church Father is transferring to his own time the situation proper to the apostolic council. None the less Justin's report (*Dial.* 46/47) may reflect faithfully the position *circa* 150.

[5] Cf. for the more recent position, W. Kümmel, "Das Urchristentum", *ThR*, 1948, 28 ff.; 1950, 26 ff.

most important point: none of these groups entirely rejected the idea of a mission to the Gentiles.

The Pharisaic conservative party in Jerusalem (τινὲς τῶν ἀπὸ αἱρέσεως τῶν Φαρισαίων πεπιστευκότες, 15: 5) regarded circumcision as a *sine qua non* and defended the complete validity of the Mosaic law for all Christians whether of Jewish or Gentile stock. They considered that σωτηρία (15 : 5) was linked to circumcision, which on Jewish lines they regarded as the "seal of election" (cf. Rabbi Aqiba in Mekh. Ex. 19: 5), and analogous to the acceptance of neophytes into the Jewish *berith*. In this matter the Christian Pharisees espoused the stricter views of the school of Shammai.[1] There was also a more moderate middle group to which Peter and James, if we are to believe Acts, belonged. This group, while adhering to the idea of the primacy of the Jewish position, was prepared to make concessions to the Gentiles in regard to the obligations of the law, and in particular yielded ground on the question of circumcision. For its standpoint it could appeal to the views of Rabbi Joshua (Baraita Yebamoth 46a), who held that proselytes need not be circumcised provided that they underwent the rite of baptism.[2]

As the spokesman of the middle group, James finally carried through a compromise solution, which followed the lines of synagogue missionary practice. The so-called apostolic decree (which Acts gives three times, 15 : 20 ff., 28 ff., and in a shortened form, 21: 25) must, as I have shown elsewhere,[3] be regarded as a Jewish–Christian version of Noachide minimum obligation of the law, which the rabbinic "Halakha" imposed upon the σεβόμενοι τὸν θεόν. This earliest Christian church law gave up circumcision, as it did the full *Kashruth*, and in its canonical textual form[4] singles out only four Mosaic requirements, interpreted in a ritualistic sense: the abstention from meat sacrificed to idols (εἰδωλοθύτων), from the flesh of animals not ritually slaughtered (αἵματος), from animals which had been ensnared and killed (πνικτῶν), from the contraction of marriage in forbidden degrees and from unchastity (πορνείας). H. Waitz[5]

---

[1] Cf. my quotations in *TheolJchr*, 259, notes 2, 3.

[2] Further non-rabbinic sources for this view still possible in the time of Paul in Klausner, *op. cit.*, 53 ff. and 319 ff.

[3] *TheolJchr*, 259 ff.

[4] Cf. G. Resch, *Das Aposteldekret nach seiner ausserkanonischen Textgestalt untersucht*, Leipzig, 1905, 19 ff.; H. Lietzmann, *Amicitiae Corolla*, London, 1933, 203 ff.; W. G. Kümmel, *Spiritus et veritas*, Festschr. f. K. Kundsin, Eutin, 1953, 83 ff.

[5] "Das Problem des sog. Aposteldekrets", *ZKG*, 1936, 227.

has convincingly shown that in this order they were taken from Lev. 17–18. From the customary Noachide count of seven have been omitted the prohibition of blasphemy, of robbery, of bloodshedding, and the positive command of justice, doubtless because such injunctions were not controversial and their general recognition was taken for granted.[1]

A very acute exegesis has proposed to see a difference of teaching between the two leaders of this group: it is said that James entertained with reluctance the formula of agreement which he himself proposed (it is pointed out that Peter, in his speech in Acts, refers to ἡμεῖς while James says αὐτοί) and that he satisfied his conscience by indicating the eternity of the Mosaic law. Differing from the Peter of Gal. 2: 11, he reserves for himself and circumcised believers the validity of the Mosaic law *in toto*, because he clings to the conception of it as a soteriological factor; whereas for Peter, the exponent of a "programme of Jewish moderation" (Lietzmann), it was much more a matter of national custom simply.

I would not care to take these fine distinctions too seriously, for what seems to me more important is the fact that Peter, like James, belonged to the same harmonizing middle group in the Jerusalem Council. Influenced by Hegesippus's description and Ebionite church traditions, I was, however, formerly uncertain as to whether James was not to be considered plainly as the head of the "Christian Pharisee" party in the first church. It now seems to me certain that the historical James was never such, that only after his death was his figure embroidered in a Judaizing way, was he made into the "Pope of Ebionite fantasy" (Th. Zahn).[2] His intention at the Jerusalem Council was obviously only to remember the Jewish Diaspora, which was to be evangelized, and which from early generations had rallied to the authority of Moses (15: 21).

As a result of these considerations, important corrections have to be made to the picture of early Christianity drawn by the Tübingen school. The differences between Paul and the prime apostles— "those of repute" (δοκοῦντες 2: 2) and the "pillars" (στῦλοι 2: 9)

---

[1] Whoever will not accept this can, of course, base himself on the decree of Lydda akin to the Noachidic laws, to the effect that in times of religious persecution the rabbinic law concerning conditions of distress may permit transgressions of the law—with the sole exceptions of idolatry, incest, and murder (Sanh. 74, Jer. Sanh. II, 6—21b—and Arakhin 15b). Cf. Venetianer, *Die Beschlüsse zu Lydda und das Apostelkonzil zu Jerusalem*, A. Schwartz-Festschrift, Vienna, 1917, 417 ff. But it all comes pretty much to the same thing!

[2] As regards the historical James, the arguments of G. Kittel (*ZNW*, 1942, 98 ff.) against Lohmeyer seem to me conclusive: I cannot at all follow his early dating of the Letter of James ascribed to the Lord's brother.

as they are seriously, yet with a slightly ironical ring, termed in Galatians—become less significant. For they can no longer be defined as the instigators of disturbance in the missionary churches, but rather those who came to Antioch, the τινὲς ἀπὸ 'Ιακώβου of Gal. 2: 12—probably the same as the παρείσακτοι ψευδαδελφοί of 2: 4—must be regarded as messengers of Jerusalem extremists, the ζηλωταὶ τοῦ νόμου of Acts 15: 5.[1] With them, the Judaizers, the actual ancestors of the later Ebionites, Paul was engaged in bitter and far-reaching strife, as we shall show. There were indeed differences between Paul and the στῦλοι, perhaps even serious divergences of outlook, but no enmity and above all no "unbridgeable gulf". Such a state of affairs did not even occur with Peter on the occasion of the episode at Antioch, which Acts passes over in silence. It is only in Ebionite legends that it emerges. Peter, who was accustomed to table fellowship with the Gentiles, merely had misgivings and was weak-minded on the occasion. The same situation is noted eight years later (A.D. 56) according to the "we" report of Acts 21: 18 ff.—for James and the πρεσβύτεροι are expressly contrasted with the ζηλωταὶ τοῦ νόμου. Their tactically shrewd proposal (redemption of our poor Nazarites) was intended to reconcile Paul with the rabid Judaizers who accused him of forsaking the religion of Moses.

Thus I come to the conclusion that the right hand of fellowship (Gal. 2: 9), with which the στῦλοι admit Paul to the apostolic circle, signifies their honest recognition (v. 7) of the Pauline mission to the Gentiles, their acceptance of the fact that Paul was entrusted with the gospel to the Gentiles, just as Peter was entrusted with its preaching to the circumcision. It meant that the two men were in co-operation rather than in conflict, and that James as the moderator of the church gave his blessing to the arrangement, to the great displeasure of the intransigent "zealots for the law" in Jerusalem. The regrettable incident in Antioch was merely episodic, occasioned by uncertainties about the correct procedure for mixed Christian communities. Even in the later years of the decade there was no substantial change, for otherwise Paul's intention of himself bringing to Jerusalem the collection taken in Macedonia and Achaia, in

---

[1] This opinion has many champions; cf. only the commentaries of Preuschen, Wendt, and Loisy, also G. Kittel, *op. cit.*, p. 98: "According to both our available sources, Acts 15 and Gal. 2, the authorities of the Jerusalem church are not to be equated with the 'intrusive false brethren' who denounce Paul as a heretic and stir up trouble; they are men who are prepared to accept Paul's report, and on the basis of it come to the conclusion that he is preaching the genuine gospel and that his work is to be recognized and affirmed."

Corinth and Rome, for the leaders of the church, and of thus fulfilling his obligation (Gal. 2: 10) as Jerusalem's messenger for this
purpose (שליח ציון)[1] would be unintelligible. Only if we assume
a genuine understanding between Paul and the στῦλοι could the
apostle have made known this intention to his churches (Rom. 15:
25 ff.; 1 Cor. 16 : 4; 2 Cor. 8–9).

The Tübingen conception of a deep gulf between Paul, on the
one hand, and James and Peter, on the other, which Baur, Schwegler,
Volckmar, Hilgenfeld and their followers conjured up on the basis
of the biased Jewish–Christian writings of the next generation, does
not stand the test of impartial examination, and cannot possibly
have reflected the real historical situation. Such a gulf is true only
of the Pharisaic group of Judaizing Christians who were probably
strongly represented in Jerusalem. That the Tübingen school may
have been right inasmuch as the στῦλοι, contrary to the account in
Acts, inclined in their heart towards this group, may nevertheless be
granted. In so far as we are dependent for the decision of this
question on the report of the author of Acts, we must always bear in
mind its predominant tendency: to conceal by its mode of presentation the inner divisions of the apostolic age, and largely to legitimate
the Pauline Gentile churches.[2]

The only question that remains to be considered is whether and
to what extent Paul, the exponent of a universalism emancipated
from the Mosaic law, actually dealt with the injunctions of the
apostolic decree in his missionary practice. According to the report
of Acts, he did not intervene in the Jerusalem discussions, but only
reported his missionary successes. In Gal. 2, where he at most
speaks between the lines of an arrangement which was painful to him,
he seems, according to the terms of v. 6, to dispute that any injunction
was given him at all. It is hardly likely that he will have felt the
compromise solution of Acts 15—most investigators assert in virtue of
Acts 21: 20 that he was not in Jerusalem at all—to be binding on
him for his later missionary journeys (cf. 1 Cor. 8: 8; 10: 27).
Whether its injunctions, occasioned by the questions in Antioch
(15: 2) and hence in the first instance intended for Antioch, Syria,

---

[1] On the idea of the Sheliach-Zion, which has long been maintained, see Klausner,
op. cit., p. 342.

[2] Cf. the judgment of Lyder Brun, "Apostelkonzil und Aposteldekret", *NTT*, Suppl.,
1920, 43. The new work of Joh. Munck, *Paulus und die Heilsgeschichte*, Aarhus, 1954, turns
historical truth upside down through its polemic against traditional Tübingen views and
exaggerates out of all proportion certain correct opinions. Cf. W. D. Davies, *New Testament Studies*, 1955/56, 60 ff.

and Cilicia (15: 23) were in fact applied there or in other missionary churches, and if so, for how long, is a matter on which we have no sure knowledge. In the following period the mass of new Christian converts who penetrated the Diaspora churches were no longer under pressure from Judaizers and certainly were unable to make anything of these injunctions.[1] It is probable that the apostolic decrees were only in fact followed in the limited area of Jewish-Christian missionary propaganda.[2] And according to the assertion of Justin (*Dial.* 46–47) even among Jewish Christians there was still, *circa* 150, an uncompromising and a more flexible tendency in questions relating to the Gentile mission.

(b) *Conflicts in regard to the idea of the apostolate*

The main differences, however, between Paul and the primary apostles lay in another sphere. They were concerned with the question of apostleship and in the last resort with the legitimacy of Paul's apostleship. This was obviously a genuine problem and one which was taken up by the Judaizers and exploited in a spiteful spirit. Since we shall discuss the position of the latter and their background in a special section, it is only now a question of explaining the actual material differences between Paul and the Jerusalem college. We shall begin with an inquiry into the original idea of the apostolate held by the first church, in so far as it is still recognizable from the Lucan description:

According to the well-known account given in the Gospel of Luke, Jesus at the very beginning of His ministry designated His twelve disciples as apostles (6: 13 and par.). The list of their names is formally put forward both by the synoptics and in the Acts of the Apostles. They received their status from Jesus Himself, with whom they dwelt; it is to them the Risen Lord appears (Mt. 28: 18 ff.) and they who are commanded to go out into all the world. Luke also ends his gospel (24: 47–49), and begins the Acts of the Apostles (1: 8) with Jesus' missionary charge to the twelve, whom He describes as His witnesses ($\mu\acute{\alpha}\rho\tau\upsilon\rho\acute{\epsilon}\varsigma$ $\mu o\upsilon$). It is quite plain that the title of apostle as the highest description of rank in earliest Christianity was limited to the twelve, and I suppose that this reflects the

---

[1] Cf. on this point, further, the study of K. Boeckenhoff, *Das apostolische Speisegesetz in den ersten fünf Jahrhunderten*, Paderborn, 1903.

[2] Some examples of the horror of meat offered to idols, blood and things strangled in Gentile Christianity of the 2nd century have been collected by E. Haenchen, *Die Apostelgeschichte*, Göttingen, 1956, 418 ff.

oldest view of the character and status of the Christian apostle.[1] The apostles are they who stood closest to the earthly Jesus and therefore had for the faithful the value of authentic witnesses to the occurrences of His life and all that happened after His death. Paul too seems at least to grant the fact that before him there were apostles in Jerusalem (Gal. 1: 17). Thus the apostolate was a closed circle: they were μάρτυρες who had been associated with the teaching office of the earthly Jesus, and with whom alone the Risen Lord had eaten and drunk (Acts 10: 41). In contrast with them, Paul, through his experience on the Damascus road, became a witness only to the resurrection of the Lord, not a witness to the earthly life of Jesus.

The question of the essential marks of an ἀπόστολος had already at a very early stage caused a deep division within primitive Christianity. It is clear that the college of the twelve considered with James that the eye-witness character of the chosen disciple, the actual living together with the earthly Jesus, was the utterly exclusive sign of the apostolic dignity. This is confirmed also by the report in Acts about the choice of Matthias as a substitute (Acts 1: 21 ff.), a story which strongly suggests the closed character of the circle of the twelve. In Galatia there took place a first attack on the equality, in kind and value, of Paul's office with that of the twelve, on the grounds that Paul had not, like the latter, enjoyed human contact with the earthly Jesus. Kümmel[2] supposes that it was not Paul's vision of the Risen Lord which was doubted, but only the idea that it mediated his call to the Gentile mission. And because the apostolic office of this late-comer seems to have been problematic from the first, his champion, the author of Acts, even *post festum*, endeavours to base his apostolic authority on the commission of the church at Antioch, which was his point of departure (Acts 13: 1 ff.), and on Barnabas, who had introduced him to the church (9: 27). This, however, completely alters the idea of an apostle, as compared with Jerusalem standards. And in truth Paul put forward to the first church quite a new conception of apostleship, so constructed that it was capable of proving the legitimacy of his own apostolic status. Paul opposed to the principle of belonging to the most intimate circle of Jesus' friends, as expressed by the church

[1] Against H. Frh. v. Campenhausen's valuable study: "Der urchristliche Apostelbegriff" (*Studia Theologica*, Lund, 1948, 105 ff.). Campenhausen is of the opinion "that Luke has followed in his report later linguistic usage and then wrongly transposed it to Jesus Himself and His time".

[2] *Kirchenbegriff und Geschichtsbewusstsein in der Urgemeinde und bei Jesus*, Uppsala, 1943, 9.

in Acts 1: 21–22, a principle relevant to the new post-messianic situation: the principle that it was now no longer a question of knowing Jesus after the flesh, but only of witness to the Risen Lord (2 Cor. 5: 16).[1]

For him personally there was linked with this new principle the significance of a special mission, a charge laid upon him personally by the Risen Christ. He was in consequence commissioned with the task of proclaiming the gospel to the Gentiles (Rom. 1: 1; 11: 13; 15: 16; Gal. 1: 16; 2: 6–8, etc.). By the will of God he has been called ($\kappa\lambda\eta\tau\acute{o}s$) to be an "apostle of Jesus Christ"; as he says in the majority of the openings of his letters, he has been inducted into the office of $\delta o\hat{v}\lambda os$ $X\rho\iota\sigma\tau o\hat{v}$, which plainly connotes an instrument or agent.[2] He answers his opponents in Galatia by affirming that his apostleship is independent of men, because it springs from a special revelation of Christ, which has been conferred on him (Gal. 1: 11–12). His apostleship does not stem from human authorization ($o\vec{v}\kappa$ $\acute{a}\pi$' $\grave{a}\nu\theta\rho\acute{\omega}\pi\omega\nu$ $o\grave{v}\delta\grave{e}$ $\delta\iota$' $\grave{a}\nu\theta\rho\acute{\omega}\pi ov$), but solely from the command of Jesus Christ and His heavenly Father (Gal. 1: 1). God effected an $\grave{a}\pi o\kappa\acute{a}\lambda v\psi\iota s$ $\tauo\hat{v}$ $v\acute{\iota}o\hat{v}$ $\theta\epsilon o\hat{v}$ $\grave{\epsilon}\nu$ $\grave{\epsilon}\mu o\acute{\iota}$, and it is from this source that his apostolic office derives (Gal. 1: 16). Those of Jerusalem were compelled to recognize the equality of his rank with that of the older apostles.[3]

As contrasted with the Jerusalem idea of apostleship as constituted by the eye-witness, Paul represents a charismatic and broader conception of the apostolate, which includes also those who have received a special mission from the Risen Lord.[4] Such a circle would obviously go beyond that of the twelve apostles, with the addition of James and himself (cf. 1 Cor. 12: 28; Eph. 4: 11). "Who in the opinion of Paul may have belonged to it apart from Peter and Paul cannot now be decided."[5] In any case a keen conflict might well arise with regard to the inclusion of this or that Christian missionary.

Hence Paul understood by apostleship something quite different

---

[1] This view has often been expressed since Baur. More recently Lietzmann, Schlatter, Sass, and Käsemann have seen in the text about the Christ the basis of Paul's conception of the apostolate.

[2] Cf. G. Sass, "Zur Bedeutung von $\grave{a}\pi\acute{o}\sigma\tauo\lambda os$ bei Paulus", *ZNW*, 1941, 31 ff.; A. Fridrichsen, *The Apostle and his Message*, Uppsala, 1947, 3: "When Paul in Romans introduces himself as a $\kappa\lambda\eta\tau\acute{o}s$ $\grave{a}\pi\acute{o}\sigma\tauo\lambda os$ he characterizes himself as an eschatologic person."

[3] Details in Rengstorff, Art. "$\grave{a}\pi\acute{o}\sigma\tauo\lambda os$", Kittel, *WB*, I, 443; G. Sass: *Apostelamt und Kirche*, Munich, 1939, 23 ff.

[4] Cf. W. Kümmel, *op. cit.*, 7.

[5] Campenhausen, *op. cit.*, 106.

from the Jerusalem leaders.[1] While he recognizes the latter as the στῦλοι,[2] the conflict of opinion with regard to his apostolic prestige in Galatia and Corinth (cf. section 4) led him to raise the claim of being the last and decisive link in the apostolic chain (1 Cor. 15: 8 ff.). This is the argument he puts forward against the primitive tradition (1 Cor. 15: 3b–5) which apparently insisted that the appearances of the Risen Christ had closed with the appearance to the twelve and James.[3]

However, it does not seem to me that the circle of the twelve or the στῦλοι as their organ made a direct attack on the apostleship of Paul. There is no evidence in the sources for such an idea. The situation is rather that the twelve were clearly much impressed by the missionary successes of Paul. No doubt the Judaistic emissaries who penetrated his churches and attacked his apostleship referred to the appearance which his churches wore, and used the Jerusalem conception of the apostolate in order to undermine the legitimacy of the status claimed by Paul. Hence his bitter remarks about the "reputed pillars" (δοκοῦντες στῦλοι, Gal. 2: 9), his gibe at the "superlative apostles" (ὑπερλίαν ἀπόστολοι, 2 Cor. 11: 5; 12: 11), who were contrasted with him as though he himself had no rank.

This material difference in the conception of the apostolic office, which was sharpened in a provocative way by the Judaistic extremists who were obviously interested in stirring up strife, implies a more radical divergence of view. Karl Holl (*op. cit.*, 61 ff.) sees here the emergence of a difference in the idea of the church: the legally orientated idea of the Jerusalem church, based upon personal relation to the earthly Jesus and compatible only with the apostleship as an office, and the more "spiritual" idea of Paul, who builds on the operation of the Spirit in Christian believers, and compatible with an inspired apostleship. Maurice Goguel[4] accepted this thesis and developed further this divergence in ecclesiastical outlook, pointing to its origins in a difference in Christology. Among the men of Jerusalem, the consciousness of the presence of Christ guiding the church

---

[1] This is disputed in the new work of P. Gaechter, S. J., *Petrus und seine Zeit*, Innsbruck, 1958, in favour of a harmonizing survey such as catholic exegetes prefer.

[2] C. K. Barrett, *Paul and the "Pillar" Apostles*, Studia Paulina in honorem Joh. de Zwaan, Haarlem, 1953, 13, proposes to take στῦλοι in an eschatological sense as "the pillars of the eschatological temple". This is not probable.

[3] Cf. K. Holl, *Der Kirchenbegriff des Apostels Paulus in seinem Verhältnis zu dem der Urgemeinde*, Ges. Aufs. II, Tübingen, 1928, 44 ff.

[4] "L'apôtre Paul a-t-il joué un rôle personnel dans les crises de Grèce et de Galatie?" *RHPhR*, 1934, 461–500; further, "Einige Bemerkungen über das Problem der Kirche im NT", *ZSTh, ol.*, 1938, 525–543.

by His Spirit faded into the background, because their thought was directed to the earthly rather than to the Risen Christ, and they aimed at filling the time up to His expected return by an exposition of His teaching. On the other hand, Paul, whose activity flowed from the resurrection of Christ, spoke of a Christ who was alive and present to believers by His Spirit, with the consequence that in the power of the Spirit the latter were able to anticipate the aeon of the future. The passages of Paul's letters which are relevant here (e.g., Rom. 16: 25–26; 1 Cor. 2: 7–10; Eph. 3: 3–9) regard the possession of the Holy Spirit as the key to divine mysteries ($\beta\acute{a}\theta\eta$ $\tauo\hat{v}$ $\theta\epsilono\hat{v}$). This is a theme which was also very widespread in the Qumran literature. In this respect Paul, even in the matter of terminology, clearly stood in the same stream of traditions as the "sects".[1] Of course there are reports of "spiritual" phenomena outside the Pauline churches. To maintain his thesis logically, Goguel should account for the relevant texts of Acts as interpolations. But he is right in so far as the later Jewish Christians are concerned, who seem no longer to have been aware of any special charismatic gifts among believers. Obviously family relationship with their predecessors in the Jewish-Christian sphere had made such experiences unnecessary for them.[2]

In the field of early Christianity there were indeed differences of Christological outlook and divergent views of the church, but they can hardly have developed from the discrepancies in the idea of apostleship, however great the meaning of these discrepancies may have been. But so far as I can see, the sharpening of these discrepancies into a real antithesis was not the intention and work of the $\sigma\tau\hat{v}\lambdao\iota$ or the twelve; it was rather the work of those Judaistic extremists who involved Paul in severe struggles.

4. PAUL AND THE JUDAISTS

(a) *General characteristics*

What do we know about this party of Judaizers who intervened in Galatia and Corinth? In the Gentile-Christian Galatia they appear as emissaries from Jerusalem with the authority of inspectors, yet who gave them this authority is not clear (2: 4); $\ddot{o}\sigma\tau\iota\varsigma$ $\dot{\epsilon}\grave{a}\nu$ $\hat{\eta}$, he will have to bear his judgment, cries Paul (5: 10). In Antioch they

---

[1] Cf. now J. M. Allegro, *Die Botschaft vom Toten Meer*, Frankfurt, 1957, 114 ff. (*The Dead Sea Scrolls.*)

[2] Cf. Schoeps, *TheolJchr*, 293 ff.

appear as ambassadors of James (2: 12) who call Peter to order, requesting him to be so good as to adhere to the recently promulgated church law about food rites, and not to get ensnared in attempts at conciliation. In Corinth they show themselves to be emissaries of the Jerusalem church, authorized by letters of credit (2 Cor. 3: 1).[1] It is probable that these letters had not been issued by James, as I formerly supposed (*TheolJChr*, 124) with Baur and others influenced by the Ebionite legends, but by leaders of the Jerusalem Judaistic group, who were the real ancestors of the Ebionites. The context of affairs as a whole does not permit us to make the original apostles themselves responsible for incidents in Corinth, which was even Holl's opinion. Precisely when we practise tendentious criticism in Baur's sense, it appears that the original apostles were put forward only for the purpose of attacking the missionary to the Gentiles, and that Paul feels no need to launch an invective on the former themselves; he wishes only to assert as against his assailants the equality of his status. It seems to me that one of the most recent interpreters, namely Ernst Käsemann,[2] has most properly explained the historical context of 2 Cor. 10–13:

> The original apostles are only indirectly concerned in the conflict, in so far as their authority is exploited against Paul. This in itself makes his position uncomfortable enough, and puts him on the defensive. For he cannot deny a certain pre-eminence of the στῦλοι. But for that reason alone there is no need for him to allow his authority to be impugned by his adversaries. Thus there sounds an ironical undertone in the term "superlative apostles" by means of which Paul expresses both recognition and aloofness. Neither can Paul dispute the authority of the original church which is completely expressed in the letters of commendation. The protection and tactics adopted by these enemies was a shrewd move on their part. It is just because of that that the struggle implies such a serious menace to the apostleship and existence of Paul. He must to a large extent accept the presuppositions of his opponents and yet destroy the consequences which they infer. He must unsparingly deal with the intruders in Corinth, while at the same time not coming into conflict with Jerusalem and the original apostles. He must as far

---

[1] About the ἐπιστολαί συστατικαί cf. Baur in *Theol. Jahrb.*, 1850, 163 ff.; *Paulus* I, 314, who connects with this passage the information of special *testimonia Jacobi* in the Clementine novel (Rec. 4: 35). The sending of delegates with special powers to collect taxes from the Diaspora for Jerusalem was a custom which was maintained until the 5th century, as can be abundantly shown; cf. Klausner, *op. cit.*, 342; Campenhausen, *op. cit.*, 100 ff.

[2] "Die Legitimität des Apostels, eine Untersuchung zu 2 Kor. 10–13", *ZNW*, 1942, 33–71.

as possible keep the latter out of the quarrel, and in fact he brushes them very lightly with his emphasis on his equality of status. (11: 5 and 12: 11.)

Wilhelm Lütgert[1] has given quite a different explanation to the effect that Paul was not concerned in Corinth with Judaizers but with "libertinist ecstatics and gnostics", hence with people of quite a different type from the Galatian παρείσακτοι ψευδαδελφοί. Lütgert's interpretation can claim in its favour that in Corinth, according to 1 Corinthians, a wild "spiritual" enthusiasm had become rife and had had as its consequence antinomism. We know too, of course, from 1 Cor. 1 that in this church there was a strife of parties, that alongside the followers of Paul, Apollos, and Peter there were also people who simply inscribed "the Christ" on their banners (1: 12). But this so-called "Christ party" remains, in spite of the penetrating attempts of Baur, impossible to characterize; it cannot have been Judaizing, as Baur and many others have proposed, though it may have been gnostic.[2] But I feel Lütgert's thesis to be one-sided in its emphasis; the polemics which zigzag through the two Corinthian letters are on the whole clearly against Judaizers. Of course in the first letters one of the tendencies opposed seems to have been gnostic.[3] But the chief adversaries must have been Judaizers. 2 Cor. 11: 22 plainly grants them the titles Ἑβραῖοι, Ἰσραηλῖται, σπέρμα Ἀβραάμ. According to 11: 15 they introduced themselves with obvious emphasis as διάκονοι δικαιοσύνης. These Corinthian intruders would never have been able to undermine Paul's prestige had they not been able to appeal to a real authority, indisputable in Christian eyes, namely that of the mother church.[4] And in fact they preach "another Jesus" and "another gospel" (11: 4) than that which is preached by Christ's apostle to the Gentiles.

But what was the appearance of this other Jesus and this other gospel of the Judaizers? It is not possible to discover this from the invectives of the Corinthian letters alone. We get farther if we also take into account the characteristics of these Galatian enemies. And

---

[1] *Freiheitsgeister und Schwarmpredigt in Korinth, ein Beitrag zur Charakteristik der Christuspartei*, Gütersloh, 1908. K. Lake, Windisch, Munck, etc. have followed Lütgert.

[2] Perhaps it was both, as Bo Reicke (*Diakonie, Festfreude und Zelos*, Uppsala, 1951, 271 ff.) supposes, seeing their heirs in the Corinthians on account of the suggested tendency to a docetic Christology (283 ff.).

[3] Cf. apart from the commentaries of J. Weiss and H. Windisch, R. M. Grant, "The Wisdom of the Corinthians", *The Joy of Study*, 1951, 51 ff.

[4] It is hard to understand why Joh. Munck, *Paulus und die Heilsgeschichte*, Aarhus, 1954, will not see this.

we see fully into the matter if we compare later Jewish-Christian documents, which in the form of a sources document of the pseudo-Clementines—as I believe I have already shown in my writings—have preserved for us the anti-Pauline arguments of these very Judaizing enemies in Galatia and Corinth.

(b) *The situation in Galatia*

At the time of the composition of Paul's letter the situation in Galatia was characterized by the same conflict as, according to Acts, had brought confusion to Antioch; the question was whether circumcision was necessary to salvation. Paul tells us that the Judaizing emissaries wished to compel the Galatians to undergo circumcision, so that they themselves might play an important part in the sight of men, i.e., their commissioners. They wish to "glory in your flesh" (6: 13) and thus furnish a proof of the success of their mission. But they understand success only in a quite external sense, for the neophytes, the περιτεμνόμενοι, are not really won over to the way of life under the law; οὐδὲ αὐτοὶ νόμον φυλάσσουσιν, on which Lietzmann comments thus: as non-Jews they are not yet masters of the technique of fulfilling the law. But after the second intervention of Paul in Galatia the intruding agitators had almost succeeded in their purpose and persuaded the Galatians of ἕτερον εὐαγγέλιον, i.e., the doctrines of Jewish Christianity. In point of fact this consisted in the requirement of circumcision (5: 2, 12),[1] which, however, clearly did not imply an obligation to fulfil the whole law (5: 3). Further, the Judaizers wished to introduce ἡμέρας (Sabbaths), μῆνας (calendar months), καιρούς (Jewish festivals), ἐνιαυτούς (probably jubilee years); 4: 10.

The answer to this attempt to win over Greeks to the Jewish way of life is the impassioned letter to the Galatians. Paul represents to the Galatians the utter folly of their lapse from the true faith to a righteousness of the law. "Having begun with the Spirit, are you now ending with the flesh?" (3: 3.) There follows scriptural proof of the righteousness which springs from faith derived from the justification of Abraham, and for the lifting of the curse of the law through Christ's death on the cross (3: 6–14). After an allegorization of the conclusion of the two covenants initiated by God, there

---

[1] In v. 11 these opponents intimate, however, that his procedure is inconsistent and that in other cases he recommends circumcision, all of which seems to refer to the scene with Timothy (Acts 16).

follows the challenge to hold fast to Christian freedom and not to allow the yoke of enslavement to the law to be fastened on them. For the ταράσσοντες (1: 7), it is suggested, wish to subjugate them to circumcision only because they themselves wish to escape the persecution which the true gospel of Christ draws upon its preachers (6: 12).[1]

This appeal was obviously crowned with success, for the Galatians remained a Pauline Christian community (cf. 1 Cor. 16: 1). This question, which in Galatia and Antioch was a burning one, seems to have lost its actuality for the Greek churches some years later; at least it is no longer raised by the Judaistic emissaries, who have certainly not changed their point of view, in the equally Greek-Christian Corinth. Here the case is rather that a fundamental attack *ad hominem* is made to the effect that he is using his eloquence to please men (1: 10) and the attack is prepared for by the malicious deliberate creation of an atmosphere hostile to him in Galatia. The attack now gains its peculiar effectiveness from the fact that those discrepancies in the idea of the apostolate which we have already considered are taken up by his opponents and exploited for the purpose of disputing the legitimacy of his status and undermining his work. This may be inferred especially from the impetuosity with which he defends himself in the last chapters of the second Corinthian letter. The deep insight which Baur shows in the chapter on the Corinthian letters in his work on Paul has in this respect suggested the way to historical knowledge.[2]

(c) *The situation in Corinth*

The mood in this city is much livelier; it has often been felt that the actual opposition of viewpoints receives an added harshness from the irritation of personal susceptibilities. In the final chapters of 2 Corinthians the tone constantly changes. Paul's line of argument hovers between a contemptuous dismissal of his opponents, apologetic attempts to make a thorough refutation of their views, and biting ironical polemic, which but ill conceals his inner disturbance. So he draws his sword against the boastful spirit of the Judaizers and at the same time sings the praises of his

---

[1] In Philippi, using a mocking heathen word, he had even traduced circumcision as κατατομή (Phil. 3: 2). He did not go so far with the Galatians.

[2] This must be firmly held to as against pan-gnostic fantasies—cf. W. Schmithals, *Die Gnosis in Korinth*, Göttingen, 1956.

valour both in performance and in suffering as an apostle of Christ
(11: 23 f.).

What was so offensive to him in his adversaries' reproaches in
Corinth? Nothing more nor less than ἀφροσύνη, the suggestion that
he had become mad with overweening conceit. The whole section,
2 Cor. 11: 1—12: 18, turns on this point. With cutting irony Paul
begs them to be willing to bear with his folly a little longer. "I repeat, let no one think me foolish; but even if you do, accept me as a
fool, so that I too may boast a little. What I am saying I say not
with the Lord's authority but as a fool, in this boastful confidence"
(11: 16–17). The exacerbated tone betrays how his enemies' blows
had hit hard: they allege that his boasting knows no limits (10: 13),
he has become crazy with boasting (12: 11), he has tampered with
God's word (4: 2), his gospel is veiled (4: 3). And indirectly it is suggested that he is preaching himself (4: 5); that he proclaims a different Jesus, a different gospel, and has a different spirit. To these
reproaches are added slanderous statements: his travel plans cannot
be relied on (1: 15–17), he is a weakling (10: 1; 11: 21), an arrogant
writer but personally a coward, his preaching by word of mouth is
useless (11: 6), his personal presence ineffective (10: 1, 10). And
Paul himself must admit that he is no speaker (ἰδιώτης τῷ λόγῳ, 11:
6), he can achieve nothing by ὅπλα σαρκικά, such as boldness,
bravado, etc. (10: 2 ff.). But the criticisms go much deeper: they
take exception to his boundless self-praise (εἰς τὰ ἄμετρα καυχᾶσθαι,
10: 13, 15), which is coupled with spite (ὑπάρχων πανοῦργος 12: 16);
his suspected avarice (7: 2; 12: 17 ff.), his walking after the flesh
(10: 2); all of which shows only that his μέτρον τοῦ κανόνος (10: 13)
is false, his δοκιμή questionable (10: 18). His claim to be Christ's
(Χριστοῦ εἶναι) is the real problem (10: 7). But in their own
opinion those who are proud of being Hebrews, Israelites, the seed
of Abraham (11: 22) enjoy priority (5: 16) in personal discipleship
to Christ. He, however, appears to derive his vocation to the
apostolic office from his own intrinsic strength (3: 5).

Paul gives the following answer to this bombardment of accusa-
tions: those who thought thus were directing their attention only to
outward things (10: 12); they are ἐν προσώπῳ καυχώμενοι καὶ μὴ ἐν
καρδίᾳ (5: 12). Had he really become an ἄφρων in his speeches, the
Corinthians themselves would be to blame as not having taken under
their protection one so heavily attacked (12: 11–18). Moreover, he
considers that he is not in the least inferior to the ὑπερλίαν ἀπόστολοι
(11: 5). For this reason he claims equal right with the superlative

apostles to live at the cost of the churches to whom he preaches the gospel.[1] But what are the real facts? He proclaims Christ without taking a recompense (11: 7), while his adversaries aimed at profit. This, however, is no wonder; for his enemies are servants of Satan who have disguised themselves as servants of righteousness, just as Satan can clothe himself in the guise of an angel of light[2]—which he obviously means in a magical sense. Οἱ γὰρ τοιοῦτοι ψευδαπόστολοι ἐργάται δόλιοι (11: 13—they are people of this kind: false apostles and deceitful workmen).[3] In addition, they are also falsifiers of God's word (2: 17) and violent plunderers of the church (11: 20). He does not need any testimonials from authorities; the Corinthian church constitutes his letter of recommendation.

Most important of all is the 12th chapter, which contains the essence of the whole conflict: although boasting is of no avail, he must come to speak of the ὀπτασίαι καὶ ἀποκαλύψεις κυρίου (12: 1). For since it is a question of these as the marks of his belonging to Christ, he asks his enemies: Οὐχὶ 'Ιησοῦν τὸν κύριον ἡμῶν ἑόρακα; (1 Cor. 9: 1) and since his Damascus experience—the final appearance of the Risen Lord (1 Cor. 15:8)—is obviously not believed in, he appeals to an ecstatic vision which took place fourteen years previously, within the period of his Christian discipleship, when he was caught up to the third heaven.[4] By this reference he implies to the Corinthians that such a visionary was also capable of seeing the Lord. But no doubt on account of the temptation to self-praise, he again restrains himself (v. 6), saying that arrogance about the ὑπερβολή τῶν ἀποκαλύψεων is in his case obviated by a "thorn in the flesh, a messenger of Satan, to harass me, to keep me from being too elated" (12: 7). This unusual and apologetically-meant statement has been mostly understood as referring to a severe illness (leprosy, hysteria, convulsions, depres-

---

[1] He justifies this by custom (1 Cor. 9: 7–8) and "Halakha" (vv. 9–12), using the hermeneutic method *a minore ad maius*, finally also by the usages connected with the sacrificial cult (v. 13). Cf. Baur, *op. cit.*, 300 ff. I consider it as settled that older research with and after Baur was right in asserting the pre-eminence of the στῦλοι in the Jerusalem church (contrary to the views of some more recent critics).

[2] For this probably old apocalyptic idea cf. Schoeps, *AfZ*, 62.

[3] The denunciations in Philippians allude to the same people: ἐργάται κακοί and even κύνες (3: 2); their Jewish righteousness is σκύβαλα (dung, 3: 8).

[4] As is well known, this report was paraded by the "History of Religion" school in support of their claim that Paul was to be understood as a Hellenistic "pneumatic" (Reitzenstein, etc.) who had penetrated the mysteries of gnosis (Bultmann). But this is partial and prejudiced, for many rabbis were "pneumatics" and had ecstatic experiences. The belief in the actual presence of the Holy Spirit is similar to rabbinic belief in the indwelling of the Shekinah. Cf. references in A. Marmorstein, "Der heilige Geist in der rabbinischen Legende", *ARW*, 1930, 286 ff.; Davies, *op. cit.*, 211 ff.

sions, etc.).[1] However, he does not go so far, as would have been understandable in this struggle with his enemies, as to give a justification of his apostolate based on his capacity for ecstatic experiences. Rather he expressly repudiates any estimate of his character grounded on the ecstatic visions he has disclosed[2] (v. 6). He appeals to the evidence of facts: the evangelized Corinthians (σφραγίς μου τῆς ἀποστολῆς, 1 Cor. 9: 2) are the attestation of the genuineness of his apostolic ministry to which he refers. Here the spirit-inspired σημεῖα τοῦ ἀποστόλου are invoked: "The signs of a true apostle were performed among you in all patience, with signs and wonders and mighty works" (2 Cor. 12: 12). These are the charismata connected with the outpouring of the Holy Ghost (Rom. 15: 19; Gal. 3: 5). In consequence, he has been endowed with the gift of glossolaly more than all others: "I thank God that I speak in tongues more than you all" (1 Cor. 14: 18). But he adds: "In church I would rather speak five words with my mind in order to instruct others, than ten thousand words in a tongue" (v. 19).[3] In fact, it has been his special mission to declare the θεοῦ σοφία ἐν μυστηρίῳ (1 Cor. 2: 7), for ἡμῖν γὰρ ἀπεκάλυψεν ὁ θεὸς διὰ τοῦ πνεύματος (v. 10).

If now we take a detached survey of this whole polemic, it is this visionary gift of Paul which stands out, attested not only in Corinth but also by Acts (16: 9–10; 17: 23–24); it remains clear that he has seen Christ ἐν ἐκστάσει (Acts 22: 17) and that his preaching seems to depend on these very ὁράματα καὶ ἀποκαλύψεις. In fact, it is just this Spirit-derived character of his apostolic ministry—he calls it an office of the Holy Ghost (1 Cor. 12: 4)—which has made him so suspect in the eyes of his Judaizing opponents. They insist that he is an ἔκτρωμα, immature and abortive, no genuine apostle, one born out of due time. This abusive phrase of his opponents, which he

---

[1] On this question of his illness, quite unimportant in itself, a mass of mostly psychologizing literature has been written. In parenthesis I would only like to point out that if in fact Paul is mentioned in the Talmud under the name Gehazi—some indications suggest this—then he was leprous, for this is asserted of the Talmudic Gehazi (Sanh. 107b; Sota 47a).

[2] Cf. Rengstorf, ἀπόστολος, Kittel, WB, I, 441 ff. Käsemann, op. cit., 35, points out that the report of the mysteries in 2 Cor. 12 must be seen in conjunction with that other Corinthian mystery, glossolaly, of 1 Cor. 14, as belonging to the same category.

[3] M. Dibelius, Botschaft und Geschichte, II, 158, comments: "If he puts personal mystical experiences behind the gospel message to all, he does not do so for pedagogic or pastoral reasons, but because for him Christianity and the apostolate are practically coincident. The mystical experiences are there but, without Paul needing to suppress them by self-mastery, they are cloaked by God's claim on His apostle."

takes up in 1 Cor. 15: 8, must have been the real keynote of the whole Judaizing polemic.[1]

5. THE REFLECTION OF THE STRUGGLE IN LATER JEWISH-CHRISTIAN WRITINGS

That this understanding of the Judaizing attack must be the correct one may be seen from later Jewish-Christian documents, which, as I have shown, preserve the early arguments of the Jewish emissaries from the Pharisaic group in Jerusalem and suggest exactly what their polemical intervention in Galatia and Corinth was all about. The oldest part of the pseudo-Clementine literature, which in my opinion contained or edited fragments of a lost Ebionite Acts of the Apostles and clearly implies a knowledge of the Pauline letters, is in fact related to these conflicts.[2] Paul, here described according to Gal. 4: 16 as $\dot{\epsilon}\chi\theta\rho\dot{o}s$ $\ddot{a}\nu\theta\rho\omega\pi os$ or *homo quidam inimicus* and concealed under the name Simon, is for the writer a sort of Antichrist. According to the reproach of their fathers (Acts 21: 21), he taught $\dot{a}\pi o\sigma\tau a\sigma\dot{\iota}a$ $\dot{a}\pi\dot{o}$ $M\omega\nu\sigma\dot{\epsilon}\omega s$, he was a $\psi\epsilon\nu\delta a\pi\dot{o}\sigma\tau o\lambda os$ and preached a gospel of lies.

In the pseudo-Clementine texts, which carry the polemical tone to the point of the scurrilous, the whole argument culminates in a coarse repudiation of the legitimacy of his apostleship. Here the strict Jerusalem limitation of the apostolic office to the circle of the twelve is insisted on, for a thirteenth apostle is just as unthinkable as a thirteenth month of the year (Rec. 4: 35). In a debate in Laodicea (invented of course by our author) referred to in Hom. 17, Peter disputes in a way characteristic of the Judaizers that Paul could possibly have seen the risen Christ. Obviously it is a question of the same principle which the canonical Peter had stated at the time of the choice of Matthias (Acts 1: 21 ff.)—the principle that the criterion of apostleship was the ability to bear testimony to the earthly Jesus. Hence the $\dot{a}\pi o\kappa a\lambda\dot{\nu}\psi\epsilon\iota s$ $\kappa\nu\rho\dot{\iota}o\nu$, which is the testimony that Paul has to show, can have no claim to objective

---

[1] The word is certainly connected with the struggle for his apostolic dignity, and is intended to denote the abnormality of his experience of a call. Harnack already saw this, *SAB*, 1922, 72: Paul seized on the word and twisted its sense. It means, however, that he is really unworthy because at the time when the other disciples and apostles saw the Lord, Paul was persecuting them. Cf. on $\ddot{\epsilon}\kappa\tau\rho\omega\mu a$ also A. Fridrichsen, *Paulus abortivus*, Festschrift für O. A. Danielsson, Uppsala, 1932, 79 ff.; C. Schneider, Kittel, *WB*, II, 463 ff.

[2] The most recent study of A. Salles, "La Diatribe anti-paulinienne dans le Roman Pseudo-Clémentin et l'origine des K Π", *RB*, 1957, 544 ff., supposes that this anti-Pauline polemic was fixed immediately after the year 70.

validity, because they are merely phenomena of the subjective consciousness. In fact, they are angrily rejected by the Clementine Peter as sheer manifestations of an evil demon, or a spirit of lies. Peter deliberately produces the following argument in answer to a question of Simon-Paul as to whether the direct revelation of God through vision (ὀπτασία) is not a more powerful proof (ἱκανωτέρα) than evidence dependent on human judgment (ἐνάργεια, Rehm's emendation of the MSS. ἐνέργεια):

> The personal knowledge and the personal instruction of the true prophet gives certainty; vision leaves us in uncertainty. For the latter may spring from a misleading spirit (πνεῦμα πλάνον) which feigns to be what it is not (Hom. 17: 14–19).

In illustration of this, a series of Biblical visions are quoted by Peter, which had the character of dreams; the righteous man however needs no visions in order to learn what he has to do.

> To the pious in their earthly lives truth comes not in dreams or visions (ἐν ὁράματι ἢ ὀπτασίᾳ) but in the full consciousness of the waking mind. It was in this way that the Son was revealed to me by the Father. Hence I know from my own experience the meaning of revelation (τίς δύναμις ἀποκαλύψεως). As soon as the Lord asked who men considered Him to be, I said at once: "You are the Son of the living God" (Mt. 16: 16). And He who pronounced me blessed on this account, told me first that it was the Father who had revealed this truth to me. Since then, I have known what revelation is; namely, the discovery of truth without instruction, vision or dream (ἀδιδάκτως ἄνευ ὀπτασίας καὶ ὀνείρων; 17: 18).

Then the Clementine Peter gives the polemical practical application of his principle, in that, while despite all his scepticism about visions of Christ he grants that such are possible, he continues:

> If Jesus has become known to you through visions then it is only in such wise as in His anger He grants visions to His enemy (ὡς ἀντικειμένῳ ὁ Ἰησοῦς ὀργιζόμενος).[1] How then can any one be instructed through a vision so as to be capable of teaching? And if you object that it is possible, how is it then that the Master spent a whole year with us teaching us with our minds fully awake? How are we to believe that He in fact appeared to you at all (κἂν ὅτι ὤφθη σοι—cf. I Cor. 15: 8: ὤφθη κἀμοί). How can He have appeared to you when you believe the exact opposite of His doctrine? (ὅποτε αὐτοῦ τὰ ἐναντία τῇ διδασκαλίᾳ

[1] The scriptural basis is obviously Num. 12: 6–9, where God in wrath declares to Aaron and Miriam that if there arises a prophet among them, he will reveal himself by dreams and visions. But God disclosed Himself to Moses visibly as to a friend (στόμα πρὸς στόμα ἐν εἴδει, 17: 17–18).

83

φρονεῖς). If however you have become an apostle as the result of an appearance which lasted but one hour, then you should proclaim and expound His teachings, you should love His apostles, and not quarrel with me, who was with Him on earth. You have opposed me (ἀνθεστήκας —cf. Gal. 2: 11: ἀντέστην) who am an unshakeable rock, the chief pillar of His church (στερεὰ πέτρα καί θεμέλιον ἐκκλησίας, cf. Mt. 16: 18). Were you not my adversary, you would not calumniate me, and despise my preaching, with the result that I do not find the response of faith to teaching which I have heard directly from the mouth of the Lord, as though I stood condemned (κατεγνωσμένος: again, Gal. 2: 11) and you were highly praised.[1] When you call me κατεγνωσμένος you are arraigning God, who revealed Christ to me; you are impugning the Lord who because of this revelation to me pronounced me blessed. If you really wish to work for the truth, then first of all learn something from us, learn what Jesus taught us, and as a disciple of truth become our fellow worker (συνεργὸς ἡμῶν, cf. 1 Cor. 3: 9: θεοῦ γάρ ἐσμεν συνεργοί) (ch. 19).

Whoever reads for the first time this discourse of the Clementine ·Peter[2] will immediately feel two things. Firstly, that here the Peter of the New Testament has become the most violent opponent of Paul and that a bitter reminiscence of the scene at Antioch is obviously latent here.[3] Secondly, that the discourse must present in compact form all those arguments of the Judaizers reflected in the Pauline letters. There is no doubt, however, that this polemic is expressed in a diction and makes use of ideas and traits which are only possible in the second century at the earliest. The arguments are clearly aimed at gnostics who have invoked in their defence the visions of Paul. It seems to me equally certain that the author of this highly artistic literary document had before him the letters of Paul and the canonical Acts. Hence we are faced here with a much later stage of anti-Paulinism. None the less, it seems to me that we are justified in the assumption that the old arguments of the Judaizers against Paul (which were perhaps summed up in an older, now

[1] This is one of the few places where the new edition of the Homilies by B. Rehm has really improved on Lagarde's text: σου εὐδοκιμοῦντος for ἐμοῦ ἀδοκίμου ὄντος.

[2] In the passage Hom. 18, 6–10 Paul is violently attacked by the Clementine Peter—and that with regard to his missionary method. Here the reproach is that he speaks only to please men (ἀρεσκόντως τοῖς παροῦσι ὄχλοις, probably an allusion to Gal. 1. 10; 1 Thess. 2: 4) and teaches improperly.

[3] In Ep. Petri 2, 4 Paul is accused of giving a false account in Gal. 2: 11 ff. But all this is legendary, as must be admitted. There is no real indication in favour of the Tübingen standpoint that Peter developed an anti-Pauline activity in the Judaizing sense, or even for the supposition that the *contretemps* in Antioch led to an actual rupture between the two. Cf. H. Windisch, "Das Urchristentum", *ThR*, 1933, 291 ff.

vanished document) have here been utilized and preserved. In our previous section we have tried to convey them from those intimations which Paul gives us in his letters. But the literature to which we are now referring first gives them colour and continuity. Let us recapitulate the most important points:

The opposition of the Judaizers was in the first instance directed not against Paul's Damascus experience, but rather against his constant appeal to the vision and probably to others also, in order to legitimate his apostolic dignity and the character of his gospel, which deviated from the preaching of the older apostles.[1] Hence it is again a question here of that fundamental divergence of views as to what constitutes an apostle which we have already noted, on the basis of New Testament sources, as the cause of the differences between Paul and the circle of the twelve. Here, however, the Judaizers who regard companionship with the earthly Jesus and instruction by Him as alone constitutive of the apostolic dignity, pass over to a sharply aggressive attitude. They deny that ὀπτασίαι καὶ ἀποκαλύψεις of which Paul (2 Cor. 12: 1 ff.) had boasted can furnish any qualification for apostleship; also they indignantly reject Paul's claim (2 Cor. 5: 16) to understand the message of Jesus better than Peter, a claim which in the Clementine text (17:14: ὡς ὑπὸ ὀπτασίας αὐτοῦ ἀκηκοὼς τὸν λόγον) is actually made, and they insist on the unreliability of visions, which are unverifiable and in which a spirit quite other than God may be revealed.[2] Simon the sorcerer too boasts of his ascension, thanks to gnosis, in the world of unfathomable light (Rec. 2: 61 ff.), just as Paul speaks of his ecstatic transport into the third heaven.[3] But the Peter of this document stresses the point that genuine revelation means the discovery of truth apart from dream or vision. The wording ὡς ἀντικειμένῳ ὁ Ἰησοῦς ὀργιζόμενος seems to suggest that here Paul, by a perversion of his own words, is meant to be represented as the ἀντικείμενος against whom he himself had warned the Thessalonians (2 Thess. 2: 4).[4] The decisive fact is the claim of the first

---

[1] Cf. also R. A. Lipsius, *Die Quellen der römischen Petrussage*, Kiel, 1872, 38.

[2] The aversion to such circles in this strongly OT writing rests probably on such texts as Deut. 13: 3: you shall not listen to the words of that prophet, or that dreamer of dreams, for the Lord your God is testing you, etc.; Zech. 10: 2: dreamers tell false dreams, etc. Further details *TheolJchr*, 426 and also E. L. Ehrlich, *Der Traum im AT*, Berlin, 1953.

[3] Cf. Bousset, *Hauptprobl.* etc., *op. cit.*, 314; he imputes to Paul a knowledge of magical practices.

[4] This connexion was entertained by Lipsius, Schmiedel, Waitz and others. 2 Thess. 2: 4 was generally understood in the early church to be a warning against heresy. ἀντικείμενος is a translation of שׂטן, cf. Schoeps, *TheolJchr*, 131.

apostle that there is no other gospel but the one which the disciples of Jesus learnt from the lips of the Master Himself. The falsity of Paul's apostleship is clear from the fact that he does not expound the teachings of Christ, that his system of thought is the opposite of those teachings. For this reason Peter has felt compelled to denounce him, and to expose him as ἀντικείμενος, the great enemy of truth, who has twisted even his own words "by many expositions aimed at the dissolution of the law" (Ep. Petri 2: 4).

Paul was regarded at least by the successors of the old Judaizers as the adversary, the ἐχθρός, in fact as Antichrist (Rec. 3: 61). He is described by them, no doubt in sarcastic reference to Acts 9: 15 (σκεῦος ἐκλογῆς), as a vas electionis maligno. Of course he himself in Rom. 9: 22 had spoken of σκεύη ὀργῆς, an expression probably imitated from LXX Jer. 27, (50) 25. Judaists have a horror of his ἄνομος καὶ φλυαρώδης διδασκαλία (Ep. Petri 2: 3) and pillory his εὐαγγέλιον ψευδές. From the Ebionite point of view, Peter and James, in contrast with Paul, represent the true, the νόμιμον κήρυγμα. Just as the ἐχθρὸς ἄνθρωπος in his Jewish period agitated for a cultically distorted Mosaism, later he became an enemy of every law. As formerly he had frustrated by his intervention the efforts of the first church and of James to effect the conversion of the Jews to a lex mosaica per Jesum prophetam reformata, so after his conversion he remained the persecutor of the true law.

For this reason Rec. 4: 34–Hom. 11: 35 establishes the principle that "no apostle, teacher or prophet" should be accepted who has not previously submitted his kerygma to James.[1] Of Simon-Paul it is asserted that "under the pretext of proclaiming the truth in the name of the Lord, he is in fact disseminating error". Hence the last editor of this document, Georg Strecker,[2] rightly observes: "The recognition of a legalistic kerygma (Ep. Petri 2: 3) necessarily led to a denial of the rightfulness of Pauline preaching."

Unfortunately the pseudo-Clementines have preserved for us only very fragmentary sections of older Jewish Christian writings, which as sources have been worked over by their redactor and as such are no longer properly accessible to us. Hence we do not know, though many indications suggest it, whether these sources did not also contain the Judaizers' polemic against specific Pauline theology. Many conclusions a posteriori may be drawn from their own doctrinal posi-

---

[1] James as the vicar of Christ appears also in the newly discovered Coptic gospel of Thomas (v. 11 in Leipoldt's numbering).

[2] Das Judenchristentum in den Pseudoklementinen, Berlin, 1958, 196.

tions as I have tried to work them out.[1] We shall apply and discuss this *Theologica* with all due caution at relevant points in the course of our dissertation. In any case I think I have shown that it is useful to take this pseudo-Clementine literature into account in order to gain a proper understanding of the position of those Judaizing enemies whom Paul came up against in his missionary activity. Since the days of Baur, Lipsius, and Hilgenfeld, this has ceased to be done. I hope that this essay will help to tear away the veil from the Clementines!

No doubt there were besides the Judaizers yet other opponents whom Paul had to deal with in his mission. But their complexion remains obscure, and we must here pass them over. This is true at least for the main Pauline letters; as for the Deutero-Pauline literature, Ephesians and Colossians, the position is different. There powerful gnostic movements are discernible, and such gnostic doctrines and heretic teachers may certainly be characterized. That task, however, lies outside the scope of this book.[2]

In conclusion, may it be said that within primitive Christianity the position of Paul was to an extraordinary extent questionable and subject to debate. We are able to see matters only with our own eyes, not with the eyes of Paul's contemporaries. To the latter it would no doubt have seemed very improbable and indeed fantastic to suggest that Paul's gospel would triumph and conquer the world, while the Jewish Christians themselves would be left by the way and a few generations later would even be termed heretical. Paul and his theology was at that time only one current among several and not even the most important. In point of fact it gained a foothold in the church only after the year 70.[3] .Paul himself had a militant disposition, and became involved in severe struggles. Apart from the latter, the elaboration of what we to-day call Pauline theology would hardly have been made. The church owes to the situation of struggle in which Paul was implicated the best and most characteristic of its possessions.

[1] Cf. lastly my essay "Die Pseudoklementinen und das Urchristentum", *ZRGG*, X, 1958, Vol. I.

[2] Most recent studies on this circle of problems are: E. Percy, *Die Probleme der Kolosser- und Epheserbriefe*, Lund, 1946; G. Bornkamm, "Die Häresie des Kolosserbriefes", *ThLZ*, 1948, 11–20 (now in *Das Ende des Gesetzes*, Munich, 1952, 139–156).

[3] S. G. F. Brandon, *The Fall of Jerusalem and the Christian Church*, London, 1951, 126–154, has rightly emphasized this in his book which in other respects is often open to criticism. Cf. my review in the *Journal of Eccles. History*, III, 1953, 102 ff.

3

THE ESCHATOLOGY OF THE APOSTLE PAUL

THE whole of Paul's theology and consequently the faith of Christendom is dependent on the interpretation of the world situation *post Christum natum* given by Paul. This new situation may be summed up in one sentence: the Messiah who should come at the end of the age has in fact come, though the end of history is still delayed. Χρονίζει ὁ κύριός μου ἔρχεσθαι (Lk. 12: 45). No one knows how long this delay will last. Paul wrote his letters for the intervening time, gave directions to his missionary churches, and explained to believers the meaning of the critical age in which they were living. He viewed the Messianic events within the framework of Jewish expectation; but since in his view things had developed differently from that which Jewish expectation foresaw, he had to give a full reinterpretation of the change and its meaning. It seems to me that this fact must be the Alpha and Omega of every objectively true account of Paul, which hence can take as its point of departure the standpoint of "thoroughgoing eschatology" (Wrede, Schweitzer, Werner, Buri, etc.).

I. HISTORICAL SKETCH OF JEWISH ESCHATOLOGY

The special form of Paul's eschatology can be explained only if we see it in connexion with the previous history of Israel's eschatological expectations. The attempt to derive his eschatology from Hellenism I consider to be misguided. What one might call perhaps, in the style of Hellenistic mystery religions, a "Messiah mysticism"—or with Schweitzer a "Christ mysticism"—we shall see to emerge from a specific direction which, in the light of his special presuppositions, Paul was impelled to give to the traditional Jewish eschatology. We will begin therefore with a short sketch of pre-Christian Jewish eschatology, where Paul with his whole mentality was thoroughly at home.

Eschatological expectation is extremely old and probably is an integral part of the oldest contents of the people of Israel's faith.[1] Its real position in this scheme of faith can be appreciated only if, rejecting a merely dogmatic or phenomenological view which would consider it as an isolated phenomenon, we view it from the standpoint of saving history and in the light of God's covenant with His people Israel.[2] The essence of this covenant is God's command to Israel, expressed in the royal proclamation from Sinai, to embody the sovereignty of God on earth: "You shall be my own possession among all peoples; for all the earth is mine, and you shall be to me a kingdom of priests and a holy nation" (Ex. 19: 5, 6).

We regard the pre-exilic history of Israel as an attempt to realize this aim. The period is governed by the serious intention of realizing the terms of the covenant on the soil of the holy land, of embodying it as a theocratic institution, a divine state. Since, however, the demand of absolute theocracy clashes with the natural self-will of the individual and of the people as a whole, who wish to express their pride in history, a tension arises which gives birth to eschatological expectations. The realization of God's kingdom on earth comes to grief through the stubborn self-will of natural man, and therefore its champions must expect it from some future event. Martin Buber, to whom we owe this insight into the "existential depth of the paradox of all original and immediate theocracy", has uncovered the theocratic crisis in his work *Königtum Gottes*, "Kingship of God", on the occasion of an analysis of the Book of Judges:

> The audacious attempt to embody a theocracy must lead to an outbreak of the tensions latent in every people. But those who in this struggle represent the cause of God's kingdom as opposed to the motives guiding history, experience therein the first shuddering awareness of eschatology (143).

The crisis of the theocratic ideal is seen in the fact that the people were unable to endure the pure invisible kingship of God, that as a

---

[1] We are inclined with Buber, *Das Kommende*, Band 1, *Königtum Gottes*, Berlin, 1936 (1955), to date the origin of the Messianic hope quite early, perhaps even already in the period of the Judges, contrary to Wellhausen and recently Mowinckel (*He That Cometh*, Oxford, 1956). Gressmann too (*Der Messias*, Göttingen, 1929, 172 ff.) thinks it pre-prophetic and dates it from at least the time of David.

[2] Cf. J. Hempel, *Das Ethos des AT*, Berlin, 1938, 202: "Belief in a covenant between God and His worshippers is older than the Israelite religion, but in it and in it alone has it become a sustaining thought. The God of Israel is the God of the covenant. But because for it the conclusion of the covenant implies not a statement about God but the statement about Him, which describes His being more firmly than any other, the 'ethical schematization' of its religious belief stems from the field of law."

concession to human weakness God gave Samuel the seer the command to institute and anoint a human king. In this turn of events the basic paradox of the Israelite kingship becomes visible.

> The one who expresses the apostasy of his people, is at the same time God's representative through whom God, in spite of this lapse, by His own power wills to execute His will and to lay the foundations of His kingdom. For God does not surrender to the king His sovereign Lordship—but to embody His divine kingship is the task which He imposes on the earthly king.[1]

The attempt to fulfil this command and its failure in the face of human impulses and the motives of history fill the centuries of Biblical monarchy in Israel and Judah.

> The history of the kings is the history of the anointed king's failure to fulfil the meaning of his anointing. From this source alone is Messianism, faith in an anointed one who shall fulfil the meaning of his anointing, to be understood.[2]

According to 2 Sam. 7: 12 ff., God promised King David that his kingship should last for ever. History, of course, turned out differently. But for that very reason the memory of that brilliant early period, the era of King David, became the "seed plot of Israelite Messianic hopes".[3] The expected Messiah was to be of David's seed,[4] and his work was to be the restoration of the ancient splendour. Thus far we may understand the emergence of the specific form of the Messianic hope in the exilic and post-exilic periods[5] to be an

---

[1] Thus Margarete Susman, "Saul und David", *Der Morgen*, VI, Berlin, 1930, 177.

[2] Thus M. Buber, *Kampf um Israel*, Berlin, 1933, 101. For the 2nd volume of his *Königtum Gottes*—not yet published—he announces the fulfilment of this theme.

[3] So W. Eichrodt, *Theologie des Alten Testaments*, I, Stuttgart, 1957, 339. (E.T. in preparation, *The Theology of the Old Testament*.)

[4] Ὑιὸς Δαυίδ as a Messianic title is found probably for the first time in the Psalms of Solomon 17: 23 written shortly after the end of Pompey at Pharsalus 48 B.C. The promise of an eternal kingdom to the house of David (Ps. Sol. 17: 5) was part of the traditional Israelite consciousness (cf. 2 Sam. 7: 16) and is expressed in the Messianic prophecies of most of the prophets. How far the self-affirmations of David in the Psalms have influenced the later portrait of the Messiah should sometime be carefully studied. In Yalqut chadash 143, Nr. 59 David's life is once called מעין דוגמא של משיח. About David as a Messianic figure cf. the (incomplete) material in W. Staerk, *Soter II*, Stuttgart, 1938, 56 f.

[5] For the earlier period it is true that "la figure messianique est probablement absent des prophéties préexiliques", to quote Jean Héring: *Le Royaume de Dieu et sa venue*, Paris, 1937, 57. This is true so long as we distinguish the figure of the Messiah from the Messianic hope.

expression of frustrated expectations of the historical kingship.[1] This connexion with the figure of David, to whom even early eschatology transferred the mythical expectation of the return of a paradisal king, might well be described with Gressmann as the "historization of a myth".[2]

Since the researches of J. Wellhausen and his school, which gave such eloquent testimony to the complex influences at work in the "historical" period, we know that the origins of all eschatological expectation are to be found in the disappointment of hopes focused on earthly history, i.e., in the resigned recognition that any imminent realization was impossible. Despair of earthly history caused what was impossible in the present either to be transferred to the future or to be projected into the sphere of the unearthly and supernatural, and in consequence the figure of the ideal king, whose return was looked for, became moulded by the process of mythical creation. Thus the Messiah, which originally denoted only the Israelite king as the anointed vicar of God, became a figure destined to appear in the future. At the same time the process of mythical embroidering, of transfiguration in an unearthly light, began, although in our extant traditions the stage of a real incarnation of God, conceptually fixed, was never reached.

The traditional Messianic expectation was substantially political in character. Under the rule of a scion of David, men expected the restoration of the covenant and the final fulfilment of God's will on earth. The ruined booth of David was again to be raised up (Amos 9: 11); the kingdom arising from the stump of Jesse would then materialize (Is. 9: 6; 11: 1). In the age of salvation David would have a righteous branch which would inherit the throne of Israel (Jer. 30: 9; 33:15, 17; Ez. 37: 21 ff., etc.). But

> the leader of Israel in the day of salvation would be only an executive officer under God Himself the Saviour of Israel (Is. 49: 7), the divine author of this salvation. From God alone comes healing. The Davidic king appointed by God is no Messiah in the sense that he contributes by his deeds or achievement to inaugurate this great day.[3]

[1] It should be stressed, however, that the originally purely political idea of the משיח, Gk. Χριστός, which before the exile might have been applied to any anointed monarch, was narrowed down to an eschatological meaning only in the Hellenistic Roman period. It never lost entirely its original political colouring, as is shown by the superscription on the cross of Jesus.

[2] *Der Messias*, 279; cf. further Joh. Hempel, "Glaube, Mythos und Geschichte im AT", *ZNW*, 1953, 103 ff.; S. Mowinckel, *He That Cometh*, Oxford, 1956, 152 ff., etc.

[3] Thus appositely Ludwig Koehler, *Theologie des Alten Testaments*, Tübingen, 1953, 228. (E.T. *Old Testament Theology*.)

If we leave out of account the Servant passages in Deutero-Isaiah in which we might well see indicated the spiritual ideal of a suffering redeemer (this will be treated in detail in the next chapter) we must come to the conclusion that the eschatology of the prophets did not suggest a transcendent but a thoroughly earthly state of well-being, with a corresponding Messiah, who was to be political in significance in so far as he was destined to gather together the outcasts and to bring about the glorification of Zion.[1] What is said in Jer. 31–32 about the new covenant, and in both Isaiah and Ezekiel about the renewal of the heart and mind, does admittedly imply a wondrous new penetration of God into His creation, perhaps its restoration to a former paradisal condition; but it does not signify the end of earthly history. This current of eschatological expectation has in view nothing other than the final fulfilment of the divine will and the establishment of God's kingdom on the whole earth—consequent on the failure of historical courses and a new inthrust of the divine. The content of this expected time of salvation is: God will be King, He will alone be sovereign, His name the only name (Zech. 14: 9). But there is no allusion to a resurrection of the dead, to an end of death, or to a winding up of history with recompense and punishment from the world beyond. The Messiah is viewed not as a person with supernatural powers or as a divine deliverer, but merely as the executive officer of God; generally speaking, the Messianic kingdom is more important than the person of the Messianic king.

Israelite prophecy is to a large extent concerned with this type of Old Testament expectation, which might be described as the genuinely Biblical type. Here the focus of hopes is not the Messiah as a saviour springing from the supernatural world, but rather the goal of the divine ordering of history is the Messianic kingdom which is to be set up under the rule of a prince of peace who shall be of David's seed. In particular, after the return from exile (520 B.C.) and the failure of the expectations centred on the Davidic Zerubbabel, the figure of the Messiah fades away more and more into the background, giving place to the vaguer Messianic expectation—again with the exception of the special case in Deutero-Isaiah. Not until centuries later among the Tannaites did it spring up again, reflected in the poetic figure of King David *redivivus* or the Messiah

---

[1] The interweaving of political and metapolitical motives distinguishes the eschatological hope from its beginnings, as the Shiloh prophecy Gen. 49: 10 shows. Hence many controversies of OT scholars on these questions—we may think only of the opposite opinions of Sellin and Gressmann—may be reduced to terminological differences.

ben David, for only then began the mythical idealization of the first Israelite king. But the early Tannaites too stand within the prophetic tradition in so far as their predominant expectation was of the Messiah as the ideal king, the champion of peace and the perfect fulfiller of the law. Of course the focus of their expectation, like that of the synoptic Jesus too, lay in the Messianic age itself, in the kingdom of splendour adorned with the rich colours of oriental fantasy; and for this reason the figure of the Messiah himself, his characteristics or his function as the mediator of salvation, faded into the background of their thought.

The Messianic expectation of the early Tannaitic period coincides to a large extent with the longing to regain lost political power, with the result that an essentially earthly conception of the Messiah as David's son linked itself to the symbol of the eschatological prince of peace who was to inaugurate an ultimate divine kingdom of Israel in this world. Hence we must be clear about the fact that while the expectation is certainly that of a final age, it is a new aeon of this world's history that is expected, not the end of history; in any event, it is a kind of Messianic interim kingdom. The Messiah-King is considered as God's forerunner, and the last things remain solely in the disposal of God Himself. Thus gradually a time scheme of three parts was elaborated: this world—the days of the Messiah—the future world. This scheme might be considered characteristic of the Tannaite period also.

Alongside this scheme inherited from the past of the Bible, and current in the period of Jesus—no doubt adhered to more firmly among the Palestinian Jews than in the Diaspora—there is distinguishable, from the 2nd century B.C., another more supernatural trend of eschatological expectation, possibly arising from Persian influence. According to this second trend of thought, the Messiah was in fact awaited as a Saviour and His appearance was expected to coincide with the final events of a cosmic catastrophe. We refer to the eschatology of the Book of Daniel, which was adopted by Enoch and IV Ezra and receives plainer outlines and colours only in those later writings. This body of apocalyptic literature was much more calculated to harmonize with the speculation of the apostle Paul.

The Book of Daniel, belonging to the 2nd century, the last book of the Biblical canon, may have received its final form between 168 and 164 under the impact of the desecration of the temple by Antiochus Epiphanes. Here we meet the unusual figure of the *bar enash*, the "Son of Man" who comes with the clouds of heaven (7: 13–LXX ἐπὶ τῶν νεφελῶν)—a figure which has been a puzzle to researchers.[1] IV Ezra 13 also knows this visionary man around whom Daniel had still left the veil of secrecy, and presents him as an apocalyptic redeemer figure. The Similitudes of the Ethiopic Enoch (En. 37–71) give to the conception a formal eschatological title. Hence they free him from the traditional pattern of Davidic eschatology.[2] From the start the "Son of Man" has nothing to do with Messianic expectations arising from the sacral kingship originating with David.[3] Rather he is a pre-existent heavenly being which the apocalyptists derived from Iranian conceptions of an archetypal man (thus Bousset, Reitzenstein, Schaeder, Kraeling, Sjöberg, etc.) which they transformed in a Jewish way and fitted into the traditional Messianic pattern. This new conception, however, essentially modified the character of hopes for the future.

In contrast to the old national eschatology, the apocalyptists introduced an essential significant change into Messianic thought by implanting within it a cosmological dualism. This led to the development of the so-called doctrine of the two aeons (this aeon and the future aeon); a doctrine which became current about the middle of

---

[1] I would like to repeat here a theory which has not been well received by research, and which R. Eisler in his assuredly problematical book Ἰησοῦς βασιλεὺς οὐ βασιλεύσας, Vol. II, Heidelberg, 1929, 668 ff., has brought forward for discussion. This theory might throw some light on the origins of the mysterious figure in Daniel. Eisler has pointed out that in 1 Chr. 3: 24 the last member of David's house is called Anani and that עֲנָנִי (abbreviation of עֲנָנְיָה, God has answered) was perhaps confused by popular etymology with עָנָן (cloud), so that the expected last member of David's line in Dan. 7: 13 appears under the name of "son of the clouds". In fact, the Targum on 1 Chr. 3: 24 names Anani the king, the Messiah, who will reveal himself. The apparently sole place in scripture which has accepted this relation, Tanchuma B. Toldoth 20 (70b) answers the question: Who is the Anani of 1 Chr. 3: 24? "The king, the Messiah, for it is written . . ." thus notably following the text of Dan. 7: 13. Perhaps also Targ. Jer. on Ex. 12: 43 and even 2 Macc. 2: 8 have helped in the formation of this idea. Cf. also Eugène Dabrowski, *La transfiguration de Jésus*, Rome, 1933, 90.

[2] This development within apocalyptic has been pointed out by P. Volz, 35, 1 (*op. cit.*). As against his claim: "Rabbinic theology does not use it (the title Son of Man)" and that of von Gall (βασιλεία τοῦ θεοῦ, Heidelberg, 1926, 410): "We find not the slightest trace in post-Christian synagogue theology of the eschatological idea of the Son of Man", I draw attention to an Amoraic dialogue from the 2nd half of the 3rd century in Sanh. 97a: Rabbi Nachman said to Rabbi Isaac: "Have you perhaps heard when the בר נפלי will come?" The latter replied: "Who is then the בר נפלי?" The former exclaimed: "The Messiah!" No doubt here the בר נפלי means the "son of the clouds", but, as the rest of the dialogue shows, the two Amoraim no longer understand the Messianic title, which obviously belongs to an earlier stage of the tradition, and by popular etymology they explain it by reference to Amos 9: 11 as "son of the fallen".

[3] Cf. E. Sjöberg: *Der Menschensohn im äthiopischen Henochbuch*, Lund, 1946, esp. VII.

the 1st century B.C.[1] and which Leo Baeck[2] has characterized in the following way:

> Whereas Messianic thought among the Biblical prophets expressed itself in the feeling of a tension between the present and the future, between what now exists and what is coming to be, here it is expressed in the consciousness of opposition between this world and what lies beyond it. The "coming age" is here no longer a day of realization towards which hope is directed—*yamim ba'im*—but a world disclosed in vision—*olam habba*. If in the former case the expected one towards whom hopes are turned is a shoot of the house of David, who will fulfil the ideals conceived historically, here he is an unearthly being who from the heights of heaven will bring all history to a close. Whereas the dimension of longings in prophetic thought is a horizontal one, here it is vertical; a fact which constitutes the very essence of apocalyptic.

In apocalyptic literature, with its visionary pictures of the super-sensible world and the riot of colour with which it depicts future events, we are thus confronted by a clear sense of the distinction between this aeon and the future aeon transcendently understood. In contradistinction to the Biblical idea of divine monarchy, the מלכות שמים now increasingly becomes a transcendental concept, in fact a thoroughly post-messianic concept, for apocalyptic thought conceives the advent of the Messiah as taking place before the ἔσχατον. מלכות שמים is something more and other than the inauguration of the final Israelite kingdom under the rule of *Mashiach*, the prince of peace of David's line. It is also certain that the expectation of the *malkhuth shamayim* was older and more important than the ideas of a coming Messiah, and that the two things may not be identified with each other.[3] The apocalyptic figure of the "Son of Man", the בר אנש, utterly transcends the Messiah of traditional national eschatology, for it has been freed from all popular political traits. The "Son of Man" is a figure springing from the transcendent world; his emergence from hiddenness indicates the imminence of the other-worldly in its total distinction from the this-worldly. In particular, we find that in the

---

[1] The statement of Hillel in Aboth 2, 7 is one of the oldest witnesses to the use of the expressions: עולם הזה — עולם הבא. Further texts in G. Dalman, *Die Worte Jesu*, Leipzig, 1930, 121 ff., and P. Volz, *op. cit.*, 65.

[2] "Der Menschensohn", *MGWJ*, 1937, 19.

[3] Cf. K. G. Kuhn in Kittel, *WB*, I, 570 ff.; Philipp Vielhauer, *Gottes Reich und Menschensohn*, Festschrift für G. Dehn, Neukirchen, 1957, 72.

Book of Enoch a sort of ideal pre-existence is ascribed to the Son of Man.[1]

In the Messianic consciousness of Jesus there was apparently a fusion between the Messianic figure of the Son of David and the *bar enash* or *ben adam* who was to come on the clouds of heaven,[2] and on this point His mind remained shrouded in mystery.[3] Even in the pious Judaism of this period, the two trends of speculation were mostly conjoined without any sharp conceptual distinction.

What is certain is that this type of eschatological thought which leads to a transcendent reinterpretation of the Messianic idea $\epsilon i s$ $a i \hat{\omega} v a \ \mu \acute{e} \lambda \lambda o v \tau a$ was deeply harmonious with the conceptual world of Paul. Even Palestinian Judaism in the time of Jesus assimilated permanently into its stock of doctrine the apocalyptic idea of an *olam habba* with all its kindred hopes of a radical world transformation, the resurrection of the dead, and the inbreak of the other world. And this assimilation took place despite the fact that the works of the apocalyptic authors were not canonized, but were disesteemed as apocryphal.[4] In particular, we should not fail to recognize that apocalyptic meant a disparagement of earthly things, was inclined to a deep pessimism with regard to earthly history,[5] which after the destruction of the temple was made more acute by the deliberate metapolitical function of hastening the decline of political Messianism. Clearly this development culminated in the period 70–135, for the Bar Kokhba rebellion had collapsed and the nationalistic intransigent rabbis—above all Rabbi Aqiba—on account of their

[1] On the whole problem of the Son of Man in the Book of Enoch cf. R. Otto, *Reich Gottes und Menschensohn*, Munich, 1934 (E.T. *The Kingdom of God and The Son of Man*), and E. Sjöberg, *Der Menschensohn im äthiopischen Henochbuch*, Lund, 1946. T. W. Manson, "The Son of Man in Daniel, Enoch and the Gospels", *Bulletin of John Rylands Library, Manchester*, 1950, 184, prefers to say "pre-mundane election" rather than "pre-mundane existence".

[2] Héring, *op. cit.*, 142 ff.: "What Jesus expected was the advent of the heavenly man 'on the clouds of heaven', who would inaugurate in the visible world the Kingdom of God, and He intimated His own future identity with this extraordinary personage." Similarly also A. Fridrichsen, *Människosonen och Israel*, Till G. Aulén, Stockholm, 1939, 112.

[3] R. Otto above all, *op. cit.*, 179 ff., has explained the Messianic self-consciousness of Jesus as that of the Son of Man, of whom the Book of Enoch constantly speaks, in anticipation. But it seems to me extremely questionable to what extent and whether we should work with a highly elaborated Son of Man tradition, brought into currency through the Book of Enoch and reaching Jesus through baptismal sects. The secret revealed at the end of the book (ch. 105, 2), namely that the pre-existent Son of Man to be manifested in the future is in fact the Son of God—parallel to the Matthean equation 16: 13 with 18—looks too much like a Christian interpolation.

[4] Thus apocalyptic literature became apocryphal, and in M. Sanh. X, 1, Rabbi Aqiba denies any share in the future world to anyone who reads apocryphal writings.

[5] Cf. N. N. Glatzer, *Die Geschichtslehre der Tannaiten*, Berlin, 1933.

miscalculations had to pay with their lives for their political Messianism in the time of Hadrian's persecution.

For our period at all events, the years 30–60, both as regards Palestine and the Diaspora we have to reckon with a mingling of the political-Messianic trend of expectation and apocalyptic-eschatological hopes. The former may well have been predominant in the powerful Sadducean party. But there never was a unified scheme of thought about the last things, nor any fairly representative doctrine, especially as regards a Messianic interim kingdom. For this reason it would probably be vain to attempt to introduce any system into this medley of concepts and hopes, with the idea of neatly distinguishing characteristic forms of the eschatological outlook in Pharisees and Sadducees, in Palestine and the Diaspora. All that we can note is a shift of emphasis from the political to the metapolitical during and after the Hadrianic period. For this reason even the distinctions between the Messianic time and the *olam habba* were mostly effaced.

2. PAUL AS INTERPRETER OF THE POST-MESSIANIC SITUATION

Having sketched the previous history of eschatological hopes and distinguished its two main currents, we must now try to analyse the problem presented by the 1st-century situation, so as to determine the characteristics of Pauline eschatology, which clearly offers us something quite new.

All Jewish eschatology was and is exclusively concerned with the future. From this point of view it makes no difference whether the *yamim habba'im* is understood as a this-worldly future embodying a glorious divine kingdom of Judah, as is the case with the prophets and later the Psalms of Solomon, or whether it is expected as a transcendent event, as the resurrection of the dead, the last judgment, and eternal life, as is the case in apocalyptic and probably also in Jesus' conception of the kingdom. Lastly, many combinations are known to us, as a result of which the eschatological terminology of the Tannaitic period is fluid.[1] In the main a process in two stages is envisaged: first appears the reign of the King-Messiah, fulfilling political hopes, but temporally limited, and only at its conclusion

---

[1] Cf. J. Klausner, *op. cit.*, ch. 2 and *The Messianic Idea*, 416 ff., where many examples are given to illustrate the fluidity of the meaning of such terms as ימות המשיח, עולם הבא, לעתיד לבא in rabbinic writings.

begins the revelation of the wholly transcendent.[1] The conception is seen expressed for the first time in the Book of Daniel, which brought into fashion speculations about the aeons. The ten-week apocalypse of the Book of Enoch (91: 12–17; 93) is one of the oldest witnesses to an age of salvation before the end. Through Enoch, Baruch, and IV Ezra, which envisage the Messianic kingdom as lasting 400 years, the doctrine then gained a footing in official Jewish teaching.

The books of Daniel and Enoch, where the situation throughout is somewhat ambiguous, seem to place the event of the resurrection of the dead at the beginning of the Messianic kingdom, while the apocalypses of Baruch (30: 1–4) and IV Ezra (7: 26–33) place it at the end, and conceive it as the event which effects the transition from the ימים של משיח to the עולם הבא. The older scheme, wide-spread in Hellenistic Judaism (cf. Volz, 38: 5), sees the future world ushered in by the days of the Messiah (IV Macc. Test. XII Patr. and, doubtfully, Daniel and Enoch's metaphorical discourses—chs. 37–71), while the later scheme (IV Ezra, Apoc. Baruch and some Tannaites)[2] reckons the days of the Messiah into the עולם הזה. The question asked in IV Ezra 6:7: "When will the critical division of the times supervene, when will the end of the first aeon and the beginning of the second take place?" was a question which many Jews in this period were asking (cf. Mt. 24: 3; Lk. 17: 20 f.). Common to all these writings, which try to answer this question, is the idea of the חבלו של משיח (pre-Messianic sufferings) as characteristic of the last days of the aeon. As regards the last judgment, some writers suggest that God Himself will be the Judge (Daniel, Baruch, Ass. Mos., Test. Levi); others that the Messiah will perform the function (Enoch and probably IV Ezra).

The eschatology of Paul is linked with this kind of speculation about the aeons, but is distinguished from all forms of Jewish specula-tion by the fact that in consequence of the resurrection of Jesus from the dead it considers the eschaton to have already begun. From the future is still to be expected only the consummation, consisting in the final victory over death, the last judgment which will take place on the return of the Messiah (1 Cor. 4: 5; 2 Cor. 5: 10) and finally, in

---

[1] A well-known distribution in the Judaic theology of the aeons is as follows: 2,000 years Chaos, 2,000 Torah, beginning at Sinai, and 2,000 years of the Messianic age (Sanh. 97a; Jer. Megilla 70d; Pes. Rabb. 4a–c). Only afterwards comes the world of the future which is wholly Sabbath, eternal rest, as it is expressed in Tamid VII, 4. On the whole subject see G. F. Moore, *Judaism*, II, 323 f., and Billerbeck, IV, 2, 799 ff.

[2] Material in Billerbeck, IV, 2, 972.

the restoration of complete sovereignty to God (1 Cor. 15: 24), so that God in the *olam habba* may be all in all (1 Cor. 15: 28). For Paul the Messianic kingdom has already begun, the Messiah-Son of Man has already come into the world, the resurrection of the dead is already in operation, what is yet to eventuate is only the transformation of creation from perishability to imperishability, the final destruction of the power of death, the parousia and the last judgment. Paul regards his own time as that of the חבלו של משיח, as the last days of the עולם הזה, in which, however, the τέλος τῶν αἰώνων (1 Cor. 10: 11) has already appeared. In this transitional epoch in which Paul and his churches are living—we are now accustomed to call these decades of his activity the "apostolic age"—the *olam hazzeh* and the *olam habba* are already mingled, thus indicating that the Messianic age of salvation has dawned. This mingling of the two ages constitutes the distinctive eschatological standpoint of Pauline theology. Thus it becomes clear that Paul could only link up with that form of eschatology which transferred the resurrection of the dead to the end of the Messianic age (cf. Baruch ch. 20–30; 40: 3; IV Ezra 7: 26–44). The Messianic age itself, the age of the apostle, then becomes an interim stage, a transition to the *olam habba*. To understand all this we must remember that Paul viewed world history as a cosmic whole, which with the apocalyptists he divided into aeons (cf. also below, ch. 6: 2).

If we are to understand the eschatology of Paul aright—and it contains the whole Christian conception of saving history—we must make its apocalyptic presuppositions[1] more central in his thought than is usually done. It is understandable that for this aspect of his work critics confine their attention mainly to his first Corinthian letter and the two letters to the Thessalonians—his specially eschatological letters which also refer to the parousia of the Messiah. The idea that, while in Jesus the Messiah has already come, this coming does not coincide with the "end of the days", shows plainly that Paul was a theologian who thought in terms of the aeons, who saw a gulf between the מלכות המשיח and the עולם הבא—a gulf beyond which lay the last judgment and the resurrection of the dead.

This doctrine of the two aeons may be shown to exist in apocalyptic literature from the first century B.C. (the Ethiopic and Slavonic

---

[1] On the difficulties of the eschatological question for the history of Christian theology, cf. J. Kiss, "Zur eschatologischen Beurteilung der Theologie des Apostels Paulus", *ZSTh*, 1938, 379 ff. Recently also Kümmel, Cullmann, Michaelis, and especially F. Flückiger, *Der Ursprung des christlichen Dogmas*, Zollikon, 1955, who question the whole approach of A. Schweitzer and his pupils.

Enoch).[1] The interim period of the Messianic age: Βασιλεὺς βασιλῆι φιλός μέχρι τέρματος ἔσται αἰῶνος (Sib. III, 75) has been described in detail in IV Ezra 7: 26 ff. and Apoc. Baruch 29–30, as a mere preliminary period of 400 years, fulfilling nationalistic-political hopes of opulence and salvation, and leading into the transcendent coming aeon.[2] Even in the rabbinic writings this doctrine, which was at the root of the older national eschatology, was retained, but the expected Jewish nationalistic fulfilment was made subordinate to the universalistic hope. This must have been the inner reason for the division into two periods of the end of the age.

Accordingly, the older traditions concerning the days of the Messiah fix a very short interval for the interim period, namely, forty years (R. Eliezer ben Hyrcanus: Bar. in Sanh. 99a; R. Aqiba: Midr. Teh. on Ps. 90: 15; Tanch. Eqeb 7b, Pes. Rabb. 4a). The two Tannaites, commenting on Ps. 95: 7, derive this time indication from the messianically understood v. 10 (forty years I loathed that generation) and from Deut. 8: 2 by a parallelization with the forty years in the desert.[3] The Damascus Document too (9: 29) knows an interval of forty years between the death of the "unique teacher" and the appearance of the "Messiah from Aaron and Israel"; likewise we meet with the forty years as a final respite, followed by the destruction of all evil, in a newly discovered Qumran fragment on the theme of Ps. 37: 10.[4] Lastly, the final war against the sons of darkness is said to be destined to last forty years. Now these indications of a short interim period found in the older stage of tradition are of extreme interest because they show that the early Tannaitic idea of a short preliminary Messianic period preceding

---

[1] Cf. Bousset, *op. cit.*, 242 ff.; Staerk, *op. cit.*, II, 141 ff.; Volz, *op. cit.*, 64 ff.; R. Löwe, *Kosmos und Aion*, Gütersloh, 1934; H. Sasse in Kittel, *WB*, I, 206.

[2] The same time period is given by Rabbi Dosa (Sanh. 99a). The figure 400 comes from a combination of Gen. 15: 13 with Ps. 90: 15. It is interesting to note that a Syriac MS. in IV Ezra 7: 28 (Violet, *Visio*, III, 5, 3) has the short period of thirty years; Violet, of course, supposes (*Comm.* 11, 74) a misreading of the figure in the insecure state of the text. Baruch seems to present the same picture of the two final aeons; but the exact position has been obscured by a repeated editing of the vision. For further occurrences of the doctrine in the apocalyptic writings cf. Volz, *op. cit.*, 23, 5c.

[3] Other and far longer periods are given by Rabbi Eliezer ben Hyrcanus (of 400 and 1,000 years). Cf. details in Volz, 36, 10b; Billerbeck, III, 826. The later rabbinic indications go up to 7,000 years. Also we should take into account the various pre- and post-Hadrian datings; cf. Klausner, *op. cit.*, 27–33 and *The Messianic Idea*, 424 ff. On the whole subject, H. Bietenhard, *Das tausendjährige Reich*, Zürich, 1955, 44 ff.

[4] Cf. J. M. Allegro, "A Newly Discovered Fragment from Qumran", *Pal. Expl. Quarterly*, 86, 1954, 71.

the coming aeon was known in Paul's circle and was fairly wide-spread. If Paul and his followers supposed that they were living in this Messianic interim period, which would soon be concluded by the return of the Messiah and the resurrection of the dead, there was nothing very unusual about the supposition.

But for Paul there emerges a problem to which no answer was fore-seen in the tradition, and the significance of which Albert Schweitzer in particular (*Mystik* chs. 5 and 6) has isolated as basic to the apostle's whole scheme of thought. This problem, which with Walter Köhler we might call an anxiety problem and which turns his aeon-theology into an aeon-psychosis, is as follows: must not the death of those who have experienced the Messianic kingdom and who have been privileged to share in the Messianic glory be a funda-mentally different death from that of all other men? Obviously this problem was answered by Paul in the affirmative, for he modified the traditional doctrine of the resurrection, as we shall at once see, in order to adapt it to this unforeseen situation. Paul probably held the widespread notion that the interim stage of the Messianic kingdom would be only of short duration. Like Aqiba and Eliezer ben Hyrcanus, he will have reckoned with forty years at most.[1] Hence he regarded the death of Christians as only a special excep-tional case, for in a short space of time death itself, the last enemy, would be destroyed (1 Cor. 15: 26).

The eschatology of Paul was not orientated towards a far distant future, but like all genuine eschatology was an expectation centred on a near future: "to wait for his Son from heaven, whom he raised from the dead, Jesus who delivers us from the wrath to come" (1 Thess. 1: 10). "Rejoice ... the Lord is at hand" (Phil. 4: 4, 5). For this aeon is συνεσταλμένος, the appointed time is short (1 Cor. 7: 29).[2] The whole creation sighs and longs for this τέλος as the ἀποκάλυψις τῶν υἱῶν τοῦ θεοῦ (Rom. 8: 19).[3] What the expectation of the parousia means for Paul has been clearly explained by Franz Overbeck:[4]

[1] Interesting is the fact that in Rom. 13: 11 Paul thinks the day of salvation nearer than when he and the Romans became believers, that the dawn of that day is approaching. "The night is far gone, the day is at hand" (13: 12). At the time of the composition of the letter about twenty-five years have elapsed, and only fifteen years separate him from the parousia.

[2] The commentary of Joh. Weiss suggests the meaning that God Himself has brought forward the terminal date.

[3] Cf. Syr. Baruch Apocalypse 85: 10, "The approach of the times is here, in fact almost already past."

[4] In the collection of fragments *Christentum und Kultur*, Basel, 1919, 57 and 62, published from his literary remains.

Paul was spurred on by the disquieting thought that the proclamation of the gospel must be speedy and that the time granted for it had narrow limits; for the risen Jesus had been snatched away from the earth for a short while only; His return would take place within the briefest spell, within a few years, if not weeks or days. . . . Paul may be said to have carried over to the Gentile world that feeling of imminent world destruction characteristic of the Jews. . . . For the Jews their eschatology was the first and the last word of wisdom, and this Paul forced upon the Gentiles.

Paul imagined the parousia of Jesus in terms taken from the Son of Man tradition as we find it in apocalyptic and rabbinic literature: Jesus the Kyrios would come down from heaven accompanied by His mighty angels in flaming fire, and thus would judge the world (1 Thess. 4: 16; 2 Thess. 1: 7–10), which elsewhere is affirmed only of God (Ass. Mos. 10: 7; Enoch 1: 3 ff.; IV Ezra 7: 33; Sib. III, 308). Accompanying features, such as the cry of command, the voice of the archangel and the heavenly trumpet (cf. also 1 Cor. 15: 52), are equally attested in Jewish writings, as also the coincidence of the general resurrection with this event. And this expected "Day of the Lord" will break forth quite suddenly; it will come as Paul figuratively expresses it in 1 Thess. 5: 2, "like a thief in the night". Rabbinic figures are very similar (cf. the Baraita in Sanh. 97a).

We should misunderstand the apostle's letters as a whole, and the governing consciousness from which they sprang, if we failed to recognize that Paul only lives, writes, and preaches, in the unshakeable conviction that his generation represents the last generation of mankind. Through Christ's death on the cross the world too has been crucified (Gal. 6: 14) and begins now to pass away.[1] The old aeon is still in force, but it is already crumbling (1 Cor. 2: 6). For upon this generation the end of the ages has come (1 Cor. 10: 11: τέλος τῶν αἰώνων = קץ הימים). The form of this world is passing away (1 Cor. 7: 31), in fact the old has already faded (2 Cor. 5: 17). It is clear that Paul no longer reckoned with a second generation of believers, and his recommendation of the single life (1 Cor. 7: 24 ff.) seems to confirm this.

The resurrection of Jesus guarantees for him the resurrection of *all* men, for if the dead are not raised, then Christ Himself has not risen from the dead (1 Cor. 15: 13). For Paul it is indubitable that

---

[1] This interpretation of Gal. 6: 14 by 1 Cor. 7: 31 is given by M. Werner, *op. cit.*, 189, perhaps too far-fetched.

the βασιλεία τοῦ θεοῦ, the Messianic kingdom, has already begun, because Jesus as the "first fruits of those who have fallen asleep" (ἀπαρχὴ τῶν κεκοιμημένων) has risen from the dead, and His resurrection will be followed by that of Christians and the rest of the dead (1 Cor. 15: 23). If even among Christians cases of death have occurred, which seem to show that faith has not protected believers who have fallen asleep from the power of death,[1] then Paul answers the vexed and offended Thessalonians by reference to a word of the Lord: "For this we declare to you by the word of the Lord (λέγομεν ἐν λόγῳ κυρίου), that we who are alive, who are left until the coming of the Lord, shall not precede those who have fallen asleep. For the Lord Himself will descend from heaven with a cry of command, with the archangel's call and with the sound of the trumpet of God. And the dead in Christ will rise first; then we who are alive, who are left, shall be caught up together with them in the clouds to meet the Lord in the air; and so we shall always be with the Lord" (1 Thess. 4: 15–17).

When Paul wrote his first letter to the Corinthians he considered the advent of the *olam habba* to be imminent, and believed that some of his contemporaries would witness this breaking in of the other world (15: 51). He therefore expected such to experience an immediate transition to the putting on of the glorified body without the intermediate stage of a divesting through death (15: 53), i.e., he expected the parousia to occur in their lifetime. In the interval of a year or so which lapsed between this and the writing of the second letter there occurs that change in his outlook[2] which leads him to adopt the alternative possibility of a delay in the parousia and consequently the continued reign of a still uneradicated death (5: 1 ff.; also Phil. 1: 23), and hence to consider that in general the resurrection must be expected only after death.[3] Moreover, the

---

[1] Earliest Christianity must have felt as a severe shock the dying of believers before the second coming of Jesus, otherwise Paul would not at first have explained deaths in Corinth as a divine punishment for unworthy behaviour at the Eucharist (1 Cor. 11: 29–32). Cf. Schweitzer, *op. cit.*, 93, who also discusses the problem of the Corinth disbelievers in the resurrection.

[2] On this cf. E. Teichmann, *Die paulinischen Vorstellungen von Auferstehung und Gericht*, Freiburg, 1896, 59 ff. Rabbinic ideas about the resurrection of the body—parallels to Paul; cf. 1 Cor. 15: 35 with the statements by Rabbi Eliezer ben Hyrcanus in Pirqe d. R. Eliezer—have been studied in the little-known but valuable work of I. Löwinger, "Die Auferstehung in der jüdischen Tradition" (*Jahrbuch für jüdische Volkskunde*, 1923, 74 ff.).

[3] Cf. Héring, *op. cit.*, 242: "The doctrine of the resurrection *post mortem* is certainly an innovation imposed by the brutal fact of a delay in the parousia and the numerous deaths in the church."

heavenly garment may not be put on immediately at death, but the body must wait for a period "naked" in the grave. For the end is still being delayed (2 Thess. 2: 6), but εἴτε ἐνδημοῦντες, εἴτε ἐκδημοῦντες . . . θαρροῦμεν (2 Cor. 5: 8 and 9).

But the problem is by no means solved merely by saying that the "future of the Lord" is still awaited, and that death has not ceased to hold sway. It is to the credit of Albert Schweitzer that continuing the line of thought of Teichmann, Kabisch, and Wrede he has correctly understood the way in which the resurrection problem emerges. Schweitzer and after him M. Werner have indicated the decisive deviation of Paul from the traditional eschatological scheme, which still governed the ideas of primitive Christianity. Both before and after Schweitzer it has been far too little noted that Paul, who with his apocalyptic-rabbinic doctrine of the two aeons sees death conquered only at the close of the Messianic kingdom, was simply compelled to assume two different resurrections. The same, of course, is true of the Revelation of John (20: 4–6). Otherwise the difficulties which have emerged at this point for the thought of the apostle would remain insoluble. If the future Messiah has already, before the advent of the kingdom, existed, died and risen again as man, then this event—unforeseen in the traditional scheme—must somehow be brought into line with the assumption (which follows Baruch and IV Ezra) that believers, as the elect in the last generation of the Messianic kingdom, find themselves to be living in a resurrection form of existence even though they are obviously still under the dominion of death.

Paul, the interpreter of the post-messianic situation, was led by this antinomy, so difficult of solution, into characteristic ways of thought which subsequent generations find difficult to accept. His solution is somewhat as follows: if with the death of Jesus the passing away of the old world has begun and the change of aeons has been effected, then this implies that His resurrection has ushered in the Messianic age. With His parousia there will take place at the close of the interim kingdom the general resurrection of the dead, and its centre will be the new Jerusalem in Palestine. Those who have died previously will enter into the new resurrection body, together with believers who survive to this point of time. All will then in place of the old body of dust receive a σῶμα πνευματικόν (1 Cor. 15: 45–47). Hence some will be invested with a new δόξα without intermediate stage, others only after having been divested through death (2 Cor. 5: 2 and 4). The former will be the elect of the last generation who survive to this event.[1] Here are doubtless two different ways of experiencing death and resurrection.

Paul calls it a μυστήριον (1 Cor. 15: 51) that at the sounding of the last trumpet those who still live will experience transformation. At the same moment the dead will also rise (v. 52). After death as the last enemy has been destroyed (v. 26; an act in the last judgment itself according to Rev. 20: 14) the kingdom will be committed by the Son to the Father (v. 24). Thus in 1 Corinthians Paul sees the last things happen in a specific order, in fact he speaks plainly of a gradation of resurrections: ἕκαστος δὲ ἐν τῷ ἰδίῳ τάγματι (1 Cor. 15: 23). The committal of the kingdom to the Father is thus the third and last τάγμα.

Since I interpret these difficult contexts in the same way as Albert Schweitzer, I would like to quote the following relevant passage from his work for the purpose of further elucidation:

Since Paul supposes that the members of the kingdom live like their Messiah in the resurrection mode of existence, he can solve the otherwise insoluble problem of the fate of those who have died before the second coming of Jesus by affirming that they will rise again. . . . Only as those who are in Christ can believers who are alive at the time of the parousia be transformed from a natural mode of being to an imperishable one; only because believers who have fallen asleep are the dead in Christ (1 Thess. 4: 16; 1 Cor. 15: 18; 15: 23) are they not dead like other people but possess the capacity to be the first to rise again on the return of their Lord. Paul's thought is that believers mysteriously share the death and resurrection of Christ and in this way are delivered from the natural mode of their existence and constitute a class of beings apart. When the Messianic kingdom breaks forth, then those who are still alive are not natural men like others but such as through their dying and rising again with Christ have become capable of rising from the dead before other men. Because the supposition that dead believers are already risen into the Messianic kingdom and that survivors are simultaneously transformed into eternal life, constitutes for Paul a difficult problem, he is compelled to propound for its solution the mystical doctrine of a dying and rising again with Christ. Hence his mysticism remains unintelligible because pointless, so long as the

[1] 1 Cor. 15: 23 will have to be completed by 1 Thess. 4: 16. Probably Paul imagined all this in the mirror of the Apocalypse of Baruch 49-51, e.g., the fact that the just are transfigured by the radiance of the heavenly world without having to die (it was also the garment of Adam before the fall; cf. details in my book: Urgemeinde-Judenchristentum-Gnosis, 48). Thus for the just the normal thing was the transition to the other world without death.

peculiarity of his eschatology, and the difficulty it implies of affirming a resurrection mode of life for the Messianic kingdom, is not appreciated (*Mystik* 98 ff.).

These theses of Schweitzer have not remained without criticism.[1] But the mode of being of the elect in the Messianic kingdom, where the power of death remains unbroken, implies a serious problem which called for special efforts of thought on the part of the apostle. Moreover, Paul had to bring into coherence his interpretation of the saving death of Jesus as an act of redemption with faith in the redemption which was to mark the coming aeon. The post-messianic situation has its inherent difficulties. Paul considered the resurrection of Jesus as meaning for the believer something other than a transport into heaven, such as is, for instance, reported of Moses and Elijah, and frequently appears in apocalyptic writings. Such transports meant only a conservation for the ultimate age; here on the contrary: "Resurrection from the dead only occurs when the supernatural aeon had dawned. If Jesus has risen, this means for the one who dares to think that already supernatural world time has broken in. This is the point of view of Paul."[2] Thus far it does not fall outside the framework of Jewish eschatological possibilities, where the general resurrection of the dead follows the advent of the Messiah, which ushers in supernatural world time, and continues until the close of the Messianic transitional period.[3] It is probable that Paul assumed for the resurrection of the dead the same interval of time (forty years) as for the Messianic period. The forty-year interval for the Messianic time and the resurrection was later at any rate traditional.[4]

If now we wish to express the position in rabbinic categories, we should say: the stipulated time period ימים של משיח has already begun with the advent of the Messiah. But the Messiah has died and has risen again—an event which in Jewish eschatology is not provided for or foreseen. It implies that the end of the Messianic

---

[1] Cf. the modifications by J. Héring, "St. Paul a-t-il enseigné deux résurrections?" *RHPhR*, 1932, 300 ff. Héring claims: "The resurrection of the elect before the Messianic kingdom is unknown in Judaism." In point of fact it is not unknown but in the school of the Amoraic Rabbi Elijah it is sharply rejected (Sanh. 92a). Attempts at a doctrine of two resurrections are found from the beginning of the 3rd century even in rabbinism. But they are formulated differently because they have to solve another difficulty.

[2] Schweitzer, *Mystik*, 98; cf. also W. D. Davies, *op. cit.*, 288 ff.

[3] This has also been declared by Rabbi Bertinoro on M. Sanh. X. 1.

[4] Medieval Jewish calculations of the day of redemption often rest on old traditions. Details in I. Löwinger, *op. cit.*, 55 ff.

age, קֵץ הַיָּמִים, the imminent τέλος τῶν αἰώνων (1 Cor. 10: 11), and therewith the transition to the עוֹלָם הבא, is already casting its shadow. With the first resurrection from the dead the first signal has been given for the general resurrection on the day of the Lord. The special situation of the Christian in this post-messianic interval determines the special form of Pauline eschatology.[1] The problem of the death of believers made necessary, for the logically consistent thought of the apostle, the singular assumption of a dual resurrection for this special class of men who through their faith in the advent of the Messiah have become Christians and therefore in their lifetime anticipate by faith the life of the world to come. They enjoy the privilege called טַעַם מֵעֵין הָעוֹלָם הבא (foretaste of the future world). For the concrete life of this special class of Χριστιανοί this means that they are already delivered from the present evil age (Gal. 1: 4), that for them the αἰὼν μέλλων no longer lies in the future merely.[2] Paul did his utmost to proclaim this glad message as the gospel on his extensive missionary journeys. It was just the fact of the imminence of the kingdom which drove him to tireless missionary activity and the founding of churches. His journeys took him from Jerusalem to Macedonia, from Illyria to Italy and perhaps even to Spain, that the number of Christians might ever increase and that the peoples might no longer have the excuse of not having heard the word (Rom. 10: 18).

If we thoroughly consider this situation we must conclude without more ado that Paul's picture of Jesus was inevitably different from that of the immediate disciples of the Lord, that it was no longer the man Jesus but the Christ, the God-man, who could have significance for the faith of those living in the post-messianic age.

Without anticipating, we may say at present that the new life is still hidden, is "a reality which awaits consummation" (Rom. 8: 19 ff.; 2 Cor. 4: 16–18; Phil. 3: 11 ff.).[3] In other words, the consummation will come when Jesus, who after His earthly life was not simply transported into heaven but passed through death and resurrection, in order to impart to all Christians a share in this experience, will come again in glory as the Christ, the Consummator.

---

[1] Cf. now also J. N. Sevenster, "Einige Bemerkungen über den 'Zwischenzustand' bei Paulus", *NT Studies*, I, Cambridge, 1955, 291 ff.

[2] Hence Bultmann in his most recent study, *Geschichte und Eschatologie*, Tübingen, 1958, (E.T. *History and Eschatology*), can justly say: "In primitive Christianity history was swallowed up in eschatology. The primitive church understands itself not as a historical but as an eschatological phenomenon" (42).

[3] Thus Oepke in Kittel, *WB*, II, 335 (ἐγείρω).

His return will mean the breaking in of the βασιλεία τοῦ θεοῦ to which God has called Christians (1 Thess. 2: 12).

Hence the figure of the Messiah must undergo a transformation in Paul's thought. This figure, if we may say so, is mythically moulded in Paul's vision. The logia of Jesus recede behind the authority of the facts that Jesus had risen, though the kingdom has not yet come. We have already sufficiently emphasized the meaninglessness of the earthly life of Jesus for Paul's vision of the Christ. Paul does indeed mention the fact of the humanity of Christ, but the earthly life itself he does not value. For thinkers of the "History of Religion" school,[1] this was an important point of orientation. For Paul, communion with the risen Messiah was something *toto genere* different from companionship with the Jesus who walked on earth. Indirectly he counters those who appeal to the sayings of Jesus with the momentous principle: "Though we have known Christ after the flesh, yet now henceforth know we him no more" (2 Cor. 5: 16, A.V.). This, however, must imply:[2] we may not now know Him in this way, for the Jesus of the flesh belongs to the past; the Christ is no longer an earthly figure. The risen, "spiritual" Christ belongs no more to the realm of the fleshly sons of Adam. For the new aeon of the πνεῦμα that is now dawning, the earthly life of Jesus is no longer relevant. From the Risen Christ believers have received the Holy Spirit as a guarantee, ἀρραβών (2 Cor. 1: 22; 5: 5); as first fruits, ἀπαρχή (Rom. 8: 23) of the consummation which is to come. With the resurrection of the Kyrios, a new act of the drama of saving history has opened; the transformation of this aeon into the future aeon, of earthly existence into the unearthly has already begun. In Jesus the first man has risen from the dead, an event which constitutes a token and pledge that the ultimate age has in fact been inaugurated.

These considerations now make it plain that Paul substantially transformed the message of Jesus Himself. From the standpoint of his thought, which embraced the whole process of saving history, he necessarily judged the world situation differently from the way it appeared to the thought of Jesus. Jesus had certainly been aware that His death was an essential component of the חבלו של משיח,[3] because the kingdom could not come until that death had taken place. If Jesus suffers a death which God accepts as the equivalent

---

[1] Cf. Wrede, *op. cit.*, 53 ff., Brückner, *op. cit.*, 41 ff. and *ZNW*, 1906, 114 ff.; Leisegang, *op. cit.*, 27, etc.

[2] The understanding of this difficult sentence is notoriously debated; Windisch distinguishes six different interpretations.

[3] Corresponding Greek: ὠδῖνες (Messianic woes) Mt. 24: 8; Mk. 13: 8.

of the pre-messianic woes, then that death ushers in the kingdom. That Jesus expected His resurrection to follow from such a death—intended to be a λύτρον ἀντὶ πολλῶν (Mk. 10: 45)—is plainly declared in Mk. 14: 28, where on the way to Gethsemane he says to His disciples: "But after I am raised up, I will go before you to Galilee." For his preaching Paul already has behind him this prediction which, of course, in this form never materialized. In consequence of the total change in the world situation resulting from post-messianic time, quite other eschatological problems and quite a different view of the Messiah emerged for him. Paul reinterprets the traditional doctrine of deliverance; for the Messiah does not simply appear, but has already existed as man, and by His death and resurrection has inaugurated the resurrection of the dead. The result was a "self-contained Christ metaphysic".[1]

For these reasons it is quite off the point to try to discover Hellenistic or gnostic influences on his thought such as might explain his eschatology. On the contrary, we must recognize that the apostle has amplified boldly but consistently his insight into the contemporary situation as regards the process of saving history. While his thought on the subject mythicized the figure of Jesus, it did not dissolve the historicity of Jesus. The Jesus according to the flesh whom the synoptics attest has receded fully into the background (He is described as son of David only in Rom. 1: 3, and once incidentally in the pastoral letters—2 Tim. 2: 8) and His place has been taken by the Jesus of the Spirit, by the pre-existent Messiah-Son-of-Man, who according to Phil. 2: 6 ff. was in the form of God before He became fully man.[2] Christ was the man of heavenly origin (1 Cor. 15: 44–49). From 1 Cor. 10: 3 ff. we learn that in His pre-existent form of manifestation He was the rock from which water poured, and from which the Israelites drank in the desert—an image which Philo also employs in application to the logos (*Legum*

---

[1] A formulation of E. Lohmeyer, *op. cit.*, 145. It appeals to me more than Schweitzer's much over-emphasized and ambiguous "mysticism" or "objective Christ-mysticism".

[2] Dibelius says on Phil. 2: 5–11: "The thought expressed by the words ἑαυτὸν ἐκένωσεν springs ultimately from the ancient story of the God who lays aside his glory in order to descend into the deeps of the underworld, i.e. the myth of the descent into hell. This myth was perhaps elaborated on Iranian soil, whence it was transferred to Christ." E. Fuchs (*Christus und der Geist bei Paulus*, Leipzig, 1932, 93) speaks of a redeemer myth of Hellenistic gnosis clad in an ethically Jewish form. E. Lohmeyer assumes as a source a pre-Pauline psalm stemming from late Judaic apocalyptic, concerning the Son of Man, which does not exclude a foreign source. Finally E. Käsemann (*ZThK*, 1950, 360) interpreted this hymn as a creed and its *milieu* as baptism. J. Héring's exegesis of the words οὐχ ἁρπαγμὸν ἡγήσατο in 2: 6 (*Die biblischen Grundlagen des christlichen Humanismus*, Zürich, 1946, 32) as meaning that Christ did not strive after equality with God is not very convincing.

Allegor. 2: 21; 3: 96; *De Cherubinis* 127; *De Conf. Ling.* 34, etc.).[1] The equation of Christ with the Greek logos is very near to the thought of Paul. Even if we disregard Col. 1: 16, where Christ is pictured as the agent or mediator in the process of creation, the text 1 Cor. 8: 6: "One Lord, Jesus Christ, through whom are all things and through whom we exist" is very significant in this regard.[2] Since, however, Paul's eschatology remains closely related to history, he does not arrive like John at a theology of the pre-existent logos which in its essence is non-historical and leads to pure mysticism.

The intrinsic reasons for which the preaching of Paul differed from that of Jesus, and which caused it to become the doctrine of Christendom, have thus been indicated. The exalted Christ of Pauline thought became the Saviour of Christian theology and of the Christian church. This Pauline doctrine was born out of the need of a church which lay between the resurrection and the return of the Lord. To propose to reconstruct from it the portrait of the original Jesus would be an impossible undertaking. For Paul He has become the Kyrios, the Lord of the worlds, and must be viewed as such. But that it should be possible for each individual Christian during his lifetime to enter into a real relation with this κύριος Χριστός—a relation effecting salvation—was Paul's firm intuition from the start. And this is the basic eschatological implication which he gave to his doctrine of the sacraments. We must now discuss this theme.

3. THE ESCHATOLOGICAL MEANING OF THE SACRAMENTS OF BAPTISM AND THE LORD'S SUPPER

Paul found as a firmly established custom in the primitive church the initiatory rite of baptism and the repeated celebration of the Lord's Supper. But he imparted to these customs quite a new meaning

[1] The "rock in the desert" belongs (Aboth 5: 6) to the ten things which were created on the last day of the week of creation. Jewish sources do not make it refer to the Messiah; on this rabbinic folklore cf. Billerbeck, III, 406 ff. and Ginzberg, *Legends*, III, 52. W. L. Knox, *St. Paul and the Church of the Gentiles*, Cambridge, 1939, 123, thinks this speculation arose "in the midrashic exegesis of the synagogues of the dispersion" (esp. Alexandrian). But the sources do not suffice to justify this assertion. Staerk, *op. cit.*, II, 91 thinks of rabbinic theology. Probably there lies behind it a typological exegesis of Ex. 17: 6 or Num. 20: 7 ff. But the rock (Christ) accompanying the desert wanderings is a free invention of the apostle.

[2] This sentence might be understood as a further elaboration of the Jerusalem Son of Man speculations, suggesting that the pre-existent Son of Man was the mediator in the work of creation. The idea is still singular in Paul, but became a gate of entry for later gnostic theories, which sought a point of contact in the Bible.

in that he related them to his understanding of the new historical situation. Paul in fact made of these two rites eschatological sacraments; in any case they are not for him magically efficacious antidotes to death, etc., remedies against death (φάρμακα ἀθανασίας) as would be said in the theology of Isis, and as later Ignatius (*Ad Eph.* 20, 2) does in fact call them. If believers do die before the crucial event of the parousia, baptism, as Paul understands and teaches it, assures them of ultimate transfiguration. In the understanding of the apostle, baptism and the Lord's Supper anticipate the saving gifts of the future, making them effective in the present; they are the link between the two aeons, a vehicle for the blessedness of Christians considered as the ultimate family of mankind. They are intended to neutralize the delay in the parousia, since they convey to the church the presence of the exalted Christ, and foreshadow His return.[1] By means of the sacraments, which are not to be understood on magical lines but which make operative a real event, the individual Christian enters into communion with the crucified and risen Christ. Let us now consider this in more detail:

Baptism as a rite of initiation seems to have been practised by the primitive church in connexion with the rite of John's disciples and to have been a process of immersion. No specific ordinance of Jesus lay behind it, though Paul endeavours to derive its symbolism from types of Jewish saving history, as the invocation of the crossing of the Red Sea in 1 Cor. 10 plainly shows.[2] In Col. 2: 12 it is even suggested that baptism is meant to replace circumcision; it is plainly described as the "circumcision of Christ" (v. 11). And on account of Ex. 4: 24–6 circumcision always contains associations of sacramental sacrifice.[3]

The Jewish origin of Paul's interpretation of baptism (not of course verifiable in the letters) may have been Jer. 14: 8; מקוה ישראל מושיעו where the ambiguous מקוה (hope: baptismal water) permits the interpretation that Israel's Messiah is its baptismal spring. This rabbinically possible interpretation[4] Paul did not,

---

[1] Some important remarks on this are to be found in L. Baeck, *Das Evangelium als Urkunde der jüdischen Glaubensgeschichte*, Berlin, 1938, 38 ff.

[2] That Paul developed this typology independently of models is the opinion of P. Lundberg, *La typologie baptismale dans l'ancienne Église*, Uppsala, 1942, 135 ff. Origen was the first once more to view the crossing of the Red Sea as a symbol of Christian baptism. Cf. J. Daniélou, *Sacramentum futuri*, Paris, 1950, 152 ff.; K. Wessel in *RLAChr*, IV, 376 ff.

[3] Cf. G. Vermès, "Baptism and Jewish Exegesis", *NT Studies*, 1958, 308 ff.

[4] Rabbi Aqiba seems to attack it (Paul?) when he quotes M. Yoma, VIII, 10, Jer. 17: 13 (and not 14: 8) in order to suggest that God is the מקוה of Israel—and not the Messiah.

however, as we have said, explain to his missionary churches, pre-ferring ideas which had always been familiar to Greeks in order to make clear to them that baptism εἰς Χριστόν or εἰς τὸ ὄνομα Χριστοῦ was effective in establishing real communion with Christ. That he was promptly misunderstood by the Corinthians (cf. 1 Cor. 10: 1–13) in the sense of magic, is neither here nor there. His own intention is quite clear: baptism as a ceremony of sealing for Christ (σφραγίς is a well-known initiation term in the mystery cults) is meant to foreshadow in the present the salvation of the future, because it implies both the natural and the supernatural stages in the eschatological drama. Baptism gives to the believer, even though he should die before the event, a guarantee of his deliverance from imminent world judgment. Paul gave "an interpretation of the rite of immersion on the lines of the mystery religions" (Oepke) in order to have a point of contact in his preaching with the adepts' experience in the Hellenistic mystery cults, where the sacrament became an echo of the destiny of the divinity. Paul brings Christian baptism home to the Greeks by speaking of it on similar lines as a dying and being buried with Christ in order to rise again to a new life with Christ.

The saving meaning of the death of Jesus was brought by Paul into line with the mystery rite of sacramental participation in the death of a deity. This brings on to the horizon the Hellenistic con-ception of rebirth, which is also reflected in the pastorals (e.g., Tit. 3: 5) and in the Gospel of John (3: 5) Paul declares: "As many of you as were baptized into Christ have put on Christ" (Gal. 3: 27; cf. also Rom. 13: 14). The Galatians who read this must have felt that they were being reminded of the putting on of a divine garment well known to the religion of Isis—a garment which makes its wearer immortal or even deifies the adept. For the essence of this mystical rite of the garment was that an act of deification conceived as real was being celebrated.[1] The same applies, if we are to believe patristic testimonies, to consecration rites proper to the Hellenistic mysteries, especially in regard to the Eleusinian baptism *in regenerationem*, which is meant to lead to a divine rebirth of the baptized.

---

[1] Cf. C. Schneider, *Geistesgeschichte des antiken Christentums*, II, 201. Among the older literature the following are still important: W. Bousset, *Kyrios Christos*, 149 ff.; A. v. Stromberg, *Studien zur Theorie und Praxis der Taufe*, Berlin, 1913; J. Leipoldt, *Die urchrist-liche Taufe im Licht der Religionsgeschichte*, Leipzig, 1928, and R. Reitzenstein, *Die Vorge-schichte der christlichen Taufe*, Leipzig, 1929.

Of course the thought of Paul develops on quite different lines. For him, baptism is certainly not a natural process unrelated to historical events. The sacrament of baptism has become possible only because the day of salvation has dawned. Baptism is now meant to effect for believers a real participation in the body of Christ, and to bring them to share the death and resurrection of Christ as a saving event (Rom. 6: 3–5; Col. 2: 11–15; 3: 1 ff., etc.). The similarity of the mysteries, a fact to which Schweitzer closes his eyes, remains nevertheless fatal; Osiris baptism dissolves the adept in his god.[1] And the Isis consecration rites, about which we are well informed, thanks to Apuleius (*Metamorph.* XI, 21 ff.), have to be understood as something in the nature of voluntary death.[2] Certainly baptism takes place not in the name of Isis, Osiris, or Attis, but in the name of the Messianic Saviour. For this reason alone it is different. But with the characteristic piety of the mysteries, it too is none the less a sacrament, something which did not before exist in Judaism, and something which Paul could have derived neither from rabbinism nor from Hellenistic Judaism.

Rudolf Bultmann (*Theol. NT,* 134) has given a satisfactory definition of a sacrament in the sense which the ancient world attached to the term:

> An action which by natural means brings into operation supernatural forces, mostly by the use of spoken words which accompany the action, and which by their mere utterance according to the prescribed formula, release such forces. . . . The idea of a sacrament rests on the presupposition that supernatural forces may be linked to natural earthly objects and to spoken words as their vehicle and mediator.

In this sense the sacraments are for Paul the media of salvation; they make effectual the essence of Christian redemption; dying and rising again with Jesus Christ.

In primitive Christianity the sacrament was considered to express, in fact to canalize, the efficacious action of the Holy Spirit. For this reason it was more than a symbol, it was a miracle-working event. This is clear from the phenomenon of vicarious baptism about which we are told in 1 Cor. 15: 29. If it is possible, as

---

[1] Cf. J. Leipoldt, *Sterbende und auferstehende Götter,* Leipzig, 1923, 36; C. Schneider, *op. cit.,* I, 123.

[2] Cf. Reitzenstein, *ARW,* VII, 406 ff.; *Kyrios Christos,* 149 ff.; M. Dibelius, *Die Isisweihe des Apulejus und verwandte Initiationsriten,* Heidelberg SB, 1917, 4, now *Botschaft und Geschichte,* II, 30–79.

happened in Corinth, to be baptized as a substitute for a dead person, in order to convey to such a one the supernatural powers which the sacrament releases, then the sacrament comes very near to a magical action. This "heathen superstition" which Paul did not abolish or—as Wernle thinks—expressly permitted, is in fact attested for us in certain gnostic circles.[1] On the other hand, the sacrifices of the post-Pauline Taurobolia offer no analogy in this respect; that living people should undergo a consecration on behalf of the dead is not elsewhere known. In any case, what is here in question is a quite unique dilemma: it is desired that the dead of the last generation of humanity should still be able to participate in the newly established holy sacraments.

Schweitzer's judgment[2] on the situation is as follows: "The result from the standpoint of the history of religion is quite remarkable: the apostle thinks sacramentally, his teaching is even more in the style of the mysteries than the mystery religions themselves." But the character of the sacramental is here different from that which prevails in the atmosphere of the mysteries. "Here the *mise-en-scène* of the Greek sacramental faith is lacking. How unritualistic must the Eucharistic meal have appeared since it could degenerate into a wretched, undisciplined feasting. . . . Paul preaches the sacraments, but does not feel himself to be a mystagogue. On the contrary he maintains the cultic sobriety of the Jewish spirit" (*ibid.*). Lastly, Pauline baptism has quite another meaning; it implies a cleansing from sin and a consecration of the baptized. Purification from sin is expected to flow from sacramental immersion; this was the common Christian outlook. Paul too speaks of sins being washed away in baptism (ἀλλὰ ἀπελούσασθε, 1 Cor. 6: 11) and hence of a symbolical participation in the death of Jesus by baptism (Rom. 6: 5).

For Paul the positive effect of baptism consists in its conveying the gift of the Holy Spirit. This association of baptism with the reception of the Spirit is common to early Christianity (Acts 19: 1–6). Possession of the Spirit not only provides evidence of communion with the Lord, but mediates also, as we have seen, a participation in His dying and resurrection. Βάπτισμα εἰς τὸν θάνατον means that Christians are buried with Christ and are raised again from the dead (Rom. 6: 3–6). This belief simply cannot have arisen from Jewish baptism, which was supposed to cleanse from sin. Lietzmann also notes this

---

[1] Citations in Lietzmann's *Kommentar*.

[2] *Geschichte der paulinischen Forschung*, Tübingen, 1911, 166 ff. Schweitzer describes vicarious baptism as a phenomenon linked to the imminence of the end (169).

and concludes that Hellenistic beliefs are here reflected (*Komm. Röm.* 6: 3). Likewise Bultmann comments (*Theol. NT*, 138 ff.):

> This interpretation springs doubtless from the Hellenistic churches, which understood the initiatory sacrament in which they were instructed on the lines of the initiatory sacraments of the mystery religions, whose meaning was that the adept shared in the destiny of the cult-god who had suffered death and risen to life again, like Attis, Adonis and Osiris.

To understand the fate of Jesus as constitutive of a cult and to interpret the cult as a sacrament which brings the participant into communion with the cult deity, so that the fate of the latter is valid for him too—this is a Hellenistic idea proper to the mystery religions. The fate of the deity visualized and celebrated in the cult is intended to be conveyed to the adepts, and to effect the transformation of their being.[1]

Subsequently to Paul this mystic interpretation of baptism led to the idea of regeneration (παλιγγενεσία) and illumination (φωτισμός). If the original tradition only related purificatory baptism to the resurrection of Christ, later this was combined with the idea of a sprinkling by the blood of Christ—the Jewish expiatory sacrifice. As Bultmann also sees (142) this development was attended by the danger of forgetting or misunderstanding the eschatological mystical sacramentalism of Paul and of moulding Christianity exclusively on the basis of Hellenistic quasi-magical sacramentalism. In proportion as the eschatological church became a cultic church, primitive Christian eschatology became swallowed up in ecclesiastical sacramentalism. For this process of de-eschatologizing the Pauline view of baptism, the commentary of Origen on Rom. 6: 3 ff. (*Comm.* V, 8 *Rom.*) is very instructive.

The position is similar with regard to the other primitive Christian sacrament: the Supper of the Lord or κυριακὸν δεῖπνον (1 Cor. 11: 20 f.), which in Justin, Ignatius, and the Didache is called εὐχαριστία. Paul emphasizes that here we have a sacrament instituted by Christ Himself: "Do this in remembrance of me." At the same time Paul endeavours to explain the whole solemn character of the rite. In Corinth abuses crept in, because the Lord's Supper was treated as though it were a heathen sacrificial feast: some have to go hungry while others are drunk (1 Cor. 11: 21). Hence the rite must originally have been a real feast intended to satisfy the participants. Paul reminds the Corinthians of the fact that it is the death of Jesus and

---

[1] Cf. M. Dibelius, *Botschaft und Geschichte*, II, 142.

His return which on this occasion are commemorated. Here again Old Testament τύποι are visible: the feeding with manna (Ex. 16: 14 ff.) and the drinking from the water of Moses' rock (Ex. 17: 6 f.) merge with the bread and wine of the Eucharist (1 Cor. 10: 3–4). But it is not simply bread and wine which are partaken of; in a mysterious way it is also the body and blood of Christ. This conception confronts us here for the first time clearly formulated. Schweitzer comments, *op. cit.*, p. 156:

> His basic conception, namely, that the Eucharist effects or maintains communion with the glorified Christ, is quite clear. What is not so clear is how he brought this into relation with the historical words of Jesus about the bread and wine as His body and blood, and how he explained the connexion. Was his conception derived from these words, or did it spring from other sources, and merely enable him to explain the historical words?

Schweitzer answers his own question in the following way:

> The difficulty lies in the fact that the body and blood of the historical Jesus no longer exist for Paul, and that while the glorified Christ no doubt possesses a body, that body is not one through which blood flows and which can be materially eaten. To speak of the body and blood of Christ is an absurdity from the point of view of the apostle's doctrine. As regards his eucharistic doctrine he is unable to adjust the historical words with his own Christology and yet he must do so. The compromise he attempts remains obscure to us.

However we may determine the sense of the κυριακὸν δεῖπνον, the last supper of Jesus was doubtless a feast which He wished to be repeated: לזכר = εἰς τὴν ἀνάμνησιν (1 Cor. 11: 24 f.), until His parousia. The relation of the Eucharist to His death according to Luke's tradition (22: 19) goes back to His own institutional and explanatory words. But after the resurrection the Eucharist has become for the disciples an anticipation and a present realization of the Messianic feast of the blessed. This great banquet of the righteous (סעודה גדולה של צדיקים—thus Tanch. Wayyiqra 8) belongs to the eschatological events.[1] Admittedly it is not mentioned in Tannaitic sources, although it must be older than the latter, as allusions in apocryphal writings show (Enoch 60: 7–8; IV Ezra 6: 49–52; Syr. Baruch 29: 4; Test. Isaac 8: 11, 20, etc.). For Paul the last

---

[1] Cf. R. Mach, *Der Zaddik in Talmud und Midrasch*, Leiden, 1957, 207 ff.; cf. also Volz, *op. cit.*, 309.

supper of Jesus was indeed this eschatological feast. He has certainly reinterpreted the ideas handed down to him, but this does not alter the fact that they were simply a datum for him as for the primitive church, given along with Easter and Pentecost.

To the original memorial of Christ's death, Paul adds the thought of the sacramental communion of the celebrants with their κύριος. The guests at the Supper of the Lord become table companions of the exalted Christ. In this rite believers assimilate the bodily reality of Jesus; they eat His flesh and drink His blood although in a "spiritual" form (1 Cor. 10: 16–17; 11: 23–26). "The cup of blessing which we bless, is it not a participation in the blood of Christ? The bread which we break, is it not a participation in the body of Christ?" (10: 16). Hence in the bread and the wine Christ Himself is conceived to be present. The participants in the communion feast are bound together into a σῶμα, the σῶμα Χριστοῦ. Further, they become assured of sharing in the destiny of their Lord. The whole conception has ceased to be Jewish and reminds one rather of the Hellenistic mysteries. It may well be that Paul's opponents in Corinth affected a far more massive sacramentalism.[1]

C. Schneider is therefore right in suggesting (1: 70 f.) that with Paul the Eucharist becomes part of the "class of mystery cults". Doctrine, song, and prayer stem indeed from the synagogue tradition, but Paul's interpretation of the rite brings the young Christian church into line with Hellenistic mystery brotherhoods. The explanatory words in Eleusis come close to the words of institution of the κυριακὸν δεῖπνον. Paul's transformation of the memorial meal, which the first church had still celebrated as the Passover of Christ, consisted therefore in this: that the believer is to be incorporated by this means into the Body of Christ.[2] And the characteristic speculative work of the apostle[3] was simply to apply the Messianic conception of the banquet of the blessed at God's table to the post-messianic situation in such a way that, in this intervening period before the parousia, believers might be brought into fellowship with the exalted Christ through the "spiritual" essence of the transmuted body and blood (1 Cor. 10: 16). "The Mazzoh becomes the Host, the blood

---

[1] This is the opinion of exegetes such as H. v. Soden, E. Käsemann, G. Bornkamm, etc. (contrary to Lietzmann); cf. *NT Studies*, II, 1956, 206.

[2] Cf. E. Käsemann, "Anliegen und Eigenart der paulinischen Abendmahlslehre", *Ev. Theol.*, VII, 1947–48, 266: "Baptism and Eucharist incorporate the believer in the Body of Christ. For Paul this is the sheer miracle wrought by the sacraments."

[3] Bultmann (*Theol. NT*, 148 ff.) does not ascribe this to Paul himself, but makes Paul dependent on ideas stemming from the Hellenistic Christianity which he postulates.

symbol of the covenant becomes the wine, changed into the blood of the Redeemer."[1]

Hence the following may be established: Paul remoulded the Jewish tradition of the Messianic feast, which we also meet as a firm factor in the Qumran literature, in such a way that it became a cultic feast in the style of the mystery religions. He exalted it to the status of a sacrament so that the solemn feast effected communion with the Risen Christ. The fate of the Redeemer is renewed and repeated in the participants of the redemption; such is the sacramental meaning of the Christ cult. This Pauline amalgamation of ideas and traditions of heterogeneous origin, thus compounded for a short interim period, became one of several roots of the process of the formation of Christian dogma. This presents us with what is essentially a piece of Jewish-pagan syncretism. Along these lines the eschatological sacraments of Paul, which were meant to secure for believers, in the last generation of humanity, Messianic blessedness (1 Cor. 10: 11), became hellenized, and thus developed into the ecclesiastical sacraments.[2] In this way from something historically conditioned there developed what was timelessly valid. The fellowship meal, intended to give present realization to the future blessedness of Christ's return, became the regularly repeated celebration with its ritual administration of the eucharistic species, where the flesh and blood of Christ were in reality eaten and drunk. Now at the celebration of the Eucharist in the true Christian church, the bread and wine become a means of extending the incarnation of the Christ. Paul himself did not yet believe this, but, had it not been for the foundations which he laid, Ignatius of Antioch and the great church teachers who followed him would never have been able to teach their eucharistic doctrine.

4. THE JEWISH PROTEST AND THE PROBLEM OF THE DELAY IN THE PAROUSIA

In conclusion, we must now ask whether Jewish theology affords any parallels to the Pauline interpretation. First, there should be an analogy to the Christian existence of the elect in the Messianic kingdom; but the basis of this in the Jewish structure is different,

---

[1] Thus Eduard Strauss, "Paulus der Bekehrer", *Der Jude*, ed. M. Buber, 1923, 40.

[2] On the development, cf. A. Schweitzer, *Mystik*, 264–274; M. Werner, *Die Entstehung des christlichen Dogmas*, 447–451.

because the ideas and perspectives of saving history are different. To the elect gathered into the kingdom from the peoples of the world and exalted to a new status of life, there corresponds among the Jews of all times the election status of the "kol Yisrael", for it likewise implies a separation, in essential contradistinction, from the peoples of the world.[1] This too in the terminology of Schweitzer is an "objective mysticism of facts". But it stands at the beginning of history and in the promise to Abraham constitutes that history, whereas in Christianity it is an election for the end of history or more precisely for a participation by faith in an anticipated end. In both cases the event of election separates from the world, the special relationship with God brings about a new condition of being. In virtue of its election Israel is called apart from the peoples as a זרע אמת, whereas the Gentiles proceed from the זרע הטומאה (Tanch. נשא 13—Buber 16a). Hence what is predicated in Christian theology of Christ, namely that He is the seed of truth, is predicated here of Israel as a whole, which thus is raised to a special status of salvation and grace. And likewise in both cases the divine will which governs the divine kingdom is already performed by those who belong to that kingdom. But in the Jewish consciousness the Torah as the norm for the fulfilment of the divine will points forward to the future Kingdom of God, which in this case is not anticipated in history but only suggested. In so far as the Torah points beyond itself to its fulfilment it becomes a basis for the Messianic hope; the promise and the election were co-ordinated. On the other hand, for Paul and Christian theology a new aeon breaks forth in the figure of Jesus, for the end of history is anticipated in a saving event, so that the future redemption is already made a present reality for faith. This implies that the antithesis between the *olam hazzeh* and the *olam habba* is transformed into a tension between the Messianic aeon and the future consummation: the Messiah has already come and the Messiah will come again.

The depth of the contrast which characterizes the Jewish consciousness is thus weakened, for the second coming of the Lord is something different from the Jewish expectation of the Messiah. It engenders a different view of history, of which we shall speak in ch. 6. The Jews are unable to apprehend any difference of being in man or the cosmos since the coming of Jesus (for which reason they do not add "Christ"); they recognize no caesura in the course of

[1] Cf. my studies on Israel's election according to the Haggada and the medieval philosophy of religion in *Aus frühchristlicher Zeit*, Tübingen, 1950, 184–211.

history, their gaze is focused inflexibly on a future which is yet to be, and they expect everything from an event which has not yet happened. The Jews do not believe that the resurrection of a man of flesh and blood has already taken place. The *olam habba* is in their opinion as far off as ever. The question on which, as Tertullian already appreciated, the whole Jewish-Christian discussion depends, "an qui venturus Christus anuntiabatur iam venerit an venturus adhuc" (*Adv. Judaeos* cap. VI, Migne, *P.L.*, II, 612) has up to the present been answered by the Jews in the latter sense. They adhere to their rejection of the Messianic status of Jesus, because—as Origen reports (*De Princ.* IV, 8) of the Jews of his day—they do not consider that the Messianic prophecies which they interpret literally were fulfilled in Jesus.

Martin Buber [1] has expressed this Jewish feeling in 20th-century terms:

> We do not perceive any caesura in history. We recognize in it no middle term, but only an end, the end of God's ways, and we believe that God does not interrupt His course. For us redemption is indissolubly one with the consummation of creation, with the establishment of the divine unity, no longer frustrated, suffering no contradiction, realized in the multiplicity of the world, one with the fulfilled sovereignty of God. We are unable to understand the idea of an anticipation of this consummation experienced by one section of humanity, whose souls are already redeemed.

The real objection of the Jews, which is already suggested by the sentences of Martin Buber and which we wish to see in its special application to Pauline eschatology, is, in the last resort, quite naïve in character. This objection is grounded in the fact that Paul died in the year 63 without seeing the fulfilment of his expectation. The cry of John the Baptist, like that of Jesus Himself, had been: "The kingdom of God is at hand" (Mt. 3: 2; 4: 17; Mk. 1: 15). And Paul had declared: ὁ καιρὸς συνεσταλμένος ἐστίν (1 Cor. 7: 29). The primitive church expected the end to come in their own lifetime when they prayed: μαρὰν ἀθά (1 Cor. 16: 22). The disciples of Jesus certainly expected that the end of historic time would coincide with His death. That this failed to materialize meant the fundamental disappointment of Jesus' Messianic movement, but it did not mean that it collapsed in despair, resignation, or absurdity. It is a quite

---

[1] *Die Stunde und die Erkenntnis*, Berlin, 1936, 154. Similar view in Shalom ben Horin, *Die Antwort des Jona*, Hamburg, 1956, 99: "The Jew recognizes in the wickedness of this world no enclaves of redemption."

unique phenomenon in the history of religion that from the disappointment of this expectation of the end there arose a new beginning and the initiation of a new historical process. The disillusionment was compensated and the focus of attention was transferred to the plane of dogma. That this was at all possible is due to the work of Paul, and that constitutes to a large extent the significance of Pauline theology. This theology, which arose from the fervent expectation of a still awaited event, had to come to grips with the *factum brutum* of the delay in the parousia and developed *ad hoc* in order to master the situation and to transfer the event to a more distant future. Paul became an author in order to explain this delay in the parousia, in order to remove the difficulties of believers, and to obviate the assaults of unbelievers. It was in this way that he became the first theologian of Christendom.

Since, however, subsequent generations of Christians were still faced by the same unsolved problems, since in spite of their fervent hopes they still walked by faith and not by sight, and the interim period still lasted, there took place that well-known development of the early Christian consciousness which led to the formation of the catholic church. About this movement a pupil of Martin Werner, Fritz Buri,[1] has commented as follows:

> The actual disappointment brought about by the non-appearance of the end at the time of the death of Jesus or during the first generation of Christians, was principally overcome by the maintenance of the eschatological tension through ecstatic experiences. Conversely these ecstatic experiences, among which Easter and Pentecost belong, are only understandable in the context of the eschatological situation of tension, i.e. they have real significance only for those living in the New Testament eschatological atmosphere. . . . This had attained such a degree of intensity that at first it could make up for the lack of objective fulfilment. This happened not by the renunciation of hopes of an imminent end, but . . . by the supposition that the transformation of things had already come into effect through the death of Jesus. . . . Paul shares with Jesus the eschatological evaluation of His death and resurrection; but because the latter events have happened, he comes to make affirmations which were far from the mind of Jesus. The change of aeon effected by the death of Jesus, but not yet fully apparent, created for the first church a unique historical situation. The old and the new aeons became intermingled. Like a wedge the new aeon thrusts into the old, and though still invisible it constantly tends to supplant the old.

[1] *Die Bedeutung der neutestamentlichen Eschatologie für die neuere protestantische Theologie*, Zürich, 1935, 27 ff.

Much discussion has taken place about the question of the delay in the parousia so much emphasized by the school of "consistent eschatology".[1] Martin Werner has very impressively attributed to it the rise of Christian dogma; and has found some followers among the Swiss (Buri, Neuenschwander, H. Babel, etc.); but other Swiss theologians, such as Michaelis, Cullmann, Flückiger, have sharply contradicted the thesis. The opponents of "consistent eschatology" have urged that it tends to overlook all those New Testament texts which imply the assurance of present salvation. Stauffer adds further that Werner and his school have dramatized far too much the non-fulfilment of eschatological hopes, for the failure of eschatological expectations was normal at the time.

It seems to me in fact impossible to disregard the emphasis in the preaching of Jesus to the effect that the coming rule of God is even now breaking forth, and that therefore eschatological events are effectively present (C. H. Dodd, realized eschatology).[2] Hence it is supposed that the whole system of apocalyptic calculations did not interest Jesus (Lk. 17: 20 ff.). Yet this does not apply to Paul, because for him the critical change of aeon is already a fact of the past. Hence it is misguided to attempt to compare the eschatology of Jesus with that of Paul. For Paul, expectation of the end and disappointment at its failure to come are the real facts: the situation confronting him is the delay in the parousia which has continued up to the present. Paul felt all the pain and harshness of this disappointment, as did the Qumran sect (cf. *DSH*, 7: 5 ff.), but he deduced from it an appeal to intensify the certitude of faith that the last judgment was near and would certainly come, as Hab. 2: 3 suggests.

Oscar Cullmann[3] has attempted to dispose of Martin Werner by suggesting that the parousia and its delay was not central, that the central fact was the resurrection of Christ, the factuality of the saving event itself. However eloquent Cullmann may be, he cannot dispel the scandal that world history after the resurrection of Christ has proceeded just as before. The failure of the parousia, which event

---

[1] Cf. E. Graesser, *Das Problem der Parusieverzögerung in den synoptischen Evangelien und in der Apostelgeschichte*, Berlin, 1957; O. Cullmann, "Parusieverzögerung und Urchristentum, der gegenwärtige Stand der Diskussion", *ThLZ*, 1958, 1 ff.

[2] Cf. R. Bultmann, *Geschichte und Eschatologie*, Tübingen, 1958, 36 ff.; H. Windisch, *Paulus und Christus*, 440 ff.; W. Kümmel, *ThR*, 1948, 108 ff., and *Verheissung und Erfüllung*, Zürich, 1956, 20 ff. But Kümmel too is convinced that Jesus "had reckoned with a longer or shorter time between His death and parousia".

[3] *Christus und die Zeit*, Zürich, 1948, 73 ff. (E.T. *Christ and Time*.) In his later works Cullmann often insisted on his objection.

might have prevented this, should have been explained. From the standpoint of profane history nothing else is apparent but that a new witness to salvation has entered history, around which the Christian church has evolved. But the fact that history proceeded on its way set in motion the whole theological thinking apparatus of the first Christian generations. And here Paul, the interpreter of the aeons, was the decisive mind.

There can be no question that the objective course of world history has belied New Testament eschatology. Buri says even:

> This is recognized to-day by any one who is able to bring a historical understanding to New Testament eschatology. People speak of the change in the prophecy of Jesus resulting from the fact that "a long historical process followed on His ascension" (Schlatter) of the time limits (Althaus) of that expectation, of the cosmic situation of early Christianity which is unrepeatable for us (53).

In the 1st century A.D. the non-appearance of the parousia was first seen as a problem by the ἐμπαῖκται, to whom the second letter of Peter refers (3: 3 f.), and who made it a subject of mockery that the fathers had died and everything had gone on as before. The failure of the parousia led to the expectation of judgment after death. It led, above all, to the genesis of the catholic church, which, with the consoling thought that before God a thousand years are as a day (2 Pet. 3: 8), was able to incorporate the eschatological expectation into its religious system. It was Paul who made this possible, because in his doctrine were laid the bases for interpreting the prolonged interval between the Epiphany and the Parousia both as a unique series and as one which had lasting implications. Later (cf. final chapter) the understanding of Paul's true doctrine became blurred for several centuries. The catholic church in the interests of apostolic succession had to orientate itself on Petrine rather than on Pauline bases.[1] And the church of the Reformation tore from its eschatological context Paul's doctrine of justification—"only a fragment in the whole structure of Pauline ideas, a polemical point of view unconnected with ethics"[2] and nursed it as if it had been the vital heart of Paul's preaching.

[1] Cf. Erik Peterson, *Kirche*, Munich, 1929, 11: "Paul did not belong to the twelve, and in this fact is implied the limits not of his apostolic reality but of his apostolic legitimacy. This is the reason why Paul presents a different appearance in the church from Peter." Similarly, J. Wagenmann, *Die Stellung des Paulus neben den Zwölf in den ersten zwei Jahrhunderten*, Giessen, 1928, 298: "Himself a man of the second generation, Paul did not offer an immediate link with Jesus."

[2] Buri, *op. cit.*, 155.

To-day no Christian, as Werner[1] said in an early work, "can quite simply come to grips with real Paulinism". Every scholar of the 20th century who is anxious to make a considered judgment must pay heed to the eschatological confinement of Paul's system of thought. He will thus understand why the catholic church had to build its structure not on Paul, but in virtue of the coming of the Holy Spirit on Peter as the head of the twelve (Mt. 16: 18) and he will be inclined to assent to Erik Peterson's judgment:

> The church is by its very existence a proof contrary to the concrete eschatology of the Jews. The church is of course a church of the Gentiles . . . and so the church exists only under the presupposition that the advent of Christ is not immediately imminent, in other words that concrete eschatology has been eliminated, and replaced by the doctrine of the last things (5).

This de-eschatologizing of the Christian message also made the division of the last times into two periods quite pointless. Since the days of the apostolic age were not the last days, the church once more identified the Messianic time with the future world, and it was awaited as the time of Christ's return.

As for the Jewish counter-position to Paulinism, the *factum brutum* of the delay in the parousia (cf. Luke's words χρονίζει ὁ κύριός μου ἔρχεσθαι, 12: 45) gives rise to the objection which is both the most naïve and the most Jewish. The world has gone on as before and the end of history is no nearer. No change has taken place in the substance of the world. No dead man is resurrected, no ordinance of the end of time has become visible in world time, and no prophetic vision has really been fulfilled. Rather instead of peace there is war, instead of righteousness there is injustice, instead of redemption, a brute struggle for power, etc. And what element of newness has Christianity really brought into being? A theology initiated by Paul, instead of a new condition of the world, a new doctrine about a reality still unfulfilled—and of course the Hellenistic cult of sacraments derived from other sources, unknown to Judaism, and conceived as an anticipation and materialization of this still awaited reality.

And yet, in spite of everything, this little is much; for in faith the peoples of the world have gained direct access to the *olam habba*—something which Judaism could not give them or at least has not given them. The factual existence of the church is the new and

---

[1] *Der Einfluss der paulinischen Theologie im Markusevangelium*, Giessen, 1923, 167.

positive factor. But the condition of the Jews has remained the same —*ante* and *post Christum natum*—as has also the material condition of the world. The year 70 implies a far deeper incision into Jewish history than the year 30 or 33.[1] But for the world outside Israel the latter date signifies something. Ishmael has become what Isaac is; since Christ, the Gentile peoples have found their election, the way out of heathendom to God the Father through Christ the Son.

This yields quite a new picture of the process of saving history, for which Judaism has remained indebted to the world. Since Christ, the Gentiles too have gained access to the God of the fathers who revealed Himself on Sinai—and that without any violation of Jacob's rights as firstborn—for they have been called to tread their own Christian path. We shall have to speak in more detail in ch. 6 of this new picture of saving history *post Christum natum* as of the conjunction of two historic covenants.

[1] Cf. my study "Das Jahr 70 in der jüdischen Religionsgeschichte" in the volume *Aus frühchristlicher Zeit*, Tübingen, 1950, 144–183.

4

THE SOTERIOLOGY OF THE APOSTLE PAUL

Introduction : the state of the problem

IN the preceding chapter we have tried to show how the apostle Paul, using his eschatological sources, fashioned Christian eschatology as a doctrine concerning the state of the world in the interim Messianic period between the Epiphany and the Parousia.

In this chapter we propose to show how the soteriology of the apostle, arising from legitimately Jewish material, could be moulded as the Christian doctrine that through the death and resurrection of the Son of God man's atonement and reconciliation to God has been effected. As a basis for our discussion we will recapitulate the doctrine reflected in Paul's letters and thought out on the basis of the situation of the believing Christian placed between the resurrection and the second coming of Christ.

The personal experience of the apostle and the effective content of his preaching may be summarized as follows: Jesus of Nazareth, springing from the Davidic line (ἐκ σπέρματος Δαυεὶδ κατὰ σάρκα; Rom. 1: 3), spent His short life in Palestine, died on the cross for our sins, rose from the dead, and appeared to His disciples, to a large crowd (500 brethren), then to James, then to all the apostles, and finally to himself (1 Cor. 15: 3–8). He has ascended into heaven, where He sits on the right hand of God, and whence He will shortly come again on the clouds of heaven as the Son of Man. This man Jesus was born, when the time was fully come, of a woman (Gal. 4: 4), but was established as Son of God with power through His resurrection from the dead (Rom. 1: 4) and was the Son of God ἐν ὁμοιώματι σαρκός (Rom. 8: 3). He relinquished His divine glory, embraced the life of earthly poverty (2 Cor. 8: 9), assumed the form of a servant and humbled Himself even to the death of the cross. "Hence God exalted him and gave him a name above every name." God raised the crucified and buried One to new life, exalted Him to the highest throne at His own right hand, gave Him the name above every name, κύριος (which is the most frequent designation of Jesus with Paul) before which all that is in heaven, on earth, and under the earth bows the knee (see Phil. 2: 9–11). Further: "For our sake he made him to be sin who knew no sin, so that in him we might become the righteousness of God" (2 Cor. 5: 21). The atoning death of Jesus the Messiah, the Χριστός who was sacrificed for our sins (Rom. 4: 25), became our expiation, and ransomed humanity from sin. Θεὸς ἦν ἐν Χριστῷ κόσμον καταλλάσσων ἑαυτῷ (2 Cor. 5: 19). The dying of the Son of God effects the redemption of the cosmos, and of humanity as a whole, for in Christ's death on the cross the world has been crucified (Gal. 6: 14) and has begun to pass away.

This is in brief the quintessence of Pauline soteriology. It is not the teaching of Jesus Himself. A New Testament scholar has pregnantly formulated the distinction in the following way: "Jesus foresaw His passion, but did not explain it. Paul however had to explain the cross." [1] Paul's explanation has become the fundamental doctrine of the Christian church.

When a Jew hears for the first time the Pauline doctrine of the atoning death of the Messiah on the cross, thus summarized, it seems to him something as remote from and contradictory to the Jewish world of ideas as could possibly be conceived, as having no analogies nor sources in Jewish writings. And the fact that an atonement of humanity through the death of the incarnate Son of God appears impossible from a Jewish point of view springs from this, namely, that the idea of the Son of God in its Pauline form takes us outside Judaism. However, I shall have to show that the apostle's trains of thought are not without preparation in Judaism, or at least that true Jewish elements can be analysed whose combination alone leads outside Judaism and reminds us of heathen mythological modes of thought. In fact, at the basis of this soteriological dogma there lie the following Jewish ideas, which we shall proceed to investigate:

1. The meaning of suffering and of a vicarious atoning sacrifice.

2. The picture of the suffering servant of God in Isaiah 53 and the idea of a dying Messiah arising therefrom.

3. The *Aqedath Isaac* and its problems as the ultimate pattern of thought. The significance of this for Paul has least of all been recognized.

[1] Kümmel, *ThR*, 1954, 156, in "Wiedergabe eines Gedankenganges von Goguel".

I. THE ATONING SUFFERINGS OF THE RIGHTEOUS

The decisive question for us is: how far has Paul's idea that Jesus made a vicarious atoning sacrifice for humanity a foreshadowing in the theory of sacrifice and suffering proper to the Old Testament and the rabbis?

First of all it must be said that suffering (יסורים literally, chastisements) was highly valued in Judaism of every period. This is already shown by the stereotyped formula with which an assessment of suffering in many places of scripture is commonly introduced: חביבם יסורים. In particular, after the year 70 a whole theology of suffering arose, chiefly connected with Rabbi Aqiba. Here the substitutionary and atoning character of suffering has been built up into a system.[1] Pious individuals suffer bodily pains as penance, and these are regarded as expiatory for their own and also for others' sins.[2] The pains and chastisements of the Israelites are understood as an expression of the love of God, who grants them the power of atoning for their wrong doing.[3] According to a late Tannaite, there even falls a ray of divine glory on him who is overwhelmed by suffering.[4] In the substitutionary theory of the later Tannaites, elaborated after 70, suffering is pre-eminently a means of atonement. Thus said Rabbi Nehemiah, a pupil of Aqiba: חביבים יסורים for chastisements expiate even more than sacrifices. Sacrifices expiate with money values, but chastisements with the body, for in Job we read: skin for skin (2: 4; Sifre Deut. 6: 5; Mekh. Ex. 20: 23 and parallels).[5]

---

[1] A compendium of Tannaitic statements about the value of suffering is found in Mekh. Ex. 20: 23 and in Sifre Deut. 6: 5; a systematic treatment of the theme in W. Wichmann, *Die Leidenstheologie*, Stuttgart, 1930; E. Sjöberg, *Gott und die Sünder*, Stuttgart, 1938, 169 ff.; E. Lohse, *Märtyrer und Gottesknecht*, Göttingen, 1955, 29 ff.

[2] מותת הצדיקים מכפרת (Makkoth IIb, Sukkoth 52a, Moed Qatan 28a) is a frequent Talmudic maxim, as many stories show. Cf. that of Rabbi Nahum from Gumza (A.D. 90) in Taan. 21a or of the widow of Rabbi Ishmael ben Simon according to Eccl. R. 11: 2 and parallels. The pious secure Israel by their lives and effect expiation (Tanch. 132b. par.). Cf. also Marmorstein, "Zur Erklärung von Is. 53", *ZAW*, 1926, 264 ff.

[3] Mishle Rabba 13, 24: Because God loves the Israelites, he chastises them in this aeon by empires so that their sins may be expiated (Source Eliezer ben Hyrcanus? Similarly, R. Nehemiah, Tann. of the 3rd generation, in Sifre Deut. 6: 5). Such pains are called (e.g., Berakh. 5a) יסורים של אהבה and are intended to atone for sins: whom God loves. He chastises by suffering. Similar views are reflected in the apocalypses (Bar. 78: 3; IV Ezra 8: 47, etc.).

[4] Rabbi Jose ben Yehuda (Tann. of the 5th generation *circa* 180) in Sifre Deut. 6: 5 (32).

[5] The prayer of Rabbi Shesheth in Berakhoth 17a points in the same direction. Rabbi Simon ben Jochai declares that all the good which Israel enjoys has been granted only in consequence of the meritoriousness of sufferings (Mekh. Ex. 20: 23 etc.).

The conception of vicarious sufferings is very ancient and has its roots in the Biblical institution of sacrifice, as is shown by the old pious expression of veneration typical of the Mishna, אני כפרה (thus Rabbi Ishmael in M. Negaim II, 1). This expression was apparently taken up by Paul himself (Rom. 9: 3). Whoever makes this exclamation declares that he is ready to "take upon himself in vicarious fashion the sufferings which may strike others because of their sins, to suffer them in their stead and in their favour" (Billerbeck). Thus it is reported of Resh Laqish (*circa* 250) that he wishes to be an expiation for Rabbi Hiyya (*circa* 200) and his sons, on account of their merits in regard to the Torah (Sukka 20a). Or in Berakhoth 62b it is asked why God said to the destroying angel (2 Sam. 24: 16): "It is enough." Rabbi Eliezer explains it thus—by causing God to say to the angel: "Take from among them some great one, to whom their accumulated guilt may be transferred" (i.e., according to Rashi: "who is able by his death to expiate their many sins"). "In that hour died Rabbi Abishai ben Zeruiah, who outweighed more than half the Sanhedrin."

The idea that God chooses a righteous man in expiation of sins, who is regarded as a pawn for the sins of the people, seems to have been very widespread (Gen. R. 44 on 15: 1; Ex. R. 35: 4; Tanch. Wayyakhel, etc.). Thus David, Ezekiel, Job, Jonah were thought of as suffering vicariously for the sins of the whole people.[1] The idea lies also behind a series of rabbinical reports of martyrdoms, to which vicarious atoning power was ascribed. But for the most part they are post-Pauline and cautiously worded, because it was felt to be undesirable to lend support to the Christian interpretation.[2] Again with the same motive and in order to eliminate the reference of Isaiah 53 to Christ, atoning power was imputed to the death of Moses.[3]

The many allusions to this idea in the apocalyptic writings which were contemporary with or earlier than Paul have more weight for our purpose. Of especial interest in this connexion are the Assumption of Moses, the Psalms of Solomon, the Test. XII Patr. (Benjamin 3: 8—an interpolation?), and Maccabees. "God is gracious to him who takes punishment upon himself", it is said in Ps. Sol. 10: 2.

---

[1] Examples given in Billerbeck, II, 280 ff. (not all of them suitable).

[2] Evidence in H. W. Surkau, *Martyrien in jüdischer und frühchristlicher Zeit*, Göttingen, 1938; H. A. Fischel, "Prophet and Martyr", *JQR*, 1947, 265 ff., 363 ff.; E. Bammel, "Zum jüdischen Märtyrerkult", *ThLZ*, 1953, 119 ff.; E. Lohse, *Märtyrer und Gottesknecht*, Göttingen, 1955, 72 ff.

[3] Examples in Schoeps, *TheolJchr*, 95.

The thought of substitution in death is already expressed in II Macc. (7: 37–38), but the author of IV Macc., who is contemporary with Paul, says plainly that the death of the seven Maccabean boys was an expiatory sacrifice. "By the blood of those pious youths and their expiatory death, the divine providence rescued Israel which before had been so heavily oppressed" (17: 22). The petition of the priest Eliezer, 6: 29: "May my blood serve for them as a means of purification" (καθάρσιον), makes plain the back reference of the martyrs' death to the sacrifice of purification.

The understanding of suffering as expiatory in post-Biblical and early Talmudic times doubtless goes back to the Biblical idea of sacrifice as expiatory and substitutionary (אשם). This was enjoined by the covenant-God Himself as a means of maintaining His covenant (Lev. 5: 14 ff.; 7: 1; 19: 20–22). While the guilt offering implies a *satisfactio*, the expiatory sacrifice is meant to effect an *expiatio* for the sinner. Of course the Old Testament offers us no theory of expiation elaborated in detail, but so much is clear, that in contrast to all the magical exorcism rites practised in Babylonia, cultic expiation in Israel is included in the freely disposing grace of the covenant God. In the priestly law He has bestowed on Israel the expiatory sacrifice which is intended to remove all disturbances in the harmonious covenantal relation between God and Israel—apart from the sin ביד רמה—and which expressly establishes the substitutionary power of the soul of the animal for the human soul as a means procuring the forgiveness of sin: "For the life of the flesh is in the blood; and I have given it to you upon the altar to make atonement for your souls; for it is the blood that makes atonement by reason of the life" (Lev. 17: 11).

This means therefore that the soul of the animal is poured out in the blood on the altar, to make an expiation (כפר—literally covering) for him who sacrifices and who without this covering would be liable to the punishment of the holy God. In the Jewish faith blood is a means of expiation because it is the bearer of the soul. אין כפרה אלא בדם = There is expiation only through the blood (Yoma 5a and par.).[1] Hence the rite of the Day of Atonement ordained in the Torah culminates in the expiatory sacrifice by the high priest (חטאת—Yoma 55a) and in the sprinkling of the sacrificial blood on

---

[1] This understanding is shown plainly in Hebr. 9: 22 (cf. *Comm.* O. Michel), but above all in the later Jewish exegetes. Cf. Rashi on Lev. 17: 11: "The soul of every creature is in the blood, therefore I gave it as an atonement for the souls of men, that one soul should come and atone for others." I single out from the literature on the subject: J. Abrahams, *Studies in Pharisaism and the Gospels*, II, Cambridge, 1924, 184 ff.

the *kapporeth* and before the ark of the covenant, because this maximal efficacy of expiation through the substitutionary soul of the animal indwelling the blood brings man into closest contact with God.[1]

It may seem doubtful whether in the expiatory ceremonial in the Torah a *poena vicaria* is expressed. However, after the *Gezerah* of the year 70 has made impossible the further use of the sanctuary at Jerusalem which since Josiah's reform of the cultus had been the sole legitimate place of sacrifice, the expiatory sacrifice was understood in the way which is attested in the substitutionary doctrines of the following period.[2] In later centuries special liturgical surrogate usages were introduced.[3] But at a comparatively early period the idea must have arisen that the death of the righteous effects atonement in the same way as the Day of Atonement expiates sins (cf. the report about the death of Rabbi Aqiba in Midr. Prov. 9: 2; similarly in Midr. on Song of Sol. 7: 9). Rabbi Ammi (*circa* 300) developed even a special exegetical norm (Moed Qatan 28a and par.) for this connexion from the link between Num. 19 (expiatory ashes of the red heifer) and Num. 20 (the death of Miriam). In any case it was accepted as a firm rule that the death of any other being—even the death of an animal dying for me—could procure a covering (atonement) for my sins.

Now the synoptic λύτρον corresponds exactly to the Old Testament כפר. We may suppose that the atoning sacrifice of the second temple still in operation at the time of Paul—it was, of course, still

---

[1] Better than in more recent accounts, this is worked out by G. F. Oehler, *Theologie des Alten Testaments*, Stuttgart, 1882, 493.

[2] As regards the Amoraic substitution theory, that reading and study of the sacrificial laws has equal value, that penitence, kindness, and especially prayer have the same atoning effect, cf. the rich source material and interpretations I have assembled in *AfZ*, 173 ff. See also A. Metzinger *OSB*, "Die Substitutionstheorie und das atl. Opfer", *Biblica*, Rome, 1940, Vols. 2–4.

[3] The report in M. Yoma, VI, 6 may be regarded as an instance of such surrogate usage. This describes how in accordance with Lev. 16: 21 ff. the goat sent out into the desert, bearing the sins of the Israelites into a remote land, hurled itself from a rock and destroyed itself. This self-destruction, which is not indicated in the Torah, shows what was understood to be the essential element in the atoning sacrifice: a living being sacrifices its life for the sins of men. Another custom replacing that of the goat from pre-Gaonic times, much prized by the later cabbalists and practised in orthodox circles up to the present, was that of the "cock-kappara", which was performed on the day of preparation for Yom Kippur. The man takes a cock or his wife a hen (only a white one—cf. Is. 1: 18), whirls himself around it three times before slaughtering it, and utters the formula together with the recitation of verses from the Bible (Ps. 107: 10, 14, 17–20; Job 33: 23–24): "May this cock be a substitute for me and an atonement: it is to die but I shall go with all Israel to a good life. Amen."

131

celebrated in spite of the missing ark of the covenant and the *kap-poreth*—stood at the very heart of Pauline thought as the soteriological problem: how can another procure atonement for my sins? When Paul answers this question with 2 Cor. 5: 21: God has made Christ to be sin and in Him has reconciled the world unto Himself (v. 19) the expression cannot be understood otherwise than as an allusion to the laying of the hand on the animal (סמיכה) prescribed in Ex. 29: 10 (סמך) as a result of which the sacrificed animal is laden with the sins of the sacrificer and is to become a "body of sin" through the transference of guilt. This becomes still clearer when Paul in Rom. 3: 25[1] presents Jesus in His outpoured blood as the ἱλαστήριον for faith. Contrary to many devious interpretations, this can only have the meaning—to be inferred from the obvious cultic significance and reference to Lev. 16: 12–15—that Jesus is typified by the Old Testament institution of expiatory sacrifice and by His sacrifice has been appointed by God to take the place of the lost כפרת. The mercy seat (ἱλαστήριον) stood hidden behind the veil in the holy of holies (Ex. 26: 33; Lev. 16: 2). Thus Paul means: "Through Christ the way to the Most Holy has been unveiled."[2] After His blood has been shed, the empty place where formerly the divine presence inhered, as a token of the divine will to righteousness (i.e., not to leave Israel without the means of expiation), has once more been filled.

Since, however, this time it was not expiation through the blood of a conscienceless animal but through that of a man, a sinless man was required to make the sacrifice valid, in accordance with a doctrine—obviously referring to the high priestly confession of sin—of the school of Rabbi Ishmael: יבא זכאי ויכפר על החייב (the innocent effects atonement for the guilty—Yoma 43b). Paul was accepting this tradition, which must have been older than the school of Rabbi Ishmael, when he teaches that the blood of Jesus the Christ has reconciled man with God (Rom. 5: 8–9). After the example of the LXX[3] Paul transferred the central cultic expiatory idea to the ethical world. The doctrine of justification by faith which he expounds here receives its support in accessory fashion (πόλλῳ μᾶλλον)

---

[1] Both Ἐν τῷ αὐτοῦ αἵματι and διὰ πίστεως are related to ἱλαστήριον. Cf. Büchsel, Kittel, *WB*, III, 322. Recently Lohse, *op. cit.*, 151 ff., has called in question the whole understanding of this text.

[2] Thus A. Nygren, *Christus der Gnadenstuhl*, In memoriam Ernst Lohmeyer, Stuttgart, 1951, 92. Cf. on the whole sequence of thought linked with Rom. 3:24 ff.; H. Wenschkewitz, "Die Spiritualisierung der Kultusbegriffe Tempel, Priester und Opfer im NT", *Angelos*, IV, Leipzig, 1932, 182 ff.

[3] Cf. C. H. Dodd, *The Bible and the Greeks*, London, 1935, 91 ff.

from the soteriology of a Messianic ritual sacrifice. The new covenant is sealed with blood (1 Cor. 11: 23 ff.) just as much as the old (cf. Rashi on Ps. 50: 5).

The bloodstained sacrifice of Christ and its sealing with death is described by Paul, who uses the verbal substantive ἀπολύτρωσις, as a ransom (Rom. 3: 24–25). The parallel passages (Col. 1: 13 ff., Eph. 1: 7) likewise regard the blood of Christ as a ransom price or the equivalent; also those texts where the verb (ἐξ)ἀγοράζειν appears. Although the terms and images stem from the ancient custom of freeing slaves, they are linked by Paul to ideas of the Old Testament sacrificial cultus, and have become descriptive of eschatological conditions brought about by the death of Christ.[1] Similar implications are contained in the legal bond (χειρόγραφον) nailed to the cross and thus made invalid (Col. 2: 14). This image, taken from the language of Roman civil law, can be shown to have penetrated the Jewish liturgy at the time of Paul (Prayer Abinu malkenu Taanith 25d).

In general, Paul shows himself to be familiar with juristic terminology. He knows and speaks the language of Jewish law and business of his time.[2] This is also seen in the fact that he is obviously unable to conceive how God can forgive a sin, until it has been expiated by objective satisfaction. Thus in Gal. 4: 2 Paul actually describes the death of Christ by using a technical term relating to taxes, προθεσμία, indicating the period when old demands cease to be valid.

Paul's whole understanding of expiatory sacrifice, however, is dominated, over and above what has been urged, by the fact that at that time the current belief and expectation was that the Messiah would by his passion assume the office of vicarious expiation. In the Gospel of John we read: "Behold the Lamb of God who takes away the sin of the world!" (1: 29.) This implies a typological comparison of the sacrificial death of Christ with the slaughter of the paschal lamb—a comparison with which Paul was just as familiar. For Paul too celebrated Jesus as the Paschal Lamb (1 Cor. 5: 7: καὶ γὰρ τὸ πάσχα ἡμῶν ἐτύθη Χριστός) whose slaying expiates sins, when on the celebration of the exodus the lamb's blood was sprinkled on the doorposts. Probably that Old Testament text which associates the

---

[1] Cf. also Deissmann, *op. cit.*, 130 ff. and G. Wiencke, *Paulus über Jesu Tod*, Gütersloh, 1939, 42–72.

[2] An example is 2 Cor. 1: 22, where God has sealed the preachers of the Gospel and given them the earnest of His Spirit. The term used here, ἀρραβών (pledge), is a borrowing from Semitic speech, which (through the Phoenicians?) had entered Greek terminology of law and business.

lamb with sin (Is. 53: 7) influenced him,[1] especially as we have much evidence of an early Messianic understanding of Isaiah 53 within the church of the Messiah, Jesus (Mt. 8: 17; Lk. 22: 37; Acts 8: 32, etc.).

2. THE SUFFERING OF THE MESSIAH

The classical type of vicarious suffering and atoning death is afforded by the figure of the Servant of Yahweh in Isaiah 53. The reflection of this figure in the work of Deutero-Isaiah surely provides the second root of Paul's soteriology. Hence we proceed to investigate the Jewish interpretation of this figure, and further to ask whether Judaism has any knowledge at all of a suffering and dying Messiah, to whose sacrificial death atoning power is ascribed. Then we shall have to draw that graph of inner development by which the Pauline doctrine arose from Jewish possibilities, and later gave birth to the official church dogma.

We have already seen that the sufferings of the righteous were often assessed as being of vicarious expiatory value. The intervention of the righteous to plead for a sinful people was not merely a current idea in the Judaism of the apostolic age; this thought runs through Holy Scripture as a whole. Abraham wishes to intercede for Sodom and Gomorrah (Gen. 18: 23 ff.). Moses offers himself as an $\dot{\alpha}\nu\dot{\alpha}\theta\eta\mu\alpha$[2] if only God will forgive the people (Ex. 32: 32 ff.; cf. also Ps. 106: 23; Amos 7: 1 ff., etc.). And the idea culminates in the work of Deutero-Isaiah (*circa* 545 B.C., shortly before the collapse of the Babylonian kingdom) which speaks of a יי עבד who is capable of validly representing the people before God. This figure of a suffering servant (Is. 53: 4 ff.) whose chastisements are for our healing, whose wounds make us whole, who suffered death because of our transgressions, has set a problem to research on account of the twilight which half conceals it. But so much is clear, that we have here the portrait of a just man who surrenders his life as an atoning sacrifice (אשם—Is. 53: 10) not in expiation of his own sins but for the sin of the whole people.

Alongside other possible interpretations, such as the collective,

---

[1] Bousset's derivation of the lamb symbol for the Messiah from Test. Joseph ch. 19 is forced and improbable (*ZNW*, 1902, 155 ff.). On the connexion of the lamb of God with παῖς θεοῦ cf. J. Jeremias, *ZNW*, 1935, 115 ff. Further, H. Wolff, *Jesaja 53 im Urchristentum*, Berlin, 1950, 89; Kittel, *WB*, V, 700 (Jeremias); C. K. Barrett, *New Testament Studies*, 1954/55, 210 ff.

[2] An intrinsically exact parallel to Ex. 32: 32 is Rom. 9: 3. Obviously Paul's exclamation is ideal and typical—a fact which has not always been properly taken into account by exegetes.

which no doubt was first represented in Hellenistic Judaism,[1] the character was probably at an early period understood and personified as the Messiah. Thus the apocalypses of Enoch, Baruch, and IV Ezra speak of the Messiah and the Son of Man in terms which are taken from Deutero-Isaiah's portrait of Yahweh's servant.[2] The rabbinical source texts usually adduced as illustrating this context of ideas[3] admittedly belong to later centuries. But according to the Jew Trypho (Justin: *Dial.* 89, also 39, 49, 68), the pains of the Messiah were traditionally regarded by his co-religionists as being announced in Holy Scripture. In fact, the Hodayoth of Qumran also applied the servant texts to the "teacher of righteousness", no doubt in order to characterize the type as a man of sorrows.[4] Moreover, it is hardly possible that Jesus and the first church were alone in their interpretation of Isaiah 53 Messianically, and recent research has accepted the hypothesis that such ideas were widespread in pre-Christian circles. In any case there is no doubt that Jesus, in treading the road of His passion, thought of Isaiah's Ebed, saying, "He was reckoned with transgressors" (Is. 53: 12; Lk. 22: 37). His Messianic self-consciousness pictures itself in the terms of Is. 53: 10–11, which recur almost word for word as a sort of kerygmatic formula in Mk. 10: 45, so that Jesus knows Himself to be a אשם which must be surrendered to death as a λύτρον ἀντὶ πολλῶν (LXX: περὶ ἁμαρτίας, Is. 53: 10).

The fact that the very earliest church theology applied Isaiah 53, together with certain words of Zechariah (2: 10 ff.; 9: 9; 13: 7 ff.), to their Lord's way of the cross[5] is indirectly confirmed for us by the apostle Paul, who for his teaching about the sacrificial death of Jesus

---

[1] Cf. J. Jeremias, *Zum Problem der Deutung von Jesaja 53 im palästinensischen Spätjudentum*, Mélanges offertes à M. Maurice Goguel, Neuchâtel–Paris, 1950, 118 ff.

[2] Examples in J. Jeremias, *Erlöser und Erlösung im Spätjudentum und im Urchristentum* (*Bericht des zweiten deutschen Theologentages*), Frankfurt, 1929, 106 ff.; Schweitzer, *op. cit.*, 69; E. Sjöberg, "Känna I Henok och 4 Esra tanken pa den lidande Människosonen", *SEA*, Uppsala, 1940, 163 ff.

[3] For example by G. H. Dalman, *Der leidende Messias nach der Lehre der Synagoge im ersten nachchristlichen Jahrtausend*, Karlsruhe, 1887. Important also is the unpublished Berlin rabbinic work of H. Fischel on the various modes of interpreting Is. 53; an extract is found in *HUCA*, 1943/44, 53 ff.

[4] Thus by H. Wolff, *Jesaja 53 im Urchristentum*, Berlin, 1950, and H. Hegermann, *Jes. 53 in Hexapla, Targum und Peschitta*, Gütersloh, 1954; J. Jeremias in Kittel, *WB*, V, 687 ff. (παῖς).

[5] All traces of the Ebed tradition in the synoptic accounts have been discussed in their continuity by O. Procksch, *Jesus der Gottesknecht* (Gedenkschrift für A. von Bulmerincq, Riga, 1938, 146 ff.). Cf. also E. Lohmeyer, *Gottesknecht und Davidssohn*, Uppsala, 1945; H. H. Rowley, *The Servant of the Lord and other Essays on the Old Testament*, London, 1954; O. Cullmann, *Die Christologie des NT*, Tübingen, 1957, 50 ff. (E.T. *New Testament Christology.*)

expressly refers to tradition—and such reference is unusual with him: 1 Cor. 15: 3, For I delivered to you as of importance what I first received: ὅτι Χριστὸς ἀπέθανεν ὑπὲρ τῶν ἁμαρτιῶν ἡμῶν κατὰ τὰς γραφάς (cf. Is. 53: 8–9). Also in both Rom. 4: 25 and Gal. 1: 4 Paul alludes to texts from the suffering servant passages (Is. 53: 5 and 12: LXX) as in other places (Gal. 3: 13; 4: 5, etc.) where he uses the verb ἐξαγοράζειν to characterize Christ's deed of ransom. Further, the combination of words δωρεὰν διὰ τῆς ἀπολυτρώσεως in Rom. 3: 24 must be an allusion to Is. 52: 3, for these words ring like an echo of חנם תגאלו; they were ransomed as a gift (by grace).[1] Probably Paul gives us no express proof from scripture on these lines simply because the connexion was taken for granted by him as by early Christianity as a whole. The picture of the *Ebed ha-shem*, Messianically interpreted, was current in the circles in which they moved.

Hence we see that the expiatory sufferings of individual righteous men or learned men, which vicariously avail for others, is no unusual thought among the rabbis.[2] In later times it was even normally illustrated by Isaiah 53.[3] Wherever the Ebed of Isaiah is related to the Messiah, the thought of a vicarious expiatory sacrifice is present. In fact, the idea was expounded in rabbinics with reference to Isaiah 53; although it is attested in literature not before the first half of the third century, it is probably much older.[4] In the circle of the Mishna redactor (Yehuda I, 135 to *circa* 217) the בר רוד is already described as outcast or sickly חלי (Is. 53: 4).[5] The Palestinian Joshua ben Levi (Sanh. 98a) and his contemporary Rabbi Alexandrai (Sanh.

---

[1] In Tannaitic writings a Messianic exegesis of Is. 52: 3 is already attested. In 80 Joshua ben Hananiah refers to it for his statement, which is reminiscent of Paul, that the presupposition of redemption is not penitence and good works (Sanh. 97b). Also 1 Pet. 1: 18 alludes to it.

[2] Quotations in Billerbeck, II, 279–282; G. F. Moore, *Judaism* I, 546 ff.; J. Jeremias in Kittel, *WB*, IV, 858 ff.

[3] Rashi, who understands the *Ebed Yahweh* figure as a personification of Kol Yisrael, comments on Is. 53: "Israel was punished with suffering so that all the nations might be reconciled by its penal pains." Likewise Ibn Ezra: "The sins which the peoples should have done penance for, have been borne by Israel." In general terms the Talmud formulates with reference to Is. 53: 11: The death of the righteous has atoning power (Moed Qatan 28a). The learned are also often included. Is. 53: 12 is even applied to Moses, and his death is called an "expiatory altar for the whole of Israel" (Jellinek's Beth Ha-Midrash VI, 78), which brings him near to the Messianic figure of the suffering servant. Further details in Billerbeck, II, 274 ff.; Bo Reicke, *Glauben und Leben in der Urgemeinde*, Zürich, 1957, 348 ff.

[4] This is the opinion also of M. Zobel, *Gottes Gesalbter*, Berlin, 1938, 141. He suggests that this view, despite the fact that references in the Mishna and Tannaitic sources are lacking, must be qualified as very old.

[5] Obviously חלינו in Is. 53: 4 has been read as "our Cholaia".

93b) as also the rabbis born two or three generations later, Huna and Idi (Midr. Teh. 2, 7 with numerous parallels) likewise describe in detail the sufferings of the Messiah understood according to Isaiah 53. Nevertheless, this type of exegesis plays only a subordinate part in Judaic tradition as a whole.[1]

If we investigate rabbinic sources to see whether they show any knowledge of a suffering and dying Messiah we find a curious situation which has often been pointed out. Billerbeck summarized his investigation of rabbinic source material on this point in the sentence: "The ancient synagogue knows a suffering Messiah, to whom death was not appointed, and it knows a dying Messiah, of whom no sufferings are predicated, the Messiah ben Joseph."[2]

So far as the genesis of this second Messianic figure is concerned, the basis of it must lie in the dualism of the Biblical-apocalyptic ideas of the Messiah.[3] The picture of the Messiah as a warrior king leading his people to the last battle and to final victory was separated from the idea of the purely spiritual Messiah who was a saviour. The second warrior Messiah, on the basis of Messianically interpreted scripture texts (Deut. 33: 17 and by a curious exegesis Zech. 12: 10), was derived from the tribe of Ephraim—the second most powerful after Judah—and designated "Son of Joseph".[4] As one dedicated to battle he was called the משיח מלתמה and was made the forerunner of the true Messiah ben David or הגאל הגדול. The fact that the Messiah ben Joseph dies as the conqueror of Gog and Magog—a widespread symbol in Jewish eschatology for a collective anti-Messiah—(Targ. Jer. on Ex. 40: 11; Bar. in Sukka 52a, etc.) is a simple necessity following the old Talmudic law: "Two kings cannot wear the crown" (Hullin 60b). In no passage of scripture is expiatory power ascribed to this Messiah ben Ephraim's death, in which is expressed the tragic end of political Messianism,[5] nor is Isaiah 53 ever applied to the figure.[6]

[1] Cf. also the judgment of P. Seidelin, "Der Ewed IHWH und die Messiasgestalt im Jesajatargum", ZNW, 1936, 230.

[2] Cf. Billerbeck, II, 2, 273, on Lk. 24: 26.

[3] Cf. Klausner, op. cit., 96: "The dual nature of the Messiah had to be symbolized by a double Messiah."

[4] The inner contradiction in the traditional figure of the Messiah hardly needed the Messianic disaster of Bar Kokhba, as Dalman, Klausner, A. Jeremias, and others suppose, to become manifest to the world. Nor is it necessary to regard the warrior Messiah as a collective symbol of unhappy zealot leaders, as Gressmann and R. Meyer have proposed (Meyer, Der Prophet aus Galiläa, Leipzig, 1940, 81 ff.). Cf. also C. C. Torrey, "The Messiah Son of Ephraim", JBL, 1947, 253 ff.

[5] Thus H. Gressmann, op. cit., 462. Cf. also Bousset, 230 ff., J. Jeremias, Kittel, WB, V, 685.   [6] Cf. Billerbeck, II, 297.

The suffering servant of God is therefore relevant only to the Messiah ben David. He is indeed said to suffer for sin, but he does not die a sacrificial death. The pains with which, according to Rabbi Alexandrai, he is laden as with millstones (Sanh. 93b) are mostly referred to the time of his obscurity before he appears as king in glory, and is still walking the earth unrecognized as the son of man.[1] Either they are understood as part of the pre-Messianic oppression (חבלי של משיח), or they are transferred to his pre-existent life before his incarnation.[2] One of the oldest texts in Sanhedrin 88a (early 3rd century) which ascribes a meritorious character to the pains of the Messiah and probably goes back to a much older tradition,[3] names as the place of his suffering in obscurity the world city of Rome.[4] Rabbi Joshua ben Levi met the prophet Elijah, who was standing at the entrance of the cave tomb of Rabbi Simon ben Jochai. He said to him: "Shall I reach the future world?" The latter replied: "If God wills" (literally "if it pleases this lord"— Rabbi Simon related that he had seen two persons and heard the voice of a third).

Rabbi Joshua ben Levi went on to ask: "When does Messiah come?"

He answered him: "Go and ask him himself."

"And where does he abide?"

"At the gate of Rome."[5]

---

[1] This motive is not seldom found in apocalyptic and later rabbinic literature. H. Gressmann in an appendix to his work (*Der Messias*, 1929) has collected the chief variants. Now we have a monograph on the theme by E. Sjöberg, *Der verborgene Menschensohn in den Evangelien*, Lund, 1955, esp. ch. 2 (41–98).

[2] Zobel, *op. cit.*, 141–158, has collected the various traditions. As far as apocalyptic is concerned, Sjöberg, *Enoch* etc., 130 has denied a pre-existent suffering of the Son of Man.

[3] Certainly "this utilization of Is. 53 is quite isolated in the Gemara" as Lagrange (*Le Messianisme chez les Juifs*, Paris, 1909, 246) observes, but nothing justifies the supposition that it was impossible to the Tannaites. A detailed analysis of this Haggada has, moreover, been given by I. Lévi ("Le ravissement du Messie-Enfant", *REJ*, 1922 and 1923). W. D. Davies, *op. cit.*, 283, says that the whole circle of ideas is "not unfamiliar to pre-Christian Judaism". Further cf. J. Jeremias in Kittel, *WB*, V, 689; but Sjöberg, *Der verborgene Menschensohn* etc., 255 ff., denies the existence of this tradition in the apostolic age.

[4] The localization of the Messiah's concealment in Rome was probably due to the fact that an effort was made to render the event of Messianic redemption parallel at every point to that from Egypt. Pharaoh's daughter reared Moses, who was to take vengeance on her father. And so the Messiah who will take vengeance on Rome (Edom, מלכת רשאים) sits in Rome. Cf. the Jer. Taanith 64a: Rabbi Joshua said: If anyone asks you where your Saviour is, answer: In the great city of Rome, for it is written, Is. 21:11: One is calling to me from Seir in Edom.

[5] As for the decree—obviously transferred to Rome—that walled towns were barred to lepers, cf. J. Jeremias, *Jerusalem zur Zeit Jesu*, II A, Leipzig, 1935, 33.

"And how shall I recognize him?"

"He sits among the wretches who are afflicted with diseases" [Rashi comments: "they who are smitten with leprosy, and he too is a leper, for we read in Is. 53: 4–5: 'He has taken upon himself all our sicknesses, and is smitten for our sins'"], "and they all bind and unbind their wounds; but he (the Messiah) binds and unbinds only one wound; he thinks: perhaps I am desired (by God for the redemption of Israel) lest I should be hindered (by the dressing of all wounds)."

Joshua ben Levi went to him in Rome and said: "Peace be to you, my master and lord." He answered him: "Peace be to you, Bar Levi." Bar Levi continued: "When does the lord come?" He answered: "To-day." Joshua ben Levi returned to Elijah. The latter said: "What did he say to you?" Bar Levi replied: "Peace be to you, Bar Levi." Elijah: "In this way he assured you and your father of the future world." Joshua ben Levi: "He lied to me, for he said he would come to-day and he has not come." Elijah replied: "He meant the 'to-day' of Ps. 95: 'To-day if you will hear his voice.'"[1]

There are various other passages of rabbinic writings—especially later ones[2]—which suggest that the sufferings of the Messiah were a favourite theme for Haggada.[3] In any case a Messianic understanding of Isaiah 53 is just as much attested in rabbinic writings as in the gospels. But the Messiah as Redeemer who expiates the sins of mankind through his sufferings and death[4] was for a number of reasons never accepted by Judaism. Nor was apocalyptic able to take this

[1] In the midrash the whole psalm is Messianically interpreted. Messianic interpretations of verse 7 (penitence as the pre-requisite of redemption) are frequent in tradition: e.g., Pal. Taanith I, 1; Midr. to the Song of Sol. 5, 2; Ex. Rabba 25, etc. Also the Letter to the Hebrews has adopted this Messianic interpretation (Hebr. 3: 7). Cf. O. Michel.

[2] As an example we may refer to the Pesikta in the Yalqut 359, where the Messiah voluntarily takes upon himself the week of sufferings ordained by God, making only the condition that no Israelite shall be lost, and that the saving value of his work shall benefit the dead, including also abortions and those not yet born. Such opinions are frequently found in medieval Jewish traditions.

[3] This material has been clearly but incompletely assembled in Billerbeck, II, 283–292. Medieval excerpts have been given by A. Wünsche, משיח של יסורים, or The Sufferings of the Messiah, Leipzig, 1870, 36 ff.

[4] It is interesting to see that the prophetic Targum Jonathan—drawn up in the 5th century but, as is clear from Sanh. 94b, already known to Rabbi Joseph ben Hiyya circa 300—tones down the phrasing of Is. 53: 12 as נפשיה למותא מסר, which can only mean that the Messiah has incurred the risk of death but there is no question of a real dying, nor can there be, since he is understood by the Targum to be the Messiah ben David. Jeremias (Kittel, WB, V, 693) and others therefore suppose that the Targum is a polemic against Christian ideas.

step.[1] Sometimes it was replaced by the traditional doctrine of the זכות אבת (merits of the fathers), which at all times was firmly held, implying that the righteousness of the fathers would avail for the people.[2] At other times the substitute was the thought of the expiatory value of the sufferings of the righteous, of which we have spoken in Section 1, and also individual penances, which after the destruction of the temple were simply regarded as taking the place of the Biblical sin offering, and which therefore until such time as the official sacrifices were restored made unnecessary any other substitute. Moreover, the expectation of the ימים של משיח as a time of absolute salvation with the Messiah as world king excluded the idea of an expiatory death on the part of the Messiah ben David, and the fate of death was loaded on to his Ephraimitic predecessor. On the other hand, the Jews were prepared to ascribe to the Messiah ben David a time of suffering prior to his glorification, for his waiting in concealment is understood as a suffering, the delay in his parousia being due to Israel's sins. Understood in this way the suffering of the wretched mendicant Messiah afflicted with leprosy before the gates of the world city of Rome is a profound Jewish symbol, which may be set beside that of the crucified Saviour as taught in Pauline theology and by the Christian church. But it did not become a dogma, because a redeemer Messiah was never a central issue in Jewish religion.

That according to Isaiah 53 the Messiah ben David must die for the sins of mankind is an exegesis of Paul and primitive Christianity which is not elsewhere found in Jewish circles, and this interpretation of the passion and death of Jesus by the early Christians as a fulfilment of scripture became a fundamental pillar of the whole Pauline doctrine of redemption. 1 Cor. 15: 3, Phil. 2: 7 and Rom. 5: 12 ff. are the three Pauline texts which show the plainest reference to Is. 52–53. It was not the sinlessness of the Messiah (2 Cor. 5: 21), which was not unknown at least in apocalyptic writings,[3] but the idea that He who shed His blood for many (Mk. 14: 24), and hung on the cross for them, should, in spite of the form of servant which He

---

[1] Cf. Sjöberg *Enoch* etc., 132: "The Son of Man in the symbolic discourses (in the Ethiopic Book of Enoch) is not a suffering Saviour."

[2] The merits of the fathers bring about God's gracious pardon of the world's sins (Sifre Lev. Bechuqqothai 8; Lev, Rabba 36, 5, etc.), prevent the destruction of Israel which was merited by the golden calf episode (Ex. Rabba 44, 1), and play a part in many other connexions. For this doctrine see the still unsurpassed work of A. Marmorstein, *The Doctrine of Merits in old Rabbinical Literature*, London, 1920.

[3] Thus, for instance, Ps. Solomon 17: 41 says of the Messiah that he is καθαρὸς ἀπὸ ἁμαρτίας. Similarly, Test. Jud. 24: 1, Test. Levi 18: 9, etc.

assumed (Phil. 2: 7), have been the true Son of God in a divine sense
—it is this which is a σκάνδαλον for the Jews, as Paul himself judges
(1 Cor. 1: 23). Neither the Bible nor the rabbis know anything
of a divine nature of the Messiah, as we shall see more exactly in
the fourth and fifth sections of this chapter. For all these reasons
the doctrine of the suffering of the Messiah derived from Isaiah 53
has never been given in Judaism the Christian orientation of an
expiatory death of the Son of God such as would benefit humanity
as a whole. Likewise that development was excluded which beyond
Pauline teaching culminated in the ancient church dogma of the two
natures of the God-man. And last and not least, Jewish Messianism
has always expected salvation and redemption exclusively for
Israel and those from the Gentile world who joined themselves to
Israel.[1]

3. THE EXPIATORY CHARACTER OF THE *AQEDATH ISAAC*

There is, however, a third constitutive element which, as I think,
plays a decisive part in the formation of Pauline soteriology and
which oddly enough in the whole complex range of Pauline studies
has so far been little heeded.[2] This is the *Aqedath Isaac*, of equal
expiatory value according to rabbinic teaching, and which in my
opinion has provided the very model for the elaboration of Pauline
soteriology. We have only to picture to ourselves how obvious to a
one-time Pharisee, setting out to develop a doctrine of the Messianic
sacrificial death of God's messenger, would be the associations of this
symbolic happening. The *Aqedath Isaac* too is a sacrificial deed flowing from a divine command, which—in spite of the fact that it was
never consummated—had expiatory efficacy in regard to Israel's
sins.

Hence we shall quote the testimonies of tradition which certainly

---

[1] Hence J. Jeremias, *Die Abendmahlsworte Jesu*, Göttingen, 1949, 93 ff., has rightly
drawn attention to the fact that the רבים (LXX: πολλοί) in Is. 52: 14 in the whole context of the λύτρον passage is mostly interpreted by the Jews as referring to Israel, never to
the Gentiles. The texts from pre-Christian Jewish apocrypha which are supposed to
prove the opposite prove in fact nothing.

[2] Yet we should mention: Israel Lévi, "Le sacrifice d'Isaac et la mort de Jésus", *REJ*,
1912, 156 ff.; V. Aptowitzer, "Les éléments juifs dans la légende du Golgotha", *REJ*,
1924, 150 ff.; J. Klausner, *From Jesus to Paul*, Jerusalem, 1950, 253; J. Daniélou, "La
typologie d'Isaac dans le christianisme primitif", *Biblica*, 1947, 363 ff., and now the history
of the exegesis of Gen. 22 by David Lerch: *Isaaks Opferung christlich gedeutet*, Tübingen,
1950.

must have been known to Paul,[1] especially as Isaac in the 4th Book of Maccabees (7: 14; 13: 12; 16: 20; 18: 11) is considered a prototype for the martyrs, and his exaltation had already begun in the thought of Hellenistic Judaism.[2] Paul himself has not yet explicitly drawn out the typology Isaac–Christ. He only says that Christians on the pattern of Isaac are children of the promise (Gal. 4: 28; Rom. 9: 7 ff.). The Letter of Barnabas (7: 3) is the earliest evidence in Christian literature of this symbology according to which Isaac on Moriah is the Old Testament τύπος of the passion of Christ. But Clement of Alexandria, Tertullian, Irenaeus, and Origen (in greater detail)[3] are familiar with the theme: Christ was the Isaac of the gospel.[4] Melito of Sardis (*fr.* 9 and 10), Orosius (*MPL* 31, 71 ff.), Ambrosius (*CSEL* 32, 641), Augustine (*MPL* 36, 245; 41, 511), and especially Ephraem Syrus (*Opp.* 1, 171, etc.) have embroidered the theme. In Christian art also this motive played a certain role from the 4th century onwards;[5] it is met with in the frescoes which have been uncovered at Dura.[6] Hence it seems natural to assume that the atoning character of the Aqedath (Gen. 22: 9; binding) of Isaac stood out clearly in the mind of the sometime Pharisee when he was preparing himself to develop the doctrine of the Messianic sacrificial death of God's messenger. In both cases it is a question of the sacrifice of a son flowing from a divine command, only in one case the sacrifice is to be made by one who knows himself to be Messiah, and is looked upon as the one whom God has sent; in the other it is a man who is to sacrifice his only son, not God Himself—it is the father of Israel acting at the divine behest, and on that son depends the fate of Israel and the world. In both cases we have to do with the central act in the process of saving history; but the sacrifice of Isaac did not reach completion.

The midrash Rabba to Bereshith, based mainly on Tannaitic

---

[1] This tradition is thought to be old also by H. Riesenfeld, *Jésus transfiguré*, Uppsala, 1947, 86 ff., and J. Daniélou, *Sacramentum futuri*, Paris, 103.

[2] Thus Philo is able to tell of a miraculous birth of Isaac, and once even calls him υἱὸς θεοῦ (*De Mutatione Nominum*, 23, 131).

[3] The texts have been quoted by me in *AfZ*, 230 ff.

[4] In spite of these essays we should not overestimate the comparison in early patristic literature. Hence we may agree with J. Parkes, *The Conflict of the Church and the Synagogue*, London, 1934, 117: "Considering how apposite the parallel is, it is surprising that it is not used more frequently."

[5] Cf. J. Jeremias, *Golgotha*, Leipzig, 1926, 83; H. Leclercq, Art. "Isaac", *Dict. Arch. Chrét.*, VII, Paris, 1927, 1553 ff.; Th. Klauser, Art. "Abraham", *RLAChr.*, I, Leipzig, 1941, 25 ff.

[6] Cf. Rudolf Meyer, "Betrachtungen zu den drei Fresken der Synagoge von Dura-Europos", *ThLZ*, 1949, 30 ff.

material,[1] has gathered together in Parasha 56 most of the material of tradition scattered in the Talmud which reflects the current interpretation of the sacrifice of Isaac. The greater part of this material must be very old, older than the date of the testimonies quoted. On Gen. 22: 6 "And Abraham took the wood of the burnt offering", the midrash completes as though by way of introduction: "like one who bears his cross on his shoulders". The thought of the λαμβάνειν σταυρόν of Mt. 10: 38 is certainly close. On "So they went both of them together" the midrash (similarly Tanch. Wayyerah 18), which with Onkelos and Jerushalmi reads *kachado* (of one mind) for *yachdaw* (together), comments: "Abraham went to bind, Isaac to be bound; Abraham ready to slay, Isaac ready to be slain."[2] On v. 12: "Isaac begs his father even to bind him very firmly, so that he may not tremble and that the sacrifice may not become invalid" (cf. also Pirqe d. R. Eliezer, 31). The whole emphasis of Jewish tradition is placed, however, on the fact that the Aqeda constituted a temptation,[3] and was designed to test the obedience in faith of the ancestor. His readiness to make the Aqeda glorifies the divine name (thus Tanch. Wayy. 18 corresponding to Ps. 8: 5). The sacrifice itself, however, does not seriously come into consideration; the factual reality of the human sacrifice is in Jewish tradition the most unthinkable and horrifying of things.

Nevertheless, Abraham's faith is "counted to him as righteousness". Tradition teaches that from this uncompleted action flows a power of merit which was effective at the Red[4] Sea and is not unconnected with the revelation of the law at Sinai.[5] To this day it is remembered at the blowing of the trumpet blast on New Year's Day for the salvation of Israel and in the *Mussaf* prayer on the *Rosh hashana*, which is accompanied by the recitation of ancient prayers, some of which are attested from as early as the 2nd century. The

---

[1] Cf. B. Heller, *E.J.*, VII (1931): Genesis Rabba is a work of the Amoraic period still much under the influence of the Tannaitic tradition. It must have been written in Palestine about the end of the Amoraic period.

[2] In some Aqeda legends Abraham is the hero, but in the first mention of the Aqeda in the liturgy, in the *Zikhronoth Mussaf Rosh ha-shana*, it is Isaac; cf. Ginzberg, *Legends*, V, 240.

[3] Cf. the interesting discussion in Sanh. 89b.

[4] According to Mekh. Ex. 14: 15 (30a) conveyed by Rabbi Jose ha-Gelili, the Aqeda was visible at the Red Sea as an image and effected deliverance from danger.

[5] The connexion Moriah-Sinai is the object of a special tradition which claims that Mount Sinai once got separated from Mount Moriah as the Halla from the unleavened bread. In the Messianic age both mountains will again be united in thought (M. Teh. 68, 17). Similar symbolism later combined Moriah and Golgotha; cf. Syr. *Cave of Treasure*, 29, 6.

merit of Isaac is of assistance to his descendants and makes up for their sins (thus J. Taanith 65d; similar thought in Ex. R. Par. 44 on 32: 13, etc.). The Targum on Micah 7: 20 has the comment: "Reckon to our account the *Aqedath Isaac* who was bound on the altar before thee." According to Rabbi Jochanan ben Nappacha, the midrash on Gen. 22: 14 (Par. Jer. Taanith IV, 5; Pes. Rabb. 39) reports that Abraham begged as a reward for the promptitude of his obedience: "I pray Thee, when the descendants of Isaac fall into sin and are dominated by the evil impulse and no one intercedes for them, be Thou their Intercessor; may his Aqeda be remembered in their favour, and have mercy on them."

Further, the Targ. Jer. and Pseudo-Jonathan consider that the divine forgiveness of sins is based on the power of the Aqeda, and according to a Tannaitic tradition the ram that Abraham was to sacrifice was created on the eve of the sixth day of creation, i.e., among pre-existent things (Pesachim 54a). Rabbi Abbahu (Pal. Am. end 3rd century in *Rosh hash.* 16a par.) similarly bases the custom of blowing in the synagogues a blast on a ram's horn at New Year, relating it to the ram of Gen. 22: 13: "The Most Holy said: 'Blow before me on a ram's horn, that I may remember in your favour the sacrifice of Isaac, the son of Abraham, and I will reckon it to you as though you had allowed yourselves to be bound for me.'"[1] According to Rabbi Levi (Pal. Am. 3rd gen.) in Ber. R. on 22: 13 (parallel text: R. Huna bar Isaac, Pal. Am. 3rd gen., Lev. Rabba Par. 29 on chapters 23, 24), Messianic redemption was to be effected through the ram's horn: "At some future time your children will be cast from one kingdom to another, from Babylonia to Medea, from Medea to Javan, from Javan to Edom; finally, however, they will receive their redemption through the horns of a ram." There seems no doubt whatever that from the most ancient times atoning power was ascribed to the Aqeda;[2] at the time of the redaction of the Mishna *circa* 200 the texts were admittedly not yet firm, but perhaps the Aqeda had been as early as the 1st century a part of the New Year

[1] Parallel texts Pes. d. Rab Kahana Pisqa 23 and Wayy. R. Par. 9 on ch. 23, 24 complete by: "And for them justice shall be changed into mercy. When? In the 7th month—hence at *Rosh ha-shana.*"

[2] The Mishna itself (Taanith 11, 3–5) has a similar prayer text for the liturgy of the feast days, which according to the Gemara (Taanith 16a) in connexion with the ceremony of ashes was understood to be expiatory. The oldest Roman and Spanish Aboda texts are given by L. Zunz, *Die synagogale Poesie des Mittelalters*, Berlin, 1855, 136 ff. The fact that Jewish prayer books—esp. as regards the *Zikhronoth Mussaf Rosh ha-shana*, which are attributed to the Amora Rabh (3rd century)—show the expiatory value of Isaac's sacrifice as central to the Jewish faith, must be considered as well known to Christian scholars.

liturgy, since in the schools of Hillel and Shammai the order of prayers for the day was discussed according to Megilla 31.[1]

Further, Ber. R. 64 on 26: 3 (Rabbi Hoshaia) describes Isaac as a perfect sacrifice, *ola temimah*. And Cant. Rabba on 1: 14 says specifically: "Isaac lay bound upon the altar like a bunch of grapes (*eshkol ha-kopher*, an image for ransom money) because he expiates the sins of Israel."[2] Rabbi Joshua ben Hananiah (Tann. 2nd gen.) declares that Isaac shed a fourth part of his blood upon the altar (Mekh. d. R. Simon bar Jochai on Ex. 6, 2).[3] And according to Tanch. and Rashi on Gen. 22: 14 (also Lev. 26: 42) it was said: "To all future generations the ashes of Isaac are visible on the mount of the Eternal and ready for expiatory purposes." The ashes of Isaac, by which, of course, is meant those of the substituted ram, play in various ways, especially in later texts, a soteriological role. Ashes are strewn on the head on fast days in order that God may be mindful of the ashes of Isaac (M. Taan. 11, 1; Taan. 16a—Rabbi Hanina), or on the prayer desk of the synagogue as a means for obtaining forgiveness of sins (Jer. Taan. 11, 65a). The ashes of Isaac lie on the ground on which the temple at Jerusalem was built (Zebachim 62a—Isaac Nappacha); God regards them as though they were piled up on the altar of sacrifice (Tanch. Wayy. 23 and Wayyiqra R. Par. 36 on 26: 42 par.). Even to-day the Israelites pray standing on the "ashes of the lamb that was bound". Quite universally, God remembers the *Aqedath Isaac* in favour of all men, Gentiles as well as Jews. It is implied in the Tanna debe Eliyahu Rabba ch. 7 (ed. Friedm. 36— Parall. Wayyiqra r. Par. 2, 11 on ch. 1: 5). For had Isaac not been created, the world would not have been able to endure (Tanch. Toledoth 2). Lastly, we find in the Pes. of Rab Kahana Pisqa 32 (200a), which often gives us very old traditional material, the soteriological principle: in regard for the merit of Isaac who offered himself up on the altar, the Most Holy (praised be His name) will one day raise the dead. It is just this faith which Paul linked with the sacrificial death of Jesus.

[1] Cf. Lévi, *op. cit.*, 178: "The ritual of the prayers for *Rosh ha-shana* existed already in the 1st century A.D. and as the part relative to the Aqeda is integral to it, it is certain that the doctrine behind the Aqeda was already popular at this time." Cf. further Lohse, *op. cit.*, 91, who here supposes a reaction to Pauline Christology.

[2] Interpreted by J. Jeremias, *Das Lösegeld für viele Mc. 10: 45*, Judaica III, 1948, 253.

[3] Cf. what has been said above in section I about the atoning power of the blood. Once again I cite the old principle, Yoma 5a, "there is no expiation apart from the blood". Cf. also the explanation of Rashi on Lev. 17: 11; the soul of every creature is bound up with its blood, hence I gave it as a means of atoning for the soul of man, that a soul should come and make amends for another.

Hence it must be noted that the parallel to Pauline doctrine is very striking. When Paul says in Rom. 8: 32: "God did not spare his own Son but gave him up for us all", the τοῦ ἰδίου υἱοῦ οὐκ ἐφείσατο, as Origen noted (*MPG*, 12, 203), reminds us forcibly of the LXX text of Gen. 22: 16 which Paul "whose letters are saturated with LXX allusions" (Büchsel in Kittel *WB*, III, 323) probably had ringing in his ear.[1] In any case the "putting to death of Jesus for our trespasses", of which Rom. 4: 25; 5: 8–9; 8: 32; Gal. 1: 4; 1 Thess. 5: 10, and other texts speak, bears a strong resemblance to the atoning sacrifice which Abraham was prepared to make.

A further trace of this parallelism may possibly be present in the formula of Rom. 3: 25, that God προέθετο Christ as ἱλαστήριον, if we are prepared to accept the suggestion of G. Klein (*Studien über Paulus*, Stockholm 1918, 96) that in this context προέθετο offers us an association with the יראה of Gen. 22: 8. Abraham said: "God will provide himself the lamb for the burnt offering" and the link will be: "God has provided Him (Christ) as an expiatory sacrifice." Such a connexion implies for προτίθεσθαι, instead of the usual meaning "publicly put forward", "exhibit", the meaning of "propose", "resolve", "select"; a use of the word which is found in two other New Testament texts (Rom. 1: 13; Eph. 1: 9) and in the Letter of Diognetus; cf. also πρόθεσις as "intention" (Rom. 8: 28; 9: 11; Eph. 1: 11; 3: 11). The medial use of the verb is not seldom found in classical Greek (Plato *Phaedr.* p. 259d.; Polyb. 6, 12, 8). The double accusative is obviously a difficulty;[2] but the verb προορίζειν (Rom. 8: 29; Eph. 1: 5), which is closely related in meaning, suffers this construction also. Our hypothesis is, furthermore, supported by patristic exegesis.[3] Origen,[4] Ambrosiaster,[5] John Chrysostom,[6] and later Fathers (e.g., Oecumenius, Theophylactus) accept such an understanding of προτίθεσθαι as the assumed association with Gen. 22: 8 would imply.

---

[1] Cf. also the opinion of O. Michel in the commentary on this: "The wording in 8:32 reminds one of the wording in Gen. 22: 16; thus the sacrifice of Isaac is used in order to illustrate God's offering of Jesus Christ." On the word-group ἱλάσκεσθαι cf. O. Michel's discussion of Hebrews 2: 18.

[2] Hence Büchsel (Kittel, *WB*, III, 322) declares this translation "impossible".

[3] Cf. K. H. Schelkle, *Paulus, Lehrer der Väter, die altkirchliche Auslegung von Röm. 1–11*, Düsseldorf, 1956, 116.

[4] *Comm. in epist. ad Rom. 3: 8* (*MPG*, 14, 949): "*proposuit* enim intelligitur quasi prius posuit, hoc est priusquam esset. Quod enim est ponitur, quod nondum proponitur."

[5] *MPL*, 17, 180: "In Christo proposuit deus, id est disposuit propitium se futurum humano generi, si credant."

[6] *MPG*, 60, 444: ὁ μὲν γὰρ πατὴρ προέθετο, ὁ δὲ Χριστὸς ἐν τῷ αἵματι τὸ πᾶν κατώρθωσεν.

Let us now break off this detailed study and formulate once more the hypothesis which was our point of departure. Just as Paul, in common with other Christians of his time, interpreted the figure of Yahweh's Servant Messianically as the type of the suffering Redeemer, there was present to his mind with equal force the Moriah scene of the *Aqedath Isaac*, which as a pious Jew he would know thoroughly from the liturgy of the *Rosh ha-shana*, when he was preparing to develop the doctrine of the atoning power of the Messianic sacrificial death. There was need only of a slight modification—the substitution of God Himself for Abraham and of Jesus for Isaac.[1] The indications in 1 Cor. 5: 7 that Christ was sacrificed as a paschal lamb, and in Rom. 5: 9 that the outpouring of His blood has saved mankind, suggest an exegesis that was in all probability based on Jewish interpretations of the *Aqedath Isaac* current at all periods. For in the Mekhilta 8a on 12: 13 (also Ex. Rabba 17 chs. 12, 22) it is said that the saving virtue of the blood of the paschal lamb, sprinkled on the door-posts of the Israelites on passover night, is derived from the blood of the binding of Isaac, of which God is thus reminded. And the sacrifice of Isaac (typifying the paschal lamb) took place, according to a tradition which Paul probably knew, on a passover day also. If the paschal lamb was for Paul a type of Christ, then the second implicit identification is that Isaac was the paschal lamb, for according to old sources the Aqedath took place on the 15th Nisan, the day on which the passover lamb was slaughtered.[2]

All in all, it seems to me that, when he developed his soteriological doctrine, Paul—the one-time Pharisee—recollected the central significance of the Aqeda. Further, Gal. 3: 16 shows how much this train of thought preoccupied him. Of course he made out of it something quite different and quite un-Jewish. For the decisive difference is just this, that the sacrifice was not in fact completed; that God commanded it to be stopped. It is regarded by God only as if it had in reality been completed.[3] Judaism has always felt with

---

[1] In Islamic tradition Ishmael—the ancestor of the Arabs—takes his brother's place in the Aqeda. Details of the midrash are reflected again in the Islamic legend. Cf. M. Grünbaum, *Neue Beiträge zur semitischen Sagenkunde*, Leiden, 1893, 111 ff.

[2] Nisan 15 was regarded as the most important day in the saving history of Israel and connected with the Messianic hope. The birth, the aqeda, and the death of Isaac are placed on this date; the night of his birth was called the ליל שמורים, the meaningful holy night. Sources are given in R. Mach, *op. cit.*, 80-83.

[3] Cf. Ber. R. Par. 55, 5: R. Joshua of Sikhnin in the name of R. Levi: Isaac's sacrifice was regarded as if the deed had been completed, although it was not. Among medieval commentators R. David Qimchi says: "Although the deed was not performed and Isaac was not in fact killed, yet in God's sight the will was accepted as equivalent for the deed." Similarly, Maimonides, *More Nebukhim*, III, 24.

horror the thought that it might have been completed. It is not for nothing that Taanith 4a (similarly Tanch. B. Wayy. 40) interprets the word of Jer. 19: 5 "it did not come into my mind" as referring to God's abrogation of His command to sacrifice Isaac, and on similar lines the midrash makes Abraham petition God: "Swear to me that from now on You will no more prove me, nor my son Isaac" (Ber. Rabba 56 on 22: 15).

Franz Rosenzweig is one of the few in recent times who has noted this inner connexion between Moriah and Golgotha. In a letter to Eugen Rosenstock he uses it to point out the relation between the two religions and sharply formulates the difference between them in the following terms:

> Abraham sacrificed not some particular thing, not *a* child, but his "only" son [reference to Sanh. 89b] and, what is more, the son of the promise and to the God who made this promise, the content of which humanly speaking is rendered null by this very sacrifice. It is not without significance that this pericope belongs among our most solemn feast days; it is the archetypal sacrifice not of particular individuality (Golgotha), but of the people's existence as son, of all future sons. Before God we invoke this sacrifice or rather this readiness to sacrifice, and, in fact, the readiness of the father; not that of the son which is so much emphasized in the narrative [R. means no doubt the midrash?]. The son is restored to life. He is only yet the son of the promise.[1]

If we wish we may even amplify what Rosenzweig says in the following way: through the Aqeda the son of the promise became the son of God. His redemption implied redemption for the whole of Israel, as is made explicit in Taanith II, 4, 65d. His mere readiness to be sacrificed sufficed to gain atonement for his people, whereas it was impossible to make room for the theology of Christ's sacrifice on these lines. For this reason alone Paul's argument was that the benefits of the sacrificial death of Christ were not limited to Israel, but effected atonement for humanity as a whole and were destined to open up a new way to God; a point which we shall discuss in more detail in ch. 6. In any case in the thought of Paul the Aqedath of Isaac can have been only a type or shadow of the Aqeda of Jesus of Nazareth which was perfectly fulfilled. On the other hand, the meaning which Paul saw in the atoning death of Christ cannot be fully understood apart from a tacit reference to the Aqedath of Isaac.

[1] Franz Rosenzweig, *Briefe*, Berlin, 1936, 689.

THE SOTERIOLOGY OF THE APOSTLE PAUL

Isaac was already even such a מברך as Christ: a dispenser of blessing. Then in later rabbinical texts of course an Isaac-soteriology was
deliberately developed and expounded as an *answer* to Paul.

4. THE PAULINE FAITH IN THE SON OF GOD

Paul's combination of these three Jewish faith motives, the atoning
efficacy of the sufferings of the righteous, the suffering of the Messiah,
and the Aqedath of Isaac, constituted an unheard-of novelty from
the point of view of tradition. But it was not this which led to the
break with Judaism. Nor was the decisive factor the ascription of
soteriological significance to Jesus of Nazareth as Messiah, whose
death and resurrection inaugurated the final world-week. In the
Jewish view the truth or untruth of this judgment on history would in
the end be demonstrated. When barely a hundred years later Rabbi
Aqiba falsely held the armed insurgent Bar Kokhba to be the Messiah,
it was no reason to compel a secession; his mistaken judgment was
corrected by the realities of history. And even the soteriology of
blood which Paul, in harmony with the early tradition of the church,
linked to the death of Jesus for the sins of mankind (1 Cor. 15: 3 ff.),
the necessity of His suffering and dying as a proof of His Messianic
mission—all this, as we have seen, could be made intelligible if necessary with the help of scripture proofs and Jewish source material.
The thought of vicarious expiatory suffering and the *Ebed Yahweh*
which were already common in pre-Pauline church traditions provided the basis in this respect. Even the fact that Paul fused the
Messiah with the Son of Man who suffered and died, and ascribed
to this figure pre-existence, might perhaps have been regarded in
Jewish quarters as a bold speculation worthy of discussion. But the
fact that, going beyond the primitive Christian understanding of the
matter, he combined these conceptions with the Messianically understood *Aqedath Isaac* in such a way as to transfer the story from
Abraham and Isaac to the eternal God Himself and His incarnate
Son, and thus exalted the Messiah beyond all human proportions to
the status of real divinity—this is the radically un-Jewish element in
the thought of the apostle. For this there is no possibility of derivation from Jewish sources, but—if indeed it is a question of derivation
—it is impossible to refute the idea of a link with heathen mythological conceptions, filtered through the Hellenistic syncretism of the
time. We now propose to illustrate this in more detail.

We have already enlarged in detail on the fact that Paul unlike the Synoptics was orientated not by the earthly figure of Jesus, but by the exalted Christ of the Spirit. The divine mode of the being of Jesus, the supernatural origin and future of the Crucified, and therewith also His substantial divinity as Son of God—all that is the essential theme of Pauline Christology. With the Synoptics the description of Jesus as "Son of God" had doubtless its origin in the self-testimony of Jesus Himself (Mt. 11: 27), who called God His Father, as in fact was traditionally the custom of the pious (cf. Wis. Sol. 2: 18; Ps. Sol. 13: 9; Ecclus. 4: 10).[1] But on the lips of Jesus the address "Abba" was certainly meant to denote the unique nature of His relation to God. The primitive Christian title "God's Son" likewise may have only implied His elevated rank as Messianic king. It was Paul who for the first time made out of a title of dignity an ontological affirmation, and raised it to a mythical level of thought. In order the better to discern this, we shall now consider the individual constituents of Pauline Christology.

Judaism at the time was well acquainted with the thought of an ideal pre-existence of the Messiah—or rather of his name. The name, or, in modern terms, the idea of the Messiah is part of the arrangements which God at creation foresaw as necessary to the attainment of the aim of creation.[2] But a real pre-existence of the Messiah such as would have enabled the Jews to speak with Paul of a real divine humanity of the Messiah or even of the Son of Man was never taught in Judaism, not even in Hellenistic Judaism.[3]

The Davidic origin of Jesus mentioned in Rom. 1: 3, His being born of a woman (Gal. 4: 4) and being found in the likeness of men (Phil. 2: 7) almost completely vanish from the horizons of Paul's

---

[1] Cf. W. Wrede, *Paulus*, Halle, 1905, 91.

[2] According to Pesachim 54a, seven things were created before the world: namely the Torah, Teshuba, Gan Eden, Gehinnom, the throne of glory, the temple in Jerusalem, and the name of the Messiah, for it is said in Ps. 72: 17: "His name is eternal, before the sun was his name budded." There are numerous parallels. The apocalyptic writings, especially the symbolic discourses of Enoch (cf. Sjöberg, *op. cit.*, pp. 83–101), speak more frequently of a heavenly and even personal pre-existence of the Messiah-Son-of-Man, understand him (cf. IV Ezra 13: 26) as the man from the sea who for long had been saved by God for the redemption of creation, who in 13: 32 ff. is described as "my son", but who never reveals the divine–human features of Pauline soteriology. On the whole subject cf. G. Dalman, *Worte Jesu*, Leipzig, 1930, 246 ff.

[3] I agree with von Gall, who observes, *op. cit.*, 387: "Just as little as the Messiah, for the Jewish feelings of our period, can be a son of God, so little can pre-existence be attributed to him. He was only with God in idea, only his name is eternal." Or as Sjöberg, *op. cit.*, p. 82, says with regard to apocalyptic, the Son of Man is subordinated to God, but by no means equated with Him, or identified with Him.

thought behind His other origin and mode of being, behind the insistence that He is the pre-existent Son of God, and κύριος, designated thereto by the resurrection (ὁρισθείς, Rom. 1: 4; cf. 2 Cor. 5: 16; Acts 10: 42; 17: 31). Originally the title κύριος may have been a suitable equivalent of Messiah, since Χριστός was meaningless to the Greeks.[1] But for Paul He is since His resurrection Son of God ἐν δυνάμει; as κύριος He exercises since His elevation universal sovereignty.[2] And κύριος, which is also a term frequently used in the mystery cults, was already for the LXX the translation of the Hebrew name of God.[3] By the application to Him of this title in the Pauline letters Jesus is at the very least brought into close proximity with God.[4] In the Deutero-Pauline Letter to the Colossians it is even said of Christ that He stands outside the category of created beings, that He is εἰκὼν τοῦ θεοῦ τοῦ ἀοράτου, πρωτότοκος πάσης τῆς κτίσεως (1: 15). The συνέστη in 1: 17 is even reminiscent of the stoic idea of a world-soul interpenetrating the whole of nature. Further, Christ is called the πρωτότοκος ἐκ τῶν νεκρῶν (1: 18), the mystery which was hidden for ages and generations and is now first revealed (1: 26); in Him dwells τὸ πλήρωμα τῆς θεότητος and indeed σωματικῶς (2: 9).

For a characterization of the situation it is sufficient to see that all the Messianic titles of dignity of Jesus are with Paul "intended to designate their Bearer as essentially divine".[5] The usual title υἱὸς θεοῦ, which must be distinguished from the *ebed* predicate (παῖς θεοῦ) of the Jewish-Christian primitive church, was frequently combined by Paul, through typological allusions to the Christ of the Old Testament, with His pre-existence and pre-human reality (cf. 1 Cor. 10: 4) to suggest that He is the Son of God sent from heaven to perform the work of salvation. The author of the Acts of the Apostles also sums up by this title the purport of Pauline preaching (9: 20). As υἱὸς θεοῦ Jesus appears in the work of Paul "as a super-worldly

[1] Cf. N. A. Dahl, *Die Messianität Jesu bei Paulus*, Studia Paulina in Honorem Joh. de Zwaan, Haarlem, 1953, 61.
[2] Cullmann, *Christologie*, 243, is certainly right: "It is primarily a question of function, not of being." The Greek doctrine of nature and substance is far removed from Paul.
[3] W. Michaelis, *Zur Engelchristologie, op. cit.*, 61 ff., has shown by twenty-two scripture references that κύριος means for Paul the LXX name for God.
[4] It should be clear from Baudissin, Foerster, Cerfaux, Cullmann, etc. (as against Bousset and Bultmann), that the Pauline kyrios Christology flows from the piety of Hellenistic Judaism rather than from the Hellenistic cult *milieu*. Lohmeyer's Galilean hypothesis is not verifiable.
[5] Thus W. Staerk, *Soter* I, Gütersloh, 1933, 99.

being, standing in closest relation metaphysically to God".[1] The Son of David in His incarnate existence, in His "pneumatic" existence He is the Son of God, for *pneuma* with Paul denotes the heavenly sphere or its substance.

The same applies—as also to the title $\sigma\omega\tau\acute{\eta}\rho$, which is more seldom with Paul—to the primitive Christian title $\kappa\acute{\upsilon}\rho\iota\sigma\varsigma$, which Paul uses to denote in particular His exaltation and present unique position of power as the Son of God, and one who obviously bears a kind of $\theta\epsilon\hat{\iota}o\nu$ $\sigma\hat{\omega}\mu\alpha$. This removes Him from the sphere of the human, from the aeon of the fleshly, for His $\phi\acute{\upsilon}\sigma\iota\varsigma$ is filled by the working of the Holy Spirit with divine $\delta\acute{\upsilon}\nu\alpha\mu\iota\varsigma$ and has become $\theta\epsilon\acute{\iota}\alpha$ $\phi\acute{\upsilon}\sigma\iota\varsigma$. As $\kappa\acute{\upsilon}\rho\iota\sigma\varsigma$ He has assumed the form of a servant, and is therefore in His outwardly visible appearance ($\sigma\chi\hat{\eta}\mu\alpha$ = habitus) a complete man. "For to be kyrios means nothing else than to be equal to God —and that in full humanity."[2] In Phil. 2: 6 Paul speaks of an $\emph{\'{\iota}\sigma\alpha}$ $\epsilon\hat{\iota}\nu\alpha\iota$ $\theta\epsilon\hat{\omega}$ of Christ, which can only mean that "Christ was and is equal with God".[3] In 2 Cor. 11: 31 Paul relates the Jewish formula of benediction, the word $\epsilon\mathring{\upsilon}\lambda o\gamma\eta\tau\acute{o}\varsigma$ (ברוך), which applies to God, to Jesus Christ and no doubt feels no scruple in so doing. In Rom. 9: 5—where the application of the doxology and so the understanding of the text is a matter of dispute—Jesus is perhaps even called God.[4] In 1 Cor. 15: 47 Christ is described as the $\acute{o}$ $\delta\epsilon\acute{\upsilon}\tau\epsilon\rho o\varsigma$ $\emph{\'{\alpha}}\nu\theta\rho\omega\pi o\varsigma$ $\mathring{\epsilon}\xi$ $o\mathring{\upsilon}\rho\alpha\nu o\hat{\upsilon}$, which may well be understood as a fusion of the apocalyptic Son of Man tradition which prevailed in the primitive church with a form of Messianic expectation going back to the Genesis text. This is especially so if we take into account the predicate of the Messiah, connected with Genesis, to the effect that Christ is $\epsilon\mathring{\iota}\kappa\grave{\omega}\nu$ $\tau o\hat{\upsilon}$ $\theta\epsilon o\hat{\upsilon}$ (2 Cor. 4: 4; Col. 1: 15). It is also possible that Paul found such a fusion already in contemporary expectations of the end.[5]

[1] Thus Bousset, *Kyrios Christos*, Göttingen, 1913, 182. Wrede (*Messiasgeheimnis in den Evangelien*, 1901, 214 ff.) and Lietzmann (*Komm.* on Rom. 1: 4) connect Rom. 1: 4 with 8: 3 and regard $\upsilon\mathring{\iota}\grave{o}\varsigma$ $\theta\epsilon o\hat{\upsilon}$ as a title for the pre-existent Christ. But Paul uses it equally of the earthly Christ (Rom. 5: 10; 8: 32, etc.).

[2] E. Lohmeyer, *Brief an die Philipper*, Göttingen, 1928, 92 ff.; cf. also Bousset, *op. cit.*, 118 ff. and 153. The Kyrios comes very near to divinity and becomes $\acute{o}\rho\iota\sigma\theta\epsilon\grave{\iota}\varsigma$ $\upsilon\mathring{\iota}\grave{o}\varsigma$ $\theta\epsilon o\hat{\upsilon}$ $\mathring{\epsilon}\nu$ $\delta\upsilon\nu\acute{\alpha}\mu\epsilon\iota$.

[3] Stählin in Kittel, *WB*, III, 54.

[4] Cf. O. Michel in his discussion of Rom. 9: 5b in his commentary. Patristic exegetes since Origen have seen in Rom. 9: 5 a clear testimony to the divinity of Christ. Cf. K. H. Schelkle, *Paulus, Lehrer der Väter, die altkirchliche Auslegung von Röm. 1–11*, Düsseldorf, 1956, 331 ff. In 1 Cor. 8: 5 ff. Paul tones down the ascription of divinity, names only the Father God, and Christ kyrios. Cf. Joh. Weiss *Komm.* and *Das Urchristentum, op. cit.*, 363.

[5] Thus O. Michel, "Die Entstehung der paulinischen Christologie", *ZNW*, 1929, 329.

The most frequent designation occurring in his letters, Χριστός as the second name for Jesus, goes far beyond the implications of the Jewish Messianic title. It "stands on a par with what is materially expressed in the apocalyptic title *bar enash*".[1] This Christ or Messiah-Son-of-Man—Paul always uses only the Grecized form ὁ ἄνθρωπος—for Paul, originates from heaven (1 Cor. 15: 47), is the first born of the whole creation (Col. 1: 15) who participated in the creation of the world (Col. 1: 16; 1 Cor. 8: 6)[2] and who after the completion of His work on earth ascended into heaven and sits at the right hand of God (Rom. 8: 34; Col. 3: 1). At His parousia which is awaited from heaven (Phil. 3: 20) He will utter the ultimate judgment on all men (2 Cor. 5: 10).

Hence this Christ has become a supernatural being and approximates to gnostic heavenly beings who come down to earth, and was even able during the desert wanderings of the Israelites to transform Himself into a rock from which water gushed out (1 Cor. 10: 4). This heavenly Christ seems to have wholly absorbed the earthly Jesus into Himself. As pre-existent Son of God and agent in creation, He is almost a mythical figure, whose contact with the earth and earthly things is but slight.[3] The myth clearly reflected here of the heavenly man who comes down to earth points to pagan spheres and can be connected with Judaic–Hellenistic wisdom speculations only by ingenious contrivance. In any event the Jerusalem Synoptic tradition knows nothing of this pre-existence and mediation in the work of creation.

We see here how quite new thoughts and imaginations stemming from extant non-Christian forms of the myth have been transferred to the figure of the historic Jesus.

The equation of the Χριστός with God Himself, which cancels the line of demarcation between the God of the Old Testament and the Messiah, leads logically to the fact that Paul transfers all the Old Testament statements about God to the exalted Χριστός Ἰησοῦς. Thus Joel 2: 32 becomes the text of Rom. 10: 13: "every one who calls on the name of the Lord will be saved". Or Is. 40: 13 becomes:

---

[1] W. Staerk, *op. cit.*, I, 101.

[2] The same is said of the pre-existent Torah (Pesachim 54a) in exegesis of Prov. 3: 19 in Tanchuma בראשית (beginning). The Torah says here: I was the agent of God in the beginning (אמון = τεχνίτης). Here Paul seems to have replaced the hypostasized Torah by the hypostatized Messiah as the architect in creation. Knox, *op. cit.*, 113, wishes to derive this doctrine from the "syncretized system of philosophy in vogue at Alexandria". But the rabbinic sources are Palestinian.

[3] So also W. Kümmel in *ThBl*, 1940, 214.

τίς ἔγνω νοῦν κυρίου, ὃς συμβιβάσει αὐτόν in 1 Cor. 2: 16 (on the contrary not Rom. 11: 34). Or again the confession of Is. 45: 23: "As truly as I live, says the Lord, to me every knee shall bow, every tongue shall swear" (in the LXX "shall confess τὸν θεόν") is used in Phil. 2: 10, 11 (not in Rom. 14: 11) to characterize the Lordship of Jesus Christ. And that classical expression of Jewish piety from the oracles of Jeremiah, "Let him who glories, glory in the Lord", is applied by Paul in both the Corinthian letters to Christ (1 Cor. 1: 31; 2 Cor. 10: 17). All these applications of Old Testament texts prove nothing other than that the Pauline κύριος Ἰησοῦς Χριστός has been deified far beyond the circle of ideas current in the first church, has become ἰσόθεος, and has His essential being in God, whether we understand Pauline Christology on mythical lines in the light of the pre-existence of the heavenly man, or on the lines of adoptianist exaltation.

The Judaic opponents of the apostle must have received all this with discomfiture and dismay, for they were adherents of a propheto-logical Christology, from which the soteriological moment and the divinization of the Messiah were quite absent.[1] In particular, the later Jewish Christians always saw in Jesus no more than an exceptional prophetic figure like Moses, and accepted a twofold parousia, one *in humilitate* and the other *in gloria* when He would return as Messiah-Son-of-Man (cf. Rec. 1: 49; 1: 69).[2] They are so very important just because they show that the primitive Christian kerygma was capable of quite another line of development than that which Paul—and still more pointedly the Letter to the Hebrews (Christ as the heavenly high priest)—gave to it. The Ebionites, characterized by their radical protest against bloody sacrifices, would never have admitted of Jesus, the true prophet whom Moses had foretold (Deut. 18: 15) that His death was of expiatory atoning value and His blood a sacramental means of redemption. Christ's death on the cross was for them without soteriological significance, as also the virgin birth, pre-existence, and θεία φύσις clearly never gained acceptance with them. As we have seen, they were within the first church the strongest opponents of Paul; and this is true not only as regards questions of the law and missionary practice, it applies also in all severity to that Christology which irreconcilably divided the two camps.

---

[1] For details see Schoeps, *TheolJChr*, 71 ff.; *Urgemeinde—Judenchristentum—Gnosis*, 25.

[2] Cf. M. Werner, *Entstehung*, 318: "For the faith of early Jewish Christians, Jesus of Nazareth was signalized by 'power and signs' as the prophetic man of God destined to future exaltation to the dignity of the heavenly Messiah, the Messiah *designatus*. . . ."

Now in order to appreciate fully the peculiarity of Paul's soteriological Christology it is necessary to consider in detail the well-known passage Phil. 2: 5–11. This formulates most explicitly the consequences of the affirmation that Christ has His true heavenly being with God and shares all the divine attributes. Hence here the episode of His earthly incarnation appears as a self-emptying, a resignation, for vv. 6–7 should not be considered on account of 2 Cor. 8: 9 as a Marcionite interpolation (as E. Barnikol takes them). Here we are faced rather by a quoted hymn, which seems to offer a kerygmatic association of the two traditions of God's servant and the Son of Man.[1] But we ourselves are concerned with its intrinsic meaning only; which is best interpreted with F. Büchsel[2] as follows:

> The self-emptying consists in the change from equality of status with God to the extremest inequality, to equality with man: figuratively speaking, the divine form of being is changed into the servant form. He became κύριος in the form of a slave and by the death on the cross as an atoning sacrifice, the servant-Messiah became the σωτήρ of humanity. Here lies the paradox of the destiny of the Christ (Incarnation) and its resolution (resurrection).[3]

Redemption (ἀπολύτρωσις) is effected by Christ (Rom. 3: 24 ff.); atonement (καταλλαγή) has become a reality (2 Cor. 5: 18 ff.).

Hence the real content of this Pauline Christology, which far exceeds the ideas of the Jerusalem first church but is akin to Johannine Christ-mysticism, consists in the fact that the Messiah as the Son of God in the literal sense pre-existed in heaven, came into the world by self-deprivation of the divine form of His being, in order to fulfil His redemptive mission, and then again ascended into heaven. *This myth of the condescension, sacrificial atoning death, and ascension of the heavenly man is radically un-Jewish.* Of course, for particular phases of this myth there are analogies or correspondences in the Jewish sphere, especially in its Hellenistic form, but they were always intentionally expressed otherwise. On account of the importance of the matter we will briefly mention them:

First I would mention the downright hypostatization of the Torah,

---

[1] Thus O. Michel, *Zur Exegese von Philipper 2: 5–11* in Karl Heim Festschrift, Hamburg, 1953, 80 ff.

[2] *Theologie des NT*, Gütersloh, 1935, 109.

[3] Similar formulations by M. Dibelius in *ZRGG*, I, 1604, and G. Stählin in Kittel, *WB*, III, 354: "He became Ebed *YHWH*, He who is Himself kyrios (*YHWH*). . . ."

which corresponds to the special sonship of Christ.[1] There are many texts where God refers to the Law as "my daughter", e.g., in the Baraita, Sanh. 101a; Lev. Rabba Par. 20 and parallels; Ex. Rabba Par. 33; Cant. Rabba 8, 11, etc. But such texts were always meant allegorically. Jewish theology never went as far as the idea of an "only begotten daughter". The same applies to the *aggadoth*, which speak of the pre-existence of the Torah, and allow it to be "original wisdom", the builder of creation. All this is a matter of imagery; it does not permit any real transference of attributes. But for Paul the divine sonship of Jesus is no figure of speech. It is an ontic reality which cannot be explained as a mere assigning of attributes.

Secondly, we should mention certain expressions and ideas in apocalyptic writings which, as Gressmann has already pointed out, seemed to have developed the idea of divine sonship for the Messiah in association with Ps. 2: 7, even to the point of terminology. Thus Enoch 105: 2 (if this text is not a later interpolation) has: *filius meus Messias*. In some MSS. of IV Ezra 7: 28 ff.; 13: 37 f.; 13: 52, etc. "the man of the sea" is called *filius meus*. Yet it may be that in the lost Semitic original something else, e.g., עבר, stood here.[2] No doubt, in the Diaspora, narratives probably of Egyptian origin may have been current which told of a miraculous generation by the direct operation of God. Thus Philo reports (*De Cherubinis* 45–50) that Sarah, Leah, Rebecca, and Zipporah were miraculously fertilized by God. Paul's assertion of a marvellous divine generation of Isaac in Gal. 4: 21–31 must therefore have been Haggada going back to the traditions of Hellenistic rabbis.[3] Finally, Moses too was described by Philo as a θεῖος ἀνήρ, and Goodenough thinks that here we have a process of deification (cf. above, 1, 2c). The Septuagint too seems to have drawn the picture of the eschatological saviour in transcendental terms.[4] But all this is hardly sufficient for the hypothesis that Philo, LXX, or the Hellenistic rabbis by distinction from Palestinian traditions accepted a real divine sonship of some man or of the

---

[1] This has been cleverly shown by C. A. Bugge, "Über das Messiasgeheimnis in den Evangelien", *ZNW*, 1906, 108, and in *Das Christusmysterium*, Christiania, 1915, 36 ff.; but his conclusions are quite misleading.

[2] Cf. H. Gressmann, *op. cit.*, 383 ff.; W. G. Kümmel, *Das Gleichnis von den bösen Weingärtnern, Mc. 12: 1–9*, in *Mélanges offertes à M. Maurice Goguel*, Neuchâtel–Paris, 1950, 130.

[3] About its echoes in Philo cf. W. Bousset, *Jesus der Herr*, Göttingen, 1916, 83 ff. On the whole material regarding the birth of sons of God esp. in Hellenistic Egypt cf. M. Dibelius, "Jungfrauensohn und Krippenkind", *SB Heidelb. Akad. Wiss.*, 1932, now *Botschaft und Geschichte*, I, Tübingen, 1953, 1–78.

[4] For examples of translation see Volz, *op. cit.*, 205.

expected Messiah. For all Hellenistic Judaism, Christian sources which have preserved the Jewish objection to Christ-soteriology assert the very opposite.[1]

Finally, various texts of the Old Testament could be mentioned such as Is. 7: 14; Ps. 2: 7 ff.; Ps. 110: 1, etc., which might be regarded as suggesting divine sonship. But such an idea was never meant to be seriously implied by such texts.[2] "The thought of divine generation from the Virgin is not only alien to the Old Testament and to Judaism, but quite impossible within its framework."[3] Likewise the idea of a Messiah as adopted into divine sonship, and who after his exaltation becomes God, can never be attested from Jewish sources. The strict monotheism and divine transcendence with which Judaism stands or falls would never permit even for the Messiah any interruption of the norm of creation. Hence the ascension and exaltation of Jesus to the right hand of God would be impossible of acceptance in Judaism.[4] No one who knows anything of the Jewish mode of thought could imagine it possible.

Nothing is more disloyal to the Jewish intention in this matter than the way in which people have handled the so-called mythological Bible texts. As an example I will mention only the בני אלהים in Gen. 6: 2, translated by Onkelos as רבוניא (the great ones). The midrash Rabba on this text reports even that Rabbi Simon ben Jochai, a Tannaite circa 150, with an obviously anti-Christological intention cursed those who translated בני אלהים as the "sons of God". That אלהים is here to be understood in a profane sense was commonly accepted in later Judaistic writings—aside from mystical

[1] Justin, Dial. c. Tryph. cap. 49, 67, 84, 87; Origen, Contra Celsum, cap. 40, 49, etc.; Hippolyt., Refut., III, 264, 7, ed. Wendland; Jerome, MPL, XXII, 173.

[2] Such texts which fitted in with the Christian view have mostly been left aside, although formerly they were interpreted without suspicion. Cf. the list in A. Jeremias, ATAO, under Son of God, high priest, virgin birth, etc. The usual rabbinic exegesis relates the title υἱὸς θεοῦ directly to Israel, the first born son (Sabb. 31a), child of a king (Sabb. 64b, etc.). Further quotations in Brierre-Narbonne, Les prophéties messianiques de l'A.T. dans la littérature juive, Paris, 1933, 5.

[3] Thus rightly R. Bultmann, Die Geschichte der synoptischen Tradition, Göttingen, 1957, 316. (E.T. History of the Synoptic Tradition.)

[4] I do not see how this idea should have developed from the motive of being snatched away, which belongs to the theme of the hidden Messiah. None the less, we may note the idea, attested in Pes. R. Kah. 4 Pisqa 5 (by the Amoraic Rabbi Berechiah), that the Messiah can reveal himself to and then be hidden from men. The question how far we have here a parallel to Moses (both saviours disappear and return) has been discussed in an interesting way by I. Lévi, "Le ravissement du Messie-Enfant", REJ 1923 1 ff. The possible relation of this material to the Pauline belief in the parousia would require careful special study.

interpretations. A similar result follows from investigations of the repercussions of Ps. 2: 7 in Jewish literature, Dalman[1] concluding: "When God calls the Messiah His son, this is only a symbol for the focusing of divine love on him. . . . The expression has never given rise to the inference of the divine nature of the son. It is an important characteristic of Israel that it never imputed to itself or to its kings divine origin." So far as I can discover, "Son of God" as a Messianic title independently of a Messianically interpreted scripture text is not to be found in the older rabbinic literature.[2]

Hence we conclude: despite the many expressions of Messianism known to Tannaitic Judaism, despite the many eschatological speculations springing up in the synagogal sphere,[3] Judaism never knew a Messiah who himself possessed divine being, or was son of God except in a purely allegorical sense. For the Jews he always remains, as Justin attests (*Dial. c. Tryph.* cap. 43), ἄνθρωπος ἐξ ἀνθρώπων even where with reference to Daniel 7: 13 (*Dial.* 31) he is pictured as "the son of man coming on the clouds of heaven". A cult of this Messiah never existed and could not exist among the Jews, for whom the Messiah was always eschatologically imminent. Such a cult arose only in the primitive Christian church, and in the preaching of Paul it gained its deep immanent meaning for the life of believers.

What is the origin of the Pauline faith in the Son of God, seeing that there is no basis for it in Judaism? The answer is: it clearly goes back to the self-testimony of Jesus, which for good reasons (cf. 161 ff.) appeared intolerable to the Jews, because it blurs the line of demarcation between God and man, and contradicts strict transcendent monotheism, that fundamental tenet of the Jewish creed (Deut. 6: 4). Hence we see in the υἱὸς θεοῦ belief, to which Jesus himself testified according to the synoptic account—and only there— the sole decisive heathen premiss of Pauline thought. All that belongs to it and flows from it (e.g., the condescending heavenly man of Philippians, the dying with Christ, the realistic evaluation of the sacraments, etc.) is un-Jewish and akin to heathen ideas of the time.

It will probably always be impossible to locate precisely the

[1] *Worte Jesu*, 220; cf. also the work of A. Vis, *Inquiry into the Rise of Christianity out of Judaism*, Amsterdam, 1936, 21 ff.

[2] Cf. Billerbeck, III, 20. It is significant that the midrash on Ps. 2: 7 desires to understand the repellent "thou art my son" as "thou art dear to me as a son". A similar change by means of the particle כ is already made by the Targum on 2 Sam. 7: 14. The predicate "holy" is probably never used in Jewish sources of the Messiah; cf. W. Staerk, *op. cit.*, I, 47.

[3] The DSS community also is a typical Jewish institution. The teacher of righteousness received none of the many predicates (Messiah, Son of Man, son of David, of God,) which the early church and Paul gave to their Master.

genesis of this faith. Θεῖοι ἄνδρες as mediating between divinity
and humanity, and sons of God descending from heaven, were
nothing unusual in the ancient world.[1] According to the definition of
Bieler, the Hellenistic man of God was "a man with qualities and
capacities exceeding the common measure, a favourite of the gods,
and a sort of mediator between gods and men". Up to a point the
Jewish *Saddiq* might be regarded as such a one. But in Judaism it is
always a question of a metaphorical title; such beings were never
god-men descending from heaven, never σωτῆρες. In Hebrew there
is no proper equivalent for σωτήρ, at least in the sense of Messianic
soteriology. Yet in Rome of the imperial period it was quite usual
to explain a mysteriously gifted man and a saviour as a son of deity.
Ancient nature religions, especially that of Egypt, the cult legends of
Isis, Osiris, Attis, and Heracles, etc., have in this respect furnished
the model. Johannes Weiss, who refers one-sidedly to Babylonian
texts, is accordingly right in observing: "In Babylonian and Egyptian
religion, in Hellenistic syncretism, such a conception not only produces no offence, but is part of commonly accepted ideas."[2]

In the sphere of early Christianity too, a whole series of sons of
God and saviour figures appear (Simon Magus is not the only one
but the best known of them) about which we are informed not merely
by Celsus but by many other sources in the sub-apostolic age.[3]
Acute researches which have been undertaken by many investigators
—I here mention only at random Reitzenstein, Baudissin, Joh.
Weiss, Böhlig, Lösch, Wetter, Bousset, Prümm—have not succeeded
in deciding the question of genesis. Thus it has been attempted to
derive the belief in divine sonship from the Ptolemaic apotheosis
which survived in the official Roman imperial cult. Again, the extra-
Jewish, oriental use of Kyrios as a title of dignity, which is supposed
to have influenced the LXX, has been made responsible. The Egyptian–Babylonian–Assyrian system of gods has been made to bear the
brunt of the blame. An ancient oriental myth of a journey through
hell by the sun-god played a great part for a certain time. But all
these theories of derivation are unprovable and must remain always

---

[1] Cf. the material in L. Bieler, θεῖος ἀνήρ, *Das Bild des göttlichen Menschen in der Spätantike
und im Frühchristentum*, 2 vols., Vienna, 1935–36, 105–113. Also H. Windisch, *Paulus und
Christus*, Leipzig, 1934, 24–114.

[2] *Christus, die Anfänge des Dogmas*, Tübingen, 1909, 36. Ideas of sons of God have also
been studied by W. von Baudissin, *Adonis und Esmun*, Leipzig, 1911, 16 ff., as also by W.
Bousset, *Kyrios Christos*, 182 ff.

[3] They have often been collected, e.g., by G. P. Wetter, *Der Sohn Gottes*, Göttingen,
1916, ch. 1.

hypothetical. Relatively the greatest probability will always be on the side of those deductions which are inferred from the life of the apostle, and which propose for the origin of this conception the extra-Jewish *milieu* of Tarsus, the apostle's home. Thus H. Böhlig (cf. above ch. 1, sec. 1b) has tried to show the soteriological character of the cult of the Heraclean deity Sandan—a dying and rising god in whose honour every year there was celebrated a funeral pyre feast, surrounded with pomp. In fact, inscriptions speak of θεοὶ σωτῆρες. The old city deity Baal-Tarz had become, under Persian influence, Ahura Mazda, and under Greek influence Zeus. In the Augustan period the city god lent his character to Apollo, Ares, etc., but under the Greek name Heracles he became the leading deity. We are obviously faced by a vegetation god, who in the funeral-pyre feast symbolically represents the death and resurrection of nature. At bottom Sandan-Heracles is nothing other than the Syrian Adonis, the Phrygian Attis, the Egyptian Osiris, and the Babylonian Tammuz. There cannot have been a great gap between the Tarsus feasts and the mystery feasts well known elsewhere of Hellenistic saviour gods.

Yet the fact that it was actually the dying and rising god Sandan-Heracles of Tarsus who served for Pauline soteriology as the pattern of the θεὸς σωτήρ can be just as little demonstrated as the contrary. What is certain is merely the fact that the Hellenistic idea of the υἱὸς θεοῦ as σωτήρ points beyond itself to the religious syncretism of Asia Minor and the intensity of the general need for salvation at the beginning of the Christian era. Beyond that we can only observe that "the extraordinary coincidence of the Christian and heathen idea of the σωτήρ exalted to the status of deity made remarkably accessible, for Paul the missionary, the heathen world of Anatolia".[1]

5. THE JEWISH PROTEST AGAINST CHRISTOLOGY

After showing the non-Jewish content of Paul's soteriology, we now turn in conclusion to the question: how did rabbinic Judaism react to the new faith in which traditional and pagan elements were combined? This question is inseparable from the other: how did the Jews react to the claim of Jesus to be the Messiah-Son-of-Man and to the Messianic doctrine of the first church? Both questions also imply the question of how Paul's teaching about Christ as Son of God was received—a doctrine which, of course, is first made explicit in the

[1] Böhlig, *Geisteskultur* etc., *op. cit.*, 168.

Fourth Gospel. We cannot in this matter look for special Jewish reactions to particular· statements of Paul, but only for the general reaction to the person of Jesus and the assertions of Christian believers.

An answer to all these questions is already given in the Synoptic accounts themselves. In the scene of Jesus' trial at night He is asked by the high priest with a solemn oath to say whether He is the Son of God. According to Mt. 26: 63 and Mk. 14: 61–62, the question is put directly by the high priest, and according to the older tradition contained in Mark, is answered by Jesus in the words ἐγώ εἰμι. However, with G. Klein[1] I consider·it possible that Jesus, as the tradition reflected in John 10: 30 shows more plainly, said originally אני והו, thereby committing a *gidduf* ·by uttering the holy hidden name of God (*Shem-hammephorash*).[2] Thereupon the high priest, hearing a blasphemy, rent· his clothes following the prescriptions of M. Sanh. VII, 5.

E. Stauffer[3] has carefully investigated ·traces of the liturgical theophany formula *Ani*· (*we*) *Hu* in Jewish writings. It seems to me to be proved that this lies behind the ἐγώ εἰμι statements, and that in the mouth of Jesus[4] it implied that He predicated of Himself divine nature, while in the ears of the high priest it sounded, of course, like a horrible blasphemy. The question was provocative, and was intended to convict the accused of blasphemy and by a ·confirmatory confession on his part·to gain a clear pretext for a conviction of guilt and sentence of punishment. We see from this that according to rabbinic law·it was not the claim to be Son of Man or Messiah which constituted blasphemy but just the assertion of divine sonship in the form of a statement about His own being implied in the *Ani* (*we*) *Hu*. Hence the result of the high priest's question was to

---

[1] *Der älteste christliche Katechismus und die jüdische Propagandaliteratur*, Berlin, 1909, 55 ff.

[2] Details about the tradition of secrecy in G. Klein, *Schem ha-mephorasch (Det förborgade Gudsnamnet)*, *ett bidrag till kännedomen om Esseismen och Urkristendomen*, Stockholm, 1902). M. Sukka, IV, 5, might suggest that not the tetragrammaton but perhaps אני והו was the hidden name of God. Klein's supposition seems to have been occasioned by a theory of Grünbaum (*Ges. Aufsätze zur Sprach- und Sagenkunde*, Berlin, 1901, 274). On the whole theme cf. my arguments in *AfZ*, 286 ff. The new study by M. Reisel, *The Mysterious Name of Y. H. W. H.*, Assen, 1957, is unrewarding.

[3] *Jesus, Gestalt und Geschichte*, Berne, 1957, 130–146. One of Stauffer's pupils has broadened the whole material. J. Richter, *Ani Hu und Ego eimi, die Offenbarungsformel "Ich bin es" in der biblischen Welt und Umwelt*, Theol. Diss., Erlangen, 1956 (Masch. Schr).

[4] Stauffer attaches great importance to the fact that Jesus never described Himself as Messiah but always as Son of Man. Cf. his essay "Messias oder Menschensohn?" in *Novum Testamentum*, 1956, 81 ff. This is of great importance for the assessment of the self-understanding of Jesus, but our putting of the question is not thereby influenced.

set in motion the machinery of formal indictment and to render unnecessary the hearing of witnesses. "Why do we still need witnesses?
You have heard his blasphemy" (Mk. 14: 62 ff.).

In the accusation of being a pseudo-Messiah the Sanhedrin would
never have recognized the right to indict of blasphemy according to
Lev. 24: 16. Only in consequence of the affirmation of divine sonship, of the suggestion that He would come again on the clouds of
heaven as the Son of Man in Daniel's vision, sitting on the right hand
of Power—hence only in consequence of His claiming for Himself
Ps. 110: 1 in a literal sense[1]—could He be properly said to have
blasphemed and to be punishable with death. The evangelical source
parries this judgment by asserting that it was soteriologically necessary, and bases it on the scripture proof which it places in the mouth
of Jesus to explain His Messianic destiny, that the Son of Man (cf. 1
Kgs. 19: 10) must be delivered into the hands of men. This "must"
is emphasized because the suffering of the Messiah stands written in
the scriptures (Mk. 9: 12). Under the impact of the destiny of Jesus
the first Christians learned to see in the passion of the Messiah His
way to glory (Lk. 24: 26; Acts 3: 18). They read His Messianic
character in His glorious sufferings, and in fact to some extent allowed it to begin only with the resurrection. This is so also for Paul,
who, as we have seen, in common with early church theology, takes
Jesus' *via dolorosa* to the death on the cross as the whole basis for his
soteriological argument: the Messiah was to die and intended to
die, and for this reason He, as Son of God, had to appear on the
earth in flesh. The whole effort of his thought was meant to bring
home this paradox, to bring together God and the world in the
crucified God-man.

The essence of this Christological doctrine and soteriological faith,
that God became man and offered up His only begotten son for the
sins of the world, is for the Jews, as Paul said, a "scandal", i.e., an
impossible faith-idea; for it violates the sovereignty and sheer transcendence of God, and in fact destroys the world. To this Christological doctrine might be applied the exegesis of the Jewish confession
of faith—"Hear, O Israel"—in the Midrash Samuel 5: 4 (also Cant.
Rabba 5: 11, etc.): "If you change to a *resh* the *daleth* in the word

---

[1] A Messianic understanding of Ps. 110: 1 is oddly enough attested only late in rabbinic
literature. For the first time by Hama bar Hanina *circa* 260; cf. Bacher, *Ag. pal. Am.*, I,
457. It is otherwise with the Ethiopic Enoch, in which there are many allusions to
Ps. 110: 1 (thus 55: 4; 64: 29). What, however, is with Enoch merely metaphorical,
Jesus expresses as concrete fact. For the early church Ps. 110: 1 was a well-known proof
text with which Paul too (1 Cor. 15: 25) shows himself familiar.

Echad, you destroy the world."[1] Because of the assertion of an incarnation of the eternal God, not only did the Sadducean high priest rend his clothes, but according to the account of John the Jews too sought to stone Jesus on account of the βλασφημία, ὅτι σὺ ἄνθρωπος ὢν ποιεῖς σεαυτὸν θεόν (10: 33; 5: 18), and likewise Stephen was stoned (Acts 7: 54–60) by a fanatically excited mob when he confessed his faith in a heavenly Son of God.

Some critics (Ed. Norden, Montefiore, Dibelius, Lietzmann, and others) suppose that Hellenistic Judaism did not perhaps reject such a faith so sharply as Palestinian. But there is no real proof of this. On the contrary, we have three generations later the relentless polemic of the Hellenistic Jew Trypho of Ephesus, on which Stephan Lösch[2] comments: "Whether Justin in his dialogue with Trypho has freely combined into a literary work real conversations such as he had had at Ephesus and elsewhere with Jewish scholars or not, there is no doubt that in the objections of Trypho to Christianity we recognize the opinions of contemporary exponents of Judaism." In chs. 43, 48, 49, 67, 71, 84, 87, etc., the theme of the discussion is constantly the *theologoumenon* of the virgin birth of the Messiah. The polemic of Trypho, who rejects as false the LXX translation of Is. 7: 14 (67: 1; 71: 3), returns again and again to the central thought of ch. 49: 1: καὶ γὰρ πάντες ἡμεῖς τὸν Χριστὸν ἄνθρωπον ἐξ ἀνθρώπων προσδοκῶμεν γενήσεσθαι.

In this protest against the faith in the divinity of Jesus the exponents of Judaism are at one with the later Jewish Christians (the Ebionites), who do indeed recognize the Messianic character of Jesus but were never prepared to admit His divinity in humanity.[3] It is certain, however, that Justin has preserved for us in undistorted form Judaic religious ideas, and not only Palestinian ones such as were bound to emerge in debates with the early church, in so far as discussions took place. Even if we are inclined to admit with Dibelius[4] that miraculous births κατὰ πνεῦμα are possible ideas in Judaic Hellenism, yet the virgin motive, legends about Mary, and the fatherlessness of Jesus are in any event un-Jewish interpretations springing from a syncretistic sphere of ideas. Moreover, for the

---

[1] With this is connected the fact that in the Massoretic text, which the Machsorim of all centuries follow, the Daleth is written in thick type and double size, so as to eliminate any misreading. Of course, to-day it is not possible to decide whether this polemic was originally directed against Christological dogma or a dualistic gnosis.

[2] *Deitas Jesu und antike Apotheose*, Rottenburg, 1933, 89 ff.

[3] The sources are detailed and discussed in Schoeps, *TheolJchr*, 73 ff.

[4] *Jungfrauensohn und Krippenkind*, 49.

decision of the question whether Hellenistic Judaism had not perhaps a greater understanding of the divine sonship it is not without significance that, in Justin, Trypho derisively plays on the ἱερὸς γάμος theme in attacking the early Christian dogma, and equates the myth of the birth of Perseus as son of Zeus and the virgin Danae with the New Testament story of the birth of Jesus: "You Christians should be ashamed to relate such things like the heathen. It would be better if you asserted of this Jesus that as man he was born of human seed, and called to be Messiah on account of his faithful obedience to the law" (*Dial. c. Tryph.* 67, 2).

There could not be clearer testimony that for the Judaism of the Diaspora also (πάντες ἡμεῖς) heathen *mythologoumenon* and Christian incarnational teaching were considered the same type of thing, that both seemed equally blasphemous from the monotheistic standpoint. Is. 42: 8: "I am the Lord, that is my name; my glory I give to no other" is a doctrine which Trypho thinks is mocked by the divinity of Christ which Justin wishes to prove from scripture (*Dial.* 65). The Jew of Celsus (Origen *contra Celsum* 1, 40) was likewise offended by the idea of divine sonship, and Origen confirms that this was the attitude of his Jewish contemporaries (1, 49). All later Jewish writers adhered to the same objection.[1]

As for the significantly scantier sources of rabbinic literature, what seems to me most grave is the uncompromising rejection of the mere thought of incarnation and ascension, as expressed by R. Jose (Tannaite 3rd gen.) in Sukka 5a: "Never has God come to earth, and never have Moses and Elijah ascended into heaven, for we read in Ps. 115: 16: 'The heavens are the Lord's heavens, but the earth he has given to the *bene adam*'." Similarly also R. Idith in Sanh. 38b, who was considered a master of dialogue with the "Minim". Further, let us mention a few examples of anti-Christian rabbinic polemic which I have to some extent already quoted in my book on Jewish-Christian debate in 19 centuries.[2] Thus we read in the Aggadath Bereshith, ed. S. Buber, par. 31 (end), which is, of course, a late homiletic midrash given by Rabbi Hilkiah (a 5th gen. Palestinian Amora *circa* 330), as an exegesis of Eccl. 4: 8: "Foolish is the heart of the liars who say that the Holy One, praised be His name, has a son. If God could not bear

---

[1] Cf. Walter Bauer, *Das Leben Jesu im Zeitalter der neutestamentlichen Apokryphen*, Tübingen, 1909, 452 ff.; for rabbinic sources see J. Bergmann, *Jüdische Apologetik im ntl. Zeitalter*, Berlin, 1908, 80 ff. For anti-Christological polemic of the Jews according to 4th-century patristic sources, cf. L. Lucas, *Zur Geschichte der Juden im vierten Jahrhundert*, Berlin, 1910, 27 ff.

[2] Berlin, 1937; 2nd ed., Frankfurt, 1949, ch. 3.

for very pain that Abraham should slaughter his son, to do which he was ready, how much less could He have allowed His own son to be slain, without destroying the world." The address of this polemic is plain. Of similar import is Jer. Sabbath 8d (cf. also Cant. Rabba on 7: 9; Midr. Samuel 5: 7): "When Nebuchadnezzar used the phrase of Dan. 3: 25: 'he is like a son of God', there came down an angel from heaven who struck him on the mouth and said: 'You blasphemer, has God a son?'" (R. Berechiah, a Pal. Am. of the beginning of 4th century). Further the midrash Rabba on Ex. 20: 2 explains: "I am the Lord thy God." Compare with this, he suggests, a king of flesh and blood. The latter reigns and has a father, or brother or son. The Holy One, praised be His name, said: "I am the first" for I have no father; "and I am the last" for I have no son; "beside me there is no god" (Is. 44: 6) for I have no brother (R. Abbahu, 2nd gen. Am. *circa* 300).[1] And Zechariah 13: 8 is interpreted by Rabbi Yehuda bar Simon: "Every mouth which confesses that there are two gods, will be wiped out and destroyed" (Deut. Rabba Par. II on ch. 6: 4). Whether in regard to this last text the polemic is against Christians or gnostics, is obscure; in any case it is a question of defending the unity of God against assault, and for this many other texts could be adduced. Thus the Tannaite Rabbi Nathan saw from Ex. 20: 2 and Is. 44: 6 answers to the "Minim" who assert that there are two powers (שתי רשיונות) (Mekh. on Ex. 20: 2).[2]

It is not surprising that the rabbinic sources quoted belong to later centuries, since they presuppose controversy with church Christians. Partly earlier are some references which relate to the historical Jesus and also belong to our context.[3] They are scattered and incidental allusions which are uncertain in historical implications. They merely give rise to the inference that the events of the year 30 were

---

[1] Similarly Eccl. 4: 8 (a person who has no one, either son or brother) has given occasion for the midrashic anti-Christological explanation: The one is God, praised be His name, to whom Deut. 6: 4 refers: The Eternal, our God, is one. And there is no second, i.e., He has no sharer in His world, neither son nor brother. But if He has no sharer, has He not a son? Because He loved the Israelites, He called them His sons (Deut. 14: 1) and brothers (Ps. 122: 8). Prov. 24: 21: "do not associate with those who change", is explained in Deut. Rabba Par. II ch. 6, 4: with such as say there is a second God. And Rabbi Acha (320) speaks of those who change, against whom the first sentence of the Shema and Eccl. 4: 8 are cited together.

[2] Similarly, Rabbi Berechiah in Sifre Deut. 32: 39; M. Sanh. IV, 4 (anonymous) and Tos. Sanh. VIII, 9. About the change in the line of opposition in the 3rd century on the emergence of the Trinitarian dogma, cf. V. Aptowitzer in *MGWJ*, 1929, 117 f.

[3] They have been studied in detail by S. Zeitlin, *Jesus in the Early Tannaitic Literature*, in Abhandlungen zur Erinnerung an H. P. Chajes, Vienna, 1933, and in critical debate with the older workers von Strack, Laible, Herford, and Klausner.

not taken very seriously by the early Tannaites, as, in general, con-
demnations of Messianic heresy at that time must have appeared
elsewhere also. Thus we learn that Jesus ha-Nosri in the mode
of thought and speech of the time was described as a man who
"allowed his food to burn", i.e., aroused public scandal and became
a recreant (Sanh. 103a, etc.). The remark that He was a wonder-
worker (Sanh. 43a) points to the possession of magical powers by
Jesus, as indicated in the ὡς ἐξουσίαν ἔχων of Mk. 1: 22.[1] It is
alleged as a basis of His condemnation that He derided the words of
the wise (cf. Mt. 23: 5 ff.), misled Israel into the ways of disloyalty
(Sanh. 107b); Sota 47b).

At the end of the Tannaite epoch—quite 150 years after the crucifixion—this is explained by Rabbi Eliezer ha-Qappar (Tann. of 5th
gen.) a contemporary of the Rabbi, redactor of the Mishna. Clearly
under the impact of discussions with Gentile Christians, he accused
Jesus of making himself a god. According to Jer. Taanith 65b and
Yalqut Shim. 1, 765 (Salonika) on Num. 23: 7 this accusation is placed
in the mouth of the Biblical Balaam, whom God permitted to prophesy that at some future date a man, the son of a woman, would arise
and would try to make himself god and mislead the world. But it
was said: "God is not man that He should lie" (Num. 23: 19). And
if such a one says he is god, then he is a liar. Again, 50 years later,
Rabbi Abbahu of Caesarea, a contemporary of Origen, says: "If
Jesus says: 'I am God', then he lies. 'I am the son of man'—his end
will disprove it. 'I will ascend to heaven.' He says it but he will not
do it" (Jer. Taanith 2, 1). And Rabbi Eliezer expounds Num.
24: 23 with reference to Jesus as follows: "Woe to him who will live
by this people which has listened to that man who made himself god"
(*ibid.*). Clearly it is the same reproach which John's gospel reported
(5: 18): "The Jews sought to kill Jesus because he made himself
equal with God." And it is the same reproach which is the ground
of the stoning in 10: 33: "because you, being man, make yourself
God."

Such Jewish reactions to the doctrine of the God-man are only
possible from the middle of the 3rd century, when the evolving great
church began to elaborate its Christological dogma on a Pauline
basis. For external reasons the reactions are mostly indirect and disguised, but their tendency is clear; namely that Pauline Christology
and soteriology is a dogmatic impossibility from the standpoint of

---

[1] Cf. the interpretation of E. Stauffer, *Jesus, Gestalt und Geschichte*, Berne, 1957, 142 ff.
(E.T. *Jesus and His Story*.)

strict Jewish transcendent monotheism.[1] Judaism of every tendency, both before and contemporary with Paul—even Hellenistic (cf. LXX Is. 63: 9)—rejected any compromise. Thus in the last analysis, as the quoted texts consistently show, the Christian doctrine of the incarnation must be utterly repudiated on the ground of the Jewish experience of God: that God as the formless cannot be embodied in any kind of form, that He as the Infinite, prior to all forms, was the Creator of every form. No haggadist ever needed to study the details of Pauline Christology and soteriology. Admittedly the latter, as we have seen, arose from legitimately Jewish sequences of thought, but their combination with the un-Jewish doctrine of the divine sonship has made any contact with Judaism impossible. In becoming fixed as the dogma of the Christian church, they burst for ever the framework of the Jewish faith. The "acute Hellenization of Christianity", so much discussed in its day, takes place at this point.

[1] On this theme cf. A. Marmorstein, *Studies in Jewish Theology*, London, 1950, 101 ff.

5

PAUL'S TEACHING ABOUT THE LAW

Introduction: Objective Presuppositions

THE Pauline understanding of the law, the most intricate doctrinal issue in his theology, has certain objective presuppositions bound up with the historical situation which Paul encountered:

When after his conversion Paul visited Jerusalem, probably in 35–36, he was there confronted by a small church believing in Jesus as Messiah. It had hardly as yet hardened into an institution, but it already practised baptism and the Lord's Supper. Paul's position in this first church seems from the start to have been distinguished from that of the other apostles by the fact that he saw a conflict where the rest, in discipleship to their Lord, saw only a harmonious combination. This combination, the law and the Messiah, was for Paul, on account of a simple "Halakha" reflection which we shall at once describe, an impossibility of thought. In his mind it shaped itself into the sharp alternative: the law *or* the Messiah.

We know from Gal. 1: 16 that already at Damascus the apostle had recognized his special task in the service of Christ to be the apostolate to the Gentiles. It is possible that Saul himself had been a missionary to the heathen, especially a preacher of Jewish circumcision, as E. Barnikol[1] supposes on the basis of Gal. 1: 13–16. This possibility is neither provable nor is it to be excluded, and it could explain the quick decision of Damascus as a persistence of the same psychological realities. After Damascus the question of the validity of the law—even apart from its Messianological problematics—became alive for him in a way which it did not for the Jerusalem apostles. The question of the applicability of the law to proselytes was difficult to answer in respect of the Jewish mission to Gentiles. For the most part it was solved by compromise (cf. ch. 6, section 1) and on this model the Jewish Christians proposed to act by insisting

---

[1] *Die vor- und frühchristliche Zeit des Paulus*, Kiel, 1929, 18 ff.

on the כשרות and ברית מילה as well as on ritual cleanness through
the baptismal immersion of proselytes explained in a Christian sense.
Paul, however, practised "complete freedom from the law" in his
missionary churches. His attitude in missionary work and his "uncompromising rejection of any obligation on the part of Gentile
Christians to fulfil the Mosaic law"[1] are based on a fundamentally
different understanding of the latter.

The story of his conflict with the Jerusalem traditionalists, reported in the Acts of the Apostles and the Letter to the Galatians,
together with its stages: Jerusalem–Antioch–Apostolic–Decree–
Corinth, need not here be repeated. As we have seen in ch. 2, 3a,
the controversy ended as far as Paul was concerned with the surrender of the Jewish-Christian prerogative on condition that his churches
recognized their duty to pay a tax to the temple in Jerusalem,[2]
and with the admission of table-fellowship as a symbol of the secured
unity of the Jewish and Gentile elements in the church. The
emancipation of developing Christianity from national-racial limits
meant that Paul had triumphed inasmuch as the most important
points of the Jewish covenantal law were recognized as without
obligation for the churches of the new covenant. His views on the
task of Gentile Christians and the role of the Jews belong to the
systematic discussion of his federal theology, which springs from
Jewish universalist expectations (ch. 6). They are also simply the
result of his post-messianic theology concerning the law, which gave
to the religion of Jesus the form enabling it to expand throughout
the world. This again determined his special position in the primitive church, and implied that the conflict on the apostolic council
was not to become a mere episode of early church administration.
Rather it brought into effect the basic consequences of Paul's doctrine about the law and its annulment through the Messiah, and this
gave a critical turn to Christian history and so to world history as a
whole.

Paul's teaching about the law is not comparable, any more than
eschatology or soteriology, with the teaching of Jesus Himself. The
polemical sayings of Jesus about Jewish observance of the Sabbath,
divorce, or ritual cleanliness do not recur with Paul. Moreover,
Paul's teaching on the point was for many centuries not understood

---

[1] Thus H. Lietzmann, *Geschichte des alten Kirche*, I, Berlin, 1953, 129 ff.
[2] Cf. the illuminating essays by Karl Holl, *Gesammelte Aufsätze zur Kirchengeschichte*, II,
Tübingen, 1928, 58 ff., on the collection for the saints in Jerusalem as an impost on the
church as a whole, underlining the precedence of the Jerusalem church.

or not correctly understood, because the rabbinic presuppositions of the apostle were lost sight of, and in particular the fact that for a Jew the problem of the abolition of the law could only be solved by the law itself, i.e., by drawing out from scripture the "true meaning of the law". All systematic expositions of Paul's doctrine of the law which attempt to explain it without wider reference, as is usually done, overlook the position of Paul within the history of the Jewish religion. Only when we recognize the latter can we understand his Christian theology in its entirety, for that theology could only be a real problem to his Jewish-Christian partners and opponents. In any case the statement in 2 Pet. 3: 16 that some things in his letters are difficult to understand is true of nothing so much as of his doctrine of the law.[1] H. Böhlig's comment, made in 1913, that Paul's attitude to the law is one of the sore points in critical studies of recent decades, is still true, for here problems completely unsolved still face us.

We shall now attempt to explain the apostle's understanding of the law, by which he usually meant the whole Torah,[2] in the light of his rabbinic presuppositions. To set a limit to our aim we must bear in mind that his letters, among which those to the Romans and Galatians deal chiefly with the problem of the law, do not contain any direct debate with the Jews, and were written not even for Jewish Christians but for mixed Christian communities of the Jewish Diaspora. Moreover, the greater part of these Gentile Christians already belonged to the circle of the σεβόμενοι τὸν θεόν resulting from Jewish missions, and they had not come to grips with the Torah itself but at most with the Noachide Torah.[3]

We now come to the real theme of this chapter. We would like again to emphasize in advance that the apostle's understanding of the law is only comprehensible and fathomable, in its deep content, when we keep our attention focused on Paul's consistently eschatological mode of thought: his "through and through teleological

---

[1] This has been emphasized too by A. v. Harnack, *Beitr. z. Einl. in das NT*, III: *Die Apostelgeschichte*, Leipzig, 1908, 211: "Paul gave the deepest but also the most knotty justification for universalism and the abolition of the law. This justification was hardly understood by any one, and was not successful with the churches."

[2] According to Gal 1: 14, the oral Torah also belongs here (i.e., the rabbinic Halakha) and is described as παραδόσεις πατρικαί.

[3] Thus the great Roman church may well have arisen from the proselyte annex of the Roman synagogue: cf. the explanation of the well-known passage in Suetonius, *Vita Claudii*, ch. 25, by Heumann as early as 1709. Bousset-Gressmann, *Religion des Judentums* etc., 81, think (surely rightly): "The problem of the Letter to the Romans is best solved if we suppose as Paul's readers a church consisting essentially of one-time proselytes." Cf. also Harnack, *SAB*, 1928, 135 ff. Further below, pp. 235 ff..

habits of thinking".[1] Any discussion of this very complex and intricate theme, if it is to succeed, must approach the subject from this angle.[2]

I. CHRIST, THE END OF THE LAW

The *abolition of the law* is a Messianological doctrine in Pauline theology.[3] It became a burning issue as a result of the recent resurrection of Jesus from the dead, as the first Christians believed. For the whole theology of the apostle is really nothing other than the re-thinking of all received notions in view of this event, expected from one day to the next, but for Christian faith already belonging to yesterday. The apostle wishes to draw and must draw the inferences of this event for his transitional generation, and hence, as Schweitzer says, he must "take into account the logical fact that the law ceases when the Messianic kingdom begins" (186). The 2,000-year era of the Mosaic law which followed on the 2,000 years of *Tohuwabohu* (Sanh. 97a, Ab. Zara 9a: Jer. Meg. 70d) has now ended and the era of the Messiah has begun.[4] The law had validity until "all things were fulfilled". Now the fulfilment has been effected. According to this midrash of the aeons, Judaism and the law have no further meaning than that of marking the end of an epoch.

Paul deduces from his faith that the Messiah has come in the person of Jesus the conclusion: "Christ is the end of the law" (Rom. 10: 4).[5] The validity of the law as a divine way of salvation has finished since the resurrection of Jesus from the dead, which proves both His Messianic status and the inbreak of the last age. For "the law is binding on a person only during his life" (Rom. 7: 1). And to anyone with a knowledge of the law, this fact implies, if he is of Jewish origin, the rabbinic interpretation: "As soon as a man is dead, he is free from the obligation of the commands" (Sabb. 30a; 151b; Nidda 61b; Pes. Rabb. 51b; Jer. Kilaim IX, 3). In fact, we have here a

---

[1] The expression of Joh. Weiss, *Das Urchristentum*, Göttingen, 1917, 329.

[2] The special studies of P. Blaeser, *Das Gesetz bei Paulus*, Münster, 1941, and Chr. Maurer, *Die Gesetzeslehre des Paulus*, Zollikon, 1941, suffer from this defect.

[3] Cf. W. D. Davies, *Torah in the Messianic Age*, Philadelphia, 1952.

[4] This calculation of the age of the world as 6,000 years, which is also found in IV Ezra 5: 55; Barn. 15: 4 and others, seems to be very old. Through Julius Sextus Africanus it was then taken over by the Byzantine chronographers. Cf. O. Linton, *Synopsis Historiae universalis*, Copenhagen, 1957, 109 ff.

[5] Even if we translated τέλος as aim or fulfilment, it would not essentially alter our interpretation.

current Jewish notion which goes back to Ps. 88: 5 (חפשי =
ἐλεύθερος) and which had been expounded by Rabbi Simon ben
Gamaliel (Sabb. 151b), who—unless a later Tannaite was meant—
was certainly known to Paul as the son of his personal teacher.

The inference which Paul draws from this principle is that the man
who is dead to this aeon has become free from the law (Rom. 7: 6),
νυνὶ δὲ κατηργήθημεν ἀπὸ τοῦ νόμου, and that in the world of the
future which has already begun with the resurrection of Jesus the
validity of the law has ceased. From the standpoint of rabbinic
thought this inference is obvious and is already drawn by the Amora
of the 4th generation, R. Joseph bar Hiyya. In Nidda 61b we read:
מצות בטלות לעתיד לבוא; a statement which must be older than its
communicator.[1] Whether Rabbi Joseph meant that in the future
aeon the whole practice of the law would cease, or whether—as
Bacher[2] in the context understands—he meant only the ceremonial law, the important point for us is that the Pauline inference
is at least represented in rabbinic Judaism. Philo also (*Vita Adam* I,
13; also *Vita Mosis* III, 22) and likewise apocalyptic writings imply
the cessation of the law in the Messianic kingdom.[3] A specially
widespread opinion in rabbinic literature is that in the Messianic era
the old Torah will cease together with the evil impulse, but that God
will give a new Torah through the Messiah. Later texts too in this
matter no doubt contain old traditions.[4] And this new law not only
plays a part in Matthew (5: 17–20)—it has also its place in Pauline

---

[1] Thus also J. Klausner, *Jesus von Nazareth, seine Zeit, sein Leben, seine Lehre*, Berlin, 1930,
376 (E.T. *Jesus of Nazareth: His Life, Times, and Teaching*); a special knowledge of the
material of tradition is ascribed to this Amora. Because of his deep knowledge of
Tannaitic doctrines he was called *sinay* (Berakh. 64a; Moed Qatan 12a), one who knows
Sinaitic teaching.

[2] *Agada der babylonischen Amoräer*, Frankfurt, 1913, p. 105, note 23.

[3] Cf. Schweitzer, *op. cit.*, 188: "Although late Jewish apocalypses do not in fact express
the idea that the law is of no further importance in the future kingdom, they are controlled
by the idea and act accordingly. Surprising as it may sound, they nowhere assert that
the law will operate in the Messianic kingdom, and never do they describe its life as that
of the perfect fulfilment of the law."

[4] The destruction of the evil impulse in the Messianic time—often inferred from
Ez. 11 : 19 and Joel 2 : 28—is a current rabbinic theme (cf. Volz, *Eschatologie, op. cit.*, 42, Ia).
Targum on Is. 12 : 3 and Othioth d. R. Aqiba (Beth ha-Midrash, ed. Jellinek III, 27):
The Eternal sits and examines a new Torah which He will bestow in the future through
the Messiah. Same point in Yalq. Shim. II, 296 on Is. 26 : 2, the source of which is
probably the *Otiyoth*; cf. Ginzberg in *MGWJ*, 1914, 165; Davies, *op. cit.*, 70 ff. In the
Midr. Lev. R. Par. 13 on 11, 1 R. Abba bar Kahana (Pal. Am. end 3rd cent.) interprets
Prov. 30: 5 thus: God spake: From me will go forth a new teaching, the renewal of the
law (*chiddush ha-tora*, cf. also Levy, *WB*, 11, 186). A short parallel in Pes. Rabb. ed.
Buber 188b. Behind lies the "Halakha" discussion of a forbidden method of slaughter.
The term *tora chadasha* is met with elsewhere, e.g., in the Yalqut on Is. 20: 2.

thought, for the νόμος Χριστοῦ of love (Gal. 6: 2) or the νόμος πίστεως (Rom. 3: 27) in fact mean nothing else. Wherever in the early catholic period there were attempts to formulate this *nova lex Christi*, the phrases of Paul were used.

Paul's teaching about the abolition of the law is, however, falsely understood if its "Halakha" basis is ignored. To this E. Benamozegh [1] first drew attention. My judgment is that Rom. 10: 4 is an absolutely exact inference from the standpoint of Jewish theological thought; but the rabbis did not share Paul's premiss that the Messianic age had begun with the death and resurrection of Jesus.

Moreover, pseudo-Messianic movements in later Jewish history made exactly the same "Halakha" presumption. It is reported of the followers of Sabbatai and the Frankists that believing the last age to have dawned with the coming of their Messiah, they declared the Mosaic law annulled. It is very instructive that sixteen centuries later the same circle of thought was traversed when it was attempted to explain the disaster which overtook the pseudo-Messiah, Sabbatai Sebi—this time not subjection to the cross, but apostasy—as an event necessary to salvation. [2] In both cases it is a question of pure aeon-theology. The Messianists do not turn against the law but reject simply the further validity of the law. We have here a purely Jewish problem of saving history, not a Hellenistic one—it is something indeed quite incomprehensible to the Greeks. [3]

Of course Paul added further pregnant reflections, retrospective considerations as to the purpose of the law and its whole meaning. Here too we can recognize common rabbinic presuppositions, although their amplification discloses the original thought of the apostle; his own personal argument with, and self-justification in face of, the law. If Paul's teaching about the law sounds so surprisingly new and non-Jewish, here again it is none the less a question of Jewish faith-ideas which have been differently and unjudaically combined and presented. As we already know, the perspective of this

[1] *Morale juive et morale chrétienne*, Leghorn, 1867, 62 ff.

[2] Abraham Miguel Cardozo, Abraham Perez in Salonika, and others taught that with the advent of the Messiah the validity of the old Torah would cease and a new Torah *de-Aziluth* (Torah of the higher world) would begin in which what was formerly forbidden would be allowed. The parallel is so striking from the point of view of the history of religion, because consequences necessary to thought are inferred from the same premisses. On these theses of Sabbatianism cf. G. Scholem, *Die jüdische Mystik in ihren Hauptzügen*, Zürich, 1957, 346–351, also Scholem's essay, "The Meaning of the Torah in Jewish Mysticism", *Diogenes*, 1956, Nr. 15, 76 ff.; cf. also H. J. Schoeps, *Philosemitismus im Barock*, Tübingen, 1952, 98 ff.

[3] Cf. L. Baeck, "The Faith of Paul", *JJSt*, III, 1952, 106 ff.

Jew who believed the Messiah to have come was quite different from that of his rabbinic contemporaries. And this is very largely true of Paul's teaching about the meaning and purpose of the law, as he developed it in a survey of the pre-Messianic time.

One of the disputed questions in the schools had been whether the Messiah would come in an age of perfected righteousness or of extreme sinfulness. Rabbi Jochanan bar Nappacha (Sanh. 98a; Pes. Rabb. 51b) said: "Messiah ben David will come only in a time whose men are either כולו זכאי, completely pious (acc. to Is. 60: 21) or כולו חייב, fully laden with guilt" (from Is. 59: 6). For Paul the question was decided in the latter sense: the Messiah has come and has not found an age of fully righteous men, hence the other opinion must have been the right one (כולו חייב).[1] This, however, brings Paul up against the difficult question as to how the law can have had a function when not only did it not make possible the coming of the Messiah, but the Messiah came in spite of the fact that the law was unable to limit sinfulness. Hence the law must have had another purpose, namely that of rendering sinfulness evident and piling up the measure of sins. Gal. 3: 19: "Why then the law? It was added because of transgressions till the offspring should come to whom the promise had been made". Rom. 5: 20: "Law came in, to increase the trespass." The intervention of the law took place between creation and redemption, centuries after the fall (Gal. 3: 17; Rom. 5: 13). Marcion, according to Origen's commentary on Rom. 5: 20, did not fail to notice the ambiguous παρεισῆλθεν.[2]

There are no Jewish parallels to this assessment of the law. G. Klein[3] pointed out that Rom. 5: 20 sounds like a paraphrase of Dan. 9: 24. The לחתם חטאות in the latter corresponds to the ἵνα πλεονάσῃ τὸ παράπτωμα in the former. Here too, as the infinitive construction shows, it is a question of completing the measure of transgressions; but this is not described as a function of the law. Such a role for the law is unknown to rabbinic Judaism. However, in Ez. 20: 25 we read of "statutes that were not good", and such radical deductions as Paul infers may have seemed to him not

---

[1] Cf. G. Klein, *Studien über Paulus*, Stockholm, 1918, 76 ff. It is supposed that this idea is older than Rabbi Jochanan bar Nappacha. The sabbatians in the 17th century had the same view. Cf. G. Scholem, *op. cit.*, 348: "From this epigram (sc. Sanh. 98a) many sabbatians inferred that since we cannot all be saints let us all be sinners." Paul never drew this conclusion, though it was drawn by his gnostic followers, like the Carpocratian Epiphanes.

[2] Cf. A. v. Harnack, *Der kirchengeschichtliche Ertrag der exegetischen Arbeiten des Origenes*, II, Leipzig, 1919, 69; Th. Zahn, *Der Brief des Paulus an die Römer*, Leipzig, 1925, 287.

[3] *Studien über Paulus*, 78.

unbiblical. There is no doubt that Judaism of the time is convinced of the general sinfulness of mankind; as also of the fact that what sinfulness is can be measured by the law and that through the law we can come to the knowledge of sin (Rom. 3: 20; 7: 7, etc.). Also the method of putting together texts which speak of sinfulness—in Rom. 3: 9-20 Paul quotes five verses from the Psalter and one from Isaiah—is in accordance with Haggada usage. Likewise apocalypses about the evils of the latter days were frequent,[1] especially immediately after 70; and Paul too in 2 Thess. 2: 3-12 gives such a one.

But the Pauline inference that the law, which could not prevent universal sinfulness, and on the basis of which no man could be justified by his works, is a law unto death (Rom. 8: 2-3; Gal. 3: 21) is one which no Jew could draw. He insists rather on the text: "For it is no trifle for you, but it is your life" (Deut. 32: 47). And Rabbi Aqiba added to the verse the comment so contrary to Paul: "When is it your life? When you concern yourselves about it" (Gen. R. Par. 1 on 1: 1). Or still more plainly in exposition of Lev. 18: 5 Rabbi Acha says likewise in the name of Rabbi Aqiba: "The commands were given only that man should live through them, not that man should die through them" (Tos. Sabb. 15, 17 par.). To the one who performs it the Torah is *sam hayyim* (a medicine of life); to the one who does it not, it is a *sam muth* (a poison), says Rabbi Joshua ben Levi: Yoma 72b.[2] Paul can prove the opposite inference not from the law itself, but only from faith in Jesus Christ, the Messiah who has come. The retrospective way of thought is the real axis of his argument. Not the meaning of scripture, but Christ is the *a priori* for his judgment of the law. The fact that what is to be proved is assumed by him, springs simply from his interpretation of the post-messianic situation. From the latter there stems the retrospective judgment that the law must have been παιδαγωγὸς ἡμῶν εἰς Χριστόν (Gal. 3: 24).

2. THE "CURSE" OF THE LAW

The only Judaic point of contact which exists for Paul and which he one-sidedly uses in Gal 3: 10-13 is the famous "curse" of the law with which the Torah threatens its transgressors (Lev. 26; Deut. 28).

[1] Such views of the miseries of the last time (*cheble shel mashiach*) and the accumulation of sins in the last days are given in Sanh. 97-98; cf. also the pre-Christian Book of Jubilees, ch. 23, 16-23.

[2] The rabbis too added more difficult conditions only when it was expected that the majority of the synagogue members could fulfil them. This is assured by Baba Bathra 40b.

Philo too (*De Exsecrationibus* 127 ff.) and all the Tannaim refer to it when they wish to describe—mostly in regard to the expected coming of the Messiah or the future world—the accumulation of sins characteristic of the time. But Paul uses the Deuteronomy text differently from the rabbis, who were able to conjoin the curse of the law with the blessing of it announced in the same chapter, and to do this in harmony with the spirit of scripture.[1] Paul's intention is to demonstrate the "unfulfillability" of the law as its intrinsic meaning; every man stands under the curse of the law because no man πᾶσιν τοῖς γεγραμμένοις ἐμμένει. Paul merely indicates this, because it is taken for granted by him. In this passage (Gal. 3: 10–13), as important as it is difficult for Paul's theory of the law, three sequences of thought are interwoven which, as original to the apostle, we must analyse more precisely, and in doing so we shall be able to expound essential components of Paul's doctrine of the law as springing from one point. Again it is the jerkiness of Paul's thought, the fact that thoughts occur to him in their stereotyped form and drive him from one circle of problems to another, which makes the understanding of him so difficult.

1. In the first place, the assertion is made as an implication of common experience (δῆλόν ἐστιν) that no man can be righteous before God on the basis of the law. "For all who rely on the works of the law are under a curse", as Deut. 27: 26 explains. The tacit underlying assumption is that in fact no man can fulfil the law. What Paul really means here may be seen from the LXX style of his quotation, for in the Hebrew text both πᾶς and πᾶσιν are missing.[2] From the discussion in Sota 37a (also Tos. Sota VIII) one can also see, however, that Paul understands Deut. 27: 26 in the light of rabbinic tradition.[3] His implied meaning, that no man can fulfil the law, is

---

[1] M. Loewy, "Die paulinische Lehre vom Gesetz", *MGWJ*, 1903, 418 ff., proposes to see in the argument of Sota 37b, which implies that the announcement of the blessing preceded that of the curse, an indirect polemic against Pauline exegesis. It should be said for the right understanding of the text that the threatened curse is applied to the failures enumerated in Deut. 27, but according to the Torah text there can be no question of a curse on those who are concerned with the works of the law. M. Noth with A. Alt comes to this conclusion (*Gedenkschrift für A. v. Bulmerincq*, Riga, 1938, 127 ff.) and points out that the LXX can only have understood the corpus of the twelve curses, whereas Paul speaks simply of the book of the law.

[2] When Oepke (*Theol. Handkomm. z. NT*, IX, 55) says that Paul changed slightly Deut. 27: 26 only formally but not in substance, he forgets that it is just this slight change which is in question.

[3] Further testimonies given in Samarit. Targum Lev. R. Par. 25, Jer. Sota 7, 21d, etc. The treatment of the text in Philo (*De Exsecr.* 127 ff.) is only a matter of generally held prophecy.

really intended to suggest the *whole* law in its 613 commands and prohibitions. It is for this reason that the curse of the law strikes every man, for—see Eccl. 7: 13—the complete observance of the law among men, i.e., among sinners, does not exist. Gal. 5: 3 confirms that he regards the fulfilment of the whole law (ὅλον τὸν νόμον ποιῆσαι) as the obligation, unrealizable in his opinion, which alone can free us from the curse of the law.

This question of the "fulfillability" of the Torah in the completeness of its commands and prohibitions does not stand entirely outside the scope of rabbinic thought. A wrestling with the same problem is seen from the behaviour reported of Gamaliel II (Sanh. 81a), who apparently considered even the 13 moral commands required in Ez. 18: 5 ff. as incapable of fulfilment: when Gamaliel came to the verse (Ez. 18: 9: he is righteous, he shall surely live) he wept and said: "Only he who follows all these commandments will live, but not he who fulfils only one of them." Of course, the contrary opinion of Rabbi Aqiba was aimed at weakening the radicalization of the law's requirement associated with Paul (ὅλος ὁ νόμος), because if such were really the case, no one in fact could live. Still more instructive is the well-known parallel text Makkoth 24a, where the same debate about the 613 requirements is the theme, Rabbi Gamaliel bursting into tears as obviously he read *kol* instead of *elleh*, while his opponents were concerned to concentrate the idea of right conduct not on the totality of the commands but on the individual command. If a man fulfils only one of the commands it is as if he had fulfilled them all (thus most plainly in the more recent parallels in Midr. Teh. 15, 7).

In any case it is sufficiently plain that the question of the "fulfillability" of ὅλος ὁ νόμος was seen as a problem even in rabbinic Judaism; only here there was no intention of a *reductio ad absurdum* of the law by the law, rather the "works of the law" as a basis for the conduct of life as a whole was regarded as the will of God. The blessing and the curse of Deut. 11: 26–28 was considered to lie within the free choice of the people according as the individual or the community fulfilled the divine requirement or not.

2. The assertion of Gal. 3: 10–11a that no one can be righteous before God through the law is proved by Paul—apart from the consideration of the intrinsic "unfulfillability" of the law—in vv. 11, 12 from the consideration that, according to the rules of Talmudic hermeneutics, the law cancels itself. Paul in fact uses the 13th *midda* (exegetical principle) of Rabbi Ishmael: שני כתובים המכחישין, i.e., if two verses are contradictory, one should find a third verse in

order to overcome the contradiction. Habakkuk 2: 4: "He who through faith is righteous shall live"[1] and Lev. 18: 5: "He who does them shall live by them" are in contradiction. Hence the question is whether works or faith yield the way to life. A Torah text and a prophetic text are here in contradiction. A further text from the Torah, which was previously quoted as a basis for the whole discussion, gives the solution, and in v. 14 is recapitulated in the word εὐλογία (the intercalated v. 13 merely continues the thought of v. 10; cf. under 3): "Abraham believed God and it was reckoned to him as righteousness." The following verses merely draw out the consequences of this solution, suggesting that the counting of faith as righteousness excludes the law (v. 18a, parall. Rom. 4: 14) as a factor, giving rise to the Messianic time, that Christ is the one seed in whom all the peoples of the earth are to be blessed as a reward for Abraham's faith-obedience. If we leave aside the problems connected with the word ἐλογίσθη,[2] then our conclusion is that the Pauline exegesis solves the contradiction brought forward for tendentious purposes by a one-sided emphasis on faith at the cost of the ἔργα τοῦ νόμου.[3]

3. Lastly, in this Galatian passage there is still a third train of thought, to be found in vv. 10 and 13, which are interrelated. For obviously v. 13, which is logically out of place here, is included by association with the similar LXX text. The word (ἐπι)κατάρατος of Deut. 27: 26 is used by the LXX also in Deut. 21: 23, where the ignominy of death by hanging on a tree is in question and the point is made that the body is not to hang overnight on the gallows, for: "a hanged man is accursed (ἐπικατάρατος) by God".[4] It is clear that previously Saul must have taken offence in this Jewish way at the

---

[1] In the form in which quoted by Paul, Hab. 2: 4 has been distorted in order to obtain the requisite opposition to Lev. 18: 3 necessary for proof from scripture. Cf. A. Schweitzer, *Die Mystik des Apostels Paulus*, Tübingen, 1930, 204: "The Hebrew text has 'the just will live by his faithfulness באמונתו'. LXX gives: 'Through my faith' (ἐκ πίστεως μου), but it understands πίστις not as faithfulness but as faith, and disconnects 'by faith' from the verb, and fuses it with 'the just' into a single idea. Thus it gets the meaning it requires: 'The one who is made just by his faith will live'." In *DSH*, 8, 1–3, faithfulness as a "teacher of righteousness" is connected with the verse. But here it is not faith which justifies but which implies the doing of the works of the law. Cf. also J. Daniélou, *Qumran und der Ursprung des Christentums*, Mainz, 1958, 132.

[2] Cf. the monograph by H. W. Heidland, *Die Anrechnung des Glaubens zur Gerechtigkeit*, Stuttgart, 1936.

[3] That Gen. 15: 6 may also be used as a proof of the opposite is shown by Jas. 2: 23.

[4] Most rabbinic exegetes understand *elohim* in *qillath elohim* as Gen. Obj., which quite changes the sense; e.g., Rashi: "For a man hanged is a cursing of God." Also R. Meir in Tos. Sanh. 9, 7. The Ebionites too according to Jerome *ad Gal. 3: 14* have this interpretation. Cf. H. J. Schoeps, *Theologie und Geschichte des Judenchristentums*, Tübingen, 1949, 76 ff.

manner of Jesus' death,[1] for which reason he cannot utter the word curse in connexion with the law without immediately thinking of the curse which the law specifically lays on him who suffers death by hanging on a tree. Hence the associations of the LXX key-word ἐπικατάρατος compel him to drop the train of new thought just begun, in order to give quite a new interpretation of Deut. 21: 23, intended to dispel the Jewish scandal at the mode of Jesus' death by crucifixion.

We are helped in recognizing the fact that a new interpretation is given here by the long-unnoticed observation of G. Klein,[2] that the *taluy* of Deut. 21: 23 has a dual significance and can mean both the "hanged" and the "elevated", as, in similar fashion, the evangelist John uses the verb ὑψοῦν (8: 28; 12: 32) to mean not only the elevation of Jesus but also the manner of His death.[3] If accordingly *taluy* were a title of dignity[4]—*taluy rosh*, meaning the head that is raised above all others (Tanch. ed. Buber Num. 1: 2), then only is light thrown on the quaint and characteristic exegesis of Deut. 21: 23 by the mysterious words γενόμενος ὑπὲρ ἡμῶν κατάρα and the use of that text precisely in this connexion.[5] The crucifixion of the Messiah was in truth His elevation, as was promised for Yahweh's servant in Is. 52: 13, and it took place in order to do away the curse of the law by the realization of that curse: "for He became a curse for us". The solution of the curse is its transformation into a blessing, as is also shown by the continuation in ἵνα, which, resuming an earlier train of thought, interprets and identifies the supposed κατάρα of the cross as the εὐλογία τοῦ 'Αβραάμ. But the crucifixion is also a proof of

---

[1] It may also be noted that the Tannaitic and Amoraic writings have never associated these verses of Deuteronomy with Jesus. But Christian sources attest the reference. Thus Jerome *ad Gal. 3: 13 ff.*: "Et nobis soleat a Judaeis pro infamia objici, quod Salvator noster et Dominus sub Dei fuerit maledicto" (*MPL*, 26, 387 ff.). Similarly Tertullian *Adv. Jud.*, X; Justin *Dial. c. Tr.* cap. 89, etc.

[2] *Studien über Paulus*, Stockholm, 1918, pp. 62–67, where there are many references to the use of the verbs *talah, rum, nasa* promiscuously.

[3] M. Güdemann, "Neutestamentliche Studien", *MGWJ*, 1893, 347, supposes also that the double meaning of ὑψοῦν goes back to the double meaning of *talah* in the style of a pun. Interesting also is Güdemann's reference to the parable reported in Pesiqta Rabbathi cap. 10, which is built up on the same pun. Cf. also in more recent literature the Comm. on John by Schlatter, Dodd, Bultmann, etc., as also G. Kittel in *ZNW*, 1936, 282 ff., suggesting that in northern Syria crucifixion was described as an "elevation". Important connexions are shown in the essay of G. Bertram, "Der religionsgeschichtliche Hintergrund des Begriffs der Erhöhung in der Septuaginta", *ZAW*, 1956, 107 ff.

[4] Cf. E. Schweizer, *Erniedrigung und Erhöhung bei Jesus und seinen Nachfolgern*, Zürich, 1955, 69.

[5] The gnostics proved other things by means of this exegesis and reference to Paul; cf. M. Werner, *op. cit.*, 190.

Jesus' Messianic status; for *taluy* connotes that the Crucified is also the Exalted, and this dual sense of *talah* echoes also in the ὑπερύψωσεν of Phil. 2: 9 when Paul in this famous text names Jesus as the exalted One, or, as we can now complete the thought, the One who was exalted through His crucifixion. By His crucifixion through which He became *Taluy rosh*, "Jesus is manifested as Messiah and as such is the end of the law."[1]

However violent this exegesis may appear—but Paul himself is violent enough—it seems to me true to the text, and more fitting to Paul the rabbinic exegete than the ingeniously contrived exegesis of Gal. 3: 13, which Zahn, Lietzmann, and others propose on the model of 2 Cor. 5: 21; especially as in our passage it is only a question of the crucifixion as destroying the force of the law, not of the crucifixion as expiatory. The latter implication belongs to quite a different circle of Paul's thought.

In the letter to the Galatians, Paul, taking as his starting-point the death of Jesus as a saving event, and surveying retrospectively the meaning of the law, concludes that it was a παιδαγωγὸς εἰς Χριστόν because scripture consigned all things to sin (3: 22a) in order that— when the time was fulfilled (4: 4)—through faith in Jesus Christ the promise should be fulfilled in those who believe (3: 22b). Christ is the end of the law because through the atoning efficacy of His blood He has satisfied the requirements of the law, and now by divine grace effects what the law could not: forgiveness of sins. As the One who fulfils the Torah, Christ is the τέλος νόμου, and in taking its place and assuming its functions He also takes over its predicates of honour and salvation. Hence the law culminates in Christ.[2]

This same chapter of the letter contains yet a further train of thought designed to lessen the importance of the law and to weaken the saving significance of the Jewish faith. Paul in fact contrasts (Gal. 3: 15–18) the law with the promise which at a prior stage of revelation had been given to Abraham, and therefore as an earlier disclosure stands nearer to the inmost will of God. This back reference, in discussing the law, to the covenant with Abraham which was more original, has an exact parallel in Jesus' reference in the question of divorce to the ordinance of creation as revealing a deeper and more original form of the will of God (Mk. 10: 1–12; Mt. 19:

[1] Klein, *op. cit.*, 67.
[2] Cf. C. A. Bugge, "Das Gesetz und Christus", *ZNW*, 1903, 105: "Christ maintains the law as a whole and in such a way that it undergoes a transformation. Thus sacrifice is merged in Christ. He is the very paschal Lamb, His sacrifice is that of the paschal Lamb, and yet the old has vanished; behold, all has become new."

1–9). This parallel, so far as I know, has not yet received the attention it deserves.[1] The promise to Abraham, who according to Gen. 12: 3; 17: 5; 22: 18 and in rabbinic interpretation is the father of all peoples, has been fulfilled "in Christ", i.e., the Messiah is the heir of Abraham.[2] Through Christ Abraham's blessing now penetrates the Gentile world (3: 14), which in v. 16 is deduced from the singular of Gen. 22: 18 (בזרעך), both in contradiction to the meaning of the word and to Biblical linguistic usage.[3] The law given 430 years after Abraham (LXX Ex. 12: 40 ff.)—the παρεισῆλθεν of Rom. 5: 20 is, moreover, an abbreviation of this Galatian exegesis—intervened between the promise and its fulfilment, "in a certain sense illegitimately (like the 'false brethren' of Gal. 2: 4), through a side door".[4] God's valid testament (διαθήκη) made in favour of Abraham and his seed cannot be undone later by the law.[5] If the inheritance becomes obtainable by the works of the law and no longer by the validity of the promise (3: 18), then in Paul's view the order of grace would be set aside in favour of the order of merit.[6] Since in this characteristic dialectical proof of the apostle, Abraham's inheritance rests on the strength of the promise, the title to that inheritance springs not ἐκ νόμου but ἐκ ἐπαγγελίας and Abraham received it ἐκ πίστεως. Conclusion: οἱ ἐκ πίστεως are the true υἱοὶ Ἀβραάμ. If we add to this line of argument Gal. 4: 21–23 it becomes quite plain that, for Paul, descent from Abraham κατὰ σάρκα is utterly to be derided,

[1] Cf. my study "Restitutio principii als kritisches Prinzip der nova lex Jesu", in AfZ, 271 ff., as also a different explanation in D. Daube, ZNW, 1957, 126.

[2] The Genesis promise was seldom understood Messianically in Jewish tradition; the usual idea is (e.g., Rabbi Eliezer in Yebamoth 63a) that Israel, or the physical posterity of Abraham, was to be a blessing to the nations.

[3] The singular זרע, seed, means posterity countless times in the OT. The plural occurs in the OT only once (1 Sam. 8: 15) and with the meaning "grain". In Gen. 22: 16 ff. the context makes it clear that the text is to be understood plurally. V. 17: "I will make your descendants as numerous as the stars of heaven." The exegesis is allegorical in the sense that it no longer takes into account the original meaning of the words and has overstepped the limits set to allegory in rabbinical hermeneutics (cf. above, p. 42). Nevertheless, there are counterparts in the midrash; cf. D. Daube, The NT and Rabbinic Judaism, London, 1956, 438 ff.; Ellis, op. cit., 70 ff.

[4] Expression of Johannes Weiss, Das Urchristentum, Göttingen, 1917, 426.

[5] That this whole parable, couched in rabbinical legal language, is lame because it makes God the testator and the promise to Abraham a juristic arrangement about an inheritance, has often been noticed. Of more interest is the question why Paul undertakes at all this abstruse attempt to justify the abrogation of the Mosaic law on the ground of the promise to Abraham, seeing that it is cancelled in Christ, according to his real belief, apart from any appeal to Abraham.

[6] Foerster in Kittel, WB, III, 783 (κληρονόμος) supposes that we have here a special polemic of Paul against a Jewish-Christian opinion (why not Jewish?) asserting that only the physical descendants of Abraham are heirs.

since the Jews insist on appealing to their descent from Abraham as a biological guarantee of their spiritual election.[1]

The final consequence of this curse of the law is for Paul the following: for the interim period up to its termination by the death of Christ, the law had regulative significance. Its interim character is seen in the fact that it was a merely provisional arrangement ("a transitory factor"—Böhlig). In order to support this Paul does not attempt to criticize the content of the law given on Sinai, but puts forward a theory as to its supposed origin, which leads him to the most reckless conclusions. He derives his "proof" from Jewish folklore, which indicates that the law was given not by God but by angels (Gal. 3: 19). This proof, as Werner (*op. cit.*, p. 201) says very aptly, is intended *in malam partem*, since the angels were obviously hostile to the Jewish people. The presence of angels at the event of the giving of the law[2] was a favourite bit of embroidery in rabbinic tradition, and was meant to enhance the glory of Sinai. But not even the fear of anthropomorphism,[3] usual at the time, could have induced a rabbi meditating on this decisive moment in Jewish history to interpose between the people and their God a mediating figure, and thus to affirm in all seriousness that the giving of the law was a work of angels.[4] The theory is not unknown elsewhere in the New Testament (Acts 7: 38, 53; Hebr. 2: 2). But the consequences as inferred by later writers in the spirit of Paul are monstrous. For Barnabas, the law of the *mila* rests on the ordinance of an ἄγγελος πονηρός. Simon Magus (Iren. *Adv. Haer.* I, 23, 3) later Cerinthus (Pseudo-Dionysius 59), Cerdo and most heinously of all Marcion[5] simply rank the law-giver God among the angels of Gal. 3: 19, who in 4: 2 appear as guardians and trustees. One of these law-giving angels was then, as is well known, identified by Marcion with Yahweh, the God of Israel, and reduced to the status of a demiurge.

But in this curious passage, Gal. 3: 19, Paul goes a step farther and seriously declares that no one other than Moses functioned as the

---

[1] This was obviously to be expressed also by the allegory of Isaac as the son of the free woman (Sarah) and Ishmael as the son of the maid servant (Hagar). Details in ch. 6, 1.

[2] Midr. Tch. 68, 18 and parall. asserts that 22,000 ministering angels descended on Sinai. LXX already translated קדש in Deut. 33: 2 by ἄγγελοι who came with God from Sinai; cf. L. Prijs, *op. cit.*, 45 ff. Josephus too (*Ant.* 15, 5, 3) knows this probably very old tradition.

[3] Cf. A. Marmorstein in *REJ*, 1927, 44 ff., and *Enc. Jud.*, VI, 644.

[4] Kittel too (*WB*, 1, 82) calls the thought "un-Jewish"; he notes the Christianization of the tradition.

[5] References in A. von Harnack, *Marcion*, Leipzig, 1924, 139–160

mediatory ($\mu\epsilon\sigma\iota\tau\eta\varsigma$) of the angels.[1] In the last analysis this means that the law springs not from God but from the angels.[2]

To sum up, we may conclude that this ancillary proof against the permanence of the law denies not merely its saving character, but in spite of Rom. 7: 12 even its revelational character. It is separated from gnosis in fact only by the mean concession $\mu\grave{\eta}$ $\gamma\acute{\epsilon}\nu o\iota\tau o$ of Rom. 3: 31. The whole thing is, of course, pure speculation, and shows not the slightest dependence on scripture or reminiscence of rabbinical opinions. It is clear that in the heat of the contest Paul had allowed himself to be driven to make assertions which on calmer reflection he could hardly have maintained seriously, if only not to run the risk of ridicule. In any case the rabbis met this attack also, which in Christian writings quickly found followers, by developing their own legendary traditions.[3] More important, however, is the fact that in Berakh. 25b (given by Rabbi Abbaye, Am. of the 3rd generation) we find the clear explanation that God did not give the Torah for the sake of ministering angels.

3. THE LAW AND SIN

If from the analysis of Gal. 3 we have inferred essential aspects in the Pauline theory about the law, which are more or less dependent on the apostle's judgment of the eschatological situation, we must now examine more closely doctrinal elements in the letter to the Romans. The first impression that might arise on the comparison of

[1] On the mediatorial role of Moses, often mentioned in later writings, cf. G. Klein, *Schem ha-mephorasch*, Stockholm, 1902, ch.: "Moses en Förebild till Messias", which however reads into the texts more than they contain. In any case it must be noted that the mediatorial idea is quite foreign to pre-Pauline Judaism. Neither scripture nor the LXX (for the opposite cf. LXX Is. 63: 9) know it; they have not even a corresponding technical term (Kittel, *WB*, IV, 605). The later סרסור comes from the language of trade and denotes the agent or broker, also the interpreter, but is far removed from any Christological use such as occurs in 1 Tim. 2: 5. It is interesting that Delitzsch suggests that Gal. 3: 19 should be translated back by סרסור and 1 Tim. 2: 5 by העמר. Irenaeus and other Fathers finally replaced Moses as mediator by Christ, whom Paul did not yet describe as $\mu\epsilon\sigma\iota\tau\eta\varsigma$.

[2] Cf. *Komm.* Lietzmann, and Oepke in Kittel, *WB*, IV, 622. In 2 Cor. 3: 5 ff. Moses as $\mu\epsilon\sigma\iota\tau\eta\varsigma$ is fantastically supposed to have realized the transience of the law and to have worn a veil over his countenance, because the $\delta\acute{o}\xi\alpha$ reflected in it was passing and the children of Israel were not to notice the disappearance of the splendour. Most recently a peculiar interpretation of this text has been given by S. Schulz ("Die Decke des Moses", *ZNW*, 1958, H. 1/2) suggesting that Paul was here attacking a Jewish-Christian tradition.

[3] According to Sabb. 88a (Joshua ben Levi), Pes. Rabb. 97a, Tanch. 51 (ed. Buber) the angels are opposed when God proposes to give the Torah to Israel through Moses. Marmorstein (*Expositor*, 1919, 103) saw here, I think rightly, an opposition to the Christian formation of legends.

these two letters, namely that Galatians is more antinomistic and Romans more concerned with the legal standpoint, is wrong. This impression is obviously connected with the different situations of those to whom the letters were addressed; situations which Paul tries to examine in detail. In Galatians Paul had to do with Judaizers who wished to reintroduce the law, whereas in Romans the greater danger sprang from a moderate antinomism which he had to resist.

As regards the question of the law, the most interesting point lies in ch. 7, which on account of a certain anthropocentric tendency has often been regarded as autobiographical. W. G. Kümmel in particular has shown the baselessness of psychological interpretations. Ch. 7 is not autobiographical, nor even rhetorical, but is to be understood symbolically as a description of the life of all Jews, including that of Saul, just as ch. 8 describes symbolically the life of all Christians, including that of Paul ἐν πνεύματι. Hence ch. 7, as Kümmel, Bultmann, Bornkamm, Dahl, and others have pointed out, represents in the first-person form a phenomenological account of Adamic man under the law, judged from the standpoint of Christian experience. Ambrosiaster called the "I" of Rom. 7 a *causa generalis*. Beyond this the chapter is intended to describe the crisis of the legalistic attitude as experienced subjectively by Paul. Thus here the abrogation of the law is developed not from an eschatological basis but from the experience of sin. In his argument Paul goes far beyond the preaching of Jesus and the synoptic tradition, but has many rabbinic parallels.

We have already had occasion to emphasize the close connexion between the law and sin. But Paul's opinion is not only that the law incites to sin and renders guilty, thus increasing sins; he also sees the relation conversely, and shows that sin, awakened by the law (7: 8) proves the law's "unfulfillability". This not only cut the ground from beneath Jewish legal righteousness but also just as much from beneath the systems of ancient philosophy which embodied the principle that the good can be taught. The meaning of Rom. 7 is as follows: spirit and flesh, will and ability, the law of God and the law of sin, are locked in an unceasing conflict in the heart of man. The struggle, which Paul depicts in semi-mythological terms, is carried on with unequal resources, because the law of God brings into operation only man's will, whereas actual conduct is determined by the law of sin, i.e., by the fleshly nature of man (7: 14–23). This description, behind which lies a conception of sin as a daemonic power which, as it were, has taken control of man, must be regarded as a striking

contribution to the rabbinic doctrine of the struggle of the יצר הרע
with the יצר טב, which obviously was a favourite theme of discussion in the age of Paul.

The usual rabbinic teaching insists on an equipoise of both impulses and claims that it lies in man's free will to decide which of the two he will follow.[1] With Rabbi Aqiba most teachers expound the idea of the absolute freedom of the human will (Aboth 3: 15) and teach that by the practice of the law man can free himself from sin (e.g., Qiddushin 81a). Man's inherent tendency to sin, which was implanted in him at birth with the *yeser hara*, is compensated by the Torah, which was adapted to the whole will and nature of man. There are, however, pessimistic opinions which register a predominance of the evil impulse. Thus in the Tannaite R. Eliezer ben Hyrcanus, who lived at the close of the 1st century, hence not much later than Paul, we have a rabbinic exponent of the Pauline doctrine of the general sinfulness of mankind. In Sanh. 101a it is reported that Rabbi Eliezer emphasized to his pupils his favourite text, which was always on his lips, Eccl. 7: 20: "Surely there is not a righteous man on earth who does good and never sins." In Arakhin 17a he expressly declares that even the patriarchs would not have been able to stand before strict justice, which, moreover, Justin also (*Dial.* 95) gives as a Jewish opinion. And from a somewhat obscure report about a "minim" controversy in which Rabbi Eliezer was involved may be recognized his opinion which as דברי של מינות was perhaps taken from Jesus, to the effect that its sinful origin adheres to the object and what springs from the unclean never loses its uncleanness[2] (cf. Tos. Hullin, 2: 24; Aboda Zara 17a varied in Midr. Eccl. 10: 8).

Other voices are raised which go farther and understand the *jeser hara* as an independently effective cosmic power, not merely as an impulse to evil but as an evil impulse conceived on almost daemonological lines, almost as an alien god dwelling in the body of man. Quite in Paul's style, the picture is drawn of man lusting for what the law forbids (Jer. Yoma 6: 4) and the lustfulness is daily renewed and

---

[1] The most important references are collected in Billerbeck, Vol. IV, on the good and evil impulses; treatment of the theme by I. Freundörfer, *Erbsünde und Erbtod beim Apostel Paulus*, Münster, 1927, ch. 1; Chr. Maurer, *op. cit.*, 36 ff.

[2] Other texts imply that the creation was corrupted by the fall and that things, perfectly created, became defective (Gen. Rabba 12, ch. 2: 4). Further cf. Moed Qatan 15b: Bar Qappara taught: My image I gave to them but by their sin they have distorted it. The restoration of things to their primal state is awaited from the Messiah (Gen. Rabba 12— Rabbi Berechiah in the name of Rabbi Samuel).

daily nourished (Sukka 52a). If the evil impulse was initially only a guest in the habitation of a human life, later it gains mastery as the בעל הבית, master of the house (Gen. Rabba Par. 22 on 4: 7). From this it is only a step to regarding the evil impulse as innate. In this connexion we adduce that the Midrash Rabba Par. 34: 10 on Gen. 8: 21 מנעריו (from his youth) explains with regard to the origin of the evil impulse: "as soon as man leaves his mother's womb". The Rabbi says even that the *yeser hara* arises before birth in man. Further, it is stressed that the good impulse is only born in man after the evil has gained control (M. Teh. 9: 2); the latter is in man as soon as he is taken from the womb (*ibid.*), the former is added only when he attains the age of thirteen years (M. Eccl. 9: 14–15; similarly 4: 14).[1] This implies that the *yeser hara* is more powerful than the *yeser ha-tob*, that it will always conquer all good impulses in any critical situation. Such meditations come very near to Pauline ideas.

The position is similar with regard to apocalyptic writings such as IV Ezra, the testimony of which is important for the New Testament period and often as typical as the expressions of rabbinic literature. In their judgment on the corruption of mankind, including the Jews, the apocalyptists often go quite as far as Paul in that they note man's inability to keep the law "on account of the law of sin in his members". In this respect we need only read IV Ezra 3: 19–21 (ed. Violet *Visio* I: 4–6): "Thou gavest to the seed of Jacob the law and to the people of Israel the commands, but Thou didst not take from them the evil heart that Thy instruction might bear fruit. For since he bore in himself an evil heart, Adam transgressed, and was overcome and likewise all who descended from him. A lasting sickness arose in the heart of the people, an ulcerating sore ($\nu\acute{o}\mu os$—a distortion of $\nu o\mu\acute{\eta}$ reading of Perle) together with the evil impulse. The good disappeared and the evil remained." In IV Ezra 9: 36–37 (*Visio* IV: 9–10) can be seen a clear parallel to Rom. 7: 14 ff.: "We who have received the law, perish as sinners together with our heart which heard that law; Thy law however does not pass away, its glory abides." Paul too believes firmly in the holiness and the spiritual character of the law (Rom. 7: 12 and 14); it is only man who perishes through the sinfulness which the law has disclosed.

All these voices which always express the same truth, often very movingly—prayer texts coming at least from the 2nd century (cf.

[1] Cf. also Jerome on Eccl. 4: 13; also now R. Mach, *Der Zaddik im Talmud und Midrasch*, Leiden, 1957, 26 ff.

Yoma 87b) should be added[1]—allow it to be clearly enough recognized that Paul's doctrine of sin was not unusual but indeed typical of his time. This is confirmed likewise by the Qumran literature, in particular the psalms.[2] More problematic are only the special turns which Paul has given to this doctrine of sin, and the consequences drawn from it.

Thus the peculiarity of Paul's idea of sin has often been seen in the identification of σάρξ (as contrasted with πνεῦμα) with ἁμαρτία, and in this regard he falls decisively outside the framework of rabbinic thought.[3] But this opinion cannot be accepted without further question. According to a doctrine of Rabbi Ishmael, the body of man springs from a place that is sinful (Lev. Rabba Par. 4 chapter 4, 1). Or take the explanation of the Midrash Num. Rabba Par. 13 chapter 7, 12 on Gen. 8: 21: "Woe to the dough of which the baker himself says that it is bad" (Doubl. Pes. R. Kah. IX, 157 ff.; R. Hiyya in Midr. Teh. 103: 14; Gen. Rabba Par. 34, 8: 21). And the opinion of Rabbi Alexandrai (Am. 2nd gen.) given in Berakhoth 17a is concerned with nothing else than the conflict between the will and the power to perform which is occasioned by the sinful flesh: "Lord of the worlds, it is open and known to Thee that it is our will to do Thy will, and that we are prevented from doing so by nothing other than the leaven in the dough" (i.e., the evil impulse in man's body). It is, however, typical of Jewish piety that Rabbi Alexandrai continues: "May it be Thy pleasure that we return to fulfil the commands of Thy will with all our hearts." Paul, on the other hand, is concerned to abide by the conflict he has observed and to understand it not as an exception but as the rule and norm (Rom. 7: 21: εὑρίσκω ἄρα τὸν νόμον) in order to show conclusively the powerlessness of the law. For any other solution apart from faith in Jesus Christ he excludes from the start.

Here in fact we come upon a real opposition, because the Pauline doctrine must be deemed erroneous from the standpoint of Biblical theology. Judaism has always held fast to the tenet that man was

---

[1] Cf. Montefiore, *Rabbinic Judaism* etc., 185.

[2] Cf. J. Hyatt, "The View of Man in the Qumran Hodayot", *NT Studies*, 1955–56, 276 ff.; I. Licht, "The Doctrine of the Thanksgiving Scrolls", *Isr. Explor. Journ.*, 1956, 1 ff., 89 ff.

[3] Thus Lietzmann, *Komm. zu Röm.*, 1933, 75; Volz, *op. cit.*, 87 (25, 6b); Bousset–Gressmann, *op. cit.*, 404 ff., think even that Paul is here introducing to Christianity a "strictly Hellenistic outlook"; similarly G. F. Moore, I, 485. The idea is not OT; cf. L. Koehler, *Theologie des AT*, 122. But the Qumran texts seem to know it, as K. G. Kuhn, *ZThK*, 1952, 217 ff., points out. Most recently on this cf. E. Schweizer, "Die hellenistische Komponente im ntl. σάρξ-Begriff", *ZNW*, 1957, 227 ff.

created to do the will of God, as it is presented in the Torah (Rabbi Jochanan b. Zakkai in Pirqe Aboth 2, 9). The right fulfilment of the law, of course, always implies the creaturely situation of the fear of God (יראת יי), which the doing of the law ever renews.[1] But Paul does not seem to know this idea of the fear of God; the terms θεοσέβεια and εὐσέβεια, which are but a pale Greek equivalent, are completely lacking in Paul. Without reference to such ideas Paul has simply understood the law as a sum of prescriptions and has played off the fact of sin as offence against the commands. But the power of sin was never able to dissipate the faith of the Jewish teachers in the "fulfillability" of the law. Paul, however, arrived at the fundamental conviction that man is basically incapable of doing the will of God. We see here a singular maiming of the will—even of the will to recognition—in the apostle, who apparently does not know the power which resides in תשובה, which according to Jewish belief of all ages is able to break the mastery of sin.[2] That the somewhat analogous idea of μετάνοια in Greek plays hardly any part in the thought of the apostle has often struck New Testament critics.[3] Unlike Jesus and the prophets, Paul did not summon to repentance; he set little value on man's freedom of decision and discounted the fact that he is able to turn again to God. The reason for this is simply that μετάνοια by its relation to the death and resurrection of Jesus was wholly subsumed in πίστις. The advent of the Messiah signified the great revolution of all things; faith in Him made the conversion of the individual soul unnecessary.

However, the view expounded by Paul in Rom. 5: 12 ff. remains wholly within the framework of Jewish theology. The text does not teach a doctrine of inherited sin in the dogmatic church sense. To read such into it, we should have to translate ἐφ' ᾧ by in quo with Ambrosiaster and Augustine, whereas according to normal linguistic use the former can only have the meaning of ἐπὶ τούτῳ.[4] The text

---

[1] I gave references in "Religionsphänomenologische Untersuchungen zur Glaubensgestalt des Judentums", ZRGG, II, 1949, 293 ff. Further below in ch. 7.

[2] Rabbinic references for the meaning of conversion in Jewish writings in my Grundlehren des jüdischen Glaubens (to appear shortly).

[3] Cf. J. Behm in Kittel, WB, IV, 1000; R. Bultmann, Christus des Gesetzes Ende, Munich, 1940, 6.

[4] Thus Zahn, G. P. Wetter, Der Vergeltungsgedanke bei Paulus, Göttingen, 1912, 68, and others. The Greek exegesis of Rom. 5: 12 ff. accepted the idea of inherited sin only from Didymus Alex., while Latin theology assumed it earlier. Cf. J. Freundörfer, op. cit., 129 ff.; K. H. Schelkle, op. cit., 173 ff.; and esp. S. Lyonnet, "Le sens de ἐφ' ᾧ in Rom. 5: 12 et l'exégèse des Pères Grecs", Biblica, 1955, 436 ff., as also A. M. Dubarle, Le péché original dans l'écriture, Paris, 1958, 121 ff.

expresses no more than the fact communicated in Gen. 2: 17 and 3: 19, namely that Adam's sin was punished by death—a statement which Paul accepts with the comment that death is the wages of sin (Rom. 6: 23).

In rabbinical writings the reason why every man must die is often deduced from the disobedience and punishment of the first man, and the consequent fate, overhanging all, of inherited death.[1] It is a mistake to suppose that such opinions are only to be found in apocryphal or apocalyptic writings.[2] The "Halakha" midrashim also contain reflections about the inheritance of death as the consequence of Adam's transgression. Let us quote here a reflection on the death of Moses attributed to Rabbi Levi (*circa* 300) (Deut. Rabba 9: 4; in abbreviated form also Midr. Eccl. 7: 13): "Moses spake thus to God: 'Lord of the world! There are 36 sins punishable by being cut off from the land of the living. If a man commits any one of them, he renders himself guilty of death. Have I perhaps offended thus? Why dost Thou threaten me with death?' God answered him: 'Thou must die because of the sin of the first man, who brought death into the world.'" The same point of view is expressed earlier also, thus by Rabbi Meir *circa* 130 (Erubim 18b) and Rabbi Jose *circa* 160 (Sifre 5: 17). The Tannaite Rabbi Yehuda ben Ilai, who belongs to the same period, interprets Deut. 32: 32 by the comment: "You are the children of the first man through whose fault you are punished with death. Death was appointed the destiny of his descendants until the end of all generations" (Sifre Deut. 323).[3]

Alongside this there is another view which bases the justification of death on actual misdeeds committed, according to Eccl. 7: 20, by every man. This view is connected with the declaration of the Palestinian Amora Rabbi Ammi: אין מיתה בלא חטא (no death without sin—Sabb. 55a; Lev. Rabba 37: 1; beginning of Eccl. Rabba). Rom. 5: 12–19 shows clearly that both these rabbinic views were well known to Paul and that he accepted them both—the doctrine of inherited death (v. 14) as also the idea that death was the punishment of actual sins committed by the individual man (v. 12b).[4]

[1] Cf. Billerbeck, III, 227 ff.; A. Marmorstein, "Paulus und die Rabbinen", *ZNW*, 1931, 271 ff.; G. Bornkamm, *Das Ende des Gesetzes*, Munich, 1952, 83 ff.

[2] IV Ezra is full of them, especially plainly in 7: 118; cf. also Syr. Baruch 54, 15, 19, etc.

[3] The question of individuals who were righteous being free from sin is thus left open, and in the case of Moses it was often asserted that he was. One Baraita (Sabb. 55b; Baba Bathra 17a) names four persons: Benjamin, Amram, Jesse, and Chileab who through the wiles of the serpent had to die, though innocently.

[4] In Syr. Baruch 54, 15 we have the same association, suggesting Jewish reflection on the problem of death.

As far as the antithesis Adam-Christ is concerned, this again is a well-known Messianological motive. Paul uses it chiefly for the purpose of showing how the death of Jesus, which certainly may not be explained by the principle of Rabbi Ammi, because of His sinlessness, breaks the chain which binds humanity to Adam the father of sin. His self-sacrificial death, the death of a guiltless man, is able in the view of Paul to expiate human sin; the failure of the law of Moses could thus be compensated and wiped out by πίστις Χριστοῦ. The idea that the future Redeemer as the ideal Adam expiates by his death the sins of the *bene Adam*, was expounded in rabbinic writings. The antitheses of Adam and Messiah, of sin and redemption, were so widespread[1] in fact that, by his insistence on the typological relation Adam–Christ, we may suppose Paul to have been appealing to his Jewish hearers through the presentation of his message in commonly accepted terms.[2] Moreover, the Ebionites gave a contrary answer, for they considered Adam not as a sinner but as the προφήτης ἀληθής, who possessed the Holy Spirit (Clementina, Hom. 1, 18–20; 2, 6–12; 3, 17–20, etc.). Perhaps the truth is that in this respect also they wished to attack Paul, by glorifying the first Adam whom Paul had discredited.

In our argument it is important to note that the customary Jewish opinions about the supremacy of the inclination to sin were represented not only by apocalyptic, as research since Bousset has commonly supposed, but also and equally by the rabbis. In his exposition of such opinions in Rom. 5 and 7—from a different angle in Rom. 1 : 19–32—the essential aim is to bring out the madness of mankind so that the redemption wrought by the Messiah may shine the more brightly against this dark background. But again and again the Jewish problem crops up tormentingly as to what can be or can have been the meaning of the law against this fact of universal sin. We have already in part learned the answer of Paul. In Rom. 5: 20

---

[1] Cf. the demonstration from texts in B. Murmelstein, "Adam, ein Beitrag zur Messiaslehre", *WZKM*, 1928, 242 ff., and 1929, 51 ff.

[2] The parallel passage 1 Cor. 15: 45–49 offers another train of thought, namely that Christ is a person of universal significance and like Adam is the ancestor of a new, second stream of humanity, taking its rise from His resurrection. On this cf. Schweitzer, *op. cit.*, 165, and J. Daniélou, *Théologie du Judéo-Christianisme*, Tournai, 1958, 355, who sees here a continuation of the Adam tradition of Enoch (48, 3). Striking also is the speculation, discussed in the midrash Gen. Rabba Par. 8 on 1: 27 (Amoraic in origin) as to whether Adam was created in the likeness of the עליונים (upper beings) or of the תחתנים (lower beings). Paul decides that Adam stems from the תחתנים, the Messiah from the עליונים, since he says: ὁ πρῶτος ἄνθρωπος ἐκ γῆς χοϊκός, ὁ δεύτερος ἄνθρωπος ἐξ οὐρανοῦ (1 Cor. 15: 47).

the law which was powerless to alter the situation created by Adam's fall, powerless to check or divert the flow of evil consequences, had no other function than that of increasing the mastery over human life which sin had attained. Hence even in the Letter to the Ephesians the law can be described as a hostile thing ($\check{\epsilon}\chi\theta\rho\alpha$, 2 : 14) and especially as regards the plurality of its $\dot{\epsilon}\nu\tauo\lambda\alpha\acute{\iota}$ and $\delta\acute{o}\gamma\mu\alpha\tau\alpha$.

In the train of thought in Rom. 7: 7 ff. sin is further defined as the object of a recognition which the law has brought about.[1] The anthropocentric orientation of the idea of sin, noticeable here, is already marked in the LXX and seems to have been a special characteristic of Judaic Hellenism. In any event the awareness of sin as $\dot{\epsilon}\pi\iota\theta\upsilon\mu\acute{\iota}\alpha$, in the light of לא תחמוד, the 10th commandment, which even the rabbis regarded as an important criterion of the fulfilling of the law,[2] is described by Paul from a psychological angle as the special effect of the law. We are here faced by a Pauline passage of thought which many commentators regard as devious, for the apostle, in seeking to clarify the "Halakha" presuppositions of the idea חשב $= \lambda o\gamma\acute{\iota}\zeta\epsilon\sigma\theta\alpha\iota$, asserts that sin is recognized as sin only through the law, and that as "dead sin" ($\dot{\alpha}\mu\alpha\rho\tau\acute{\iota}\alpha$ $\nu\epsilon\kappa\rho\acute{\alpha}$, i.e., $\chi\omega\rho\grave{\iota}s$ $\nuo\mu\omicron\upsilon$) it cannot be imputed to man. Cf. 5: 13: "Sin is not counted where there is no law." This in fact corresponds to the rabbinic distinction between conscious and unconscious sin (ביד רמה— בשגגה), an idea which lies behind Num. 15: 29–30 and Lev. 4: 2, 13 ff. Paul is thinking in these categories when he speaks of a "dead sin" which is awakened to life through the law. When Paul continues: "the very commandment which promised life proved to be death to me" (7: 10) there may be adduced a curious rabbinic parallel to this lament. In Pes. Rabb. 107a, in association with Jer. 20: 7, Israel addresses God as follows: "Lord of the world, Thou hast too much exhorted me, until with the divine law a yoke of decrees has been placed around my neck, through which I have become guilty. Had I not received the law, I would have been as one of the heathen nations for whom there is neither recompense nor punishment." As the text continues we find that the reproach of "over-persuasion" and "stupefaction" laid at the door of God is

---

[1] On the anthropological problems here arising see, apart from the basic work of W. G. Kümmel and the essay of Bultmann, "Römer 7 und die Anthropologie des Paulus", *Festschrift für G. Krüger*, Giessen, 1932, the work of G. Bornkamm, *Das Ende des Gesetzes*, Munich, 1952, 51 ff., and D. Stacey, *The Pauline View of Man*, London, 1956.

[2] Cf. the statement of the Amora (4th century) Rabbi Jakum in exegesis of Jer. 3: 9: whoever fails to keep the last commandment, לא תחמוד, is to be considered as failing in all ten commandments (Pesiqta Rabbathi 21–107a).

grounded in the consideration that in the case of the ten commandments transgression is not punishable with death, whereas in regard
to various other points of the Torah it is, examples being quoted.[1]

The whole train of thought in Rom. 7 is summed up in the introductory sentences: "Do you not know, brethren, that the law is
binding on a person only during his life?" And v. 4: "Likewise, my
brethren, you have died to the law through the body of Christ. . . ."
To this there is a still more clearly formulated parallel in Gal. 2: 19
ff.: "For I through the law died to the law, that I might live to God.
I have been crucified with Christ, it is no longer I who live but Christ
who lives in me . . ." etc. Clearly behind both texts there lies the
"Halakha" already discussed, namely that the obligation of the law
ceases as soon as death supervenes. Paul means that in accordance
with this "Halakha", valid for all men, the Messiah in His death has
died to the law and is no longer subject to the obligations of the law.
Through the Messiah's resurrection, this has a practical meaning for
all those who through faith and baptism (Rom. 6: 3) have shared
His death and entered with Him into the new age. Thus all Christians are freed from the law.

All this is further illustrated by Paul in a comparison drawn from
the Talmudic law of marriage. Since the husband (the law) has
died, the wife (Christ) can no longer be called an adulteress if she
is united with another partner. The Christian has been united to
another, "to him who has been raised from the dead" (Rom. 7: 4).
This means ἐγὼ γὰρ διὰ νόμου νόμῳ ἀπέθανον and corresponds in
fact—naturally not in the Pauline parable—to the definitions of the
Mishna Qiddushin 1: 1 (explained in Qidd. 13b) to the effect that
death, as far as legal obligations are concerned, is comparable with
divorce.[2] The tendency of this example is strongly reminiscent of
doctrines which Paul's teacher has bequeathed, and which no doubt
Paul once made his own. For both Gamaliel I and his son Simon
left behind them teachings aimed at facilitating re-marriage (M.
Yebamoth, XVI, 7, also M. Gittin IV, 2–3, in regard to the con-
veyance of letters of divorce).

In any event as regards this question of the law and death, the
Pauline νυνὶ δὲ κατηργήθημεν ἀπὸ τοῦ νόμου of Rom. 7: 6 is very
close to the בטל מן מצות of Rabbi Simon ben Gamaliel (Sabb.

---

[1] Since the Yalqut of Jer. 20: 7 takes this text in somewhat abbreviated form, it is hardly
possible that there is any Christian interpolation: cf. Loewy, *op. cit.*, 536.

[2] It is possible that in the tale of Imma Shalom and the "philosopher" in Sabb. 116b
there lies an answer to this Pauline doctrine. Since, however, the text appears to be
mangled, the sense is not clear.

151b).[1] But the latter understands the principle that death frees us from the law in a different way from the sense in which it is applied by Paul. The Pauline inference is, of course, completely unrabbinical, and is argued in the light of his idea that the Christian man has with Christ died to the law and thus has become freed from it (Rom. 7: 6). It is also illuminated by his view already discussed that the law fails in face of sin, with the result that the διὰ νόμου of Gal. 2: 19 receives a dual meaning, suggesting also that with death obligations towards the law have ceased. The conclusion then is: whoever after the coming of Christ pleads the validity of the law, denies the saving significance of the death of Jesus Christ and nullifies God's grace (Gal. 2: 21; 5: 24). He has not understood the nature of the new age that has dawned (4: 8–11).[2]

4. FURTHER JEWISH COUNTER-POSITIONS

We have now studied the whole complex of thought which was developed from the introductory principle of our discussion—"Christ is the end of the law". Although we have tried to mention from time to time the Jewish counter-positions, we now propose to investigate further Jewish reactions to Paul's abrogation of the law, and to amplify them by the method of confrontation.

As we have already seen, for each link in the Pauline argument a Jewish counterpart can be indicated. The sole difference is that each inference deduced from the premisses proved unacceptable from a Jewish point of view; the power and prevalence of sin was very well known, but Jewish theologians constantly adhered to the admonition: "Sin is couching at the door; its desire is for you, but you must master it" (Gen. 4: 7). The problematic character of a complete fulfilment of the law was well enough realized, but the Jews have never despaired about the "fulfillability" of the law, and have never allowed its sacred character to be violated. Rather against antinomists of the type of Paul or even of a Rabbi Eliezer ben Abuya, the Mishna Sanhedrin XI, 1 expounded by Rabbi Eliezer of Modaim has been insisted on: "Whoever violates the sacrosanct, desecrates the feasts, whoever openly makes his neighbour's face turn pale, whoever undermines the covenant of our father Abraham, or falsely

[1] Cf. M. Loewy, op. cit., 342 ff.

[2] Exactly the same view was developed by the Sabbatian theologian, Abraham Perez (1668) in the tractate *Magen Abraham*, which suggested that in the redeeming Messianic age, i.e., then in the kingdom of Sabbatai Sebi, every one would become a sinner who should still keep the law in the rabbinic sense. Cf. Scholem, op. cit., 342 ff.

interprets the law, has no lot or part in the future world, even though he were a master in the knowledge of the law and had good deeds to his credit." For those who are "antinomists" on principle and despisers of the law of whatever kind are in fact to "uproot what for Israel is a hedge against sin" (Jer. Berakhoth 6a). Or as Tos. Hullin 2, 22 (Parall. Jer. Aboda Zara 2, 40b; B. Aboda Zara 27b; Eccl. Rabba 1, 8) in the name of Rabbi Ishmael communicates: "Retribution comes at last to every one who pulls down the walls of the wise; for it is written: 'A serpent will bite him who breaks through a wall'" (Eccl. 10: 8).[1]

If it be true that Paul appears in the Talmud under the name Gehazi (Sanh. 107b; Sota 47a) as Travers Herford and H. J. Schonfield thought, then the Jewish opinion of Paul would be that formulated by Rabbi Jochanan about the faithless servant of the prophet Elisha, namely that he was incapable of repentance, after not only sinning himself but also deliberately misguiding others into sin. A suspicion of anti-Pauline polemic also clings to the text—Ruth Rabba 3—who "made himself peculiar in regard to circumcision and the law" (exegesis of Prov. 21: 8).[2] The Book of Ruth and probably also the midrash on the book were read and studied at the feast of revelation.

And now we come to the last and most radical difference which emerges with regard to the aim of the law. Paul had framed the question in such a way that the answer, which he had ready *a priori*, was implied in the question. For this end he declared that a partial function of the law, which the rabbis used occasionally for homiletic purposes, was the very essence of the law. Thus he affirmed, on the one hand, that the law was intended to make manifest and increase sins, on the other, that it was intended to justify man and was unable to do so. This was already known to IV Ezra (9: 36 ff.). But if this is intended as an essential answer by a Jew—even a sometime Jew— it is an impossibility. Every child of the Jews, whether the Diaspora or the Judaism of Palestine is in question, knows that the law had no other purpose than that of being given by God in order to be kept and not transgressed, in order to increase resistance to sin and not

---

[1] It is clear from the context (*Halakha contra Minim*) that it is here a question of an anti-Christian polemic. Cf. A. Schlatter, *Die Kirche Jerusalems von 70 bis 130*, Gütersloh, 1898, 8 ff.; S. Zeitlin, *Chajes-Festschrift*, Vienna, 1933, 298, dates the assertion around 116. Later the destruction of the temple was also referred to the neglect of circumcision and of other laws as its cause and so in the last resort to Pauline Christianity (Jer. Sanh. 10, 29).

[2] Cf. L. Baeck, "The Faith of Paul", *JJSt*, 1952, 3; on the problems of the anti-Minim controversy in general, see Schoeps, *Religionsgespräch* etc., 48 ff.; 57 ff.

augment sin. And this applies equally to the 20th century and the 1st. But the most essential point in the Jewish understanding of the law is that God gave it to the people of His choice, in order to bind Israel closely with God, because the holy God through the law wishes to render His people holy.[1] Thus the midrash makes God address Israel in the words: "Let it be clear from the keeping of the commandments that you are a people holy to Me" (Sifre Deut. 53b–75b). The laws are called "a token of God's love for Israel", the "yoke of the law" (על המצות) is described as the "yoke of the kingdom of heaven" (Aboth III, 5; M. Ber. II, 2, etc.). It is for this reason that the first Psalm speaks of joy in the law of the Lord (1:2). But Paul with his presuppositions would not have been able to join in the celebration of the feast of the Torah.

As far as the plurality of commands is concerned, it is declared: "If God gives a new law for Israel, he confers holiness on it" (R. Isi ben Yehuda, Tann. 2nd century in Mekhilta Ex. 22:30; variants—R. Hanina ben Aqashiah in Makkoth II, 16). And if Paul in view of the plurality of the commands, which the last named rabbi had based on Is. 42:21, affirms that because of the connexion of ἁμαρτία and σάρξ they are not capable of fulfilment, he is controverting the Jewish doctrine about the purpose of the law and the inner relation between the law and sin. This is expressed most pregnantly by Qiddushin 30b: "The holy One, blessed be His name, spake to Israel: 'My children, I have created the evil impulse, and I have created the Torah as a remedy against it. If you concern yourselves with the Torah, you will not be surrendered to the power of sin.'" (Doublet Baba Bathra 16a: the Holy One created the evil impulse, but He also created the Torah as a remedy against it.)

This idea was so deeply rooted that it prevented the development of a doctrine of inherited sin in Judaism. Because the children of Israel, the seed of Abraham, were chosen to receive the Torah, they were freed from the situation created by the transmission of sin, which in several Haggadoth is accepted as true of the heathen outside Israel. Most striking in this connexion is the Haggada about the pernicious beastliness of the snake, to which I have referred elsewhere.[2] The consequences of the fall were said to have been transmitted among the non-Jews, but were lost among those who stood on

[1] On this rabbinic function of the laws, cf. along with other authors A. Marmorstein, op. cit., 209 ff.
[2] AfZ, 203, where I have classified this Haggada in the circle of ideas about Israel's election, but it must not be misinterpreted in a physiological sense.

Sinai, because the Jews possess the Torah as a protective and saving resource against the power of the evil impulse. The Jew has only to begin to attack it by the deeds of the law, and God will surely lend His aid as He has promised according to Pes. R. Kah. 25 (Yalqut Hosea 532 on 14: 2): "My children! The evil impulse is like a big rock! Grind it down and in the end I will abolish it from the world."

If, however, it is a question of the struggle between the sinful body and the law of the spirit (νόμος πνευματικός—ἕτερος νόμος ἐν τοῖς μέλεσιν) as depicted so vividly in Rom. 7: 14–23 and which is equally known among the rabbis, then the Jewish answer is a prayer to God that the conflict may be resolved by a moderating of the evil impulse. "The prophet said to Israel: 'Repent.' They answered him: 'We cannot; the evil impulse so masters us.' He answered them: 'Tame your impulses.' They replied: 'May God soften them.'" (Sanh. 105a.) And similarly we read in Seder Eliyahu Rabba 62: "Sinners say: 'Creator of the world! It is well known to Thee that we are enticed into sin by the *yeser hara*. Take us in the arms of Thy great mercy as those who are fully repentant.'" But because Paul does not know the Jewish belief in the power of turning again to God, he does not understand that the question of the fulfilment of the law is in the last resort unimportant. For whether the law is fulfilled by man or not, the mere intention to fulfil it brings man close to God, because that intention is man's affirmation of the covenant, which precedes the law.

For this reason too the Pauline doctrine of justification: ἐξ ἔργων νόμου οὐ δικαιωθήσεται πᾶσα σάρξ (Gal. 2: 16; Rom. 3: 20), considered from the standpoint of the rabbinic understanding of the law, stems from a partial aspect of the law wrongly isolated from the saving significance of the law as a whole. Protestant exegetes do well to distinguish between the place of this doctrine in Paul's thought and its role in the theology of Luther. Luther's outlook was non-eschatological, and he did not understand what it really meant in the scheme of Paul's thought—namely a fragment of a doctrine of redemption, a polemic doctrine connected with the *abrogatio legis* and unconnected with ethics, a doctrine which may be understood only against the background of the very imminent parousia but not as a timelessly valid truth.[1] "By taking the doctrine of justification by faith as a point of departure, the understanding of Paul's world of thoughts

---

[1] Cf. Bultmann, *op. cit.*, 5, and the remarks of F. Buri, *op. cit.*, 155 ff. Here are the essential merits of Schweitzer and his school of "consistent eschatology".

196

became unintelligible.''[1] Since nevertheless with W. Wrede the process of purging Paul of Lutheran contaminations was started, the one-sided Lutheran interpretation of the Pauline doctrines of justification and forgiveness may be said to have been painfully overcome.[2]

It is certainly a rabbinic opinion that man comes to judgment and is judged according to the measure of his works. But justification which discriminates, which renders man meritorious (cf. M. Makkoth III, 16), can, of course, spring only from God, who—contrary to Pauline doubts (Gal. 3: 22 ff.)—has given a law intended to create life and blessing, and to lead to a life of righteousness which in truth flows from the law itself. The ἔργα νόμου intercede for us at the bar of judgment just as the ἁμαρτίαι are our accusers. This is a favourite thought with the rabbis, frequently and variously expressed. Although sometimes audacious expressions about reward and merit have crept in, yet the favourite contrast between a Jewish piety based on works and the sense of merit, and, on the other hand, Pauline justification by grace, is an over-simplification of the situation. Critics should at last free themselves from this old theme hawked about in Christian apologetics and no longer seek to depreciate Jewish piety, which in fact, contrary to what they think, has appreciated very highly the לשמה-laws.[3] Otherwise one easily falls into the fatality of having to agree that Paul, despite his polemic, is very much at home in categories of thought about reward and merit,[4] within which he sometimes describes the deeds of Christ also. Above all, the essence of the law as a Biblical revelation of the will of God can never be recognized if we think along these lines, for God wills to be sanctified by the law which He has proclaimed, as we read: "You shall be men consecrated to me" (Ex. 22: 31). The Mekhilta explains this as follows: "If you are holy, then you belong to me" (Rabbi Ishmael). The consequences of this must be expounded in the last section of this chapter.

Thus we come to the conclusion that for Paul the Pharisee of

---

[1] Schweitzer, *Mystik*, 215.

[2] F. Flückiger, *Die Entstehung des christlichen Dogmas*, Zollikon, 1955, 52, throws light on this.

[3] Only recently there have been indications that this convenient scheme is too simple and not at all adjusted to information from the sources. Important in this respect is the fine work of the Swedish scholar Erik Sjöberg, *Gott und die Sünder im palästinensischen Judentum*, Stuttgart, 1939, esp. 23 ff. and 188 ff.

[4] For the numerous references cf. H. Preisker in Kittel, *WB*, IV, 726 ff. μισθός; G. Bornkamm, *Der Lohngedanke im NT*, Gütersloh, 1947, and now the monograph of G. Didier, *La rétribution dans la morale de St. Paul*, Paris, 1955.

Tarsus—as also for Philo of Alexandria[1]—the law was no longer a living possession. And this for the obvious reason that he had ceased to understand the totality and continuity of the Berith-Torah. But according to tradition the whole people—600,000 strong—stood on Sinai and accepted the law *in toto* as the seal of God's covenant, to be valid for all future generations. Of all this there has remained for Paul only the "righteousness of the law" as a *theologoumenon*. The תורה קדשה was reduced by him to the scope of the ethical law, which he understands as a law intended to make righteous, and which, he concludes, it is unable to do, since man is not righteous but a sinner. This moralization of the Torah, this legalistic emphasis which is already found in the LXX, must have been a special characteristic of Hellenistic Judaism.[2] In face of this preponderance of the ethical commands, the ritual and ceremonial ordinances in the Torah, the מצות = ἐντολαί and גזרת = δόγματα lose their sacramental significance. Above all, the Jewish sacrament of the covenant, the circumcision of the flesh, was spiritualized by Paul into a circumcision of the heart (Rom. 2: 28–29)[3] and that contrary to the Jewish-Christian standpoint (formulated in Acts 21: 21). He can obviously do this very cavalierly because, like Philo,[4] he sees the reality of the covenant only as an abstraction, and he misunderstands its symbolism as a covenant pointing to the law of holiness. The obligations of food laws and the strictness of the command to keep the Sabbath (Col. 2: 16–17) are consequently for him—since the law is no longer valid—only σκιὰ τῶν μελλόντων, mere shadows of the future reality which is Christ (Col. 2: 17), practically therefore a negligible quantity. Even if the Jewish Christians still keep these laws, they have no special significance for them, and for the Gentile Christians no meaning whatever. "All who have sinned without the law will also perish without the law, and all who have sinned under the law will be judged by the law"; so argues Paul (Rom. 2: 12) in a passage which is intended to reduce *ad absurdum* the so-called "righteousness of works".

Hence the law has become a matter of indifference. For Paul this implies on principle a maintenance of the *status quo*, each believer

[1] Cf. I. Heinemann, *Philos griechische und jüdische Bildung*, Breslau, 1932, 482 ff.
[2] Cf. C. H. Dodd, *The Bible and the Greeks*, London, 1935, 61 ff.
[3] Cf. Art. Περιτομή, Kittel, *WB*, VI, 82; more detailed treatment in the older work of H. Wenschkewitz, "Die Spiritualisierung der Kultusbegriffe im NT", *Angelos*, 1932, 70 ff.
[4] The fact that the *Mila* is the sign of the covenant (Lev. 12: 11) is no longer known to Philo, who in the best manner of enlightened rationalism thinks of it as a hygienic preventative measure (*Spec. Leg.* I, 1 ff.).

adhering to the state which was his before his Christian conversion (1 Cor. 7: 17, 20, 24). For Jewish Christians the law continues to have validity, for which reason Paul caused Timothy, the son of a Jewess, to be circumcised. In his own life, Paul obviously remained consistently faithful to the Torah (a point which has been emphasized by the English exegetes Davies, Parkes, etc.). For practically the question of freedom from the law only arises in regard to Gentile Christians who do not need to bind themselves to an ordinance of the old and dying aeon, an ordinance which previously had meant nothing to them. And while for Jewish Christians the practice of the law was still normal and right, yet even for born Jews it had become, after the advent of the Messiah, an ἀδιάφορον, i.e., irrelevant. Were they still to insist on it, were they after baptism to yield themselves again to the law as the means of salvation, as no doubt the ψευδάδελφοι of Gal. 2: 4 required, then they would become severed from Christ (Gal. 5: 4). For it is impossible to be in Christ and in the flesh at one and the same time (1 Cor. 10: 20–21).

Fundamentally the norm now is as an exegete has expressed it: "Neither as a way to salvation, nor as a plainly obligatory rule of life, may the law be made valid for the Christian church. The fulfilment of its commands, in so far as they are not absorbed in the command of Christ and of the Spirit, has become an *adiaphoron*."[1] Hence the law in its totality, *qua* law, is considered by him to be antiquated. The acceptance of the idea that an exception should be made for the moral law in the narrower sense—thus the decalogue—is non-Pauline later church doctrine, the roots of which lie in the Letter of Barnabas, and the early apologists.[2] In fact, there remained over to early Christianity, as is shown by Acts 15: 20, and 29, out of ὅλος ὁ νόμος only a Noachide minimum of four interdicts.

This Pauline attitude, sharply defined in the letters to the Romans and Galatians, and which motivates his conduct at the apostolic council, led to the final break with contemporary Judaism. For Judaism might have endured a Messianic sect in its midst, but could not tolerate the abrogation of the Mosaic law of holiness, on which in the last resort its own Jewish consciousness of the covenant was based. And this applies not only to Palestinian Judaism but also to that of the Diaspora, for "whoever declared the law to be a transitory factor, had no further share in the Jewish inheritance. The Jews of

---

[1] L. Brun, "Der kirchliche Einheitsgedanke im Urchristentum", *ZSTh*, 1937, 107.
[2] Cf. my arguments in *AfZ*, 153 ff.; further also in ch. 7, 2 of this book.

the Diaspora above all, hence the LXX Jews, anathematize such a one."[1]

Paul furnished a solution to the problem of the law which in the last resort rested on a misunderstanding, to which we shall return in the last paragraph of the chapter. The solution also shows many inner contradictions, though there is no need to sort them out. Of course a Christian who relied on Paul for information about the meaning and purpose of the Torah as an instrument of the Jewish covenant would receive a picture that was a complete travesty. This travesty has, of course, made history, and was to some extent the cause of the dilemma of the early church in the matter of the law. Only few critics have seen these questions clearly, and those who have clarified them most have been adherents of the "History of Religion" school. It is for this reason that I would like to conclude this section with an assessment of the situation by the author just quoted: "Paul does not attain his object in regard to his arguments about the law. Without doubt he distorted the character of the law and did not really get to grips with it."[2]

5. FAITH AND WORKS

Paul's struggle against the Jewish law was the necessary consequence of his presuppositions. The dualism which so strongly characterizes Pauline thought: flesh-spirit, sin-righteousness, etc., is now well known to us from Qumran writings too.[3] But Pauline dualism is eschatological in structure, and in the last analysis is based on his fundamental dualistic position: the aeon of the law—the aeon of Christ.

It was for this reason that Paul had to do battle with the law regarded as a principle of salvation. For in the interim period between the resurrection and the parousia in which Paul believed himself to be living and teaching, the old authority of the law could not subsist alongside the new authority of the Messiah who had come in the flesh. Otherwise Christ would have died in vain (Gal. 2: 21).

---

[1] Cf. H. Böhlig, "Zum Weltbild des Paulus", *Memnon*, Vol. V (1911), 191.

[2] H. Böhlig, *Die Geisteskultur von Tarsus* etc., *op. cit.*, 166.

[3] On Rom. 3: 20; Gal. 2: 16 Hodayoth IV, 32 ff., offers a clear parallel: "I know that righteousness belongs to no man. To the highest God belong all the works of righteousness." In the concluding psalm of the sect scroll we read: "My justification depends on the righteousness of God, which is eternal." Cf. also M. Burrows, *Die Schriftrollen vom Toten Meer*, Munich, 1957, 275 ff. (*The Dead Sea Scrolls.*) Further references have been collected by Sh. E. Johnson, "Paul and the Manual of Discipline", *HThR*, 1955, 157 ff.

His conflict with the Jewish-Christian thesis that the death of Christ, while admittedly an atonement for the sin and guilt incurred by transgressions of the law, upheld in fact the ancient status of the law, was carried out not from the standpoint of a Gentile Christian antinomism but rather as the natural result of his Messianological convictions.[1] This Messianic dogmatism induced him to assemble all those features of the law which indicated that it would be cancelled in the Messianic age. Every criterion suggesting that the law was inadequate for salvation was emphasized in order to disperse with the old covenant for intrinsic reasons, and to make the sun of the new covenant shine the more brightly. If then the Mosaic law whose validity was limited temporarily could be shown to be no longer the divinely appointed way of salvation, if Christ as the end of the law and the content of the new covenant could be shown to have taken its place, then the legal principle of life through obedience to the Torah could be replaced by the new principle of life through faith in Christ.

The characteristic fixation of the apostle's mind on the Old Testament is shown in that he cannot develop his principle otherwise than as he finds it proved in the Torah itself. And not only does he find it proved, but he thinks he is able to show that it is the true meaning of the Torah. His proof is conducted by his pointing to the figure of Abraham, venerable to every Jew as his ancestor, and through whose merits in fact the world subsists (Gen. Rabba Par. 35, etc.). In particular, in Judaic Hellenism the glorification of Abraham as the pattern of steadfastness in faith was somewhat paraded as being adapted to the needs of Gentiles whom it was desired to convert. (Cf. ch. 6, section 1.) According to Philo, Abraham embodied faith as the ἡ τῶν ἀρετῶν βασιλίς (De Abr. II, 39):[2] "To free oneself completely from all earthly goods, and to believe in God alone, is the mark of a high and heavenly spirit, unfettered by earthly ties" (Quis rerum div. heres 93). Paul shared this opinion of Philo, only he went far beyond Philo's idea of faith as fidelity to the law. The centre of gravity in Paul's argument is that righteousness can be attained apart from the law and as a pure gift of grace, just as was promised to Abraham. For faith was reckoned to him as righteousness when he was still in an uncircumcised state (Gen. 15: 6); the

---

[1] Various patristic sources have preserved for us the Jewish-Christian protest against Paul's apostasy from the law, already voiced in Acts 21: 21. I quoted and interpreted them in *TheolJChr*, ch. III A, par. 2, 135 ff.

[2] The connecting passage is a rapturous eulogy of Abraham's faith: cf. also *De Praem. et Poen.* II, 142, etc.

question of circumcision arises with regard to him two chapters later. The confident trust in the promise which is older than the law, was in itself already sufficient for the attainment of righteousness. Hence, deduces Paul, true righteousness springs from faith and not from the law (Rom. 5: 20). "For we hold that a man is justified by faith apart from works of law" (Rom. 3: 28).

But this new tearing asunder of polarities, this absolute opposition between faith, on the one hand, and the law, on the other, quite contrary to the continuous meaning of the Biblical narrative, has always been unintelligible to the Jewish thinker. None the less, the categories in which Paul thinks and argues are thoroughly rabbinic. Thus Midr. Teh. 27: 13 and 94: 17 (Doubl. Gen. Rabba Par. 74 on Gen. 31: 42) conceptually distinguishes a merit or a righteousness flowing from faith: זכות אמנה—δικαιοσύνη ἐκ πίστεως—in the terms of Ps. 27: 13, from a righteousness which stems from the law: זכות תורה—δικαιοσύνη ἐκ νόμου—in the terms of Ps. 119: 32. But here the two kinds of righteousness or merit are set alongside each other, and not played off against each other. There is no occasion for such an attitude unless it is desired to prove the priority and superiority of faith over against the law. And it is precisely this which Paul wishes to do.

The central meaning of faith in the Old Testament is quite clear. The Old Testament term האמין never admits a spiritualized interpretation, but always connotes trust in the sense of fidelity. For scripture knows only one alternative as regards man's position in face of God, His covenant and His law: namely, fidelity or infidelity. Faith means obedience towards God. The modern conceptual antithesis: faith or doubt, is just as little known in scripture as the Pauline antithesis faith or works.[1] In post-Biblical writings this view of faith has rather sharpened,[2] and the Haggada changes many texts where clearly fidelity is meant, so as to make them refer to faith.[3] In this matter I approve the description which in his day A. Meyer[4] gave:

[1] Cf. A. Schlatter, Der Glaube im Neuen Testament, Stuttgart, 1905, 9–80, who proposes to see a change only in the later writings of the Canon.

[2] For Josephus cf. A. Schlatter, Die Religion des Judentums nach dem Bericht des Josephus, Gütersloh, 1932, and for Philo the Diss. of M. Peisker, Der Glaubensbegriff bei Philo, Breslau, 1936.

[3] Thus the Pauline distortion of Habbabuk is not isolated, the Qumran Comm. on 2: 4, Tanchuma 16b, Mekhilta on Ex. 14: 31 and Ex. Rabba Par. 23 have it also. The same thing is observable in the Targum translations. Not without reason does the midrash on Song of Sol. 4: 8 distort the peak of Amana, by a simple change of pointing, into the peak of faith.

[4] Das Rätsel des Jakobusbriefes, Giessen, 1930, 137.

Especially marked is the emphasis on faith in the centuries before and after Christ, and Christianity itself is an outcome of this emphasis of Israel on faith. The idea of faith stemmed from the idea of fidelity, of loyal adherence to God and His law. As the law insists on works, so faith becomes a zealous obedience in the matter of fulfilling the law, and its individual prescriptions. It is joy in the law and faithfulness to the law even in the most minute points.

Rabbinic Judaism even—contrary to the opinion of Montefiore—held a doctrine about the relation of faith and works, which, however, should not be over-emphasized. The well-known discussion of Makkoth 23b about the *Iqqarim* of the Torah, which concludes with the principle of Hab. 2: 4 (the just shall live by faith) set up as a basic principle by Rabbi Nachman ben Isaac (died 356) shows plainly enough that the rabbis understood the distinction between faith and works, and the superiority of the former. This, however, is already a relatively late reflection, no longer corresponding to classical Jewish piety which was orientated more towards יראת יי or שמים. The fear of God is the characteristic creaturely attitude, corresponding in Judaism to what Paul calls πίστις. This is implicit behind the performance of all the laws, and constitutes what alone is required of man. "And now, Israel, what does the Lord require of you, but to fear the Lord your God" (Deut. 10: 12). "Fear God and keep His commandments, for this is the whole duty of man" (Eccl. 12: 13). How Judaism conceived the relation of faith and works is best expressed by the rabbinic opinion that at the last judgment good works apart from the fear of God will avail nothing, since the latter is the presupposition behind the six sections of the Mishna (Sabb. 31a). Likewise the Letter of James—James drew on the same Jewish sources as Paul—with its tendency to combine the two factors in contrast to Paul, represents contemporary Jewish opinion which no doubt prevailed in the Jerusalem church.[1] And the later Ebionites thought with regard to the mission of Christ the "true prophet", that He taught the forgiveness of sins through good works (Hom. 3: 26).

The ancestor Abraham was according to Jewish ideas, just as much as for Paul, the great pattern of fidelity and steadfastness.[2] Rabbinic

---

[1] A. Meyer, *op. cit.*, 108: "James has old traditions, Paul is the modern."

[2] The pertinent texts have been examined in O. Schmitz, *Abraham im Spätjudentum und Urchristentum*, Festgabe für A. Schlatter, 1922, 99 ff. (esp. Mekh. Ex. 14: 31; Ex. Rabba Par. 23; Cant. Rabba 4: 8) and quoted in Billerbeck, III, 199 ff. Testimony for Philo in M. Friedländer, *Die religiösen Bewegungen innerhalb des Judentums im Zeitalter Jesu*, Berlin, 1905, 362 ff. See now *Cahiers Sioniens*, special number, 1951, vol. 2, *Abraham Père des Croyants*.

sources also declare that Abraham's righteousness flowed from his faith. The old Sanhedrin president Rabbi Shemaiah (1st century B.C., hence pre-Pauline) expressed this opinion (Mekh. Ex. 14: 31). It is certain, however, that there were other views. It is possible that in the well-known principle of Rabh based on Gen. 26: 5 (Yoma 28b, Mishna Qidd. IV, 14) that Abraham fulfilled all the later commandments even before they had been proclaimed, we should see a polemic against the interpretation of Shemaiah and Paul.[1] But in any event the figure of Abraham, both in Palestine and the Diaspora, was the great pattern and symbol of faith; Paul knew what he was doing in linking his argument to this figure venerated by all. The question whether the faith of Abraham was understood in Judaism as a work on the same level as the works of the law—or even if superior, still as a work—is a question framed from without, and springing from the ideas connected with the Lutheran doctrine of justification. The collection of sources made by Strack-Billerbeck on Rom. 4: 13 *ad usum delphini* merely hinders the correct orientation. The question "faith or works" could not have been posed in the sphere of a Judaism bound by Holy Scripture.

Typical of Jewish piety is a sentence of Rabbi Nehemiah (Tann. *circa* 150) in the Mekhilta on Ex. 15: 1: "He who fulfils a commandment in faith merits highest praise before God." Further passages of the Mekhilta speak of the power of faith: so long as Israel does the will of God and believes in Him who gave Moses the commandments that were to be obeyed, God will do marvels for it and give it victories (Ex. 17: 11), God will pardon it (Ex. 12: 7), and it will be healed (Ex. 18: 4), etc. We shall only be able to elucidate this matter if we break through the terminological nominalism. By πίστις Paul obviously means a different kind of faith from the faith involved in the Biblical–Talmudic אמנה. For Paul's faith alone makes possible for him the membership of a community which the Pharisees from the standpoint of their faith would have to call a community of sinners.[2] The Pauline faith is not trust in the Biblical God, but is faith in the sacral event (already discussed) of Christ-soteriology, which he assesses as a saving disposition of God. With Paul the faith of the pious believer (in the Messianic status of Christ) replaces the

---

[1] The usual explanation of the anachronistic sentence as due to the clumsiness of rabbinic thought seems to me inadequate. M. Joel, *Blick in die Religionsgeschichte*, II, Breslau, 1883, 174 ff., supposed that this attack on Paul had its secret point. But the pre-Christian Book of Jubilees knows this version too.

[2] Shrewd though aphoristic observations on this in M. Dibelius, "Zur Methode der Paulusforschung", *ThLZ*, 1933, 288.

Jew's fidelity to the law and becomes the sum of all truth and wisdom.

The next stage in the development is that Paul postulated of this new kind of believing a righteousness proper to it, and it is important to grasp his thought in its original form, since it has been obscured and disfigured by the Lutheran interpretation of it as an *opus operatum*. For it is certainly not true that the majority of Pauline texts which treat of faith admit of the interpretation: "Justification not on the basis of the works of the law, but on the basis of faith in the forgiveness of sins which the death of Jesus Christ has made possible." On the contrary, many texts speak of faith as though it had the character of a meritorious achievement.[1] Further, this teaching about the righteousness which flows from faith and excludes the works of the law was not formulated by Paul—as we have noted in the previous section—as a timeless truth, but as something valid only for the short transitional period in which the apostle believed himself to be living. The eschatological $\nu\hat{\upsilon}\nu$ of Rom. 3: 21 implies the situation created by Christ, in which this new righteousness is possible.

Even so, the doctrine is the "product of an unnatural sequence of thought", the outcome of a "sophisticated logic".[2] It is to be understood only in the light of the attempt to represent the life of the believer as resting on the pure grace of God in contrast to the rabbinic degeneration into a formal kind of righteousness, which misuses the fulfilling of the law to the end of self-praise. Paul reproaches the Jews with $\kappa\alpha\acute{\upsilon}\chi\eta\sigma\iota\varsigma$ (Rom. 3: 27), with the fact that they oppose their own righteousness to the $\delta\iota\kappa\alpha\iota\sigma\sigma\acute{\upsilon}\nu\eta$ $\tauο\hat{\upsilon}$ $\theta\epsilonο\hat{\upsilon}$ (Rom. 10: 3). Just as the Greeks seek to attain their own wisdom, so the Jews hanker after their own righteousness, in order to win thereby a merit of which they may boast before God.[3] True righteousness which discloses itself as the righteousness of Christ in the act of faith can be bestowed only by God, and then makes man righteous too. This is what Paul understood by justification by faith. Paul had already fought against faith in one's own righteousness in Rom. 2: 17–29;

---

[1] Cf. H. Braun, *Gerichtsgedanke und Rechtfertigungslehre bei Paulus*, Leipzig, 1930, 79 ff.

[2] These judgments of value are in Schweitzer, *op. cit.*, 220. Other assessments of the Pauline doctrine of justification in H. Grundmann, "Rechtfertigung und Mystik bei Paulus", *ZNW*, 1933, 52 ff.; H. D. Wendland, *Die Mitte der paulinischen Botschaft*, Göttingen, 1935; H. W. Heidland, *Die Anrechnung des Glaubens zur Gerechtigkeit*, Stuttgart, 1936; Dibelius-Kümmel, *Paulus*, 104 ff.

[3] Cf. R. Bultmann, *Theol. NT*, 255–266.

and in the section 7: 7–25 his intention is to reduce it to the absurd by his doctrine of justification, by teaching that obedience to the law can never lead to righteousness, that the latter must be bestowed as the gift of grace.

The tendency to establish a human claim over against God and to replace the Old Testament religion of grace by a human religion of merit is already observable in the LXX (cf. above, ch. 1, 2b). Thus far Paul is here attacking rather the Hellenistic Judaism of his origins than real rabbinicism. He confronts Hellenistic Judaism with the sovereignty of God and divine grace by which the sinner for Christ's sake is viewed as righteous in the last hour of judgment.

Most Christian interpreters are pleased to suppose that in grace, considered as the saving deed of God, Paul discovered quite a new point of view and a new principle. This, however, is not the case. In reality Paul was only expressing in his own words an old Jewish doctrine. Precisely in reference to Abraham and divine grace we can quote Gen. Rabba Par. 60 on ch. 24: 12: Rabbi Haggai said in the name of Rabbi Isaac (*circa* 300): "All need divine grace; even Abraham, for whose sake grace is operative in the world, needed grace." And in Pesiqta Rabbathi 98b it is said with regard to the boasting of good works which Paul condemns: "Even when we consider our pious deeds, we are ashamed of their pettiness as compared to the greatness of God's mercies towards us." Poverty in meritorious deeds is a lasting condition of humanity which can only invite God's mercy (Pesachim 118b).[1] From Ex. 13: 19 is deduced as a divine saying: "Whoever has, to him I give of his own; whoever has not to him I give in vain" (Tanch. B. ki-tissa 16; Ex. Rabba Par. 46 par.). And the midrash on the psalter causes King David to address God in these words: "Some trust in their own good works, some in the works of the fathers, but I trust in Thee, although I have no good works. Do Thou hear me!" (M. Teh. 141, 1.)

Thus it seems to me that faith or works is a question wrongly framed. The difference between Christian and Jew in this matter emerges only when, as already emphasized, we inquire into the character of the faith of which Paul speaks. Obviously Paul means a different kind of faith from that which is known to Judaism. When

---

[1] There are numerous texts in scripture showing that man is pardoned by God without any merit on his part and given a reward in the other world. One needs only to open the Jewish prayer book. Yet cf. also G. Klein, *Studien über Paulus*, 82 ff.; A. Marmorstein, *The Doctrine of Merits in Old Rabbinical Literature*, London, 1920, 56 ff.

Mekhilta Ex. 14: 31 deduces by *kal wachomer* that he who believes in the faithful shepherd Moses is to be equated with the man who believes in God Himself, the application of the saying to Jesus as Messiah would be a Jewish-Christian *theologoumenon*,[1] but not a Pauline one. For, as we have noted, Paul sees in Jesus not a second Moses, but the υἱὸς θεοῦ substantially distinct from Moses and all the prophets. Rather, justification by faith for Paul is a being in Christ, and implies a quite specific way of being brought about by God and expressed in the phrase ἐν Χριστῷ. This being in Christ which he opposes to the being under the law—an inherited Jewish formula[2]—is according to Schweitzer's luminous study "a linguistic abbreviation for participation in the mystical Body of Christ", an expression conveying that "the elect share with Christ in the same bodily fellowship".[3] Thus with Christ a new aeon of the Spirit begins, and the "being in Christ" signifies at the same time an eschatological event.[4] The life "in Christ" is for Paul a first fruits of the reign of the Holy Spirit, and so implies a real renewal of life. This is the Pauline doctrine which we see expressed in Rom. 8: 12 ff. and Gal. 5 and which alone makes fully intelligible the significance of the death and resurrection of Christ.

It is clear that Paul understands in a quite actual ontic fashion this status of belonging to Christ which stands under the signature of the ἔσχατον. It is this approach alone which gives to those instruments whereby the initiate passes into and is confirmed in his new state, namely the sacraments, their Christian character. They fulfil the function left vacant by the law. We have discussed in detail the eschatological aspect of the sacraments above, ch. 3, and have pointed out that they are intended to counter the delay in the parousia and to render present and efficacious to the church the exalted Christ, foreshadowing His second coming. In this connexion there is, however, another point of importance: the doctrine of baptism is developed by Paul in Rom. 5; 6: 4 ff. out of the doctrine of justification.

[1] About Moses as the prototype of the Messiah and the Jewish-Christian *theologoumenon*: Jesus Christ–novus Moses, all that is needed has been put together in my book, *TheolJChr*, 87–98; 110–116. To-day I would more strongly stress the pattern character of the desert period for the saving events of the Messianic age, as implied in Micah 7: 15.

[2] Cf. Lohmeyer, *Grundlagen* etc., 141 ff., and Lohmeyer's pupil W. Schmauch, *In Christus*, Gütersloh, 1935, 161 ff.

[3] *Op. cit.*, 123. Cf. also W. Bousset, *Kyrios Christos*, 148 ff., and W. Weber, *Christusmystik*, Leipzig, 1924, 82 ff.

[4] Cf. R. Bultmann, "Kirche und Lehre im NT", *Zwischen den Zeiten*, 1929, 27 (*Glauben und Verstehen*, I, 171; E.T. *Essays, Philosophical and Theological*).

This connexion is described by O. Michel[1] in the following terms:

> Justification and baptism condition and secure each other mutually. The dual question of Rom. 6: 1, 15 shows the necessity of avoiding the danger lest the reception of grace or baptism should be understood as anything but the death of the old and the birth of the new man. In this sense the doctrine of justification requires the completion of baptism as a confirmation of . . . the saving event. By the emphasis of the imperative Pauline theology precludes a false sacramentalism such as would endanger the meaning of justification.

Paul teaches as follows: the old Adam is crucified with Christ and the aeon of the σάρξ is superseded by the aeon of the πνεῦμα. Now the body of sin is done away (Rom. 6: 6). However, the fact that the Christian has died to the flesh means that he has also died to the law, since the latter was adapted to the flesh (Gal. 3: 3; 2: 19; Rom. 7: 6). Whoever is led by the Spirit no longer stands under the dispensation of the law (Gal. 5: 18).[2] Where the Spirit of the Lord is, there is liberty (2 Cor. 3: 17). It is, however, wrong to suggest, with Gunkel, Bousset, and others, that Paul moralized the doctrine of the first church about the activity of the Spirit. The case is rather that for Paul the prophecy of Ezekiel has found fulfilment (36: 26), in that the "stony heart" has melted before the power of the new Spirit which brings to birth a new creation in Christ (Rom. 8: 2). The Messianically expected περιτομὴ καρδίας of the καινὴ διαθήκη has been realized in the fellowship of Christ, and the περιτομὴ κατὰ σάρκα of the old covenant has been done away. The Christian man made capable of ἀγάπη is the true fulfiller of the law (Rom. 13: 10); the whole Torah is fulfilled in the commandment of love (Gal. 5: 14). Rom. 13: 10 and Gal. 5: 14 show clearly that Paul in quoting Lev. 19: 18 has isolated a כלל (basic principle of the law), as was customary in rabbinic practice. Jesus too in His discussion with the scribes about the chief commandment (Mk. 12: 28–34 and parallels) mentions love of neighbour as such a כלל.[3] "Thus Paul is com-

---

[1] *Komm. z. Römerbrief*, Göttingen, 1955, 140; similarly also H. D. Wendland, *op. cit.*, 46 ff.

[2] The significance of the pneuma for Pauline theology was one of the most important and well justified theses of W. Bousset and the "History of Religion" school; cf. G. W. Ittel, *ZRGG*, 1958, 77 ff.

[3] Cf. G. Lindeskog, *Die Jesusfrage im neuzeitlichen Judentum*, Uppsala-Leipzig, 1938, 226 ff.

pletely at one with Jesus; the real requirement of the law is love, in which everything else is contained."[1]

The new principle of salvation, implying an existential link between the believer and the exalted Christ—as also the converse, that Christ lives through the Spirit in the Christian—is a kind of teaching which has no basis in Jewish writings. Paul has in fact developed it independently on the basis of his Messianology. The novelty of his outlook is conditioned by the novelty of the post-messianic situation, arising between the resurrection and the parousia of the Messiah. The genesis of the whole structure is plain: the Messiah was Son of God—which is the sole un-Jewish point in Paul's thinking which explains all the other doctrines that have no parallel in Jewish writings; if we like, it is the Hellenistic premiss of his thought, though there is not the smallest reason to explain its logical inferences by referring specially to Hellenistic habits of thinking.

In order to elucidate the consequences of his Christology for the problem of the law, we may note the following points: the divine sonship of Jesus is expressed also as δs $\dot{\epsilon}\nu$ $\mu o\rho\phi\hat{\eta}$ $\theta\epsilon o\hat{\upsilon}$ $\dot{\upsilon}\pi\acute{a}\rho\chi\omega\nu$ (Phil. 2: 6). If a man is united by faith with the God-man, then he is in Christ and Christ is in him. Thus in 1 Cor. 1: 30: $\dot{\upsilon}\mu\epsilon\hat{\iota}s$ $\dot{\epsilon}\sigma\tau\epsilon$ $\dot{\epsilon}\nu$ $X\rho\iota\sigma\tau\hat{\omega}$ $'I\eta\sigma o\hat{\upsilon}$. The bodies of Christians are members of Christ (1 Cor. 6: 15). And in 1 Cor. 12: 27 the Christian church is called the Body of Christ, whose members are the individual Christians. The church is $o\dot{\iota}\kappa o\delta o\mu\acute{\eta}$ $\tauo\hat{\upsilon}$ $\sigma\acute{\omega}\mu a\tauos$ $\tauo\hat{\upsilon}$ $X\rho\iota\sigma\tauo\hat{\upsilon}$ (Eph. 4: 12).[2] $\Sigma\hat{\omega}\mu a$ $X\rho\iota\sigma\tauo\hat{\upsilon}$ means that the spiritual body of the exalted Lord embraces all Christians as its members. Thus the church is the Body of Christ.[3] In the last analysis the $\sigma\hat{\omega}\mu a$ $X\rho\iota\sigma\tauo\hat{\upsilon}$ idea in Paul, as A. Oepke[4] saw quite correctly, rests on the Jewish thought of God's people.

The suggested relationship may, however, be expressed conversely also: $\dot{\epsilon}\nu$ $\dot{\epsilon}\mu o\dot{\iota}$ $X\rho\iota\sigma\tau\acute{o}s$ (Gal. 2: 20); Christ dwells in believers (2 Cor. 13: 5); until we arrive at the pure mysticism of Christian existence, which is indicated in the $\mu o\rho\phi o\hat{\upsilon}\sigma\theta a\iota$ of Gal. 4: 19 (Lietzmann translates: until Christ has become incarnate in you). In consequence, the final result of all the intertwined thoughts of the apostle in respect of the law is this: the old type of relation with the divine mediated by

---

[1] Thus R. Bultmann, "Jesus und Paulus", op. cit., 75.

[2] Cf. Ph. Vielhauer, Oikodome, Munich, 1939, 90 ff.; O. Michel, Kittel, WB, V, 142 f.; G. Bornkamm, op. cit., 113 ff.

[3] For this too there are Jewish prototypes: people of Israel: one body. Cf. the references in N. A. Dahl, Das Volk Gottes, Oslo, 1941, 226 ff., and recently the study by P. Bonnard, "L'église corps de Christ dans le Paulinisme", RThPh, 1958, 268–282.

[4] Das neue Gottesvolk, Gütersloh, 1950, 224.

the law which brings the Jew face to face with God and is realized in the fulfilling of the commands, is now superseded—to speak in Hegelian terms—by the new situation "in Christ", by a new and more intimate relationship which enables man to share in the divine nature through the Incarnate Son. The new principle on which this participation rests is faith, which has annulled for Christians the old principle of the law that bound the Jew to his God.

Only in this sense can Paul speak of a νόμος Χριστοῦ (Gal. 6: 2), of the love which constrains Christians to carry each other's burdens, or of a νόμος πίστεως (Rom. 3: 27). He implies that faith is the true content of the law (νόμον ἱστάνομεν, 3: 31). In Christian love the law first gains its real πλήρωμα, by that alone is it comprehended (ἀνακεφαλαιοῦται, Rom. 13: 9 ff.). He contends that he has never inculcated an ethical indifferentism such as some blasphemously desire to impute to him. He has never suggested that we should do evil that good might come (Rom. 3: 8; cf. also 6: 1). It is only certain gnostics who have deliberately misunderstood him thus. On the contrary, he gave to the Thessalonians for the regulation of their communal life a διδαχή condemning ἄτακτοι who exploit the expectation of an imminent parousia for the recommending of an idle lolling about (2 Thess. 3: 11). Further, he drew up precise catalogues of vices, about which he warns Ephesians and Colossians (Eph. 5: 1–5 and ch. 6; Col. 3: 5–9 and ch. 4).[1] Likewise he specifies to the Romans what is to be understood by τὰ μὴ καθήκοντα (שלא בהוגן) or that which is not fitting (1: 28 ff.).[2]

If now we consider the content of his exhortation to the Thessalonians: the maintenance of the sanctity of marriage, desistence from unchastity, avoidance of cheating in trade (1 Thess. 4: 2–6), we are quite within the normal sphere of Jewish social ethics. No doubt his further appeals: brother love (v. 9), peace and mutual forbearance (5: 15), do remind us of the Sermon on the Mount and the Lord's Prayer. But the ethic of the Sermon on the Mount and the spirit of the Lord's Prayer do not take us outside Judaism, they rather enable us to penetrate within it.

In general, Paul in his exhortations shows himself to be an expert in missionary practice, who frequently gives very reasonable directions and decisions plainly adapted to the mentality or the special

---

[1] About these cf. K. Weidinger, *Die Haustafeln, ein Stück urchristlicher Paränese*, Leipzig, 1928, and the thorough study of A. Vögtle, *Die Tugend- und Lasterkataloge im NT*, Münster, 1936.

[2] Cf. G. Klein, *Der älteste christliche Katechismus und die jüdische Propagandaliteratur*, Berlin 1909, 72.

situation of those to whom he is addressing himself.[1] Paul considers that the way of the Christian life must avoid the opposite dangers of a soul-destroying literalism (2 Cor. 3: 6) like that of the Jewish Christians, and a spirit of freedom from the law rising to orgiastic enthusiasm, such as found champions in Corinth. At bottom Paul means by freedom from the law an inner sovereignty of spirit, and an independence of the goods, the customs, and the usages of this world. These things can no longer fetter the man who is inwardly free. Paul's formula coined for the use of the Corinthians of "having as though one had not" (1 Cor. 7: 29) refers not merely to the question of how marriage should be regarded, but also to the whole attitude of the Christian with regard to the ordinances and goods of this world. The stoic solution of ἀταραξία may sound similar, but has quite different roots. Paul's detachment from the world springs entirely from his relation to Christ, for the world in this its last stage of existence has become unimportant; wherefore existing arrangements and duties should no longer be changed (1 Cor. 7: 27 ff.).

Hence we have the impression that Paul no longer takes so very seriously the daily worries of his followers and friends, and that he himself is more inclined to compromise than to dogmatize in human affairs. None the less, Paul made catalogues of the vices against which he wished to warn believers and of the virtues which he recommended to their attention. All this is done quite in the style of the Jewish catechism tradition,[2] and is independent of stoic scholastic traditions.

In fact, all Paul's exhortations, even the first chapter of the Letter to the Romans, are in the last resort but illustrations and concrete amplifications of the principle: "The law is holy and the commandment is holy and just and good" (Rom. 7: 12). The exclamation which follows, μὴ γένοιτο—best translated "God forbid!"—is intended to refute all who suppose that he wished to attack the intrinsic goodness of the law. The carnal mind which rejects the law is enmity against God (Rom. 8: 7).

None the less, the context of meaning in which all this stands is equally clear: for the many reasons which we have discussed in this chapter, the important issue is now no longer the law but the act of

[1] H. Preisker, *Das Ethos des Urchristentums*, Gütersloh, 1949, 172 ff., has convincingly interpreted a series of examples in which rationalistic-utilitarian motives of the apostle are visible.
[2] Cf. E. Lohmeyer in *Komm. z. Kolosserbrief*, 54 ff. (Col. 3: 17—4: 1); K. Weidinger, *op. cit.*, 12 ff. Also the sectarian Manual of Discipline of Qumran (4: 2–14) offers a list of sins and merits comparable with Gal. 5: 19–26.

faith, the believing decision for Christ, for the Messiah who has come. Paul expresses this quite clearly: "Whatever does not proceed from faith is sin" (Rom. 14: 23). This "faith", however, is the antithesis of all formal concrete fulfilling of the law, for it is rooted solely in the heart's confident trust in God's grace (Rom. 4: 4); it is in no way a human achievement or ability, not even—to speak with A. Deissmann [1]—"the prior condition of justification, it is the very experience of justification". This is, of course, no Judaic אמונה; in fact, it depends on no human conduct whatever, it is a new mode of human existence arising through Christian πίστις and the consequent participation in the being of the God-man. The elect become, through the love of God, co-heirs with Jesus, so that He is the first-born among brothers (Rom. 8: 29).

It is only within this context of meaning that the following judgment is true: *Pneuma* has overcome *gramma*, the law as *gramma* is only the external fixation of precepts which make man a transgressor but cannot change or renew his being. Now, however, the possession of the Spirit is the decisively new factor, for the Spirit is the Author of the Christian community. The Spirit promised by the prophets as the gift of the last age (cf. Is. 32: 15–18; Ez. 26: 26 ff.; 37: 5 ff.; Joel 2: 28 ff., etc.) has been imparted to all believers. His efficacious operation in the community (1 Cor. 12: 6–11; 14: 25) shows that the last age has dawned; it is ἀρραβών (2 Cor. 1: 22; 5: 5), ἀπαρχή (Rom. 8: 23), even though the consummation is not yet. And further, in the words of the apostle: "Therefore if any one is in Christ, he is a new creation" (καινὴ κτίσις, 2 Cor. 5: 17),[2] he is a new man (Col. 3: 10), he walks in newness of life (Rom. 6: 4).

If we wish to call this event mystical,[3] then this mysticism of being-in-Christ is obviously the Christian co-relative, based on belief in justification, to the Jewish thought of election,[4] which has passed into the Christian faith in the καινὴ διαθήκη (2 Cor. 3: 6), the new Israel of God (Gal. 6: 16). On this matter we shall have more to say in the section that follows.

---

[1] *Paulus*, Tübingen, 1925, 132; cf. also W. Michaelis, *Rechtfertigung aus Glauben bei Paulus*, Festgabe für Deissmann, Tübingen, 1927, 116 ff.

[2] It should be noted that this terminology is not un-Jewish. Of the Messianic generation it is said, in connexion with Ps. 102: 19 (Midr.; Pes. R. Kah. P. 28 par.) that God will make of it a new creation.

[3] That it is preferable to avoid this ambiguous term I have shown in my introductory survey (cf. above, p. 46). Not only has Schweitzer exposed himself to every kind of misunderstanding by the repeated use of it, he has even been led astray into the naturalistic-ontic circle of ideas; cf. also O. Karner, *op. cit.*, 182.

[4] An essay in this approach has been made by F. Zilka in *Angelos*, 1932, 48 ff.

6. PAUL'S FUNDAMENTAL MISAPPREHENSION

We have now clarified the most important points in Paul's doctrine of the law, which is closely connected both with anthropology (the experience of sin) and with soteriology (faith, works, justification). At particular junctures we have also tried to explain Jewish teachings, in order to establish whether and in what way Paul deviates from them or surpasses them. In this essay we have noted the complete absence of certain basic ideas of Judaism, such as *Yirath Adonai*, *Teshubhah* and freedom over against the evil impulse. But the real problem lying behind all this has not yet been systematically treated: the problem whether Paul really did justice to the faith of his fathers, or whether the problematics with which he was concerned did not in fact obscure this faith from his vision. Did Paul rightly understand the law as the saving principle of the old covenant?

I think that we must answer this question in the negative, for in my opinion Paul succumbed to a characteristic distortion of vision which had its antecedents in the spiritual outlook of Judaic Hellenism. Paul did not perceive, and for various reasons was perhaps unable to perceive, that in the Biblical view the law is integral to the covenant; in modern terms was the constitutive act by which the Sinai covenant was ratified, the basic ordinance which God laid down for His "house of Israel". In the first place it was given in order to bind the Israelite people to its covenant God as His peculiar possession (עם סגלה). The maintenance of this ordinance, the proving of this constitutive act, is required of every member of the people in order that the covenant might be really embodied in Israelite life at all times and in all places.

Now when Paul speaks of the Jewish νόμος he implies a twofold curtailment, which was obviously customary in the Diaspora: in the first place he has reduced the Torah, which means for the Jews both law and teaching, to the ethical (and ritual) law; secondly, he has wrested and isolated the law from the controlling context of God's covenant with Israel. We will, of course, grant that in consequence of the post-Biblical inadequacy of normative doctrine even in the schools of Palestine, there hardly existed clear ideas about the relation of Torah and Berith, and it was scarcely realized that what Paul calls νόμος i.e., ὅλος ὁ νόμος, represented in fact the instrument of the Berith, the organ and foundation of the covenant. In order to be able to appreciate the falsity of the sharp antithesis, *the law and Christ*, we must first consider the truth about this relation of law and covenant, then the ominous reduction of it in Hellenistic Judaism (dependent on the LXX) to which Paul by his origins belongs. Hence the point is a failure to appreciate the *berith* as the basis of the fulfilling of the law—a failure which was part of Paul's fateful inheritance.

The situation within the Torah itself is as follows: the collection of laws promulgated by Moses on Sinai at the command of God is called in Ex. 24: 7 ספר הברית (Book of the Covenant), just as the decalogue written on two tables of stone at God's command is called in Ex. 34: 28 דברי הברית, the words of the covenant.[1] In Num. 15: 31 *berith* is synonymous with *miswa*, often later with *torah* (2 Kgs. 17: 15; Hos. 6: 7; 8: 1, etc.). Deuteronomy shares this view in respect of the decalogue (4: 13; 5: 1 ff.; 9: 9 f.). And when under King Josiah the deuteronomic book of the law was discovered (2 Kgs. 22) in the report which follows about its solemn acceptance by the people it is expressly termed the "Book of the Covenant" (23: 2), and its text, the "words of the Covenant" (23: 3).

Accordingly, the covenant and the law stand in a clear relation with each other. Firstly, as regards the form of the covenant: Israel is the people of the covenant, and its partner is God as the King of the Israelite people. As Max Weber[2] and Martin Buber[3] have luminously shown, the *foedus iniquum*, which represents merely the idea of an alliance between God and one nation of the earth, has become by God's free election will and grace on Sinai a *foedus aequum*. As a theopolitical event the Sinaitic *berith* is a sacral legal act of reciprocity, in the contraction of which both partners stand on one platform and speak on equal terms, recognizing each other (Deut. 26: 17–18). This expresses fairly pregnantly what is to be understood by the election of Israel.[4]

The content of the covenant is God's commission to Israel in the royal proclamation from Sinai to embody the sovereignty of God on earth: "You shall be my own possession among all peoples; for all the earth is mine, and you shall be to me a kingdom of priests and a holy nation" (Ex. 19: 5–6). The entire pre-exilic history of Israel may be regarded as an attempt to realize the covenantal constitution on the soil of Palestine and to embody it in a theocracy. This constituent act of the Sinaitic covenant is the ordinance which God lays

[1] Cf. A. Büchler, *Studies in Sin and Atonement in the Rabbinic Literature of the First Century*, London, 1928, 3 ff.

[2] *Ges. Aufsätze zur Religionssoziologie*, III, Tübingen, 1921, 81 ff.

[3] *Königtum Gottes*, Berlin, 1938, 111 ff.

[4] Cf. H. J. Schoeps, *Aus frühchristlicher Zeit*, Tübingen, 1950, 191 ff.

down for His own house of Israel. It is expressed in the form of law and statutes intended to bind the people of Israel as a עם סגולה to its covenant God. This is in particular the deuteronomic conception, which connects law and covenant very closely. The people maintain the covenant inasmuch as they observe the laws. And the reciprocal character of the covenantal partnership comes to expression in Deuteronomy by the fact that God's blessing and curse are made dependent on the attitude of the people, its maintenance or otherwise of the laws (Deut. 28: 1 ff., 15 ff.). Strict adherence to the covenantal constitution is required of every member of the people so that the covenant may be effectively realized; the salvation of the individual depends on this. "You shall therefore keep my statutes and my ordinances, by doing which a man shall live" (Lev. 18: 5), i.e., he will stand in the living divine fellowship of salvation and holiness.

It is important for us to note that the binding character of the *berith* obviously consists in this, that man stands under oath to observe the law. Hence the law is the constituent act of the covenant, which, as a manifestation of God's election-grace to the man who is faithful, produces sanctification. For the law's requirement of holiness (Lev. 19: 2) flows from the binding relationship with the holy God who requires man to reflect His holiness. The prophets speak very aptly of Israel's transgression of the law when they say that it has broken the eternal covenant (Is. 24: 5). For the classic consciousness of ancient Israel the law was the basic act constituting the covenant, a constitutional act effected by God and as such regarded as unchangeable and irrevocable. Admittedly these are modern ideas of law, which are not directly reflected in the Bible, but they correspond approximately to the visibly growing situation in the evolution of Israel.

Hence we see that covenant in the Old Testament has the character both of history and of revelation. The covenant is concluded so that the people might be and remain God's people. It serves to maintain the laws of God, just as the laws serve to maintain God's covenant which they are intended to illuminate. The members of the covenant (*confoederati*) stand under the guidance of God and are obliged to render obedience. There exists a genuine relationship of contract—expressed in a Roman legal formula, a *mutua obligatio*—which is indissoluble and unredeemable. In this covenantal league of Israel with God, religious and juridical aspects are so closely linked as to be identifiable.

Early post-canonical writings, such as the Book of Jubilees, dating probably from the third century B.C.,[1] clearly subordinate, in this important sense, law to covenant, the latter as the promulgation of Moses embracing all the statutes (23: 16; 30: 21 ff.; 33: 19, etc.). In the Maccabean period the expression βιβλίον διαθήκης even gains currency to denote the written law (1 Macc. 1: 57; Ecclus. 24: 23); the διαθήκη is described as the νόμος ζωῆς καὶ ἐπιστήμης (Ecclus. 45: 5, 15). This becomes still more plain in the Zadokite charter of the new covenant of Damascus, where the laws are simply called covenantal precepts, and the constitution the covenantal ordinance, while believers who follow the law receive the description: "those who walk in God's covenant", המתהלכים בברית. *Berith* becomes an epitome of the ordinances of the covenant to which Moses committed the people—a timeless quantity.[2] In Hebrew, both Biblical and post-Biblical, it retains the character of reciprocity, so that not only on the part of God has there been an inviolable declaration of the divine will, but man too has been bound by certain decrees, and committed by certain duties and rights.[3] Hence the Israelite *berith* has not only the significance of an order of grace, of divine institution, but also that of a covenantal charter, the determination of statutes and laws to govern the life of the Israelite people. The Mekhilta Ex. 20: 6 invoking Deut. 28: 9 establishes the point: "By covenant is meant nothing other than the Torah." In other words, the Torah is the body of the *berith*; in its 248 commands and its 365 prohibitions according to rabbinic enumeration, the *berith* is embodied as a manifestation of the divine will; the "ethical schematization of faith in God", as Joh. Hempel[4] expresses it, was carried out in Israel with the help of ideas of law and right.

The Greek translation, however, διαθήκη, used almost exclusively in the LXX for ברית, shows a shift of emphasis which has often struck the attention of critics (Riggenbach, Lohmeyer, Behm, etc.). The voluntary pact involving mutual obligations has become an authoritative legal disposition rather like a testamentary decision familiar to Greek civil law, from which the profane use of the term derives.[5] One must certainly admit that "διαθήκη in the LXX is

---

[1] Cf. S. Zeitlin in *JQR*, 1939, 1–31; W. F. Albright, *Von der Steinzeit zum Christentum*, Berne–Munich, 1949, 345 ff. (*From the Stone Age to Christianity*.)

[2] For apocryphal and pseudepigraphic literature, references are given by W. D. Davies, *Paul and Rabbinic Judaism*, London, 1948, 261.

[3] Cf. W. Eichrodt, *Theologie des Alten Testaments*, I, Leipzig, 1957, 28 ff.; Ludwig Koehler, *Theologie des Alten Testaments*, Tübingen, 1953, 49 ff.

[4] *Das Ethos des Alten Testaments*, Berlin, 1938, 202.

[5] Cf. J. Behm, Διαθήκη in Kittel, *WB*, II, 129.

not an unambiguous term, but hovers between the meanings of covenant and arrangement". But, as Eichrodt rightly alleges, the emphasis lies elsewhere than in the Hebraic *berith* or the English covenant. In the LXX use "the idea of reciprocity has ceased to exist".[1] Διαθήκη in the LXX (e.g., in the promise to Abraham also, Gen. 15: 18; 17: 2 ff., etc.) can hardly be translated as *foedus sive pactum*; the meaning seems to me to fluctuate only between *testamentum* and *statutum*—though it still has the subsidiary meaning *promissio*. The translators Aquila and Symmachus, who are more strongly rooted in rabbinic tradition, have therefore used the more exact term συνθήκη in texts which are important for God's covenant with Israel.[2] But we cannot agree with Lohmeyer when he says that the LXX translation διαθήκη is religiously more valuable because the free ordinance of divine grace is a nobler conception than that of a juridical pact which is expressed in ברית and συνθήκη. The aim of our argument is precisely to show that this term *berith* suggests the inner legal structure of Old Testament revelation, which is effaced in the LXX and distorted in the New Testament.

The LXX translation on account of its broad and free character has had, theologically, serious consequences. For, as early as Philo, God's covenant with the patriarchs and the people of Israel—which was the result of an agreement between two parties—was transformed into a one-sided declaration of the divine will in the sense of testament (a symbol of grace) or else in the sense of revelation of the divine nature (thus *De Mut. Nom.* 53; *De Somn.* II, 223 ff. on Gen. 6: 18).[3]

Philo is the first of a long series of writers for whom it may be shown that the use of the LXX alongside of or in place of the original text has led to a distortion of the classical Jewish teaching. The whole of the literature of Judaic Hellenism consequently discloses a rationalization or spiritualization of the laws of the Torah such as in either case deviates from Jewish faith-ideas.[4]

Now Paul, as W. Bauer[5] rightly observes, is entirely dependent on

---

[1] E. Lohmeyer, *Diatheke, ein Beitrag zur Erklärung des neutestamentlichen Begriffs*, Leipzig, 1913, 80.

[2] Aquila in 15 and Symmachus in 23 cases give συνθήκη for *berith*. Cf. Jerome on Jer. 11: 2: "Notandum est, quod verbum *berith* Aquila et Symmachus semper factum, LXX et Theodotion testamentum interpretati sunt."

[3] Cf. I. Heinemann, *op. cit.*, 481 ff. with references, and H.J. Schoeps, "Rund um Philo", *MGWJ*, 1938, 271 ff. and 276. Lohmeyer's criticism of Philo is out of date.

[4] Cf. the many references for this in P. Dalbert, *Die Theologie der hellenistisch-jüdischen Missionsliteratur*, Hamburg, 1954.

[5] *Griechisch-deutsches Wörterbuch*, Berlin, 1950, 331 ff.

LXX usage, and understands διαθήκη as a one-sided declaration of the will of God, an arrangement which God has made and authorized. Behind this lies the thought that God drew up a testament in our favour, in consequence of which we were entitled to expect an inheritance (κληρονομία, Gal. 3: 18; 4: 1 ff., etc.). Paul goes so far as to describe believers as the "heirs of God and fellow heirs with Christ" (Rom. 8: 17).[1] If we disregard the distorted picture in Gal. 3: 15 ff., where Paul uses διαθήκη in the sense of testament according to Hellenistic law, and tries to illustrate a saving event by a figure drawn from the sphere of civil law, he uses the term more in the sense of a divinely authorized arrangement. When in 2 Cor. 3: 14 he speaks of the παλαιὰ διαθήκη, which is superseded in Christ, διαθήκη becomes for him a sort of collection of ancient statutes identified with the νόμος, while the καινὴ διαθήκη is equated with justification which includes the forgiveness of sins. Παλαιά 'and καινὴ διαθήκη become for Paul the antithesis between Judaism and Christianity, and indicate the stark contrast between the religion of the law and the religion of grace. Because Paul had lost all understanding of the character of the Hebraic *berith* as a partnership involving mutual obligations, he failed to grasp the inner meaning of the Mosaic law, namely, that it is an instrument by which the covenant is realized. Hence the Pauline theology of law and justification begins with the fateful misunderstanding in consequence of which he tears asunder covenant and law, and then represents Christ as the end of the law.

Our essay started from this central point in Paul's teaching about the law, and to it we have finally returned.

[1] As regards the latent motives for this formulation cf. A. Deissmann, *Paulus*, Tübingen, 1925, 137.

6

PAUL'S UNDERSTANDING OF SAVING HISTORY

Introduction: The Missionary

THE apostle Paul became a missionary to the Gentiles κατ' ἐξοχήν because of his expectation that the day of universal salvation was nigh. It is to be supposed that Saul the Pharisee of the Diaspora was such a missionary before his conversion. F. C. Baur has pointed out that Paul must be regarded as a representative of the universalist hopes of his period. Thus there is much to be said for E. Barnikol's[1] assumption based on Gal. 5: 11, ἔτι περιτομὴν κηρύσσων, that before his Christian baptism he had practised the calling of a Jewish preacher of circumcision. In Gal. 1: 14 Paul says himself that in comparison with his contemporaries (the γένος of young Pharisaic theologians) he was a zealot, an enthusiast for the traditions of the fathers, and hence for the whole corpus of the law. For this reason he chose as his special task the persecution of Jewish Christians in and around Jerusalem, and brought them to prison and death, as at least Acts 26: 10-11 would have us believe. But after his conversion this Pharisaic zealot became a zealot for freedom from the Mosaic law.

Throughout his life the same prophetic promises were the impelling force behind his activity, the promise that in the Messianic age the nations would join Israel in the worship of its God, to serve this God side by side with Israel after their lips had been cleansed (Zeph. 3: 9).[2] For to His servants (i.e., according to the midrash, the righteous from among the peoples) God will give another name. This and other prophetic texts may very early have filled the soul of the young Saul. His quick decision after Damascus to become a Christian missionary to the Gentiles suggests that he saw his old task in a new light, and was thus determined to hasten the coming of the

---

[1] *Die vor- und frühchristliche Zeit des Paulus*, Kiel, 1929, 18 ff.

[2] This Zephaniah text has even been understood (cf. Aboda Zara 24a) not only as a renunciation of idolatry on the part of the Gentiles, but positively as their participation in the spiritual wealth of Israel. Further references in Volz, *op. cit.*, 258 ff. (par. 44, 7e).

parousia. For the prophetic promises must be literally fulfilled, seeing that the Messiah had now come and must be the "light of the peoples". But the great majority of the Israelites did not recognize their Messiah, on the contrary crucifying Him and casting the promises to the winds. These events were not foreseen in prophecy, at least not according to the traditional understanding. As a result many thoughts crowd upon the mind of Paul, thoughts which for the most part find their answer in Rom. ch. 9–11.

The Christian conception of saving history, considered as the history of God's dealings with mankind, the redemptive work of the Messiah for the nations, the destiny and the future of the one people —such are the problems which the apostle is concerned to solve. From his own personal insight into the sweep and continuity of the divine saving work, Paul has given a luminous answer to these questions; one might even say that he has sketched out a theodicy, i.e., an explanation and justification of the ways of God which to mortal eyes are so inscrutable. With his theology which embraces the whole scope of saving history, Paul thought to uncover God's plan both for time and for that which lies beyond time. His answer has proved epoch-making and in fact has fundamentally determined the course of world history. But in order to understand its meaning and to be in a position to appreciate its significance as a whole, it is necessary to characterize Jewish universalist hopes which were entertained in the century before the destruction of the temple, and to sketch in outline at least the inner problems of the Jewish mission to the heathen.

I. THE JEWISH UNIVERSALIST HOPE AND THE PROBLEM OF THE MISSION TO THE HEATHEN

To judge by what our sources and tradition teach us, the century of Jesus and Paul was the century of Jewish history which fostered a universalistic hope without parallel in any century before or since. For Messianic expectation of the time was not confined to Israel. The salvation of the peoples—for whose redemption the high priest at the feast of tabernacles was accustomed to offer seventy bullocks according to the table in Gen. 10—was equally the concern of the Tannaites. Whole rabbinic circles were opposed to the particularism of Ezra and insisted that the gates of the law should be opened wide so that the nations of the earth might enter. The word of Isaiah: "Open the gates, that the righteous nation which keeps faith may enter in" (26: 2) was understood right up to the 4th century as a word of vigorous inspiration for the mission to the heathen. Rabbi Meir (*circa* 150) added (Sifre) to Lev. 18: 5: "my statutes and my ordinances by doing which a man shall live", the explanation: "The text does not speak of priests, Levites or Israelites, but of just men. This teaches us that even a non-Jew, if he concerns himself about the Torah, is as much to be esteemed as the high priest" (Parall. Baba Qamma 38a; Sanh. 59; Aboda Zara 3a). Of course according to the Jewish view it is impossible to become a priest or Levite unless one is a Jew by descent, but any foreigner or heathen can become a Saddiq, for יהוה אהב צדיקים (Midr. Teh. 146, 8). Likewise the midrash Mekhilta belonging basically to the 1st century gives on Ex. 22: 21 the explanation: "The *gerim* are beloved, for in every place where they are named they are named as Israelites." This is deduced from a comparison of many texts which use eulogistic predicates of Israel in reference to the *gerim*, and it concludes with quoting Ps. 146: 9: "The Lord watches over the *gerim*." This text in the psalms is also explained in Lev. Rabba Par. VIII ch. 5, 6 as meaning that there is no difference at all between Israel and the proselytes.[1]

This universalistic inspiration bore fruit, and in the century of the Hasmonean ascendancy gave rise to Jewish missionary propaganda. About the actual scope of this it is difficult for us to-day to form a clear idea. For in the first place, in the period of the Jewish war and the destruction of Jerusalem the rabbis' friendly attitude to proselytes abruptly changed, while secondly, the Jewish successes in the missionary field gave way without a struggle to nascent Christianity. Nevertheless, we know that the Diaspora, hence Hellenistic Judaism, was the chief participant in this missionary propaganda, which is very well attested by ancient authors (Seneca, Tacitus, Suetonius, Horace, Juvenal, Dio Cassius, Strabo, Josephus, etc.).[2] Likewise the New Testament informs us that at that time Pharisaic missionaries compassed land and sea to make proselytes (Mt. 23: 15). For Horace (*Sat.* 1, 4, 142 ff.) the Jew forms the very prototype of the urge to proselytize.

The number of the Jews and their associates during the apostolic

[1] The Yalqut interprets similarly "thy priests" (429 on Is. ch. 26) in connexion with Ps. 132: 9: they are the righteous from among the nations. Centuries later the Spanish philosopher of religion Isaac Arama explained the Talmud text Sanh. 105a in such a way that "every truly pious man was an Israelite" (*Aqedat Isaac* Pf. 6 ed., Venice 1480, f. 172b).

[2] Cf. H. Gressmann, "Jüdische Mission in der Werdezeit des Christentums", *ZMR*, 1924, 169–183; sources in Schürer, III, 167 ff.; Moore, I, 323 ff.

age, according to calculations which have a high degree of probability, must have amounted to around $4\frac{1}{2}$ millions or 7 per cent of the total population of the Imperium Romanum.[1] Hence this means that every fourteenth or fifteenth man in the Imperium Romanum was a Jew, and in Egypt at the time of Vespasian every seventh or eighth. This goes far beyond the limits of those who were Jews by descent. It is not without reason that in Talmudic discussions there was anxious debate about the fact that Judaism was like an *issah* (mixture) (Qidd. 69b; 71a). We know positively that the Jewish world mission won many proselytes even in the highest strata of society. Josephus tells us that the Empress Poppaea Sabina at the court of Nero became a God-fearer (*Ant.* 20, 8, 11) and that a large circle of like-minded people gathered round her whose interests she represented at court. After her death she was not burned according to Roman custom, but embalmed in the manner of foreigners. Further, in the time of Claudius and Nero, on the borders of the empire in the direction of Parthia, King Izates II of Adiabene on the upper Tigris was converted to Judaism with his whole house. Josephus (*Ant.* 20, 2–3) was especially proud of this triumph of missionary endeavour. Hence there is no reason to be suspicious of the claim of Philo (*Apion*, II, 39): "There is not a single Greek or barbarian city, not a single people, to which the custom of Sabbath observance has not spread, or in which the fast days, the kindling of the lights, and many of our prohibitions about food are not heeded." In *Ant.* 14, 7, 2 Josephus has proudly invoked the assertions of the Roman Strabo in respect of the considerable spread of Judaism in the Diaspora.

The reason for these missionary successes is probably to be seen above all in the powerful attractions of an imageless worship of God for the world of the mystery religions, so overladen with symbolism, especially as the latter itself began to develop certain tendencies towards monotheism. Further, we should take into account the unusually close connexion in Judaism between religion and ethics, as well as the venerable age of Jewish traditions.[2] Not least many may

---

[1] Cf. Th. Mommsen, *Römische Geschichte*, V, Leipzig, 1894, 489, 578 (E.T. *The History of Rome*); A. v. Harnack, *Die Mission und Ausbreitung des Christentums*, I, Leipzig, 1924, 13; further the monographs by B. J. Bamberger, *Proselyting in the Talmudic Period*, Cincinnati, 1939, and W. G. Braude, *Jewish Proselyting in the First 5 Centuries of the Common Era*, Providence, 1940, 11 ff.; Davies, *op. cit.*, 113 ff.; M. Simon, *Verus Israel*, 334 ff., 351 ff. As regards the different computations cf. W. Foerster, *Ntl. Zeitgeschichte*, II, Hamburg, 1956, 232 ff.

[2] Cf. Deissmann, *op. cit.*, 174 ff.; H. Preisker, *Ntl. Zeitgeschichte*, Berlin, 1937, 290 f.; P. Dalbert, *Die Theologie der hellenistisch-jüdischen Missionsliteratur*, Hamburg, 1954, 23 ff.

have been influenced by the advantage which the acceptance of Judaism offered of belonging to a *religio licita* of the Imperium Romanum.

The chief literary representatives of the missionary idea were the authors of Judaic Hellenism, such as the Sybillines, the Wisdom of Solomon, the Letter of Aristea, Philo, Josephus, and others. But even the short tractates *Derekh Eres Rabba* and *Zuta* contain enthusiastic appeals of the school of Rabbi Aqiba to the Gentile world. There were probably besides special catechisms adapted for the use of converts, or manuals of guidance for their instruction, which according to various narratives of the Gemera were presumed to be known by those desirous of acceptance (Sabb. 31a; Rosh hash. 17b). There may even have been a whole *Derekh Eres* literature—an idea which has in particular been championed by G. Klein,[1] who wished to see a pre-Talmudic missionary programme in writings of the *gaonaic* period such as the *Tanna debe Eliyahu*. To-day critics are more reserved with regard to such suppositions. But a literature which in connexion with the Noachidic commands has produced moral rules of life, has drawn up catalogues of virtues and vices, and made effective use of the "two ways" scheme, is still extant even to-day in various fragments and commentaries. Even in the LXX (e.g., on Prov. 4: 27) the important image of the two ways as possibilities of human existence, so widespread in Hellenistic popular ethics, is to be found reflected. Since Alfred Seeberg[2] it has for some time been considered as settled that behind the first six chapters of the Didache (1: 3—2: 1 is of course a Christian addition) there lies a Jewish proselyte catechism of the two ways, which was intended to emphasize the so-called golden rule of Hillel in the negative form (whatever you would not wish to be done to you, do not to your neighbour; Did. 1: 2). More recent critics (J. Muilenburg, J. A. Robinson, A. Vögtle) assume of course a dependence on Barnabas 18–20; but this question has not yet been decided.[3]

Apart from the Didache, the older Sibyllines which disregard the ceremonial laws (e.g., 2: 238 ff.; 4: 24 ff.; 162 ff. and especially

---

[1] *Der älteste christliche Katechismus und die jüdische Propagandaliteratur*, Berlin, 1909, 1 37 ff.

[2] *Der Catechismus der Urchristenheit*, Leipzig, 1903; *Die Didache des Judentums und die Urchristenheit*, Leipzig, 1908.

[3] The existence of such a proselyte catechism is regarded negatively by W. Michaelis in Kittel, *WB*, V, 99 (ὁδός); positively by B. Altaner, *Patrologie*, Freiburg, 1958, 44, who sees in the basic writing (ch. 1–6) the "oldest Christian document of the sub-apostolic age". Recently a connexion with the disciplinary scroll of Qumran has been suggested; thus J. P. Audet, *RB*, 1952, 219 ff.

8: 393 ff.),[1] as also the problematic didactic poem of the Pseudo-Phocylides, in which J. Bernays saw reflected a detailed codex of duties typical of Hellenistic Judaism, may have been originally camouflaged writings of the Jewish missionary propaganda of Alexandria. That Paul knew such writings or the views expressed in them, as Klein (*op. cit.*, 184 ff.) assumed, may be presumed from his exhortations.[2] But they were not, it is to be supposed, a direct source for him. What he says in Rom. 1: 18 ff. and 2: 14 ff. about the natural knowledge of God which the heathen have, and which has been described as *theologia naturalis*, need not therefore be considered absolutely as a Judaicized stoicism. It can equally well be *Derekh Eres* teaching, ventilated in the Jewish missions of the time, a teaching such as showed humanity the way from Noah to Moses—hence twenty-six generations before the Torah.[3]

In this matter the so-called Noachidic laws play a part. They can best be understood as an abridgment of the Torah for the use of proselytes, upon whom Jewish missionaries desired to impress the necessity of obeying the law considered as reflecting the kingly rule of God. It is well known that tradition developed from the injunctions to Noah, the father of all men after the Flood and at the same time the representative of the principle of law, a minimum of *mishpatim*, the observance of which guaranteed even to the pious from among the nations a share in the future world.[4] It is true that the number of these has never been fixed, but most usual was the reckoning of seven in the Sanh. 56, Aboda Zara 64b, Tos. Ab. Z. IX, which established as Noachidic the prohibition of idolatry, of blasphemy, of unchastity, of bloodshedding, of robbery, of enjoying the flesh of living animals, as well as the positive command to act justly. Hence a number of critics suppose that these norms, stemming from a "Halakha" minimum requirement and originally no doubt applied to aliens in the Jewish state, were extended in post-

---

[1] On their ethical aspects and resemblance to early Christian methods of preaching cf. J. Klausner, *op. cit.*, 165.

[2] As against Michaelis, *op. cit.*, 92, cf. Davies, *op. cit.*, 135: "We can be sure that Paul would be familiar with ethical maxims and social conventions which the Rabbis propagated and that he used these in his training of Christians."

[3] The opinion of Billerbeck and Lietzmann on Rom. 2: 14–15 that the idea of the heathen unwittingly fulfilling the law, in virtue of their conscience, is foreign to rabbinic scholars, is incorrect when stated thus sweepingly.

[4] According to Maimonides (Tr. Melakhim XI), any Gentile is pious and will share in the life of eternity, if he recognizes the seven Noachidic laws and tries hard to fulfil them.

Biblical times to the mass of semi-proselytes.[1] By this means basic ritual rules, facilitating life in common with them and table fellowship, were secured. A series of universally applicable ethic Haggadoth and general precepts of wisdom and virtue fostering a moral way of life replaced the requirement of the largely cultic Mosaic law for the attainment of the status of σεβόμενοι τὸν θεόν, and thus inculcated among the Gentiles the right way (*Derekh Eres*) of a life well-pleasing to God.

In the circles of Hellenistic Judaism from which Paul sprang, liberal-mindedness and large-heartedness towards the Gentiles must have been most marked. In many quarters the decision to turn away from heathen myths, to accept the belief in one God who created the world, and the will to embrace a moral way of life, must have been deemed sufficient for acceptance as a proselyte. This at any rate clearly emerges from Philo's work *De Nobilitate*. Hence in the sphere of Hellenistic Judaism it was commonly taken for granted that among the heathen there were doers of the law (Rom. 2: 14) who had the true circumcision of the heart (2: 29). But when Paul goes on to say that all men can discern with the eyes of reason (1: 20) God's power manifested in the created world (ἀπὸ κτίσεως κόσμου—τοῖς ποιήμασιν) the statement reflects the thought of Is. 26: 9 ff. and the same thought recurs in Seder Eliyahu Rabba, namely that God has revealed to all men His righteousness (the lex naturalis, *Derekh Eres*) and that all those who change the truth into a lie (1: 25) are destroyed.[2]

We must now come to the most important question, that of the structure of the Jewish missionary propaganda of the time, as it had resulted from the peculiar position of Judaism midway between a nation and a religious community. In general, it was not desired to make of the Gentiles complete Jews, but rather Noachides or God-fearers, who retaining their distinctive position should be annexed to the Jewish communities. Such annexed bodies of Gentiles were especially widespread in the Diaspora, where the σεβόμενοι were allowed to gather with the regular synagogue worshippers in order to learn the Jewish law and customs. In this respect the Jews were quite large-hearted, for Philo gives the impression that the σεβόμενοι were in fact an equally justified special group of synagogue

---

[1] This has been put forward in particular by E. Benamozegh in his little-known but very significant work *Israel et l'humanité*, Paris, 1914; cf. also M. Guttmann, *Das Judentum und seine Umwelt*, Berlin, 1927, and other authors.

[2] Cf. G. Klein, *Der älteste christliche Katechismus, op. cit.*, 71 ff.

worshippers.[1] Juvenal (*Sat.* 14, 96–106) attests that such σεβόμενοι frequently became fully-fledged proselytes. Archaeological discoveries of synagogue ruins in the area of the Aegean and the coast of Asia Minor, which indicate a division of the synagogue crosswise, seem to confirm the structure of the congregation as we have described it.

Since the facts of the situation have often been misrepresented owing to a terminological obscurity which is in part due to the texts themselves, let us first discriminate here between the various groups of non-Jews who entered into a closer relation with Judaism. We must distinguish then: (1) the גר תשב = πάροικος, ξένος; (2) the ירא שמים = σεβόμενοι τὸν θεόν, or οὐρανόν; (3) the גר צדק = προσήλυτος.

1. The *ger toshab* is the Biblical squatter, "the alien who dwells in the land". He is expected to keep his foreign peculiarities, though—as long as he lives among Jews—he is obliged to observe a certain minimum of ritual, namely the seven Noachidic commands (Aboda Zara 64b). Only in so far as he does so is a position secured for him in the sacral state of Israel.[2] We must certainly admit with Arakhin 29a that, in post-exilic times, this position can only be a matter of theoretic "Halakha" which even for Israel are not practicable any longer. But one has at times the impression that later the *ger toshab* was simply identified with the half proselyte.

2. The *yire shamayim* were the mass of the Gentiles won over by the missionaries, and this group was expected to keep the most important commands: the décalogue, the Sabbath, abstinence from *nebeloth*, and payment of the temple tax (Yehuda ben Ilai in Aboda Zara 64b; R. Meir in Tr. Gerim III, 1). They must also have been committed to keep the Noachidic commands. They took part in the Jewish cult and to a certain extent practised Jewish ritual, but according to Josephus' account (*Bell.* 6, 9, 3), they were not admitted to the sacrifices. It is probable that the *yire shamayim* were more widespread in the pre-Christian period—the oldest reference to the σεβόμενοι τὸν θεόν is LXX 2 Chr. 5:6—than in the apostolic age. The Acts of the Apostles tells us, however, that Paul's missionary preaching was crowned with the greatest success among the σεβόμενοι τὸν θεόν in Antioch (13: 48), Thessalonica (17: 4), Berea (17: 12), Iconium (14: 1), and

[1] Cf. A. Bertholet, *Die Stellung der Israeliten und der Juden zu den Fremden*, Tübingen, 1896, 285 ff.; A. Berliner, *Randbemerkungen zum täglichen Gebetbuch*, II, Berlin, 1912, 37 ff.; also Bousset–Gressmann, *op. cit.*, 80.

[2] Cf. R. Meyer in Kittel, *WB*, V, 848 ff. That the גר השער (proselyte of the gate) is to be eliminated as a medieval term, has been correctly supposed by Schürer, III, 177 ff.

Corinth (18: 4).[1] It is clear that these σεβόμεν ι belonged to the foundations of the first Christian churches. We shall return in the last section to the fundamental significance of the fact that Paul won over for nascent Christianity not "pure" heathen but such as had already been to some extent converted by the Jewish missions.

3. The *ger sedeq* as the full proselyte is clearly distinguished from the second group (e.g., Mekh. Ex. 22: 21).[2] These two forms or stages of proselytism were also well known to Philo[3] (*De Spec. Leg.* I, 51 in explanation of Lev. 19: 33–34). The full proselyte undertakes to keep the whole of the Torah. The Gentile who fulfils the whole law is counted a Jew.[4] In most cases the *ger sedeq* probably passed through the preparatory and testing intermediate stage of the *yire shamayim* before being received into Judaism by the rite of initiation. Discussions arose with regard to this rite not first among modern scholars, but long ago among the rabbis.[5] Among the Tannaites, Rabbi Joshua ben Hananiah considered that after due instruction public baptism by immersion to produce ritual cleanness was sufficient for reception into Judaism, while Rabbi Eliezer ben Hyrcanus required in addition circumcision (Bar. Yebamoth 46). Rabbi Joshua probably represented the older view ("all agree to it"); but the requirement of Eliezer ben Hyrcanus was generally accepted, and thus it was settled that only circumcision made one a full member of the Jewish community. The "Halakha" generally recognized at the latest by the end of the 2nd century runs: "One is not a proselyte until one has been circumcised and has undergone baptismal immersion *b'shem shamayim*" (Yeb. 46a; Ab. Z. 59a; Tos. Ab. Z. 57a).

[1] K. G. Kuhn, Art. προσήλυτος, Kittel, *WB*, VI, 1958, 744 is surely right to suggest that Paul had the greater success with these circles because unlike the Judaists he did not require circumcision as a presupposition for salvation.

[2] Cf. on this text M. Guttmann, *Das Judentum und seine Umwelt*, Berlin, 1927, 70.

[3] Philo distinguishes between uncircumcised semi-proselytes who do not keep the Mosaic law but accept monotheism, and circumcised full proselytes. Cf. S. Belkin, *Philo and the Oral Law*, Cambridge, Mass., 1940, 40 ff.

[4] It is also notable that the Jewish Christians of the pseudo-Clementine literature understand the fulfilment of the law as the decisive criterion: "If the non-Jew fulfils the law, he is a Jew; if he does not fulfil it, a Gentile" (Ἕλλην—Hom. 11, 16). In their midway position their judgment was the best.

[5] S. Zeitlin, "L'origine et l'institution du baptême pour les Prosélytes", *REJ*, 1934, 57, asserts that baptism of proselytes was only post-Pauline. But this is not exact. Cf. further: H. H. Rowley, "Jewish Proselyte Baptism", *HUCA*, 1940, 313 ff.; Braude, *op. cit.*, 74 ff.; J. Jeremias, "Proselytentaufe und Neues Testament", *ThZ*, 1949, 418 ff.; J. Klausner, *Von Jesus zu Paulus*, Jerusalem, 1950, 472 ff.; W. Michaelis, "Zum jüdischen Hintergrund der Johannestaufe", *Judaica*, 1951, 81 ff.; T. F. Torrance, "Proselyte Baptism", *NT Studies*, 1954, 148 ff.; J. M. Taylor, "The Beginnings of Jewish Proselyte Baptism", *NT Studies*, 1956, 193 ff.

The Mishna Kerethoth II, 1 and Kerethoth 9a (Eliezer ben Jacob, Tann. 2nd gen.) adds to circumcision and baptismal immersion the further requirement for proselytes of the offering of a bloody sacrifice, which was possibly older than immersion. Not until after the time of Paul, from about the year 70, was there a general change of views with regard to missionary questions; in the second century there seems to have been a rabbinic decree directed against the indiscriminate acceptance of proselytes, and laying down grave conditions with the object of testing their character.[1]

In Paul's own time, Jewish proselytism must have reached its height. The summons to salvation (הגרים קרבים לתשבה; the heathen are on the point of being converted—Mekhilta Ex. .12: 1) rang out far and wide into the world. It was believed that the Gentiles were turning to God from the purest of motives and by divine inspiration (Mekh. Ex. 18: 6). The promise to Abraham, who was now called the father of all proselytes, אב הגרים (Tanch. Lekh Lekha VI, 32a; Jer. Bikkurim 64a; Yehuda ben Ilai) was being fulfilled. Very beautifully the Mekhilta on Ex. 22: 21 speaks of Abraham, who once had described himself as a *ger* (Gen. 23: 4): "beloved are the *gerim*, for Abraham our father was circumcised when he was ninety-nine years old". Had he been circumcised when he was twenty or thirty years old, then a *ger* could only have become a proselyte up to the age limit of thirty. For this reason God delayed the conclusion of the covenant with him until he was ninety-nine years so that *gerim* to come might not be excluded.[2] By exegesis of Deut. 29: 13–15 proselytes were expressly included in the Sinai covenant (Shebuoth 39a). In fact, it was even asserted that proselytes like the Israelites were exempted from the inheritance of original sin, from the "corruption of the serpent" (Sabb. 146a). As the "spiritual seed of Abraham" they were fully entitled to all the rights and privileges of the Jews (Jer. Bikk. I, 4). Philo too makes Abraham the very prototype and pattern of all proselytes (*De Nobil.* II, 443; *De Abr.* II, 39, etc.).

Hopes for the future typical of the school of Hillel, which controlled in undiluted form the circle of Paul's teacher Gamaliel I,[3] were those

[1] Cf. Stählin, Kittel, *WB*, V, 13 (ξένος); further also the edition of G. Polster, "Der kleine Talmudtraktat Gerim über die Proselyten", *Angelos*, 1926, 18 ff. The basis of the tractate is early Tannaitic.

[2] About Abraham as the first to convert, cf. also Gen. Rabba on 12: 5 and 8. Also *Cahiers Sioniens*, 1951, nr. 2.

[3] Under the presidency of Gamaliel I was established *mippene darkhe shalom*, the friendly "Halakha" which said that in towns where Jews and Gentiles dwell together, the Jewish authorities should appoint guardians of the poor in the case of Gentiles also, in order to fulfil all the duties of love (Jer. Gittin V, 9).

of Biblical prophetism. Israel is to be the "light of the Gentiles" (Is. 49: 6—quoted by Paul in Rom. 2: 19); the synagogue is to be the "house of prayer for all peoples" (Is. 56: 7). At the end of the days it will come to pass that all peoples will stream to the mountain of the Lord's house in order to gain the knowledge of God (Is. 2: 2 ff.);[1] in fact, proselytes will press upon Israel. From the first Isaiah up to Malachi all the prophets expected a "day of the Lord" when Yahweh alone would reign as King over the whole earth (Zech. 14: 9). This fervour of expectation, which is still expressed with great vividness in the late wisdom writings of Jonah and Ruth, and which causes the Rabbi, redactor of the Mishna, to place the piety of the heathen Job on the same level with that of Abraham (Tos. Sota VI, 1), in fact even above that of Abraham (Baba Bathra 15b—to be sure an isolated text), was universalistic in character and insisted on propaganda among the heathen as a preparation for the coming of the Kingdom of God. Just in those circles whence Paul originated, the salvation of the *gerim* became a very special concern. In connexion with the turning of Ruth in 2: 12, Hillel's descendant Simon ben Gamaliel (Lev. Rabba 2, 8) says: "If a foreigner comes to be received as a proselyte, stretch out your hand towards him, in order to bring him under the protection of the wings of the Shekinah (קרב תחת כנפי השכינה)."[2] He himself, or at latest his children, was regarded as a full Jew.

2. PAUL'S VIEW OF HISTORY AND HIS TYPOLOGICAL EXEGESIS

In the previous section we have tried to describe the universalist hopes of the Jews at the time when Saul of Tarsus was active. He saw himself as one plunged in the struggle to win over the heathen and to secure their final conversion to the God of his fathers. He shared the faith of many of his Pharisaic contemporaries that by missionary work the coming of the Messianic time might be hastened, since the prophets had prophesied that its dawning would coincide

---

[1] This point of view is taken by Rabbi Jose (Aboda Zara 3b) and Rabbi Eliezer ben Hyrcanus (Ab. Z. 24a), who elsewhere (Sukka 28a) explains that he has never in his life taught any word in which he was not instructed by teachers, and thus here no doubt he represents an old and probably pre-Christian tradition, no doubt associated with Is. 56 : 7.

[2] We might mention here too a later similar statement in Tanch. Lekh Lekha 6 (32a): Resh Laqish (*circa* 250) said: "The proselyte, who passes over to Judaism, is more beloved of God than the Israelites who stood on Mount Sinai. If the latter had not heard the voices and the thunder, and the sound of the trumpets, if they had not seen the quaking mountains, they would never have received the Torah. But the convert comes along and without having perceived anything of all this, commends himself to God and accepts God's Lordship. Could there be any one more beloved?"

with the conversion of the nations. Since the Messiah had now appeared, the missionary task was all the more incumbent on him. His sense of history was moulded by the missionary viewpoint and his whole picture of history can only be understood in the light of his sense of a mission καθ' ὅλην γῆν. Harnack's dictum: "The resurrection spells the command to evangelize" is especially relevant to Paul, although and indeed because the earthly Jesus had limited His mission to Israel. "If he feels himself constrained to carry the good news of Christ to the whole world, it is in order to afford the elect from among the Gentiles the opportunity of attaining the state of being in Christ, and thus enabling them to fulfil their election. For this dogmatic reason he wishes to press on to Spain."[1]

In Rom. 15: 20–24 Paul announces his plan of going to Spain and proclaiming the gospel where it is not yet known; 2 Cor. 10: 15–16 also probably refers to the same matter. Hence F. Overbeck[2] is not wrong when he says, of course in an ironical tone, that Paul introduced Christianity into the sphere of history by the fact that "he fused in his thought Judaism and Jesus with His Jewish followers, and transplanted them into the world of the heathen".

In any case the situation was that after Damascus, in the light of his doctrinal convictions, the urgency of the mission to the heathen pressed even more sharply on his mind. For the Messianic age had now dawned, and it was therefore appropriate that those prophetic promises which had not yet found fulfilment should do so in the shortest possible time. The event of the parousia is bound up, for Paul, with the Gentile mission; before the realization of that event the name of Christ must have resounded to the four corners of the earth. The opinion current in liberal Jewish circles, that Paul conceived the idea of the mission to the Gentiles only after the failure of his synagogue preaching, only after the great majority of his own people had proved themselves unsuitable for· Christian evangelization, completely misunderstands the real motives in the apostle's mind. With him it is not a question of sour grapes, but of the necessary consequences of his eschatological convictions. And so he formulates thus his sense of obligation towards propaganda among the Gentiles: "But how are men to call upon him in whom they have not believed? And how are they to believe in him of whom they have never heard? And. how are they to hear without a preacher? And how can men preach unless they are sent? As it is written: 'How beautiful are the feet of those who preach good news!'" (Rom.

[1] A. Schweitzer, *Mystik*, 180.　　[2] *Christentum und Kultur*, Basel, 1919, 28.

10: 14, 15.) Paul was even prepared, in order to fulfil this end, "to those outside the law to become as one outside the law" "that I might win those outside the law" (1 Cor. 9: 21). And even in the mouth of a Hellenistic Jew this meant a great deal!

To this initiative of an intensive mission to the Gentiles on behalf of the church of Jesus the Messiah, which, he claims, gave him his title and formal office, there was now added paradoxically enough the necessity of a special mission to the Jews, since the Jews refused to recognize the Messiah and the dawning of the last age. This state of affairs, unforeseen in traditional Messianology, compelled Paul to give an independent answer to certain difficult questions—an answer which in the Letter to the Romans leads him to sketch out a new picture of the post-messianic time. This view of saving history was then taken over by the Christian church.

But before we attempt to indicate these questions and the Pauline answer to them, we must say a word of explanation about the Pauline view of history implied in the problematics of his missionary work. The fact is that Paul sees all earthly happenings as cohering with the continuity of a concrete divine plan of action. His historical understanding is never influenced by the Greek metaphysic of being, but derives always from the historical outlook characteristic of Israel. History is for him the unfolding of the divine counsel. From Adam (the author of world history) and from Abraham (the author of Jewish sacred history) all the lines of development point towards the Messiah, and since the hour of Damascus towards Jesus Christ. The very presence of Christ has been revealed to him in his historical vision as spelling the end of the reign of the law, as also the end of the law's requirements.[1] The real problem for the apostle was, however, how these things should be expressed in words. In this matter he remembered no doubt the advice of Hillel: "When you come to a town, behave according to its customs" (Gen. Rabba 48 on 18: 8; Ex. R. 47).[2] The verb κερδαίνειν in 1 Cor. 9: 19 is certainly in this connexion to be taken as a current "term in missionary language".[3] His sermons and letters are marked by a dual trend according as to whether his hearers and addressees were Jewish or Hellenistic, as to whether the address was: "Brethren, sons of the family of Abraham" (Acts 13: 26) or "Men of Athens" (Acts 17: 22), etc. For Paul

[1] Cf. G. Schrenk, "Die Geschichtsanschauung des Paulus auf dem Hintergrund seines Zeitalters", Studien zu Paulus, Zürich, 1954, 49 ff.

[2] Cf. D. Daube, "Jewish Missionary Maxims in Paul", Studia Theologica, I, 158 ff., now in The New Testament and Rabbinic Judaism, London, 1956, 336 ff.

[3] Thus J. Weiss; Daube, op. cit., 352 ff. concludes backwards to השתכר.

knows very well that the Jews require signs (proofs of power) and the Greeks seek wisdom (1 Cor. 1: 22).[1] Since, however, the majority of his missionary churches were of a mixed character, both trends are to be found in his letters and sometimes alternate with each other. In general, it is assumed that the Letters to the Romans and Galatians were determined by the discussion of Jewish problems, while those to the Corinthians and Thessalonians were inspired more by concern with Greek attitudes. But even the Corinthian Letters presuppose in the readers a "not inconsiderable Judaic culture", since the many proofs and figures drawn from the Old Testament would have been unintelligible to pure Hellenists.[2]

In discussion with the Jews the Old Testament was, of course, an instrument of proof from prophecy of special importance.[3] However much he clings to the authority of the sacred text, he does not shrink from any degree of violence in reading, even if the content of meaning is thereby changed, while at times for the sake of proving his argument the texts are simply shattered. His belief, of course, is that the veil of Moses ($κάλυμμα$) obscures the true understanding of the Old Testament texts, and that the Bible may only be rightly understood in the light shed by the $πνεῦμα$ of the Kyrios (2 Cor. 3: 13–17).[4] Hence he was concerned to derive from the texts of scripture typological indications and proofs which should enable the readers of his letters to see in the true context of meaning the new experience of salvation, and the data on which the Christian faith rested. It is for this reason that typological relations play such a significant part both in the Corinthian Letters (in 1 Cor. 10 the events of the period of wandering in the wilderness, which are said to have happened $τυπικῶς$, are put before the present generation $εἰς νουθεσίαν$, v. 11) and also in the Letter to the Romans. J. Daniélou[5] has very well defined this kind of typology in observing: "It consists in showing how past events disclose the pattern of events to come."

---

[1] Cf. K. Stürmer, *Auferstehung und Erwählung*, Gütersloh, 1953, 41–184.

[2] Cf. Bo Reicke, *Diakonie, Festfreude und Zelos*, Uppsala, 1951, 271.

[3] Cf. A. v. Harnack, *Das AT in den paulinischen Briefen und Gemeinden*, SB Preuss. Akad. Wiss., Berlin, 1928. Harnack emphasizes that in 6 of the letters (1 and 2 Thess., Phil., Philemon, Coloss., Ephes.) there are no OT quotations at all. Ellis, *op. cit.*, 11, counts 93 OT quotations in Paul, of which 87 are in the four main letters. The Pentateuch is quoted 33 times, Isaiah 25 times, the Psalter 19.

[4] Cf. J. Pépin, *Mythe et Allégorie*, Paris, 1958, 248: "This distinction between an apparent meaning which the casual reader does not get beyond, and a deep meaning accessible only to the learned, is the exact definition of allegory whatever be the context in which it is used."

[5] *Sacramentum futuri*, Paris, 1950, 4.

This typological approach to reflection on history, which became an accepted principle and gained ascendancy over the whole life of the early church, acquires particular importance in Paul's antithesis of Adam and Christ. Since Paul, thinking on apocalyptic lines, had developed a special Messianology of the aeons, Adam and Christ acquired for him in strict logical consequence the status of archontes of their respective aeons, i.e., of the periods of world time which they initiated. Accordingly in Rom. 5: 12–21 and differently in 1 Cor. 15: 45–49 he unfolded a whole cosmological scheme from the standpoint of saving history, designed to show that Adam's antitype, Christ, is the Inaugurator of a new period, namely, the final period of world time, in which the Christian Church is rooted. The universal saving significance of Christ and the new Israel of God are schemes of thought developed by him in the same typological manner from Old Testament prototypes and intimations.[1]

These typological patterns, which are central to his whole picture of history, reveal plainly that Paul read the Old Testament not simply as historical or doctrinal literature but as it were with prophetic eyes, in order to extract from it its hidden typological content and suggestions of saving history.[2] Thus the great figures and moments in the Old Testament become for him τύποι foreshadowing the events of the last age. But in contrast with Philo, who reinterpreted historical events as symbolizing processes in the human soul, Paul's typological exegesis remains firmly orientated towards τὰ ἔσχατα. It may be that the picture of history conveyed by apocalyptic had even greater significance for him than that of the Old Testament. Qumran obviously offers the closest parallels to this kind of historical thinking.

The story of Abraham, so dear to Paul, plays a great part in this scheme. We have already seen that in Rom. 4 Paul gave to the whole story of Abraham an interpretation so arranged as to be susceptible of typological treatment. Abraham, who against all reason believed in God's promises, becomes thus the type of the Christian who in the same way believes in the God who raised Jesus

[1] Cf. H. Lietzmann, *Komm. zu 1 Kor. 10: 11*: "The OT events, as far as Paul is concerned, did not happen for their own sake, but to foreshadow events of the final Messianic age, just as Adam in Rom. 5: 14 is a type of the Messiah." Cf. the important monograph by L. Goppelt, *Typos, die typologische Deutung des AT im Neuen Testament*, Gütersloh, 1939, as also R. Bultmann, "Ursprung und Sinn der Typologie als hermeneutischer Methode", *ThLZ*, 1950, 206 ff.

[2] Hence E. Peterson, *Was ist Theologie?*, Bonn, 1926, 17 ff., has rightly said: "The Prophets of the old covenant prophesy the future, those of the new covenant prophesy from the past. Hence allegory belongs essentially to their method of exegesis."

Christ from the dead. The deliberate typological treatment becomes still clearer when in Gal. 3: 16 from the singular phrasing of the promised blessing to Abraham and his seed is extracted the meaning —naturally contrary to the sense of the text which refers to the physical descendants of Abraham, thus to Israel—that here a particular individual, namely Christ, is being announced. The conclusion which Paul draws from this is that only Christ and those who abide in Him are the heirs of the blessing promised to Abraham. As the new seed of Abraham called into existence by a wonderful vocation they form, as it were, a newly fashioned humanity. Christians freed from sin—and at this point Paul does not shrink from applying his typological treatment to the Passover rite itself—are compared in 1 Cor. 5: 6–7 with a fresh lump of dough (ἄζυμοι). By this typological treatment Paul opens the long line of ecclesiastical authors who have denied to the Jewish people their election privileges and promises, transferring them to Christianity as the new Israel of God by the simple device of typological–allegorical exegesis.

Paul expresses the same idea polemically in the passage Gal. 4: 21–31, which is allegorical rather than typological, and which has been discussed in detail by Michel, Goppelt, Ellis, and others. In the figures of Abraham's two wives who represent the two covenants we have here the clearest allegory (Paul describing it as such in v. 24) in the whole of the New Testament, which otherwise has remained for the most part typological. The conclusion of this passage is again that the new Christian community is the Israel of God whereas the old Israel has been rejected of God. In the Letter to the Romans a whole series of prophetic oracles are cited in support of the idea (Is. 65: 1; Hos. 2: 23; Joel 2: 32, etc.). In point of fact those oracles referred to the restoration of the people of Israel who had been temporarily banished, but they are understood by Paul to mean that God has called men not only from among the Jews but also from the Gentiles.[1] In order to justify these audacious views, Paul made use of a principle[2] which the rabbis used only sparingly and hesitatingly for such purposes: מעשה אבת סימן לבנים. Paul must have seen

---

[1] For Paul's method of using OT texts at times in his preaching to the Gentiles, his sermon at Antioch described in Acts 13 is illuminating; it consists in a short sketch of the history of Israel adapted for missionary ends, and culminating in the doctrine of the forgiveness of sins mediated through the death and resurrection of Jesus.

[2] Cf. J. Bonsirven's judgment (*Exégèse Rabbinique et exégèse Paulinienne*, Paris, 1939, 324) on Pauline exegesis: "His typological method is what distinguishes him most deeply from the preachers of the synagogue. His Christian faith alone revealed to him the whole profound significance of the OT and its symbolic meaning!"

in this principle the justification for a typology which—conspicuously in 1 Cor. 10—simply dissolves the facts of history in what follows from them. Thus far Friedrich Nietzsche was right when he wrote in *Morgenröte* (Aph. 84):[1]

> What can one expect of the after effects of a religion which in the centuries of its foundation performed this unheard-of philological farce in regard to the Old Testament? I mean the attempt to withdraw the Old Testament from the Jews by asserting that it contains nothing but Christian doctrine and belongs in truth to the Christians as the true people of Israel, whereas the Jews had merely arrogated its possession to themselves. The Christians gave themselves up to a passion for reinterpretation and substitution—a process which cannot possibly have been compatible with a good conscience. However much Jewish scholars protested, it was affirmed that everywhere in the Old Testament the theme was Christ and only Christ.

The rightness or wrongness of this declaration will have to be decided by Paul's assessment of the function of the Jewish people as conveyed to us in Rom. chs. 9–11, which are emphatically determined by typological–allegorical exegesis.

3. THE FUNCTION OF THE JEWISH PEOPLE IN ROMANS CHS. 9–11

The Letter to the Romans, which here and there bears a real conversational character, was, as we have already seen, addressed to a mixed community of Christians. Hence, in spite of the fundamentally Jewish problem of which it treats, a dual tendency of thought can be recognized. Chapters 9–11 may best be understood as an exhortation to Gentile Christians, who had previously been influenced by the Jewish mission, and had belonged to the circle of the σεβόμενοι.[2] In chs. 14–15 we see Paul taking under his protection a Jewish-Christian minority which is afraid of the majority, whereas in ch. 16: 17–18 there is again a warning about Jewish errors.

In the great chapters 9–11 Paul sketches out a theology of saving history, for he strives to unfold God's plan in time and eternity. We have here a kind of theodicy—an explanation and justification of the ways of God which are inscrutable and mysterious to mortal eyes. Here the term πρόθεσις plays a great part,[3] for Paul believes he

---

[1] *Werke*, ed. Schlechta, I, 1067 ff.

[2] Cf. Deissmann, *op. cit.*, 183; Bousset-Gressmann, *op. cit.*, 81.

[3] In addition πρόγνωσις or προγιγνώσκειν and προορίζειν belong here.' Cf. G. Schrenk in Kittel, *WB*, IV, 180 ff.; E. Dinkler, *Prädestination bei Paulus*, Festschrift für Günther Dehn, Neukirchen, 1957, 86, 98 ff.

knows the divine intention and that he is able to interpret to men God's dealings with them. Obviously going beyond the Pharisaic common sense, he believed in a divine predestination and the possibility of understanding it fully. It might even be the case that in this respect Paul stands in an Essenic tradition, for the Essenic belief in predestination which is attested by Josephus (*Ant.* 18, 1, 5) has since been confirmed by the Qumran texts.[1] In any case Paul thinks that he knows the truth with regard to the divinely governed destinies of the people of Israel whether for weal or woe. It is not by chance that he describes these destinies in connexion with the hymn about the assurance of salvation with which Romans ch. 8 closes.[2] For it is just this assurance of salvation which seems to be questioned by the destiny of Israel, since Israel's disbelief in the assertion that the Messiah had come was for Paul and for wide circles of early Christians the most inexplicable and perplexing problem to be dealt with. Hence he must know the answer better than the Jews to whom he unfolds the secret of God's ways which in his own opinion he understands.

Hence chs. 9–11 are by no means a section arbitrarily inserted into the continuity of the letter as a whole; they are, on the contrary, closely bound up with the sequence of thought which controls the letter throughout. Already in 3: 1–4 the apostle had touched upon the problem of unbelieving Israel after previously in 2: 17–20 enumerating the advantages of the Jewish Diaspora by contrast with the surrounding heathen world. This doctrinal letter dispatched from Corinth in the early part of the year 58 must have been occasioned by an inner crisis in the young Roman church. It is possible that the Jewish-Christian minority, under the impact of the successes of the mission to the Gentiles, was resisting the threat of complete suppression. The theme of the letter is the rights and wrongs of Judaism, but also of a Gentile-Christian antinomism. Attempts were being made to foist this upon Paul himself. We can find in the letter discussions on very varied points: Hellenistic philosophy, Jewish theology, and the special claims of Jewish Christians. Hence W. Lütgert[3] considered that Rom. 9–11 is much more alive if the section is understood historically rather than dogmatically, and if we take into account the intention of Paul to check a scornful attitude on the part of antinomistic Gentile Christians towards Israel.

[1] Cf. K. G. Kuhn, *ZThK*, 1952, 219 ff.; M. Burrows, *op. cit.*, 215 ff., 233, 278.
[2] So also L. Goppelt, *Christentum und Judentum im ersten und zweiten Jahrhundert*, Gütersloh, 1954, 112.　　　[3] *Der Römerbrief als historisches Problem*, Gütersloh, 1913.

This attitude on the part of Paul, however, is deeply connected with the attempt to find a new meaning in his own Judaism, for the unfolding of the true divine plan of salvation is intended to yield a new interpretation of the whole Jewish position as regards the faith. Paul is in fact convinced that he has never seceded from Judaism, since the Christian confession means for him the completion of his Jewish faith. But this position must first be demonstrated to others. "This section (Rom. 9-11) is the apostle's attempt to pursue the destiny of Israel with prophetic–apocalyptic categories of thought right into the inner shrine of God's counsels and actions."[1] We have gratefully taken into account the large body of specialist literature on these three chapters.[2]

In them Paul has endeavoured to outline and answer three weighty questions: (1) How was this obvious hardening of the heart of Israel, God's people, at all possible? (2) What is its significance for the present phase of the saving process? (3) What future is there for Israel?

1. The first question is concerned with the mystery of Jewish unbelief in face of the advent of the Messiah; it lies behind the whole complex of thought in these chapters. In particular, the confession at the opening of the section at once suggests this question, for here the apostle considers the past history of Israel as reflecting a redemptive plan and enumerates from the start the eternal signs of Israel's election: $\upsilon i o \theta \epsilon \sigma i a$ (בני בכרי: Ex. 4: 22), $\delta \acute{o} \xi a$ (שכינה), $\delta \iota a \theta \hat{\eta} \kappa a \iota$ καὶ αἱ ἐπαγγελίαι (בריתים from Abraham to Moses), $\nu o \mu o \theta \epsilon \sigma i a$ (תורה), $\lambda a \tau \rho \epsilon i a$ (עבודה), ὧν οἱ πατέρες (זכת אבות), to which finally the Messiah after the flesh belongs. The pericope 9 : 6–13, which follows this enumeration of the Jewish claims to election, tries to answer the question whether God's summoning and electing word has become ineffectual. The answer suggested runs as follows: From God's side the election has not been a mistake, and it would not be possible to call it a failure. The fact is rather that mere physical descent from Abraham is not sufficient in itself to make an Israelite an heir of the promise. The election and the

---

[1] O. Michel, *Der Brief an die Römer*, Göttingen, 1955, 256.

[2] Among more recent works we may mention: F. W. Maier, *Israel in der Heilsgeschichte nach Röm. 9-11*, Münster, 1929; E. Peterson, *Die Kirche aus Juden und Heiden*, Salzburg, 1933; K. Barth, *Die Kirchliche Dogmatik*, II, 2, Zollikon, 1942, 215–336 (E.T. *Church Dogmatics*); K. L. Schmidt, *Die Judenfrage im Lichte der Kapitel 9–11 des Römerbriefes*, Zollikon, 1947; A. Oepke, *Das neue Gottesvolk*, Gütersloh, 1950; G. Schrenk, *Studien zu Paulus*, Zürich, 1954; L. Goppelt, *Christentum und Judentum im ersten und zweiten Jahrhundert*, Gütersloh, 1954; J. Munck, *Christus und Israel*, Copenhagen, 1956; E. Dinkler, *Prädestination bei Paulus*, Dehn-Festschrift, Neukirchen, 1957.

promise do not apply to all the posterity of Abraham, οὐ γὰρ πάντες οἱ ἐξ Ἰσραήλ, οὗτοι Ἰσραήλ, but only to a part, a selection, which in v. 8 are reckoned as the "seed" (i.e., inheritors of the promise; cf. Gal. 3:29: κατ' ἐπαγγελίαν κληρονόμοι). The word λογίζεσθαι leaves it to the judgment of God as to how many and which of the children of Abraham are to be made heirs of the promise.

The apostle's approach to the matter had the effect of sundering an eschatological Israel of the promise from the empiric-historical Israel. Behind this outlook lies, of course, the prophetic word that not the whole of Israel but only a remnant will be saved, i.e., will come to inherit the promise.[1] In apocalyptic literature the theme of the remnant (relicti residui, relinqui, etc.) is a consistently used formula.[2] Rabbinic writings too have given expression to the same thought when with regard to Deut. 14:1: "You are the sons of the Lord your God", it is explained; "Only if you behave in the manner of children, if not, not" (R. Yehuda in Qidd. 36a circa 150). This limitation, however, had a different purpose with Paul from what it had with Rabbi Yehuda or any other rabbi, because Paul wishes to give reasons for the failure of the majority of Jews to accept the Messiah and so—what would have been impossible within the confines of the Jewish faith—plays off the idea of the remnant against the truth of the election which includes all Israelites, both righteous and sinners. By this means the ontic and natural character of the Jewish idea of the covenant becomes spiritualized, and the election charters of the patriarchal history can be spiritually interpreted; thus too the thesis that Isaac who was born later was preferred to Ishmael because he was the son of the promise (Gen. 18:10 and 14).[3]

---

[1] On the theological idea of the remnant as a Biblical leitmotif, cf. M. Sister, Zu Motivproblemen in der Bibel, Festschrift für Leo Baeck, Berlin, 1938, 31 ff.; J. Jeremias, "Der Gedanke des Heiligen Restes im Spätjudentum und in der Verkündigung Jesu", ZNW, 1949, 181 ff.; Herntrich in Kittel, WB, IV, 200–215; Schrenk, ibid., 215–221 (ἐκλογή); Munck, Excursus, 85 ff.

[2] References in Volz 44, 6d (352 ff.).

[3] The part played by Isaac as a type in Pauline Christology has already been discussed in ch. 4, 3. In this connexion Isaac is the "allegorical prototype of the one justified by faith" (Lietzmann). The parallel Gal. 4:21–31 which makes Isaac as the promised son of Sarah symbolize the new covenant and Jerusalem which is above, while Ishmael the son of the handmaid Hagar symbolizes the Jews and the old covenant, by its wilful distortions is sheer Hellenistic midrash speculation, against a rather obscure apocalyptic background. Sarah (perfection) and Hagar (foreshadowing) are, of course, frequent symbols in Philo, but Gal. 4:21–31 is an utter violation of the basic rule of rabbinical hermeneutics: "No word of scripture must ever lose its original sense" (Sabb. 63a). Paul justifies his procedure by the ἅτινά ἐστιν ἀλληγορούμενα of v. 24, with the suggestion that the things described have a concealed sense which is other than what the words of

The marvellous incidents connected with his birth become for Paul the proof that biological descent is no longer the valid factor, but rather the promise, in consequence of which the posterity of Abraham has been exalted from the natural to the supernatural sphere. Erik Peterson writes: "All this can be understood when we realize that Paul is concerned to bring out the distinction between the pneumatic and the natural orders" (20).

The same point is to be proved by a second example drawn from the patriarchal story. As with the sons of Abraham, so with the sons of Isaac (vv. 11–13) the divine election ($\dot{\eta}$ $\kappa \alpha \tau$' $\dot{\epsilon} \kappa \lambda o \gamma \dot{\eta} \nu$ $\pi \rho \acute{o} \theta \epsilon \sigma \iota s$ $\tau o \hat{v}$ $\theta \epsilon o \hat{v}$) was determined not according to privileges of birth or quality of character, but in God's free will to elect and summon which operated before their birth ($o \dot{v} \kappa$ $\dot{\epsilon} \xi$ $\ddot{\epsilon} \rho \gamma \omega \nu$—$\dot{\alpha} \lambda \lambda$' $\dot{\epsilon} \kappa$ $\tau o \hat{v}$ $\kappa \alpha \lambda o \hat{v} \nu \tau o s$, 9 : 11). "I have loved Jacob but I have hated Esau" (Mal. 1 : 2–3).[1] To the objection that the preference of Jacob really implies an injustice on God's part, Paul replies by referring to the sentence in Ex. 33 : 19 which places grace and judgment in the free pre-determining will of God; a sentence which all doctrines of pre-destination have always invoked.[2] This is again illustrated in v. 17 by reference to God's dealings with Pharaoh, who once persecuted the people of God as now Israel persecutes the church.[3] V. 18 then gives the logical conclusion: "So then he has mercy upon whomever he wills, and he hardens the heart of whomever he wills." Thus Paul has answered the first question by suggesting that it was always only an elect part of Israel which inherited the promises, and of this remnant the last and decisive member, the Messiah, has appealed only to the elect few.

scripture imply. Finally, I would point out that in rabbinical writings there is as yet unnoticed ironical treatment of this allegory. It is in the Pes. R. Kah. Pisqa XXII; source Rabbi Berechiah (Pal. Am. 4th gen.) in the name of Rabbi Levi (Pal. Am. 3rd gen., end 3rd century).

[1] The rabbinical exegesis of the sentence mostly rationalizes and suggests for God's hatred towards Esau the strength of the evil impulse at work in Esau (Gen. Rabba 63, etc.). There is no rabbinic typological treatment of the text with any corresponding tendency; cf. Odeberg in Kittel, *WB*, II, 957. Philo is here closer to Paul; cf. M. Friedländer, *Die religiösen Bewegungen innerhalb des Judentums im Zeitalter Jesu*, Berlin, 1905, 352.

[2] In the Jewish writings of our period such doctrines cannot be found. Echoes are found in Wisdom 12 from which Grafe, *Das Verhältnis der paulinischen Schriften zur Sapientia Salomonis*, Theolog. Abhandl. für Weizsäcker, Strasbourg, 1892, wished to derive the thoughts of Rom. 9: 15–23. Quite apart from the question whether Paul knew Wisdom at all, it seems to me that these thoughts so firmly embedded in his economy of salvation do not need any special derivation.

[3] Cf. J. Munck, *op. cit.*, 41 : Pharaoh stands for Egypt; F. W. Maier, *op. cit.*, 44, misunderstood Pharaoh as "the type of the hardening of Israel typical of his time".

2. What does it mean for the present phase of the saving process if the greater part of Israel is hardened and only a selected remnant has followed the Messiah? From the dialectical point of view the following point is of decisive significance for the present moment of the saving process: God has called the elect to glorify Him not only from among Jews but also from among the heathen. With this must be connected the question of 3: 29: "Or is God the God of Jews only? Is he not the God of Gentiles also? Yes, of Gentiles also."[1] Abraham, too, the pattern of righteousness springing from faith, the righteousness which is possible for all men, became the father of the Gentiles. While he was the initiator of the historic Israel, he became also the type of the new eschatological people of God. Every Greek can now become the seed of Abraham and the heir of the promise made to him.

Chapter 9 declares that this calling of the heathen predicted by Abraham, Moses, and Isaiah κατὰ πρόθεσις has now been occasioned by the unbelief of Israel. But in consequence of the divine patience, this summoning of the heathen to enter on the inheritance will avail to the good of the "vessels of wrath" (σκευή ὀργῆς). Scripture proof of this calling of the Gentiles is furnished in 9: 25–26 by two quotations from Hosea (2: 1 and 2: 23), which in rabbinical exegesis were never treated in the sense of a casting out of Israel and their replacement by another people.[2] But Paul deduces from his exegesis of Hosea that if not all who stem from Israel belong to the true Israel, then the consequence is that Gentiles may also belong to the true Israel of God. This summoning of the heathen into the household of God's people is the characteristic sign of the dawn of the post-messianic era. The elect Israel, following the Messiah in the path of discipleship, is the "Church composed of both Jews and Gentiles". This means, however, that the Jewish-Christian mis-

[1] Billerbeck, III, 185 rightly notes on this that the Jewish reply is a divine word given by Simon bar Jochai: "I am God over all who come into the world, but my name have I united only with you. I am not called the God of the Gentiles but the God of Israel" (Ex. Rabba 29 on 20: 2).

[2] What the Jewish exegesis of Hosea 2: 1 was, Lev. Rabba Par. II on ch. 2: 23 shows quite clearly with its plain opposition to the Christian use of the word. Hosea asks the nations of the earth: "Do you suppose because He has spoken these words to you that God is angry with you?" Hosea himself gives the answer with Song of Sol. 8: 7: "many waters cannot quench the love of God". To this are added learned sentences intended to confirm the explanation. Hos. 2: 23 in Jewish exegesis is mostly applied to Diaspora proselytes (Pes. 87b, etc.). On the later commentary by Rashi, Ibn Ezra, Qimchi see the early work of A. Wünsche, *Der Prophet Hosea*, Leipzig, 1868, 32 ff. On the whole subject, cf. Marmorstein, *Religionsgeschichtliche Studien*, I, Skotschau, 1910, 18 f. and *Studies in Jewish Theology*, London, 1950, 192 ff., as also Schoeps, *Religionsgespräch* etc., *op. cit.*, 37 ff.

sionary motto: "To the Jews first and also to the Greeks",[1] which carries a certain national pathos and which Paul himself had frequently employed, has been dissolved without residue. In the church of the new covenant there is no distinction between Jew and Greek, slave and free, male and female (Gal. 3: 28; cf. 1 Cor. 12: 13; Col. 3: 11). Paul considers that the predicate of election applicable to the Israel κατὰ σάρκα has now been transferred to the new Ἰσραὴλ τοῦ θεοῦ (Gal. 6: 16). And in 1 Thess. 2: 14 it is even said that these Christians have become imitators of the churches in Judaea who had been persecuted by the Jews who killed the Lord Jesus.[2]

The same point of view is once again expressed in ch. 10, and this time against the background of the contrast we have spoken of already between the righteousness which is based on works, and which caused the Jews to be zealous in a misguided sense, and that which springs from faith and attains its goal. This righteousness does not put to shame but rather saves (Is. 28: 16) anyone who confesses the Kyrios Jesus, invokes His name (Joel 2: 32), and sincerely believes in His resurrection. At the close of ch. 10 (vv. 18–21) the apostle again considers the possible excuse that the Jews may perhaps not have heard the gospel of Christ, and so may not have had the opportunity of embracing the faith. However, applying the prophecy of Ps. 19: 4, he declares this to be quite out of the question and adds: They have understood clearly enough, but Isaiah himself predicted the calling of the heathen and the disobedience of Israel. The present situation, he says, is nothing else than a fulfilment of prophetic oracles: "I have been found by those who did not seek me; I have shown myself to those who did not ask for me." But to Israel he says: "All day long I have held out my hands to a disobedient and contrary people" (Is. 65: 1–2). And again in ch. 11 he collects words from the Torah, the Prophets, and the Writings intended to confirm Israel's hardening of heart.

3. There remains as the third torturing question, implied in this new picture of the post-messianic age, the following: What is to be the future of Israel? What will become of the Jews? Has God cast off His people?

Paul answers: "By no means!" (11: 1).[3] The deepest ground of

---

[1] Munck, op. cit., 22, is correct in saying that this formula characterized Jerusalem Jewish Christianity.

[2] In the continuation 2: 15b Paul takes up rather astonishingly a stereotyped formula of ancient anti-semitism for which see Leipoldt, Lösch, in Komm. Dibelius.

[3] The same question is asked in Ruth Rabba IV, where God Himself answers: "I cannot do so, I can only visit on them suffering and sorrow."

this חלילה (by no means) springs from Paul's Jewish faith in the faithfulness of God, who cannot revoke covenant, law, and election, so surely as He is the God of truth, and cannot make already revealed and realized truth into a lie, not even when Israel has betrayed that truth. And so he says in 11: 29: "The gifts and the call of God are irrevocable."[1] Just as of old on the occasion of the stamping out of the worship of Baal in the days of the prophet Elijah, there remained one servant faithful to God, so in the present phases of saving history the eternal God, as already Isaiah had prophesied would happen, has provided by grace a remnant[2] (ὑπόλειμμα— 9: 27; 11: 5).

But even the vast majority are not finally reprobate; the fact is rather that a spirit of folly has hardened their hearts, so that their eyes see not and their ears hear not. The summoning of the Gentiles which in the meantime has taken place is intended not least to render Israel jealous of them. Alien branches of a wild olive tree have been grafted on to the genuine olive tree (Israel).[3] Finally, the calling of those who are not of Israel has happened because God has a secret plan in the government of the world: in part a spirit of hardening has overtaken Israel until that momentous time when the full number of the Gentiles have come in. Then it is that the whole of Israel will be saved (11: 25–26a);[4] even the branches that have been hewn off will be grafted in again, for God has the power to do that (v. 23). It is clear that Paul implies even that the Israelites as the descendants of the patriarchs have a special sanctity in election (11: 16). They belong to the genuine, ancient olive tree, and even though they have been torn asunder, can be grafted in once more in accordance with nature (11: 23–24).[5]

---

[1] Many NT critics, e.g., J. Munck, *op. cit.*, 104, shrink from the thought that Paul here wished to express the fact that God is bound legally. But it is just this which must have been the case.

[2] For Paul's treatment of the idea of the remnant, cf. Schrenk in Kittel, *WB*, IV, 215–221; O. Michel, *Der Brief an die Römer*, Göttingen, 1955, 217 ff.

[3] Cf. the explanation in A. Oepke, *op. cit.*, 217; Dahl, *op. cit.*, 242 ff.; Munck, *op. cit.*, 96 ff.

[4] The sentence πᾶς Ἰσραὴλ σωθήσεται corresponds to a rabbinic *theologoumenon*: all Israel will share in the future world (M. Sanh. X, 1).

[5] Since I find no reference to this in the commentaries, I would point out that Philo, who has developed almost the same train of thought as Paul, may be the source of the parable of the olive tree. I add here the text: *De Praem. et Poen.* II, 433: Ὁ μὲν ἔπηλυς ἄνω ταῖς εὐτυχίαις μετέωρος ἀρθεὶς περίβλεπτος ἔσται, θαυμαζόμενος καὶ μακαριζόμενος ἐπὶ δυσὶ τοῖς καλλίστοις, τῷ τε αὐτομολῆσαι πρὸς θεὸν καὶ τῷ γέρας λαβεῖν οἰκειότατον τὴν ἐν οὐρανῷ τάξιν βεβαίαν, ἣν οὐ θέμις εἰπεῖν. ὁ δ' εὐπατρίδης παρακόψας τὸ νόμισμα τῆς εὐγενείας, ὑποσυρήσεται κατωτάτω πρὸς αὐτὸν τάρταρον καὶ βαθὺ σκότος ἐνεχθείς, ἵνα ταῦτα ὁρῶντες

Paul then relates to this momentous point of time, καθὼς γέγραπται, the Messianic prophecy of Jer. 31: 33–34. The image behind these verses, as the scripture quotations show, is that of the καινὴ διαθήκη (mentioned by Paul also in 1 Cor. 11: 25) which intimates a salvation valid for Jews also: the new covenant of healing and salvation hoped for by them and promised them in scripture and now at last offered them in Christ.[1] All this implies that the second coming of Christ is most closely connected with the final conversion of the Jewish people.[2] In the older periods of the church this insight of Paul became utterly lost,[3] but since the spiritual renewal of the 17th century[4] the judgment of the Christian Church on the Jews and on their function in the saving process *post Christum natum* has been determined by Rom. 11: 25.

To sum up the chapter, the apostle finally answers the question what should be the attitude of Christians towards the Jews. His answer is dialectically framed: for the present they are indeed the enemies of God, as far as the proclamation of the Messiah is concerned, but from the point of view of their original election they are God's beloved, זכות אבות (11: 28).[5] Although they are at present disobedient as the Gentiles once were, yet the mercy which now has been showered upon the Gentiles in Christ will at the right moment be imparted to them also. This moment Paul thinks will soon come.[6] But the problem of the delay in the parousia finds its ultimate and true explanation in the still unconquered unbelief of Israel; and while this makes understandable to the churches the difficulties and obstacles of the interim period, it makes the missionary task more urgent as a preparation for the coming kingdom. The chapter ends (vv. 33–36) with a hymn-like doxology, a eulogy of the unfathomable γνῶσις θεοῦ.

τὰ παραδείγματα πάντες ἄνθρωποι σωφρωνίζωνται, μανθάνοντες, ὅτι τὴν ἐκ δυσμενείας ἀρετὴν φυομένην θεὸς ἀσπάζεται, τὰς μὲν ῥίζας ἐῶν χαίρειν, τὸ δὲ στελεχόθεν ἔρνος, ὅτι μετέβαλεν ἡμερωθὲν πρὸς εὐκαρπίαν, ἀποδεχόμενος.

[1] On the relation between Paul's understanding of salvation and the new covenant, consult, apart from various modern studies, A. v. Stromberg, *Studien zur Theorie und Praxis der Taufe*, Berlin, 1913, 81 ff.

[2] In 4th-century Judaism there still survived the opposite expectation, as Jerome reports: "Judaei et Christiani judaizantes ultimo sibi tempore repromittunt . . . ut non Judaei Christiani, sed Christiani Judaei fiant" (*MPL*, 25, 1529).

[3] Cf. the references in Goppelt, *op. cit.*, 121 and 309.

[4] Cf. H. J. Schoeps, *Philosemitismus im Barock*, Tübingen, 1952, esp. 18 ff.

[5] Cf. Bo Reicke, "Um der Väter willen, Röm. 11: 28", *Judaica*, 1958, 106 ff.

[6] This is clear from 11: 14. Paul thinks of his own work as concerned with the expected conversion of Israel, as has been correctly pointed out by an earlier author: E. Weber, *Das Problem der Heilsgeschichte nach Röm. 9–11*, Leipzig, 1911, 106.

Thus the Pauline sketch of the post-messianic time of salvation assesses the significance which may be granted to Israel in the past, present, and future, in consequence of the call of the Gentiles. It may well be said that Gentile Christianity was founded upon somewhat far-fetched speculation. To the disadvantage of the Jewish people we see here a most arbitrary typological treatment of the history of Israel adapted to the needs of nascent evolving Christianity. In any case there was much fantasy in all this,[1] and Paul himself emphasizes the incomprehensibility of God's judgments and the unfathomability of His ways (11: 33). But that Paul made himself responsible for understanding them and fathoming them, hence that he was putting forward highly subjective opinions, could not have been doubted for a moment either by himself or by those to whom his letter was addressed. As regards the use of typological–allegorical methods for historical speculation, we may agree with Walter Köhler[2] that by this means he "has freely adapted, sorted and mutilated history which seemed to plead the contrary cause". The transition from this to the assertion of the Letter of Barnabas that the Jewish people never had any covenant with God at all, and further, to Marcion's idea of the "alien God", is a very easy one. What a generation after Paul's death Ignatius of Antioch, basing himself on the οἰκονομία idea (Col. 1: 25; Eph. 1: 10; 3: 9), calls the οἰκονομία εἰς τὸν καινὸν ἄνθρωπον (ad Eph. 20, 1), the plan of salvation centring in Christ as the founder of the new humanity, was from the Pauline point of view capable of quite other developments than that which in fact was accepted as legitimate by the great church.

If finally we inquire after Jewish parallels to Rom. 9–11 it is clear that there can be none. It was by the aid of his own personal logic, contrary to the facts of history yet inwardly consistent, that he interpreted the situation which he considered to have arisen from the rejection of the Messiah: transference of the election to the new Ἰσραὴλ τοῦ θεοῦ (Gal. 6: 16): the Messianic church composed of both Jews and Gentiles, the hardening of the greater part of Israel and their final conversion to the Messiah Jesus—taken as a sort of signal of the parousia—and the fulfilment of this on the day when the conversion of the Gentiles would be complete. As we have said, many eschatological speculations of church history have been

---

[1] Cf. R. Bultmann, Theol. NT, 477: Rom. 9–11 has sprung from the speculative fantasy of the apostle.

[2] Dogmengeschichte als Geschichte des christlichen Selbstbewusstseins, I, Zürich, 1938, 12.

inspired by this outline picture, attempts to prove the truth of Paul's claims by reference to the historical situation of the Jews. The special meaning of the church mission to the Jews is most indebted to Paul when it is undertaken as a means of hastening the parousia.

4. THE PICTURE OF SAVING HISTORY IN JEWISH CHRISTIANITY

The ideas of the Judaistic opponents of the great apostle are little known—ideas which were still influential in the sub-apostolic age. This party did not renounce the task of the Gentile mission, but their efforts had little or no success except in a very small way limited both in place and time. But the Ebionites offered a picture of the process of saving history, which corresponded more closely to Jewish claims and which yet was universalistic. In *TheolJchr*, V, 5c, pp. 296–304, I have discussed in detail all the extant reports of this Gentile mission, its special structure and difficulties. We know from Origen that the words of Jesus in Mt. 15: 24: οὐκ ἀπεστάλην εἰ μὴ εἰς τὰ πρόβατα τὰ ἀπολωλότα τοῦ οἴκου Ἰσραήλ were regarded by them as having high authority (*De Princ.* IV, 22—GCS 22, 334). They too felt their missionary responsibility towards the Gentiles, though in regard to it they invoked the authority of Peter and James rather than that of Paul. But their hopeless midway position between church and synagogue, their unfavourable geographical outlook and preconceptions, and their ever-increasing sectarian tendencies prevented them from having any success. Paul was able to penetrate the Hellenistic world far more effectively than these literalistic and rigoristic Jewish Christians. From the beginning, the majority of the Gentile Christians won over and firmly established by Paul's missionary successes refused to concede their right to existence. Later, Jerome expressed the church's verdict with regard to them in the laconic formula: "sed dum volunt et Judaei esse et Christiani, nec Judaei sunt nec Christiani" (*MPL*, 22, 924). Their standpoint represented a "haeresis sceleratissima" (*ibid.*).

The picture of saving history which they unfolded, to judge from the extant fragments of the Clementine story, is unusually interesting. Their point of departure was the equation of Jesus and Moses, since Jesus in their eyes was the Messianic prophet whom God would send, like Moses himself (Deut. 18: 15). This led them to place the two saving figures in complete parallelism. Both had been sent by God in order to mediate and conclude a divine covenant with mankind. This equation of Moses and Jesus inevitably yielded a different picture of the economy of salvation from that which the church of

245

the 2nd and 3rd centuries, following in the footsteps of Paul and the Letter to the Hebrews, was accustomed to draw. It was in fact a typical picture of Jewish Christianity as a quantity standing half way between the Christian Church and the Synagogue.

The coming of Jesus was meant for the Gentiles, the revelation of Moses for the Jews. For the latter Moses was the οἰκονόμος of whom Jesus had spoken in Luke's parable (12: 42) (Hom. 2, 52). For this reason the significance of Jesus was veiled from the Jews who had received Moses as their teacher (thus Mt. 11: 25 was interpreted); but the significance of Moses was likewise veiled from those who had received Jesus as teacher (Hom. 8, 6). Since the two teachers are of equal importance, God accepts any man who believes one of the two. Faith, however, is expressed in the doing of the law of God. Everything, in any case, depends on the performance of the καλῶν ἔργων, as Jesus Himself explained (Mt. 7: 21). But from Gentiles and Jews alike is required an attitude of tolerance towards a type of doctrine which they do not appreciate; they are to practise what Jesus or Moses commanded and must ὃν ἠγνόησαν μὴ μισεῖν (Hom. 8, 7). To whom, however, it is granted τοὺς ἀμφοτέρους ἐπιγνῶναι ὡς μιᾶς διδασκαλίας ὑπ' αὐτῶν κεκηρυγμένης would be highly esteemed by God, for such a one has understood the old as the new and the new as the old (Hom. 8, 7). Hence the highest degree of virtue is the expression of love for both Moses and Jesus in the performance of good deeds. Hence the Recognitionist (4, 5), somewhat weakening the equation of Jesus and Moses, represents as the ideal requirement of religious tolerance: "Debet autem is, qui ex gentibus est, et ex Deo habet ut diligat Jesum, proprii habere propositi, ut credat et Moysi. Et rursus Hebraeus, qui ex Deo habet, ut credat Moysi, habere debet, et ex proposito suo, ut credat in Jesum, ut unusquisque eorum habens in se aliud divini muneris, aliud propriae industriae, sit ex utroque perfectus. De tali enim dicebat Dominus noster viro divite: Qui profert de thesauris suis nova et vetera" (Mt. 13: 52).

This discourse about the agreement of Moses and Jesus which is inserted in the context of Κηρύγματα Πέτρου, which presumably stems from a source akin to the latter (Hom. 8, 4–7; Rec. 4, 4–6) and which the original author causes Peter to deliver in Tripolis, is without any parallel in ancient church writings[1] and in truth is most

[1] Named by Eusebius (H.E., VI, 19, 9) only once as the title of the work of a certain Ammonius: περὶ τῆς Μωυσέως καὶ Ἰησοῦ συμφωνίας. This Ammonius was probably an Alexandrian contemporary of Origen (circa 235). Cf. Harnack, Gesch. d. altchr. Lit., II, 2, 81 ff., and Th. Zahn in ZKG, 1920, 1 ff.

remarkable. If we wish, we may see in it an example of religious enlightenment in late antiquity. One is a Jew or a Christian by the gift of God, and of set purpose one believes in the special saving virtue of the alternative belief in order to be *perfectus ex utroque* and so to comply with the requirement of Jesus. This explanation of the section Mt. 13: 52 in the light of the parable of the sower is unique, inasmuch as the old and the new in the householder's treasure are understood in a temporal sense, and the old in time (the law of Moses) becomes new, while the new (the gospel of Jesus) becomes old. Whoever stands thus in relation to Moses and Jesus is, according to Rec. 5, 34 (similarly Hom. 11, 16) the true "cultor dei, qui voluntatem Dei facit, et legis praecepta custodit". And—continue the Κηρύγματα Πέτρου—"apud Deum enim non ille, qui apud homines Judaeus dicitur, Judaeus est, neque qui gentilis vocatur, ille gentilis est, sed qui Deo credens legem impleverit ac voluntatem eius fecerit, etiamsi non sit circumcisus".[1] This discloses the final intention behind this co-ordination of Moses and Christ, this synthesis of a purified Mosaism and belief in Jesus as Messiah and true prophet: the intention, namely, that Jewish and Gentile Christianity should meet in a higher unity, that of the reformed religion of the Κηρύγματα Πέτρου, to which the world is enjoined to turn.

Jewish Christianity in its later form unreservedly affirmed the mission to the Gentiles, though naturally without surrendering Jewish prerogatives, as is shown by the Κηρύγματα Πέτρου (Hom. 8, 22; 17, 7; Rec. 1, 63; 2, 38, etc.), by the Ebionite Gospel, and the Epistolae Apostolorum, which, although not Jewish-Christian, is akin in spirit to Jewish Christianity. The Jewish Christians of Beroea who had remained faithful to the great church—the Nazareans of Jerome (*Comm. ad Is.* 8, 23–9, 3; *MPL*, 24, 128)—seem even to have considered Paul's evangelization of the heathen as a very meritorious work. But in fact, even for this broad-minded group of Christians the faith required for the Gentiles must have included an undertaking to observe the (reformed) law, and, in particular, circumcision. The form in which the homilies have come down to us does not say this specifically; if we possessed the source itself, we should be able to see more clearly the continuity with the standpoint of their fathers who sat on the Apostolic Council. In any case it seems significant that in Hom. 2, 19–20 Jesus refuses to heal the daughter of the

---

[1] The reminiscence of Rom. 2: 28 is unmistakable. H. Waitz (*Die Pseudoklementinen*, Leipzig, 1904) did not notice this variant among his NT quotations in the pseudo-Clementine works.

Canaanite woman until she has adopted the way of life prescribed by the Mosaic law (τὴν νόμιμον πολιτείαν). But conversion to the true service of God flows not from justification by faith, but "per opera bona: Et ideo nos non negligimus praedicare vobis, quae saluti vestrae scimus esse necessaria, et qui sit verus Dei cultus ostendere, *ut credentes Deo per opera bona possitis una nobiscum futuri saeculi haeredes existere*" (Rec. 5, 35).

In the centre of this discourse of Peter's[1]—plainly anti-Pauline on account of Hom. 8, 10 (the law cannot be falsified ὑπὸ ἀσεβοῦς τινος) and directed against faith without works, there stands not Christ-soteriology, but, as in the kerygmas, the Jewish confession of faith in the μοναρχία θεοῦ; 2, 19; ὅτι εἷς ἐστιν ὁ θεός; modelled on the scheme of Deut. 6: 4. Conversion to Christ and conversion to the holy God and the law of the Jews (Hom. 4, 22) are one and the same thing.

This expectation of late Jewish Christianity, that both the great religions lying at its root should coalesce in the ethic of *opera bona*, did not find fulfilment for the very good reason that neither Judaism nor Christianity can be reduced to an arid moralism, even though both wished to approve that kind of universalism. The Christ known to the great church was, for it, not ὁ ἀληθὴς προφήτης but ὁ κύριος καὶ ὁ σωτήρ, and just as little was Judaism able to negotiate about a *reductio legis Moysis*. Thus far the belief in Jesus Christ as the *novus Moses*, characteristic of the Palestinian first church as of the Ebionites of Transjordania, was condemned by the church of all times to sterility; yet the economy of salvation which this belief implies, that God —in modern terms—has concluded two covenants with humanity on Sinai and Golgotha which in the last analysis are but one—this emphasis on the juxtaposition of Judaism and Christianity in world-history marks an antithesis to the Pauline theology of the covenants which is still alive to-day and which represents an ultimate conviction of Ebionite theology.[2]

---

[1] Also the conclusion of the speech Rec. 4, 35 (in Hom. distorted from 11, 35) is plainly anti-Pauline. Cf. H. Waitz, "Die Lösung des klementinischen Problems", *ZKG*, 1940; G. Strecker, *Das Judenchristentum in den Pseudoklementinen*, Berlin, 1958, 194 ff.

[2] On a later reading of the letter of Barnabas I was taken aback to read of "certain people" who asserted that Judaism and Christianity belong in the same covenant, and against whom Barnabas warns the recipients of his letter. Is he not thinking of Jewish Christians of our stamp? The formula of Barn. 4, 6 in any case coincides with the above mentioned: ἐρωτῶ ὑμᾶς . . . προσέχειν νῦν, ἑαυτοῖς καὶ μὴ ὁμοιοῦσθαί τισιν, ἐπισωρεύοντας ταῖς ἁμαρτίαις ὑμῶν λέγοντας ὅτι ἡ διαθήκη ἐκείνων κατ' ἡμῶν. This would mean that in the period when the letter of Barnabas was written—hence already around 135—Jewish Christians were agitating for these views.

5. JEWISH IDEAS OF THE COURSE OF SAVING HISTORY

Official Judaism never rose to the height of this Ebionite view. Essays in a similar interpretation of the saving significance of the juxtaposition of church and synagogue have taken place only in recent times. Let us first, however, attempt to sketch the Jewish counter-position to Paul's ideas of the saving process. No direct replies were to be expected for the simple reason that the pre-supposition of the Pauline faith, namely that the Messiah had come and the world was in the post-messianic age, was not shared by the Jews. None the less Judaism, if not compelled to enter into a formal debate on the question, had every reason to repudiate the judgment that it was the victim of divine hardening of heart, or that it had lost its title to election.[1] The only possible answer could be the picture of the Jewish view of the process of saving history, as that had more or less clearly presented itself to the mind of the rabbis. It might be formulated in the following way:

Israel is the people of the covenant which God chose from among the nations of the earth to be His peculiar possession (Ex. 19: 5) and with whose forefathers He concluded a covenant sealed by oath (Gen. 22: 16; Deut. 7: 8, etc.). No later event—neither the Christian assertion of the advent of the Messiah, nor the destruction of the temple in the year 70, could possibly abrogate, modify, or suspend this vocation of Israel sworn by the eternal God to be God's peculiar people. Even Paul admitted this in Rom. 11: 29. No new covenant can suspend the old, and no new revelation of faith can replace the revelation of the law on Sinai. The latter was final and complete in itself, as Deut. Rabba Par. 8 establishes as a sufficient answer to Christians who deem possible a completion or replacement of the Torah by a new revelation: "We read in Deut. 30: 12: 'The commandment is not in heaven', so do not say that a second Moses might arise and bring another Torah from heaven. I bear witness to you that nothing of it has remained in heaven."[2] This very verse, Deut. 30: 12, was so interpreted by Paul and in such a sense contrary to

---

[1] The Jewish apologetics in reply to the attacks of early catholicism and the church Fathers have been assembled by myself in *AfZ*, 144 ff., 184 ff.

[2] We might here refer to the text Cant. Rabba 1, 14 probably attacking the Christian interpretation of Jeremiah, and in which Rabbi Levi (*circa* 300) in the name of Rabbi Chamas (*circa* 260) causes Abraham to express doubts before God about the covenant with Noah and other possible future covenants. God dispels these fears by referring to His promise that from Abraham's flesh righteous men should arise in every age to atone for the sins of Abraham's children.

scripture that he can no longer be excused by alleging the freedom proper to typological exegesis.[1] Paul wishes thus to buttress his preconceived idea that Christ as the object of faith has replaced the Torah, though according to Deut. 30: 14 the word of the Torah should be "in your heart and in your mouth".[2] Similarly with regard to Paul's parable of the olive tree (11: 17-24) suggesting that leaves or branches of the olive tree of Israel may be cut off. The answer of Rabbi Joshua ben Levi uses the traditional figure to bring out the opposite meaning: "As the leaves of the olive tree fall away neither in summer nor in the season of rains, just so for the Israelites there is no dying away, neither in this world nor in the future aeon" (Menahoth 53b). Further, the thought expressed in Rom. 9: 15, 17 is quite un-Jewish, for the suggestion of a "hardening from above" sounds like an automatism released by God. In that case God would cease to regard the doings of man.[3]

Quite another question, of course, is whether Israel has done sufficient justice to the fact that its covenant God is the God of humanity as a whole. Early rabbinic Judaism saw in this point a task and understood its mission to the Gentiles Messianically as a preparation for the future Kingdom of God. While the Tannaites tried to combine their ethical universalism (cf. section 1) with the cultic particularism demanded by the Torah of Israel—that of guarding the faith in separation from the peoples and being a light to the Gentiles—they thought to do justice to the exclusiveness implied in the election of Israel by making the Godfearers who were engaged to obey the seven commands of Noah only, a class apart in the fellowship of the synagogue. The fact that this arrangement, which as a compromise measure was inevitable from the standpoint of Jewish religious principle, did not in the long run suffice, is clear from the speed with which these Godfearers became Christians. Bousset[4] is right in remarking: "Christianity, which shattered the barrier between believers of the first and those of the second class, destroyed thereby Jewish propaganda." The *gere toshab* of Judaism, admitted to

---

[1] Bonsirven's opinion (*op. cit.*, 307), that such exegeses do not spring from typology but rest on heavenly inspiration, is unprovable. More probable is the opinion of Munck, *op. cit.*, 67 ff., that we have here a firm polemic against the Jewish exegesis.

[2] Cf. C. A. Bugge in *ZNW*, 1903, 95 ff., and the important but remote work of the same author: *Das Christusmysterium*, Skrifter av Videnskaps Selskapet i Kristiania, Hist. Fil. Klasse, 1914, 37 ff.

[3] Thus M. Buber, *Zwei Glaubensweisen*, Zürich, 1950, 87. (E.T. *Two Types of Faith*.)

[4] *Religion des Judentums* etc., *op. cit.*, 91; cf. also H. Lietzmann, *Geschichte der alten Kirche*, I, Berlin, 1953, 135; K. Weidinger, *op. cit.*, 13.

salvation, as it were, on an inferior level, were in consequence of the Pauline apostolic ministry equated with Jews by birth. The result which Paul fought to achieve at Antioch was just this breaking down of the wall of partition, the declaration that the Gentiles committed only to the *Derekh Eres*, or the Noachide laws, had come of age.[1] In Romans 9–11 this equalization was not only justified on theoretic grounds, but even broadened into an actual preference of the latter, since the call of God had now passed to the Gentile world. The whole of early Christian history stands under this sign, and its success was such that the missionary activities of the Jews which went on until the 5th century remained on the whole a failure, as was inevitable.

Rom. 9–11 not only gave to Christianity the theoretical basis for the rise of a universal church, but in practice led to an indifference towards Judaism which increasingly turned in on itself as though encysted. For it was the insight into the facts of history which on the Jewish side—of course together with other causes—led to a resigned self-limitation to the *status quo*, to the "hedge about the law". The question as to the salvation of the nations now concerned Judaism only in eschatology, for, as regards the present world, the Christian church had taken over the missionary task. The attitude adopted towards this church underwent many changes from the early centuries to recent times, and these I have described in my book *Controversy between Judaism and Christianity in Nineteen Centuries—the history of a theological debate (Religionsgespräch* etc., Berlin 1937, Frankfurt 1949). In broad outline this history developed "from dispute about dogma to conversations about the faith". But the dogmatic and religious–legalistic basis has remained the same in all the stages of development. And properly speaking it turns on the Jewish counterpart to the Pauline teaching contained in Rom. 9–11. This was the doctrine which Saul himself shared and which has remained the characteristic Jewish doctrine even if Paul the Christian apostle guided world history into very different channels. As the Jewish counterpart to Paulinism we will in conclusion give a systematic account of it, considering also the question of what modifications it is capable in view of the facts of history.

Judaism teaches with regard to the relation of non-Jews to God that the righteous among the nations will have a share in the future

---

[1] G. Resch (*Das Aposteldekret in seiner ausserkanon. Textgestalt*, Leipzig, 1908) considered that the apostolic decree in its oldest form was not concerned with food rules, but with moral precepts on the lines of the Noachidic laws. Cf. also G. Klein, *op. cit.*, 177 ff., and A. v. Harnack's revised opinion on this πνικτόν question (*Die Apostelgeschichte*, Leipzig, 1908, 189 ff.). The problem is still open.

world (Sanh. 105a par.; attested also in Justin *Dial.* 8). This principle has been constantly maintained in all centuries, even in the times of the worst persecutions.[1] The prevailing view receives classical expression in a sentence from the Seder Eliyahu Rabba 10: "I call heaven and earth to witness that both the Gentile and the Israelite, both man and woman, both manservant and maidservant will be judged according to their works, for all may become recipients of the Holy Spirit." What was understood by the righteous was every *goy* who keeps the *mishpatim* revealed to the second ancestor of mankind, hence the commands of Noah. Every one who rejects idolatry is on a par with the Jew (Megilla 13a). This basic principle was also codified by the codices of the Middle Ages as valid "Halakha".[2] This high regard for the just among the Gentiles went so far in times when proselytes were welcomed to associate themselves with Israel that as *gerim* of righteousness they were loaded with all the privileges and honourable titles of Israel (cf. above p. 288). But, apart from proselytism, Judaism of all ages has held firmly to the belief in one humanity and the command to love one's neighbour (Lev. 19: 18), connecting the latter with the doctrine of creation itself.

This universalistically understood command is repeatedly qualified as כלל גדול, the great basic principle of the law. Thus Rabbi Aqiba on Lev. 19: 18 remarks: "Love thy neighbour as thyself: this is a great fundamental rule in the Torah." Ben Azzai (Jer. Nedarim 9, 4) says that still greater than this rule was Gen. 5: 1: "This is the book of the generations of Adam."[3] This implies that the Biblical revelation of God is intended for all men and the descent of all mankind from Adam is still more important than the command to love one's neighbour. And the Jewish sacrificial cultus too has understood the priesthood of Israel in quite a universalistic sense, in that the priests at the *sukkoth* festival sacrificed seventy bulls for the atonement of humanity as a whole (according to the table of the peoples in Gen. 10).[4]

[1] For medieval writings cf. the sources quoted in Leopold Zunz, *Zur Geschichte und Literatur*, Berlin, 1845.

[2] Cf. Joseph Caro in his commentary on Yore Dea, 367; Beer ha-Golah on Yore Dea, 367; Choshen ha-Mishpat 34, 22, etc. More recently E. Benamozegh in *Israel et l'Humanité* has strongly elaborated this Jewish doctrine.

[3] A parallel in Ab. R. Nathan, section 16, replaces כלל (principle) by שבועה (oath) and causes Rabbi Simon ben Eliezer to say: "This word 'love thy neighbour as thyself' was uttered with a great oath, for 'I have created him'. Love him, and I will reward you in faithfulness; if not, then I will be to you a judge who punishes the evil-doer."

[4] Thus the exclamation of Rabbi Jochanan (Sukka 55b): "Woe to the peoples of the world who have suffered a loss without realizing what they have lost. As long as the temple was standing it procured for them atonement, but who will now atone for them?"

Thus the appreciation of the אמות העולם was made secure. The possibility of their being touched by the Spirit of God or sharing in the future world has never been basically denied, if we disregard certain inimical voices which may always be explained by concrete historical situations. In the words of M. Guttmann,[1] "in the whole of rabbinic literature there never was any suggestion of an exclusive religion which would make men blessed". Rather the possibility of others being converted to Judaism has always been held open, even in centuries when the missionary idea was rejected or rather had to be rejected. Secure in the possession of its special revelation, Judaism took little further thought about the formulation of a legal minimum for the salvation of the rest of humanity. Moreover, in later centuries the place of Christianity has been defined from the point of view of the Jewish law and it has been described as a שתוף (an association), i.e., a connexion of the name of God with another thing.[2] While it is true that Judaism has made no concession with regard to its own claim to the possession of absolute truth, it none the less accepted Christianity as a Noachidic possibility. Thus M. Isserles observes with regard to Shulchan Arukh, Orach Chayim 156:[3] הגויים מוזהרים על ה שתוף אין. And in Jewish medieval writing, where the relationship to the *gerim* in religious legal matters is discussed, the usual opinion is as follows: "The Christians should be considered as our brothers. They do not fall into the category of Nokhrim, Gerim and Teshubim, they stand much closer to us."[4]

Let us now quote—*pars pro toto*—as typical of the appreciation of Christianity which runs throughout the Middle Ages, a literary testimony from the last ghetto generation of Germany. Thus writes Rabbi Jacob Emden in his missive of 1757 *Seder olam rabba wezuta*: "Christianity was founded for Christians only, not as a new religion, but as the old religion, which gave to the nations the seven Noachidic commands, which they had forgotten but which were founded anew for them by the Christian apostles. Thus the heathen were forbidden: idolatry, unchastity, blood and things strangled. On the other hand they were exempted from the observance of the Sabbath and of circumcision . . . all in accordance with the prescriptions of our

---

[1] *Das Judentum und seine Umwelt*, Berlin, 1927, 168; cf. also I. Lévi, "Le prosélytisme juif", *REJ*, 1905.   [2] Cf. the references in Schoeps, *Religionsgespräch* etc., *op. cit.*, 22 ff.
[3] *Shittuf* is not forbidden to the Noachidites; similarly Tossaph. on Sanh. 63b.; Bekhoroth 2b, etc.
[4] Thus, for instance, Rabbi Isaac ben Shesheth (1400–40) in a counsel's opinion (תשבת Constantinople 1546, Nr. 119); further testimony in J. S. Bloch, *Israel und die Völker nach jüdischer Lehre*, Berlin-Vienna, 1932, 50 ff.

Torah." Further: "The Founder of Christianity benefited the Gentiles greatly by warning them away from idolatry, committing them to observe the seven Noachidic commands, and in addition giving them ethical teaching." And in the commentary on Aboth 4, 14 Emden describes the Christian Church as a "society formed according to heaven's will" and accordingly permanent.

Real attempts at a Jewish theology of history which might be placed alongside the Pauline one of Rom. 9–11 are admittedly observable here and there in the Middle Ages, especially in the work of Yehuda Halevi but also in that of Rambam and Ramban[1]—yet do not really come to systematic expression until modern times. In this connexion we should mention especially the speculative systems of that Jewish representative of German idealism, Samuel Formstecher,[2] who indirectly recognizes the world judgment on the success of the Christian mission. Formstecher regarded Christianity as a transitory mission of Israel to humanity, because Israel, in order to carry out its divine mission, had of necessity to preserve its racial purity, though it could allow Christianity to convey to the world its most essential elements, in order thus to win humanity for Israel and its law.[3] Christianity, it was suggested, dressed the ethic of Judaism in the metaphysic of the Gentile world, in order the more effectively to realize its missionary task.[4] Instead of a church composed of Jews and Gentiles there arose a church which, springing from the matrix of Judaism, existed for Gentiles, and which protects itself from its own paganism by seeking renewal through the undistorted truth of Israel. Thus the Christian Church comes to fulfil the world mission of the Jews, since the latter could not take place directly. In truth, however, Judaism is the "absolute religion of the spirit", as has been shown by the Hegelian Samuel Hirsch in an unwieldy volume of 884 pages.[5] This Jewish philosopher of religion and

[1] Cf. quotations in Schoeps, *Religionsgespräch* etc., 72 ff.

[2] *Religion des Geistes*, Leipzig, 1841. Cf. my account of the work in *Geschichte der jüdischen Religionsphilosophie in der Neuzeit*, Vol. I, Berlin, 1935, 65 ff., and also B. Bamberger, "Formstecher's History of Judaism", *HUCA*, 23, 2 (1950).

[3] E. Benamozegh, *op. cit.*, 500, has given clearest expression to this opinion by distinguishing the Mosaic law valid for all men (Noachide Torah) from the sacerdotal law valid for Israel (Sinai Torah). He explains: "The future conversion of the Gentiles, declared by the prophets, is presented as a return to the law, but to the law for all mankind and not Mosaism which concerns the Jews only."

[4] S. Formstecher, *Religion des Geistes*, 374.

[5] The exact title runs: "An account of the religious system of the Jews and its relation to heathendom and to the absolute philosophy for theologians of all confessions, together with explanatory proof texts from Holy Scripture, the Talmud and Midrashim." Leipzig, 1842.

exponent of German idealism has even adopted—though of course with changed signs—the Pauline eschatological opinion that the last day will dawn only when the last Gentile has become a Christian and so the universal church can return to its origins, i.e., to Israel.

To be sure, this Jewish theory of missions is just as speculative as the Pauline one. Moreover, it is only a philosophical interpretation of history, not a valid Jewish dogma. In the consciousness of tradition, the Jew goes no further than to say that it is better for a man to be a Christian than a heathen, because as a Christian he stands in some kind of relationship to the God of Israel. Influenced by the indirect recognition of the success of Christianity as a world mission, just before the turn of the century the Chief Rabbi of Leghorn Elia Benamozegh (one of the last significant cabbalists) advised the young French Catholic, Aimée Pallière, who on conscientious grounds wished to be received into Judaism, to remain a Christian or rather to become one self-consciously for the first time, in order thus to serve the God of Israel.[1] For it is just as undesirable that the nations should be converted to Israel, as that Israel should merge itself with the nations. Rather the "Jews remain a separate group among the peoples of the world so long as the latter have not fully embraced Christianity. For just so long will there be Jews, Christians, and heathen alongside each other."[2]

From this point of view, which yields no definition either in detail or in general outline, another opinion is possible which Franz Rosenzweig at times, and also the author of this book, have expressed. This opinion is that the Jewish revelation is final and unsurpassable for orthodox Jews, but none the less the modern Jew with a sense of realities may admit that outside Israel, and without any direct significance for Israel, there may take place in the world other revelations and other covenants. Recognizing a different faith from the deep basis of his own life of faith, Rosenzweig can even go so far as to declare that "no one from the nations of the world comes to the Father otherwise than through Jesus Christ".[3] The Jew, however, does not need to come to the Father, because as a result of

---

[1] Cf. the autobiographical account which Aimée Pallière has given in *Le Sanctuaire inconnu, ma conversion au Judaisme*, Paris, 1926, and the arguments of E. Benamozegh about Noachidism as the religion of humanity in *Israel et l'Humanisme*, Paris, 1914. Cf. also Marion Nordmann, *Aimée Pallière und die noachidischen Gesetze*, Diss. Erlangen, 1954.

[2] Thus Eugen Rosenstock, *Europäische Revolutionen*, Stuttgart, 1951, 381 ff., indirectly gives the content of his conversations with Franz Rosenzweig on this question.

[3] This very bold formula is found in Franz Rosenzweig, *Briefe*, Berlin, 1935, 73 ff. (*Brief an Rudolf Ehrenberg vom 1. 11. 1913*).

the election of Abraham he is already in contact with the Father; through the law he has real communion with God, since election and promise are by the divine will the hereditary possession of Abraham's seed. In this traditionally attested soteriology, the *Aqedath Isaac*, which by its concrete symbolization justifies the special position of Israel before God and men, acquires the same saving significance which for the Christian faith the sacrifice of Jesus on the cross has for humanity (cf. above, ch. 4, 3). Thus far the Christian assimilation by faith of the saving event, to speak in Pauline terms, can be recognized by the Jews as a way of salvation for the Gentiles. Of course the Jews have no competence to judge in these matters; in the last resort they have to accept the Christian's testimony to his faith. Moreover, the view that Jesus is a divine person in the Godhead, as taught by the church, must remain obscure to them and will sound as blasphemous to-day as it did 1,900 years ago to the high priest. The Jews remain, in fact, blind to the Godhead of Jesus. This mystery is an original Christian truth, something peculiar to the first Christians. But even though the Jews cannot believe in Christ, they can none the less acknowledge the world's faith in the redemptive power of Christ. Even if the intrinsic quality of the Christian faith remains concealed from them, they can recognize it as a saving factor for non-Israelite humanity.

As opposed to the usual Jewish opinion, such an admission, springing from a modern sense of history, that only Israel as being already in communion with the Father is to be excepted from the sphere of the church's preaching, does indeed present us with something powerfully new; nevertheless, it makes no break with the bases of Jewish tradition. So far as I can see, there is no prejudice on the part of the Jews against the salvation of non-Jews. The absolute validity of the Torah for the seed of Abraham would remain unaffected by this far-reaching admission of possible divine covenants made with non-Israelite humanity.

How far Christian dogmatic may be ready to grant the existence of an absolute revelation apart from its own, such as would except Israel from the sphere of its saving proclamation, is a question which we do not have to discuss here. It is complicated not only by the subjective opinions and conclusions of the apostle Paul and the view of history which he inferred therefrom, but also by the fact that Jesus' original sense of mission was directed towards His own people. However, the continued existence of Israel almost 2,000 years *post Christum natum*, still undisturbed in its consciousness of being God's covenant people, is testimony that the old covenant has not been abrogated, that as the covenant of Israel it continues to exist along-side the wider human covenant of the Christian Church. Whether we consider world time as pre- or post-messianic, whether we believe in a future coming or in a second coming of the Messiah, until that expected crisis in time both covenantal institutions will exist side by side with their own special self-understanding.

In any case the facts of world history do not countenance the idea of a "hardening" of Israel, but rather suggest that the synagogue has its own special knowledge of truth which has affirmed itself through the centuries alongside Christian truth. Hence more appropriate would seem a picture of world history which does justice to the views of the old Ebionites (cf. above, 4) and which presupposes an un-divided truth in God while recognizing several covenants of God with man; such covenants as those of the Torah and the Gospel, the Old and the New Testaments taken together as the book giving an authoritative account of God's dealings with mankind. For this it is necessary that they should be allowed to produce their effects as in-dependent witnesses to revelation, approached impartially, rather than that with prejudiced eyes we should see everywhere the fulfil-ment of prophecy by means of typological and allegorizing exegesis.[1] The so-called Old Testament, which for the Jews is the very Word of God, in an inward sense unappreciated by Christians who fail to read it in and for itself, spells for both Jews and Christians an eternal relatedness to God. The New Testament is glad tidings only for the nations of the world, and the latter bear witness to it in the poly-phony of the Christian churches and communities centred in Christ.

With such an understanding of the economy of salvation, we stand in obvious opposition to the view of history outlined by Paul. But we have taken into account the possibility that Paul falsely interpreted the will of God, that his understanding of saving history was a

---

[1] To quote the voices of a few modern OT scholars: W. Eichrodt, *Theologie des AT*, I, Stuttgart, 1957, 342 ff.: "Every mechanical application of OT affirmations about the coming time of salvation to the Person and Work of Christ is contradictory to the special mode of Biblical revelation which does not furnish an exclusive body of doctrine but rather proclaims a divine reality revealing itself in history. . . . It cannot be disputed that from this point of view we can no longer speak of a fulfilment of OT prophecy." Further, L. Koehler, *Theologie des AT*, Tübingen, 1953, 229: "The scion of David's house who is the leader of the holy people in the time of salvation is no prophecy or foreshadowing of Christ. The NT wished to understand Micah 5: 2 as a prophecy of Christ the Saviour (Mt. 2: 5 ff.). But OT revelation does not explicitly say so." And finally Raphael Gyllenberg (*Gedenkschrift für A. v. Bulmerincq, op. cit.*, 67): "Thus it is not allowable to read Christ into the Hebrew OT. Just as little can He be extracted from it, for He was never in it."

257

subjective judgment and an objective error. Although his view became official church teaching, the question of a revision of this might now be raised, one result of which would be to correct the church's judgment on Israel in such a way as would involve the abandonment of the church's mission to the Jews. For to speak of the blinding and the hardening of the Jews was a mistake, which might even now be rectified.

Against the thesis of an old covenant which has been superseded by the new, we here propound the argument of two world covenants, those of Sinai and Golgotha, one for Israel and one for the nations of the world; both equally valid but separate in the mind of God who turned to Israel on Sinai and to the nations on Golgotha. For He whose name Moses described as "I will be what I will be" is in the distinctiveness of His revelations ever one and the same God, who ever is to the Jews absolutely what He was when once He turned to them in grace and favour, and who ever is and will be to Christians absolutely what He became for them in mediating Himself to them differently.

The end of both covenants in the age of the Messiah will also spell the end of world time as we know it, when both covenants will be one, concluded with a new race of men. Much at the present time suggests that Paul's picture of history resting on the prophetic idea of the "remnant" is finding fulfilment to-day in regard to the historical destiny of the old covenant, which to-day, in accordance with Ez. 36: 3, שארית הגוים, is supported by a remnant of the nations (the new covenant) serving God shoulder to shoulder with the Jews (Zeph. 3: 9). This negative theology of the remnant was elaborated at the beginning of the Christian era in the movement of apocalyptic literature. To-day the time may well have become ripe once more for Messianic expectation at least within these sacred remnants of history.

Thus difference as well as affinity becomes clear: the Messianism of Israel is directed towards that which is to come, while the eschatology of the universal Christian church looks for a return of Him who has come. Both are united in the common expectation that the decisive event is still to come, that event which will disclose the consummation of God's ways with men, already partially and differently manifested in His dealings with Israel and the church. The church of Jesus Christ has kept no picture of its Saviour and Lord. But it might well be that He who comes at the end of time, He who has been alike the expectation of the synagogue and the church, will bear one and the same countenance.

7

PERSPECTIVES OF THE HISTORY OF RELIGION IN PAULINISM

I. RESULTS OF RESEARCH: TRANSCENDENCE OF JUDAISM

IN the four previous systematic chapters we have tried to show how the theology of the apostle Paul arose from overwhelmingly Jewish religious ideas. In an age of tense Messianic expectation, Saul the Pharisee, following the religious convictions which came to him as a result of his Damascus experience and believing that the Messianic event had occurred, corrected traditional eschatology and refashioned it by means of the apocalyptic teaching about the two aeons. Paul reached the certainty that with the resurrection of Jesus the *yamim shel mashiach* had dawned and that those days were strictly limited, since the parousia of the Lord was immediately imminent. All the measures he adopted in face of this situation, from the practice of eschatological sacraments to the determination of a provisional church order, were intended by him to cover an interim period only. But what was conditioned by the situation did not pass away with the situation; it was, on the contrary, stabilized by the evolving church. Thus baptism and the eucharist, practised by Paul as pro-visional only, became permanent institutions in the Christian church. The Jews, however, from the start considered Paul's assessment of the situation to be wrong. They deemed it a mistake to suppose that the world had already entered on the post-messianic age (ch. 3).

We have seen, further, that Paul referred to Jesus as Messiah certain soteriological doctrines already existing in Judaism, although he combined them with the non-Jewish faith-idea of the $\upsilon\iota\grave{o}\varsigma$ $\theta\epsilon o\hat{\upsilon}$. The Christological system thus engendered from the combination of Jewish ideas with a pagan myth reckons admittedly with the humanity of Christ, but does not do full justice to His earthly life. By his doctrine of Christ's divinity Paul oversteps the bounds of Judaism, which has never known the idea of a divine Messiah, and has never attributed soteriological functions to the Messiah. The concept of the Saviour is impossible from a Judaic point of view, and was equally impossible in the sphere of Hellenistic Judaism. In a certain sense it was the Pauline idea that the age of salvation had come which produced the figure of the Saviour (ch. 4).

This Saviour of the future world embodies the new aeon, dissolving or subsuming in itself the aeon of the Torah; with the result that the Jewish attempt to fulfil the law, which hitherto had been the sole basis of salvation, is no longer necessary. We have seen that by means of his scriptural exegesis Paul justified a whole series of deductions intended to demonstrate, sometimes incidentally, that the law had lost its validity. In this regard we found most significant the legalistic over-emphasis which suggested that Paul understood the law apart from its correlative, the fact of the covenant. Paul in fact reduced the Torah to an ethical principle intended to make man righteous and therefore a failure. Obviously the law as a whole, resting on the covenant relationship, had ceased to be a living and personal posses-sion for Saul the Diaspora Pharisee and Septuagint Jew. It was far from the mind and outlook of Saul–Paul to understand the law as the requirement of holiness (Lev. 19: 2 ff.), as the covenantal ordi-nance instituted by the holy God of Israel, whose self-revelation took this form. Christ's apostle saw in the law only an ethical norm, and the ritual and ceremonial laws had lost their sacramental meaning for him. The doctrine of justification which he developed from this one-sided view is only a partial aspect torn from the whole context of the law as a principle of sanctifying significance. It led him to set up the insoluble *aporia*: "The righteousness which springs from the law", on which the Jew prided himself, and which Paul therefore saw as the essence of Jewish piety. From this standpoint he conceived sin as a daemonic force which could be shattered by nothing short of the grace of Christ or God's saving action.

That isolation of the law from the context of the covenant, so common in Hellenistic Judaism, caused Paul to disregard the fear of God as the existential note of the creaturely situation. But only on this basis can the law be observed. It led him further to ask the question, senseless for a Jew, whether the law as a whole was "fulfill-able", and to pose it with a polemical intention. This shows, more-over, that the real Jewish presuppositions of faith: the gracious gift of the תשבה and the freedom of man over against the evil impulse, were unknown to him. All this contributed to that distortion of per-spective as a result of which Paul misunderstood the law which was the saving principle of the old covenant, and by his demonstrations and inferences arrived at the dualistic position—the Torah or Christ —which is only justifiable eschatologically and which oversteps the limits of Judaism (ch. 5).

Finally, Paul transmuted the meaning of Israel's election and replaced this by faith in Christ and the call of the Gentiles. The view developed in Rom. 9–11 as an interpretation of what the call of the Gentiles really meant for Israel from the divine point of view, also leads beyond the bounds of what is tenable even within the broadest Judaism. These Pauline positions have become fundamental doctrines of the Christian church at the cost of that eschatological expectation which was sacrificed to the delay in the parousia. There is a certain inner consistency in all this, because it has always seemed to a considering mind a great mystery that the Saviour of humanity appearing among the expectant Jewish people was rejected by them. Not only Paul, but also John and the author of the Letter to the Hebrews have tried to give explanations of this, which imply a conception of the economy of salvation and claim a knowledge of the divine plan and its various stages. Misunderstanding the theology of the law, Paul fixed the relationship of the new people of God to the old by maintaining that the election had been transferred to God's new Israel, the Messianic church formed of Jews and Gentiles; that the great majority of Israelites were the subject of a hardening process, but at the end would be converted to the Messiah Jesus, who would return to earth. This view of saving history, as we have said, has become valid church doctrine. The history of religion must take account of it, but not accept it, for that would mean (translated into its own language) speculative metaphysic. It can go no further than to note that in contrast to the Israelite *berith* of the Torah stands the covenant with humanity implied in the Christian revelation, which centres in the atoning death of the Saviour for all mankind, accepted both by Paul and the wider Christian faith (ch. 6).

Walter Köhler[1] has remarked very justly: "At the head of the Christian self-consciousness stands the apostle Paul, not Jesus nor the early church." Paul, born a Jew, became the teacher of the Gentiles, and as such he lives on in the church. "The hearts of the heathen opened to him more readily than did those of the Jews, because he was able to be a Greek to the Greeks: this must be learnt in youth."[2]

It must ever remain thought-provoking that the Christian church has received a completely distorted view of the Jewish law at the

[1] *Dogmengeschichte*, I, Zürich, 1938, 35.
[2] Eduard Schwartz, *Charakterköpfe aus der Antike*, Berlin, 1950, 217.

hands of a Diaspora Jew who had become alienated from the faith-ideas of the fathers—a view which ignores that side of it connected with the *berith* as a sanctifying ordinance and which has reduced it to a matter of ethical self-justification and ritual performance. And still more astounding is the fact that church theology throughout Christian history has imputed Paul's inacceptability to the Jews to Jewish insensitivity, and has never asked itself whether it might not be due to the fact that Paul could gain no audience with the Jews because from the start he misunderstood Jewish theology. The student of religion who takes his point of departure in the phenomena themselves will hardly consider it a matter of chance that he whose theology was based on misunderstanding has himself been misunderstood by his own followers. But the observation of this fact leads us to consider the history of the understanding of Paul within Christianity itself.

2. AN OUTLINE SKETCH OF THE INTERPRETATION OF PAUL IN CHRISTIANITY

Our conclusion therefore is that Paul had misunderstood many things. But this misunderstanding proliferated for Paul himself was repeatedly and far worse misunderstood by his own followers. It may even be asserted and proved that the whole history of the interpretation of Paul—to use Overbeck's *bon mot* which Harnack once took up—is a single chain of misunderstandings. And from the Jewish point of view the theology of the apostle Paul might be described even as the theology of multiplied misunderstanding. We propose to give a short sketch of the understanding of Paul in western Christendom.

For this purpose let us first explain the inner contradictoriness of the initial situation from which most of the misunderstanding sprang: Paul's theology did not fit into the life situation of those people whom he won over to Christianity. At bottom Paul's teaching was most calculated to help those for whom, as for himself, the law had become a problem. It essentially implied not heathen ἀνομία but Jewish zeal for the law. It was adapted only to Jews who had a zeal similar to his own. But the Ebionites, for whom it might have been seriously suited, took a different line; that of ritual reform and a deepening of the moral side of the Mosaic law. And the Gentiles, with whom the great church after the secession of the Jews had solely to deal, were simply not prepared to understand Pauline theology. They needed first and foremost a law, a realization of what was permitted or not, what was right and wrong. The discipline of the law was not for them as it was for Paul a mere stage in a process of religious development, but the first positive requirement of their new faith. "Paul's need for freedom from the law lay far beyond their horizons," K. R. Köstlin[1] rightly judged; it was in fact completely unintelligible to the Gentile Christians who streamed into the church of the new covenant.

The kernel of Paul's teaching, justification by faith, leading to the mysticism of being in Christ and the total suspension of the Mosaic law without regard to the difference between its ethical and ritual sides, was simply not appreciable by the early catholic church. This became clear very early, at bottom in the canonical Acts of the Apostles. For the author of the latter already leaves aside the Pauline doctrine of freedom from the law and the antithesis of the law and Christ, because he obviously has not understood it. He negatively reduced the doctrine of justification to the forgiveness of sins, while the expectation of an imminent end has almost completely disappeared.[2] As it turned out that the first generation of Messianic believers did not prove in fact the last generation of humanity, after Paul the eschatological interpretation of the death of Jesus had almost of necessity to be given up. The terms παρουσία and ἐπιφάνεια which originally denoted the expected return of Christ are now taken to refer to His historical appearance (2 Tim. 1: 10; Ign. *ad Philad.* 9, 2). For it is to the scepticism of a whole age that 2 Pet. 3: 4 gives expression: "Where is the promise of his coming? For ever since the fathers fell asleep all things have continued as they were from the beginning of creation."

The deductions which Paul had drawn from the saving significance of Christ's death and resurrection, for his teaching about present redemption and the operation of the sacraments, had now to be partly surrendered and partly refashioned.[3] Thus the early catholic teaching about redemption was born, for after it had given up the expectation of the parousia it could no longer understand at all the deepest part of Paul's message—viz., that the new aeon terminates the reign of the law. The great tension arising from Paul's

---

[1] "Zur Geschichte des Urchristentums", *Theologische Jahrbücher*, Tübingen, 1850, 37.

[2] From this Ph. Vielhauer concludes ("Zum 'Paulinismus' der Apostelgeschichte", *Ev. Theol.*, 1950/51, 14 ff.) quite rightly that its author stands "no longer within primitive Christianity but belongs to the growing early catholic church" and is the exponent of "an uneschatological type of Christianity which has become conformed to the world".

[3] Cf. M. Werner, *Glaube und Aberglaube*, Stuttgart, 1957, 182.

experience of sin as a daemonic power between the "unfulfillability" of the law and the longing for redeeming grace, ceased altogether to be felt by the developing catholic church. With the delay in the parousia much of the reasoning too with which Paul attempted to justify the suspension of the law, especially in respect of Gentile Christians, became untenable (cf. Rom. 10: 4). Similar parts of his letters were no longer of any interest, and became quite unintelligible, as for example the whole *status quo* problem of 1 Cor. 7: 20. Sometimes such points were radically transformed, since the mental presuppositions of the apostle were no more understood, and no longer was any distress felt about positions where Paul had wrestled in spiritual torment.[1]

The fate of Paul's teaching was thus tragic. It was modified in manifold ways; it was never retained unchanged or undiluted in early Christianity: not even by the author of the Letter to the Hebrews, who was most entitled to feel himself to be a pupil of the apostle, and who directly imitated him in turns of phrase. He edited and reproduced Pauline ideas with the help of Hellenistic exegesis. For the most part he dealt with themes which in Paul had remained either marginal or open questions, as for example the pre-existence of the Son of God or the heavenly high priesthood of Christ; other points, such as the tension between law and gospel, he consciously toned down. This latter applies also to the pastorals, the so-called Deutero-Pauline literature, which was moulded by resistance to gnostic influences. Here the acute Hellenization of the Christian gospel begins; moreover, we see already at work the moralistic disposition of the church teachers of the second century.[2] The apostolic Fathers then began to supply a whole literature of moral rules of life which could be based on the exhortations, catalogues of virtues and vices which with Paul had been only incidental in character or appeals necessitated by a definite situation. Now they become central in the church's teaching, and Paul is described with Gal. 6: 2 as a teacher of the "law of Christ". The genuine Pauline letters are increasingly interpreted in the spirit of the pastorals; about the year A.D. 100 they have essentially become "theological literature".

The great church ceased to understand that Pauline theology represents an extremist position, because its main concern was with

[1] This is discussed by M. Werner, *Entstehung des christlichen Dogmas*, 203, 233 f.

[2] Cf. H. Windisch, "Zur Christologie der Pastoralbriefe", *ZNW*, 1935, 213 ff. Windisch thinks quite rightly that sub-apostolic Christianity is less a distortion of Pauline than a continuation of Deutero-Pauline ideas. Cf. also V. E. Hasler, "Das nomistische Verständnis des Evangeliums in den Pastoralbriefen", *Schweiz. Theol. Umschau*, 1958, 65 ff.

a levelling process of compromise, and synthesis. Characteristic in this regard, apart from the letters of Ignatius of Antioch, is a writing such as the first Clementine letter, in which Roman church theology has found representative expression only thirty years after Paul's death. Here everything turns on the requirement of a life well pleasing to God and free from moral blemishes. Happy is he who emulates the example of the Creator and feels joy in his good works, confessing thankfulness to Christ.[1] Again half a century later, in the Shepherd of Hermas as also in the second Clementine letter, the attitude of righteousness by works is clearly manifest as a Christian pharisaism. Here the faith of a Paul has been utterly emptied of its content. Sin has become ignorance. The sinner is no longer shattered by the divine requirement, in order to receive his righteousness humbly as the gift of grace, but in his striving he is able to obey most of the commands and, moreover, in repentance and prayer finds an indulgent Judge. Here the faith of Paul cannot be certain of being understood, any more than Pauline Christology can be. From Clement Romanus to Clement Alexandrinus the voices unanimously ring out: Jesus was the master Teacher. The thought of the atoning sacrifice of Christ, of the redemption effected by His death, of the ransom from sin, recedes far behind that of the διδάσκαλος of believers, who instructs the latter in true knowledge, in the γνῶσις θεοῦ. Furthermore, Paul's doctrine of sin was obstructive to the very important teaching of the church Fathers on the freedom of the will.

In the second century, however, there was yet another line of development stemming from the Christological understanding of St. John's Gospel, which in many respects is akin to Paul, passing through the Letter of Barnabas with its allegorical devaluation of Jewish law and covenant and leading to Marcion, also to other more radical gnostics such as the Carpocratians, Cainites, and Ophites.[2]

The allegorism of the Letter of Barnabas is singular in this respect and is conceived *ad depravationem legis*.[3] Here the law is finally depreciated, and from Paul's radical formula: "ordained by angels through an intermediary", it is inferred that the law rests on a radical

[1] Cf. L. Sanders, *L'Hellénisme de Clément de Rome et le Paulinisme*, Louvain, 1943; L. Goppelt, *Christentum und Judentum* etc., 237 ff.

[2] J. Wagenmann, *Die Stellung des Apostels Paulus neben den Zwölf*, Berlin, 1926, 114 ff., and E. Aleith, *Paulusverständnis in der alten Kirche*, Berlin, 1937, 39 ff. The latter is in part a monograph on the theme of this chapter.

[3] Is it possible that the free-thinking heterodox Jews of Alexandria to whom Philo makes angry reference (*De Migr. Abr.* 89) were precursors of Barnabas? In this matter there is much that still needs explanation.

Jewish misunderstanding. Marcion in his antitheses between the Old and New Testaments went further by the assertion that the law was not given by the God of Jesus Christ at all but by one of the lesser demiurges. With his emphasis on the diastasis of law and gospel, of righteousness and faith, he showed acute insight into an important aspect of Paul. But as his dualistic interpretation traced this antithesis back to two different Gods, he totally misunderstood Paul. Pauline testimonies which contradict his thesis, such as Rom. 7: 12 that the law is "holy, righteous, and good", have been summarily eliminated from Marcion's gospel. Of course in making these erasures Marcion believed himself to be acting only as a faithful Pauline, fulfilling the intentions of the master by freeing his preaching from Judaistic errors. Marcion was an antinomist, and in this he took his Pauline inferences far beyond the position of Paul himself; he considered that the law hindered the faith which meant everything to Paul. Hence the law was unmoral and must be scorned and frustrated. He thought that Paul's law-free gospel was identical with the teaching of Jesus Himself, while the wretched apostles whom he considered to be in part merely confused and in part downright disloyal had translated the gospel of redemption back into legalism.

It is no part of our purpose here to describe once more Marcion's revaluations and dualism, so well known from Harnack and other researchers.[1] Marcion has become the ancestor of all *simplificateurs terribles*, and above all—if the supposition actually corresponds to his extraction—the prototype of all "Jewish anti-semites". None the less, his misunderstanding of the apostle who was so liable to be misunderstood has its deeper causes, which have made possible that myth of the Marcionites about which Origen reports (Hom. on Luke 25): in heaven Paul sits at the right hand of Christ and His one true interpreter, Marcion, on the left.

The youthful Carpocratian Epiphanes went one step further than Marcion in exploiting Paul's pessimistic view of the flesh,[2] for he did not scruple to base on Rom. 7: 7 the gnostic mystery of unchastity—"the extinction of the lights". All the extreme points in Paul's theory of the law, such as that the law brings wrath (Rom. 4: 15), incites to sin (Rom. 7: 7), first brings out the real power of sin (1 Cor. 15: 56),

---

[1] Cf. A. v. Harnack, *Marcion, das Evangelium vom fremden Gott*, Leipzig, 1924; and "Die Neuheit des Evangeliums nach Marcion", *Christl. Welt*, 1929, 360 ff. Cf. further J. Knox, *Marcion and the New Testament*, Chicago, 1942, and E. C. Blackman, *Marcion and His Influence*, London, 1948.

[2] W. Bousset has rightly perceived that there is here an essential point of departure for gnosis (see *Kyrios Christos*, Göttingen, 1905, 234).

and even increases sins (Gal. 3: 19), is subject to death (2 Cor. 3: 7), etc., were used for antinomistic purposes and were made to support a libertine, often even a nihilistic, theory. Other gnostics again (cf. *Exc. ex Theod.* 23) made Paul an exponent of "pneumatic" baptism. Of what avail here was the reservation of the pastoral letters (1 Tim. 1: 3–10) that the law is good, "if one uses it lawfully"? It was not used lawfully but with conscious malice. Thus Paul, as Tertullian rightly complains (*Adv. Marc.* III, 5), became the "favourite apostle of the heretics". But this again was nothing but a misunderstanding, for in fact antinomistic conclusions could have been drawn from the Pauline position—if at all—only as a result of his expectation of the parousia. But this was the case neither with Marcion nor with Epiphanes nor with the Cainites. And the Sabbatians of the 17th century, who were Messianic in faith, did not in fact appeal to Paul who was unknown to them, but by their own reflections they discovered for themselves the *abrogatio legis per Messiam*.[1]

Let us now return to the church Fathers and ask how they dealt with the apostle's theory of the law. The general picture would suggest that, with them, righteousness was no longer understood on Pauline lines as the righteousness of Christ disclosed to the believer in the act of faith (see above, p. 205) but as a right disposition by which man becomes righteous. No doubt the meaning which Paul attached to faith and so much emphasized did persist in the church, but faith became detached from the background of the doctrine of justification. Generally speaking, Christianity was understood as the "new word of righteousness", the *nova lex Christi*, and Christians were regarded as the bearers of the perfect ethic. Paul's thought of justification by faith faded away, and the requirement of a moral life led to the renewal of the attempt to set up one's own righteousness. With Tertullian[2] of Carthage, who became a jurist in Rome, the whole of religion is described simply in terms of a right attitude and conduct. Part of his rule of faith runs: "Jesum Christum praedicasse novam legem et novam promissionem regni caelorum" (*De Praescr.* 13, 4). Or: "lex proprie nostra id est evangelium" (*De Monogamia* 8). Tertullian is moving on the same ground as was covered by Barnabas, Hermas, and Justin when he defines the gospel as the *nova lex*, as a confirmed legalism of attitude by which man acquires merit, which Irenaeus had explained on even more radical lines.

According to Tertullian, Jesus achieved several things in respect

---

[1] Cf. Schoeps, *AfZ*, 265 ff. ("Gnostischer Nihilismus").
[2] Cf. Th. Brandt, *Tertullians Ethik*, Gütersloh, 1929; E. Aleith, *op. cit.*, 49 ff.

of the law: the earlier stage was either transformed (*demutatum*), e.g., circumcision, or completed (*suppletum*) like the rest of the law, or fulfilled (*impletum*) as prophecy, or perfected (*perfectum*) like faith itself (*De Orat.* I, 4–5). In this way Tertullian well analysed the content of the *nova lex Christi*, but he is separated from Paul's understanding of the law by an impassable gulf. With his innumerable moralistic explanations of Biblical texts he is farther from Paul than is Marcion whom he so fought against. Likewise he legitimated the typological and allegorical exegesis far beyond the extent to which Paul used it, and thus assured the victory of this so "indispensable but useless device" (Dilthey).[1]

All this becomes still plainer in Irenaeus of Lyons, although this Greek of Asia Minor reconsiders Pauline problems, such as the fall, salvation, and redemption, and makes many quotations from the apostle. We owe it to him in particular that the Pauline Adam–Christ typology was integrated into the structure of church dogma. But if possible he is still further removed from the spirit of Paul. The antithesis of law and gospel which Paul felt so strongly is supplanted in Irenaeus by a smooth harmonious saving process, at whose beginning stand the laws of nature, which alone could render men just and which the decalogue standardized. The other legal prescriptions which were added in course of time on account of the disobedience of the people, and which he calls *leges servitutis*, were suspended by the freedom of the gospel which broadened and completed the laws of nature.

Irenaeus knows nothing of Paul's distress because of the "unfulfillability" of the law, for he knows nothing of the daemonic power of sin as a debt, as guilt and doom. He does not emphasize the cross as the centre of the saving process, and his Paulinism therefore perishes on the rocks of the doctrine of justification. This he did not take over, for he was guided by the idea that man's nature is not sinful in itself, and so the Spirit of God in Christ imparted to the individual Christian rather supports the naturally good disposition than effects a radically moral transformation. Of all the Pauline points of view in regard to the law, there is only one that he really retained with understanding, namely that the Old Testament law is a παιδαγωγὸς εἰς Χριστόν. The tendency to render independent this pedagogic motif, already noticeable in Hellenistic Judaism and especially in the LXX (see ch. 1, 2b) was with Irenaeus, however,

[1] Cf. G. Zimmermann, *Die hermeneutischen Prinzipien Tertullians*, Diss. Leipzig, 1937, 6 ff.

only the expression of common church faith, already reflected in the letters of Ignatius. It was very useful for the sanctifying moralism of the catholic church, and as patristic teaching it was in the long run far more important than the other elements in the kerygma of the apostle, which was so little fruitful for the practical life of simple laymen. The whole doctrine of the atoning sacrifice of Christ recedes into the background with Irenaeus; the theology of the cross is used only for ornamental purposes. Hence Bousset[1] is quite right in asserting that Irenaeus' adoption of Pauline themes and the harmony between Paul and Irenaeus were only apparent.

Hippolytus of Rome,[2] who was a pupil of Irenaeus, proceeds on the same lines. Christian faith is with him an intensified legalism. Christ decided to wash away men's sins, but man has to contribute his own efforts to this process. Whoever obeys the holy precepts of Christ and imitates the perfection of His life, becomes like Him and is honoured by Him. The keeping of the commandments is the criterion by which one may test whether the regeneration of baptism proves effective. Hippolytus, who in pursuit of his ideal of holiness taught a rigoristic practice of penance, has also considerable significance for the use of Old Testament scriptural attestation to Christ and His evangel. But he again is far removed from genuine Paulinism just on account of his assimilation of the two testaments.

The same applies also to the allegorical–typological exegesis of the Bible practised by Clement of Alexandria,[3] who, in opposition to the gnostics, often appeals to Paul and demonstrates their serious misunderstanding of Paul. But in order to cut the ground from under their feet, he unjustifiably dilutes the Pauline theses. The optimism with which he praises the law as a factor in salvation and as a moral tutor stands in stark opposition to Rom. 7. His completions of Pauline affirmations are typical, as for example: "The just shall live by faith" completed by: "faith which is in keeping with the covenant and the commandments". Or again: "by grace are we saved" completed by "yet not apart from good works". Christ is not for him the end of the law, it is rather that the law reaches its perfection in Christ. For the intense eschatological faith of the apostle that the new aeon

---

[1] *Kyrios Christos*, 442; Aleith, *op. cit.*, 70 ff.; N. Bonwetsch, *Die Theologie des Irenäus*, Gütersloh, 1925, 80 ff.; M. Simon, *Verus Israel*, 197 ff.

[2] Cf. also A. Frh. v. Ungern-Sternberg, *Der traditionelle atl. Schriftbeweis de Christo und de evangelio in der alten Kirche*, Leipzig, 1908, 98 ff.; R. Wilde, *The Treatment of the Jews in Greek Christian Writers*, Washington, 1949, 159 ff.

[3] Cf. H. Seesemann in *ThStKr*, 1936, 312–346; F. Buri, *Clemens Alexandrinus und der paulinische Freiheitsbegriff*, Zürich, 1939, 68–72; Aleith, *op. cit.*, 87.ff.; Schelkle, *op. cit.*, 366.

dawns with the end of the law, he has no more understanding, as is the case with all these theologians. As far as possible he endeavours to bring the Old Testament law into line with the *nova lex Christi* or to make it appear congruous with the latter. Instead of the Torah he gives us a general idea of law. Paul's dualisms such as: this aeon and the coming aeon, flesh and spirit, law and faith, have no meaning for him. The law belongs to the content of the faith (*Strom.* II, 27, 2); in fact, he defends the law, which, he says, the Jews alone have not understood, and does so in opposition to Paul—and that because of the reasonableness of its content (II, 32, 3; 34, 4). Clement of Alexandria knows very well the Pauline theses, but he rationalizes them and transforms them by means of the technique of allegorical exegesis.

Similar observations would apply to the Alexandrian Origen,[1] who in his history of philosophy stands wholly on Paul's shoulders, though from the theses of Rom. 9–11 he thinks he is able to infer a kind of general world law. The *nova lex Christi*, to obey which is necessary to salvation, he describes in his commentary on Rom. 7: 19 as a *verbum breviatum*. But the thought of a partial revision of the law is as un-Pauline as possible. All these exponents of allegorical–typological exegesis have certainly used the points of view which lay ready for them in Paul, but in their use of them they show how far removed from his mind they are.

It is much the same with the rhetorician and later Bishop of Carthage, Cyprian,[2] who for the explanation of Christian baptism associates himself with the Pauline typology of 1 Cor. 10: baptism was foreshadowed by the Red Sea. But he understands as little as anyone else Paul's fundamental concern to assert that man becomes righteous by faith in Christ and not by the works of the law. The question: how do I gain the grace of God? Cyprian answers without any embarrassment—through good works. For Jesus has given a new law of moral integrity. He goes through the letters of Paul, as do most of these early Fathers, in order to discover what principles of the new Christian morality can be derived from them. Paul has to submit to the indignity of being brought forward by Cyprian in his writing *De Habitu Virginum* as the crowning witness against prevalent fashions, for it is an externalized Paul who haunts these writings. For

[1] For Origen cf. also V. E. Hasler, *Gesetz und Evangelium in der alten Kirche bis Origenes*, Zürich, 1938; E. Molland, *The Conception of the Gospel in the Alexandrian Theology*, Oslo, 1938.
[2] Cf. E. Aleith, *op. cit.*, 68 ff.

Cyprian the gospel is not a teaching which has Christ as its central content, but a collection of precepts expounded by Christ and serving the purposes of the new catholic righteousness of works.

But let us break off here, in the middle of the 3rd century, this survey of detail. That much in our dear brother Paul is "hard to understand"—"which the ignorant and unstable twist to their own destruction"—had already been complained of by the author of 2 Peter (3: 15–16), and the letter to Titus (3: 9) had indeed recommended that people should abstain from disputings about the law as being useless and unprofitable. In reality none of the church Fathers understood any longer the problem of the law as it presented itself to the mind of Paul, because none of them needed any longer to make a personal struggle to free themselves from the law. They all transformed and adapted for their own purposes the declarations of the apostle. Thus it is characteristic that Irenaeus (*Adv. Haer.* IV, 12, 4) understands Rom. 10: 4 to mean that Christ did not annul the law of Sinai but only the Pharisaic elaborations of the law. Tertullian, Origen, and others also maintained this thought, so un-Pauline, of a partial revision of the Biblical law.[1] Whatever in the law did not suit their ends they set aside in various ways by allegorical treatment; the sole legitimate way of the *abrogatio legis* through Messianology was increasingly forgotten. Without suspecting it, in Rom. 7: 14, "the law is spiritual", Paul supplied the exegetical norm not only to the Alexandrians but also to allegorical interpretation of scripture in general, with the consequence that in every favourite text the literal meaning could be replaced by a spiritual one. Thus it became possible to read into Paul's letters the whole Trinitarian doctrine, to infer from Rom. 1: 7 the essential likeness of nature between the Father and the Son, from Rom. 1: 3 the fully developed doctrine of the two natures, from Rom. 1: 20 the doctrine of the Trinity, etc.[2]

The consequences of the de-eschatologizing of Paul by the early catholic church are quite clear. We can therefore only fully agree with M. Werner, *op. cit.*, p. 234: "The whole characteristic Pauline doctrine about the law is shattered into unrecognizable fragments as a result of the development of dogma in the sub-apostolic age. No single stone remains on another." Equally is the Pauline understanding of the process of saving history perverted in the worst possible way. Thus Theodoret has simply twisted Rom. 11: 29 into meaning that God has revoked His grace once bestowed on the Jews.[3]

[1] The sources in M. Werner, *op. cit.*, 214.
[2] Cf. K. H. Schelkle, *op. cit.*, 23 ff., 26, 55, 317 ff.   [3] Cf. *ibid.*, 403 ff.

And the polemics of John Chrysostom are, as is well known, still more virulent and malicious.[1] But we cannot follow this line of development any further.

We have seen that with the exception of Marcion, who had at least some surmise of what the apostle was driving at, although he ruined it by his insistence on reading into the letters his dualistic presuppositions, none of the early church theologians had any genuine understanding of the problems with which Paul was concerned. We may summarize the main reason for this as follows:

The apostle's teaching about sin and redemption ceased to be understood because none of the Fathers was able to live through the existentially unique situation of Saul, who at Damascus became Paul. To none of them is emancipation from the Jewish law a problem, because the background against which they became Christians was heathen, and from this heathendom they wished to free themselves. Hence the apostle remained a lonely figure without a following, and the fate of his message was tragic. Since the early Christian Fathers of the church were to a large extent moralists, since they regarded faith as assent to the truth of propositions, and equated walking by faith with obedience to the commandments, they felt compelled to tone down the radical theses of the apostle. Thus the doctrine of predestination which Paul acknowledged became the paler idea of prescience; the stark alternative of the old and the new covenants was smoothed over, for Christ, regarded as a teacher of the *nova lex*, introduced a new regime which could be compatible with the greatly reduced old law. On the other hand, those mystic-pneumatic lines of thought in Paul were carried much farther by the religious thinkers of Asia Minor, and along with certain ascetic impulses they gradually developed the mysticism of being in Christ into the believer's mystical θεοποίησις. Athanasius, Gregory of Nyssa, Gregory of Nazianzus, Cyril of Alexandria, Macarius, and other teachers of the 4th century described the blessedness attainable through discipleship to Christ as ἀφθαρσία, which brings about a θεία φύσις and implies the mode of being of unearthly life.

The Eastern Church in particular developed the mystical impulses in Paul's theology, his theory of the Spirit and the gifts of the Spirit, as also his doctrine of the sacraments, while in the west his teaching about righteousness through faith had a more lasting in-

[1] Cf. M. Simon, "La Polémique antijuive de St. Jean Chrysostome" (*Annuaire de l'Intitut de Philologie et d'Histoire Orientales et Slaves*), Brussels, 1936, 403 ff.

fluence. Thus Ernst Benz[1] is not far wrong with his simplifying formula, "that the east accepted the Paul of the Corinthian Letters, while the west accepted the Paul of the Letter to the Romans". But the reason for all these changes and distortions, which at bottom are misunderstandings, must be sought in the fact that later writers ceased to understand Pauline eschatology. The non-eschatological Paul is simply unintelligible; he could not possibly find a following. Hence all his deep teaching about the law and justification, about the meaning of the death and resurrection of Christ, remained in its essence unappreciated. Thus the delay in the parousia meant that Paul's theology was totally flattened and rendered superficial.

In the following centuries too the letters of Paul, though industriously and devotedly read, seldom found understanding. In this respect he is unique in the primitive church. No other apostle had such a vividly marked theology, a personality of such sharp outline. And it is precisely this vividness of individuality which was sacrificed to ecclesiastical developments. The church was not in a position to digest such a towering figure. He must needs be stylized and assimilated to other New Testament personalities.

This line of development began in the canonical Acts of the Apostles, which places in the mouth of Paul such very un-Pauline speeches, speeches such as Peter himself might have made. This tendency became still more marked in the following centuries. Paul teaches the same doctrines as Peter and the twelve; this was a church axiom which remained unshaken until the time of Luther. In practice, this meant that Paul had been pushed into the background by the twelve. The balanced theology of the church was identified with the doctrine of the twelve, and Paul, as far as possible, was posthumously assimilated to the primary apostles. If Marcion tried to emphasize the opposition until it became a rent and fissure, a permanent cleavage, the church of the 2nd and 3rd centuries in answer to Marcion toned down the opposition until it almost disappeared. For the picture drawn of the beginnings of Christianity had to be a unified one, if only for the sake of the peace of believers' souls. The church recognized and canonized only a catholicized Paul, whom it regarded as the authorized agent and follower of the apostles. The real Paul of the New Testament letters was certainly not this; but doctrinal unity became more important than historical truth. Whether Peter was ever in Rome, whether he was martyred or not,

[1] "Das Paulusverständnis in der morgenländischen und abendländischen Kirche", *ZRGG*, 1951, 291.

he became in truth the actual founder of the great church. Thus in a way the catholic church renewed the old Jewish-Christian objection to Paul which claimed that he was not an original apostle like Peter and the twelve who were instituted by the Lord Himself, that on the contrary he joined the circle later. It wreaked vengeance on Paul by this means. Thus it was not he but Peter who became the first Pope, while Pauline doctrine was subordinated and adapted to the general teaching of the church.

Such were the reasons why knowledge of the true figure of Paul was lost, and Pauline theology persisted at most only in an apocryphal guise, until Luther discovered it anew because he saw his own religious experience reflected in that of Paul, and first understood it against the Pauline background. The Reformation truly restored the original Paul, giving him his due place and putting him at the centre of the Christian life of faith. "Ego Christum amiseram illic, nunc in Paulo reperi" (*W.A.* 2, 414). "In scholastic theology I lost Christ, now in Paul I have found Him again," is Luther's testimony. In his wrestling with a text of Paul, Rom. 1 : 17, which speaks of the revelation of God's righteousness through the gospel, it is well known that Luther rediscovered the meaning of the gospel and thus initiated the reformation movement. Of course he adhered strictly to the principle: "Christus universae scripturae scopus est", and thus found Christ reflected in the Old Testament also. By his exegesis of Paul's letters Luther developed the trend of his own theology, and became so very Pauline in outlook that he was unable to do justice to the other figures of the New Testament witness, such as that of the apostle John,[1] in their peculiar distinctiveness. Luther treated the other voices of the New Testament choir either in a Pauline sense, or critically, devaluing them, as for example the Letter of James, which he described as a letter of straw.

No one will be able to dispute the Paulinism of Luther who has really studied the bases of Luther's doctrine about justification by faith. Let us quote here a passage from the important work of Paul Althaus (*Paulus und Luther über den Menschen*, Gütersloh, 1951):

At decisive points in their theology Paul and Luther are of one mind. Luther's theology is controlled by the strict distinction between law and gospel: at this point he was schooled in the teaching of Paul. The meaning of grace, the fact that man can receive his righteousness, his dignity, and his honour only from God and God's grace—all this Luther learned

---

[1] This has been impressively shown by W. v. Loewenich in *Luther und das johanneische Christentum*, Munich, 1935.

274

from Paul. . . . The same is true of faith, its essence and meaning. What Luther teaches about faith has been drawn in its essentials from Rom. 4: faith and the promise belong together (4: 16); faith is evoked where man is confronted by nothingness and death; in such circumstances he dares to rely solely on God and honours God as true in His word, as the God who creates out of nothingness (4: 17 ff.); faith is the sole way of honouring God. Such points form the very heart of both Pauline and Lutheran theology. The *theologia crucis* which Luther adopted comes from Paul and finds its most powerful expression in 1 Cor. 1 and in 2 Cor.: God's wisdom in folly, God's power in weakness, God's life in the dying Christ, God's grace showered upon His own only through their dying with Christ, through their communion with Christ's life and death. Where else have the powerful antitheses of 2 Cor. found such an echo as in Luther?—"as sorrowing but always rejoicing, as dying and behold we live". Where has Rom. 8 resounded again so mightily as in Luther's *Price of a Christian Man's Freedom?* (14 ff.).

Of course there are great differences between them, for Luther's questions arose from a situation quite other than that in which Paul's doctrine of justification by faith had its birth.[1] Finally, Paul was a man of the 1st, Luther a man of the 16th century. Paul struggled with Judaism and Hellenism, Luther with Romanism and humanism. Luther, as is well known, was also strongly influenced by Augustine, who took even further the Pauline idea of sin, so that Luther estimated the power of sin far more pessimistically than did Paul, and that even in the Christian life. Paul was sustained by the tense expectation of the parousia, and he would have felt as strange and unintelligible Luther's formula for the Christian man who had entered into communion with Christ's death and resurrection: *simul peccator et justus.*[2] Althaus, in the work just quoted, has studied deeply the differences between Paul and Luther in respect of anthropology, and has compared them on the basis of their understanding of Rom. 7. However clear the differences, it must none the less be said that— apart from the failure of Marcion's wrong-headed attempt—Luther

[1] Schlatter (*Luthers Deutung des Römerbriefs*, Gütersloh, 1917) says the distinction has been well brought out by W. Mundle, *Der Glaubensbegriff des Paulus*, Leipzig, 1932. Cf. recently also W. Joest, "Paulus und das Luthersche simul iustus et peccator", *Kerygma und Dogma*, 1955, 269 ff.

[2] On this point F. Overbeck, *op. cit.*, 59 has written: "By its total misinterpretation of texts such as Rom. 7: 15 ff. and Phil. 3: 12, the Reformation became unable to understand truly the mind of Paul in the light of his Christian perfection. Paul certainly did not consider himself to be the persistent sinner justified only by faith—the type of Christian that Luther knew himself to be. As a member of the Christian community Paul is aware of being exalted above sin."

was the only man who restored Paul to a position of honour, and with truly epoch-making effect. Hence Protestantism has rightly been called a reformed Paulinism. Paul was the "saint" of the Reformation.

The reverse side of this is that the whole Lutheran and partly also Calvinistic doctrines of faith, justification, and election by grace were only read into the letters of Paul. This point has remained obscure to many Protestant theologians up to the present. It is not without reason that all the 19th- and 20th-century attacks on Paul, such as those of Nietzsche, Lagarde, Rosenberg, were directed also against Luther and Protestantism. If we disregard for the moment the history of Pauline research in the narrow sense, which has been sketched out in the first chapter, then we may consider these attacks as the last stage, so far, in the story of the understanding of Paul in Western Christendom.

Friedrich Nietzsche's polemic against Christianity is directed far more against Paul than against Jesus. He considers that it was Paul who corrected the teaching of Jesus and ruined the original message of Christianity. Ernst Benz rightly describes Nietzsche's hatred of Paul as "explosive and measureless". No other Christian was "in the same degree the object of Nietzsche's personal scorn, loathing, disgust, and hatred as this apostle".[1] Paul was for Nietzsche the "eternal Jew *par excellence*" (*Antichrist* 58). Nietzsche's distorted picture of Paul has attained great popularity and has been propagated in many anti-Christian writings and pamphlets. In Nietzsche's work itself it nevertheless had its level and was rooted in a total picture of history, which was fashioned by a special theory of history as a process of decadence. We will cite here a few characteristic sentences of Nietzsche about Paul:

> Paul's point of departure is the need of mystery felt by the religiously awakened masses: he seeks a sacrifice, a bloody phantasmagoria, which sustains the struggle by means of images drawn from secret cults: God on the cross, the drinking of blood, the *unio mystica* with the sacrificial victim; . . . he understood the great need of the heathen world and made a quite capricious selection from the facts of the life and death of Christ, giving everything a new emphasis and everywhere shifting the centre of gravity . . . he shattered essential and original Christianity . . .[2]

The fact that the ship of Christianity threw overboard a good deal of Jewish ballast, that it went and was able to go among the heathen—

---

[1] *Nietzsches Ideen zur Geschichte des Christentums und der Kirche*, Leiden, 1956, 36.
[2] *Werke*, ed. K. Schlechta, III, 655 (*Aus dem Nachlass der achtziger Jahre*).

all that depended on the history of this one man, tormented, pitiable, repellent both to himself and others. He suffered under a fixed idea, a question which gave him no rest, that of the real meaning of the Jewish law and the possibility of fulfilling that law. . . . Such was the first Christian, the discoverer of Christianity! Up to then there had been only Jewish sectaries.[1]

Paul logically developed this immoral view with that rabbinical boldness which always characterized him, so that it yielded the thesis: "If Christ has not risen from the dead, then our faith is vain." And at one stroke there developed out of the gospel the most despicable of all unfulfillable promises, the most immodest doctrine of personal immortality . . . Paul himself taught it as a reward![2]

Hard on the heels of the glad news there followed the worst of all: the message brought by Paul. Paul embodies the very opposite type to that of the bringer of good news; he is a genius in hatred, in the vision of hate, in the ruthless logic of hate. What has not this nefarious evangelist sacrificed to his hatred! He sacrificed first and foremost the Saviour, he crucified him on his cross. Life, example, teaching, death, the meaning and the right of the gospel as a whole—nothing existed any longer, after this forger of hate realized what things alone he could make use of. These were not reality nor historical truth![3]

A God who died for our sins: redemption by faith; resurrection after death—all these things are falsifications of true Christianity, for which that morbid crank [Paul] must be made responsible.[4]

As for Nietzsche, so also for Paul de Lagarde, the apostle Paul is the historical figure to whom is imputed the transformation and falsification of original Christianity. To this "fanatical head" Lagarde (though not H. S. Chamberlain often mentioned in this connexion) traces back the shattering and distorting of the life of Jesus, of the real essence of His person.

Paul brought into the church for us the Old Testament, under the influence of which the gospel, as far as was possible, perished. Paul favoured us with the Pharisaic mode of interpreting scripture, which proves everything from everything, and has ready resources for discovering in the text the meaning that has to be discovered, then boasting that it follows only the word of scripture. Paul brought home to us the Jewish theory of sacrifice and all that depends on it; the whole Jewish understanding of history was foisted on us by him.[5]

[1] II, 1055 ff. (*Morgenröte*, I, 68). [2] II, 1203 (*Der Antichrist Fr. 41*).
[3] II, 1204 (*ibid.*, 42). [4] III, 656 (*Aus dem Nachlass der achtziger Jahre*).
[5] *Deutsche Schriften*, ed. Karl Fischer, Munich, 1934, 68; cf. also Lothar Schmid, "Paul de Lagardes Kritik an Kirche", *Theologie und Christentum*, Stuttgart, 1935, 65 ff.; H. Karpp, "Lagardes Kritik an Kirche und Theologie", *ZThK*, 1952, 367 ff.; Benz, *op. cit.*, 139 ff.

And if anyone is so bold as to disagree with him, he launches at them his theory of hardening, declaring them blind and stubborn. Even his doctrine of justification rests on a peculiar one-sidedness of the apostle which contrasts with the original Christian approach to life. Lagarde, like Nietzsche, was most upset by the Pauline conception of sin, typical of a superfine and decadent mind. Paul would have seemed strange to the poor fishermen and craftsmen in the entourage of Jesus. "The latter," says Lagarde, "in their narrow circumstances and monotonous lives could hardly have had occasion to sin much and could scarcely have understood the tormenting feeling of failing in perfection, of ceaselessly hindering or not helping others."[1]

From this it is clear that the chief objections to Paul are of a psychological nature. The type of his personality is not pleasing to modern taste: he is too Jewish, too divided, too indignant. Such judgments culminate in that of Alfred Rosenberg, who in his notorious *Mythos des 20. Jahrhunderts*[2] has outdone Lagarde and gone a stage further in rudeness, denouncing Paul the fanatic as the preacher of international world-revolution and his doctrine as the "Talmudic-oriental aspect both of the Roman and the Lutheran churches". None of these critics has any faculty of comprehending the greatness and dynamic power of Paul's thought. They reproach him with having reduced the life of Jesus to His birth, death, and resurrection in order to make these bare facts yield Paul's elaborate theory of the redemptive death and the sacraments. The truth in this is that the unity of life and doctrine, which mystics and the spiritual-minded of all ages have always honoured as the mark of the greatness and divinity of Jesus, cannot be found in Paul's interpretation. Paul is a man of antitheses and contradictions; his thought could attain harmony only through dialectics and antinomies. But should he not perhaps appeal in this very respect to the modern consciousness? This was felt already by Luther. What to-day is described as anti-Christian feeling is, on closer inspection, for the most part anti-Paulinism. People try to rescue Jesus as the greatest and noblest of all human beings, by stripping Him of His divine attributes. It is felt that the wicked Paul was the evil genius who discovered theology, who never understood Jesus, who brought back into Christianity its Jewish element, and whose capacity for hate introduced into that religion all those ugly traits which Luther later rendered permanent.

However, this currently expressed polemical view does not go very

---

[1] *op. cit.*, 73: many other similar references may be taken from this volume.
[2] Munich, 1934 (27th–28th ed.), 74 ff.

deep. The enemies of Paul get even less near to him than his followers and idolaters. None of his opponents, not even Nietzsche, has appreciated even from a distance the intellectual vigour and fullness of Paul. In this case a deep psychological analysis is not of much use, for Paul is not concerned with psychological realities but with something quite different. I repeat what has already been said: to dissolve his experience at Damascus by psychological means is foolishness. The least we can do is to accept the faith of the apostle as such. And what is required of the scholar is that even if he does not personally believe, he should understand, the descriptions which in all sincerity the apostle gives to his faith. And this understanding must in particular be able to grasp the whole development of the apostle's thought. The latter often enough leads us into depths and abysses where Pauline metaphysic begins, which curiously enough is not even suspected by modern opponents such as Nietzsche and Lagarde, to mention only those of weight.

On the other hand, this kind of understanding is to be found within the sphere of historical and exegetical theology itself—not only Protestant but also Catholic, where in recent decades a better and deeper understanding of the apostle has developed. As contrasted with the research at the beginning of the century (Holsten, Holtzmann, Weinel, Wrede, etc.) there has emerged not least under the influence of dialectical theology a new and higher assessment of Paul in the work of Bultmann, Dibelius, Kümmel, Wendland, etc., which has had its effects even as far away as the U.S.A.[1] The critics of this new phase, however, show an attitude of reserve towards that former historian of Paul, Albert Schweitzer, to whose important book *The Mysticism of Paul the Apostle* we ourselves in our own account feel strongly indebted, however much we may differ from him. Hence we propose to conclude our present section with an extract from it which is very relevant to Paul as thinker.

> Paul has established for all times the Christian's right to think. He raises above the faith which is valid by tradition that knowledge which flows from the spirit of Christ. There lives in him an unlimited, uninterrupted reverence for truth. He accepts only those bonds which are imposed by love, not those which are imposed by scholastic authority.
> None the less he is no revolutionary. He takes his point of departure in the faith of the church, but does not admit that he must stop where the latter stops; he assumes the right to think through to the end the

[1] On this see D. W. Riddle, "Reassessing the Religious Importance of Paul", *The Study of the Bible Today and Tomorrow*, ed. Willoughby, Chicago, 1947, 314 ff.

thoughts which centre in Christ, not caring whether the knowledge which he thus attains has already come within the ken of the church and is accepted by it.

The result of this first appearance of the activity of a great thinker in Christianity, is to establish for all time the confidence that the Christian faith has nothing to fear from the power of thought, even if the latter is disturbing to tranquillity, is apt to provoke disputes which seem to promise little fruit for piety . . . Paul is the patron saint of thought in Christianity. All those who think to serve the gospel of Christ by destroying the liberty of thinking must hide their faces from him (365 ff. German edn.).

3. PAUL'S CRITICISM OF THE LAW AS A PROBLEM INTRINSIC TO JUDAISM

We have now outlined, to be sure in a cursory and inadequate way, the influence of Paul on the subsequent history of Christianity. The task now remains of asking what role Paul might have fulfilled in the history of Judaism had he remained within it. For the historian of religion it may well seem a legitimate question for consideration, to present Saul's original question about the Jewish law in its pre-Christian form and to put this question to the Jewish religion.

If we understand the matter rightly, 1,900 years ago he posed a question which tradition did not adequately answer for him as a Pharisaic theologian. We know the problem only in its Pauline setting, and so must translate it back into Judaic terms. It would then run somewhat as follows: If here and now the law as a whole does not seem "fulfillable", does not the fact perhaps suggest that the law is not an exhaustive expression of the will of God? May the fulfilling of the law of Moses be understood literally and completely as a fulfilling of the will of God?

I think that to put the question in this way is to restore it to the form in which it first presented itself to the mind of Saul, for in this form it is not compromised by terms which lead away from Judaism —terms which the Christian answer requires when it judges the law from the standpoint of the realized advent of the Messiah. Put thus, it has been a theme for discussion by Jews during the last 1,900 years; though it can only be heard and understood in times of doubt and radical questioning, as was the case in the 1st century when Hellenism assimilated Judaism and has again become the case in the last 150 years when there has again been assimilation—the intervening time being mostly under the control of the principle of the "hedge about the law". The question is whether the doing of the law must not spring from a prior attitude of faith. Not the Pauline faith in the advent of the Messiah, but faith in the God of Sinai as the pre-requisite of obedience towards the declarations of the divine will.[1] This attitude of faith was called in Biblical times "the fear of God". It was taken as a matter of course that every Jew possessed this as the law preceding all laws, which did not need to be expressly commented on. Indeed, it is mentioned in Deut. 10: 12 as the sum of God's demands on Israel, but rabbinic Judaism presupposes it as existing. It was understood that the Jews had to develop a whole polity as a substitute for the loss of the divine state, as the expression of the will of God revealed in the Torah, and related to the life of men in post-Biblical times. But it was not considered necessary and probably was not necessary to establish a special Jewish doctrine of faith on the basis of the fear of God, and in addition to the doctrine of the law.

Perhaps it has become clear only in our own times that Saul–Paul asked a decisive question determined by a border situation such as has not reappeared until the present, and for this question tradition is in his debt. Of course, the answer which he gave leads irresistibly beyond the bounds of Judaism. Our study has attempted to point out those violations of Judaism by confronting the Pauline positions with that of Jewish tradition. The enormous importance which in any event Paul's theology has for the history of the Jewish religion has been incidentally characterized in the following way by Hermann Cohen:[2] "Suspicion of the value of laws was aroused in a fundamental way by Paul, and is maintained as a living force by his criticism and polemics." What the Letter to the Ephesians calls ἐντολή (2: 14 ff.)—namely, the normalization of the individual commands of the Torah as a rule of life, can become in fact an "evil hedge". But the Jewish faith cannot follow Paul's inference when he says that the νόμος τῶν ἐντολῶν enshrined in *dogmata* "has been set aside through Christ"[3] and that therefore from the Christian point of view "those particular commands and *dogmata* about food, the Sabbath, and fasts

[1] S. L. Steinheim, *Die Offenbarung nach dem Lehrbegriffe der Synagoge*, II, Leipzig, 1856, 38, formulated this insight thus a hundred years ago: "Hence we are concerned to put forward and to demonstrate a claim directly opposite to that of Mendelssohn, namely that the OT was given not to reveal the law, but to reveal the living God, to which the law is subordinate in importance."

[2] *Religion der Vernunft aus den Quellen des Judentums*, Berlin, 1929, 399.

[3] Kittel in *WB*, II, 234; similarly also Schrenk, *ibid.*, II, 548.

were only a foreshadowing of future reality whose substance is Christ".[1] If Judaism must from its own insights into saving history reject the Messianological devaluation of the law, this very rejection, when sufficiently thought out, opens up the deep insight that the law as instruction should never be allowed to become an arid formality, because it rests on the ground of the covenant relationship. Precisely as instruction the law is not a static but an eschatological factor, because it points beyond itself to that fulfilment of the covenant when the Messiah in God's own time shall come.

The aim of the law is earthly embodiment of the holy. The will of God must be embodied on earth, and God is to be sanctified by the sanctification of man. Judaism did not need Paul to remind it that this goal can never be reached in the *olam haseh*. Just for that reason Messianic expectation persists. For the sake of this expectation an attitude of resignation is forbidden. The law is not ruined by the disillusioning actuality of sin. Rather God is the more earnestly implored to further graciously, by His commands, the sanctification of men. But even the attempt to keep the commands does not yet in itself produce the sanctification of mankind, and in perceiving this Hermann Cohen showed incomparably deep insight. For then "the commands would lose their symbolic character and take on the character of sacrifice. But we pray that God will sanctify us by His commands and cleanse our hearts."[2] The law as the expression of revelation is "the necessary form for the realization of the co-relation between God and man" (Cohen); but in the last resort the effecting of this is reserved to the Revealer of the law.

One further point must be made for a right insight into the essence of the law. In Saul's criticism of the law, which takes up the teaching of the prophets about the distinction between the ethic of the heart and the ethic of deeds, there lies an eternal warning against the desire of Judaism to fulfil the will of God often too quickly and too rectilineally; a protest against the shifting of the emphasis from the keeping of the covenant to ethical self-justification. It is not the law which makes man righteous, but God, the Lord of the covenant and the Founder of the law as a system of polity. Hence in the first place it is not the meticulous fulfilling of the law which is the main point, but the fulfilment of and adherence to the law in the faith that it is the expression of the will of the God of the covenant. The individual commands and bodies of law in scripture are essentially, and by reason of their probable genesis, collections of examples typifying the

[1] C. A. Bugge, *Das Christusmysterium, op. cit.*, 64,   [2] *Religion der Vernunft* etc., 398.

divine will rather than the complete and exclusive expression of the latter. The 248 commands (מצות—ἐντολαί) and the 365 prohibitions (גזרות—δόγματα) of rabbinical exegesis are just as little capable of enclosing the divine will of the sovereign Lord in statutory form as men of to-day are capable of feeling the importance of these 613 prescriptions without making distinctions among them.

The development towards orthopraxis as contrasted with real orthodoxy in the Talmud had the effect, however, that it became no longer possible or desirable to distinguish between the essential and unessential, the literal and the deeper understanding,[1] and thus the symbolic value of the law ceased to be understood; the fact that the community of Israel had in the law not the will of God itself but only its representation. In this connexion the word *repraesentio* may be taken quite literally as the intimation of something partially concealed. Not until the epoch of the liberal Judaism of the last hundred years have the presuppositions arisen which enable us to understand this duality and to make an end of the straightforward identification of the law and the divine will which was so typical of Talmudic Judaism. Thus Hermann Cohen has rightly sought to distinguish "the law within the law" or the "idea of the law" from the multiplicity of the particular commands, and Martin Buber has seen the relation between revelation and the commandment as that between the seal and its impression.

That there lies here a distinction which needs to be made, and even that we must distinguish between the divine Word and its human interpretation, did occasionally become clear to the old rabbis.[2] Both in the school of Rabbi Ishmael (Horayoth 8a; Makkoth 4a)

---

[1] None the less, the feeling for the difference between the letter and the spirit never quite disappeared even in these centuries. Thus Gen. Rabba Par. 19 on 3 : 2 gives a warning word of Rabbi Hiyya (*circa* 170): "Do not make the hedge about the garden too high lest it should fall in and crush the flowers." This of course means: "Do not make a subordinate thing equal in importance to the main thing." Perhaps also the exegesis of אשר שברת in Ex. 34 : 1 by Resh Laqish—"Sometimes the breaking of the Torah is in fact its maintenance, for the Holy One, praised be His name, said to Moses: Praise to you for you have broken it" should be understood in this sense (Menahoth 99b; related to it is Sifre Deut. 175). Or Jer. Terumoth 46b according to the explanation of פני מושה: "Rabbi Joshua ben Levi was rebuked by the prophet Elijah; then the rabbi asked: Have I not acted in agreement with מסרה (tradition)? Yes, answered Elijah, but is this the מסרת החסירים?" Also the explanation which depreciates the outward fulfilment of the law: "God is concerned about the heart" (e.g., Sanh. 106b) might be mentioned in this context, likewise the well-known reduction by Rabbi Simlai (Makkoth 23b) of the 613 commands to the single command of Hab. 2 : 4, which—in spite of the fact that its real point is the subject of debate—does in any event establish a distinction between moral and ceremonial precepts.

[2] Cf. G. Scholem, "Religiöse Autorität und Mystik", *Eranos-Jahrbuch*, 1957, 277.

and that of Rabbi Joshua ben Levi (Midr. to Song of Sol., 2) a distinction is made between the two first commands, which were heard by all as coming from God's mouth on Sinai, and the rest, of which only an echo could be heard while Moses articulated them. Maimonides (Moreh Nebukhim 11, 33) deduced from this that the two first commands as the basic doctrines of the existence and unity of God were the immediate precipitate of divine self-revelation. In this case the implied further inference would be that in the whole of the rest of the Torah human interpretation and explanation has played some part. This, however, is the standpoint of modern Judaism.

Only modern Judaism can appreciate once again, like Christianity, Paul's concern and the tension which he felt between the works of the law and faith, and it can appreciate it all the more because it maintains that tension and refuses with Paul to dissolve the tension prematurely by the elimination of one of its poles. The Jewish solution of it flows not from Christ but from the focusing of the two poles in God. The Jewish answer is the faith of Israel in God as the בורא עולם (Creator of the world), הנתן התורה (Revealer of the Torah), and גואל ישראל (Redeemer of Israel—and of humanity as a whole). This faith is the fundament for the doing of the works of the law. It precedes the doing of the law, which is intended only to express self-commitment to this faith and to prove obedience in the breadth and variety of life. For revelation precedes the law. It is not the law itself. Only when revelation is believed, or, in Jewish terms, when man adopts the attitude of the fear of God, can the law be done in faith. Then the question of the "fulfillability" of the law loses its sting. Quantitatively it becomes a task laid on man and an appeal to him to do as much as possible. Qualitatively it is a challenge to man's constantly renewed self-examination to see that he does the law with the right faith and disposition—which is the Jewish counterpart to Paul's insistence on faith.[1] Finally, the significance of Paul for the Jews consists also in the fact that he addressed not only Jews and Greeks, but man in general. His affirmations about man who is a sinner and who is yet capable of the right faith, concern the Jews also.

The right faith is in fact synonymous with the fear of God; and

[1] The deepest exploration of this line of thought will be found in the fragment of the correspondence between Martin Buber and Franz Rosenzweig published in the *Schocken* almanack for the year 5697 (1936/7), under the title "Offenbarung und Gesetz". My own study might be added: *Zur jüdisch-religiösen Gegenwartslage*, Berlin, 1938.

just because the latter was distorted in Paul's perspective we wish in conclusion to assess its importance as the basis of the law for Jewish thinking as a whole. Perhaps the true mission of the Rabbi Saul within Judaism itself—a mission not up to the present discharged— will be found to consist in the fact that with his criticism of the law he is able to arouse the Jews' attention to the importance of the fear of God, which they are all too liable to forget. In conclusion, we propose to give systematic historic treatment to these points, while in the spirit of objective and independent scholarship we now place ourselves on the ground of Jewish theology as formerly on that of Pauline theology, in the endeavour to reach adequate formulations and appropriate judgments.

We start with one of the few purely dogmatic sentences of the Babylonian Talmud (Berakhoth 33b) which proposes to link the prevailing scriptural belief in human liberty with divine all-know- ledge. "Rabbi Hanina said: All is in the hands of heaven with the exception of the fear of God, for it is written: 'And now, Israel, what does the Lord require of you but to fear the Lord your God?' (Deut. 10: 12.) Is, then, the fear of God a trivial matter? Rabbi Hanina said in the name of Rabbi Simon ben Jochai: The Holy God has nothing, blessed be His name, in His treasury but the treasure of the fear of God, for it is written: 'The fear of the Lord is his treasure' (Is. 33: 6)." The centrally important sentence of Deut. 10: 12, which co-ordinates fearing and loving God and walking in His ways and obviously makes them synonymous, was expounded thus by the great Jewish exegete Rashi (like Berakh. 33b): "Our teachers here tell us that all is effected by God except the fear of God."

Let us explain the position as follows: If everything comes from God except the fear of God, then that is the positive content of human freedom. For that is obviously the treasure (אוצר) in the divine treasure-house, given to man, as the Pirqe Aboth said: All is foreseen but freedom of choice is given (3, 19). The יראת יי is not a deed required by the law. It is the deed of man absolutely, which pre- cedes in importance the doing of the law and to which, of course— as we shall see—the doing of the law can lead. This is also said with desirable clarity in a sentence of Rabbi Eliezer in Sabb. 30b: "The whole world has been created merely for the sake of the man who fears God." In the concluding sentence the matter is thus summed up: "Fear God, and keep His commandments; for this is the whole duty of man" (Eccl. 12: 13). And likewise for the Jewish Christians of the pseudo-Clementine writings the φόβος θεοῦ is the mark of the true believer (Hom. 17, 11–12; 20, 2, etc.); ἀφοβία, i.e., absence of the fear of God, is the worst sin conceivable (Hom. 1, 18).

We now ask what the fear of God means for man in terms of his existential situation, and turn for an answer to the Jewish philosophers of religion.

Jewish philosophy of religion begins with Aristobulus and Philo of Alexandria. The theological thought of Philo centres strictly around the idea of creation.[1] For Philo, all testimony to divine revelation is related to the creaturely being of man and is aimed at bringing his creaturely status home to him. Cf. *De Migr. Abr.* 41: "God declares His wisdom not only by the creation of the world but also by the fact that He prefers to implant the understanding of creation in man himself." This, moreover, is in agreement with the opinion of the Tannaim as expressed in the Mishna tractate Pirqe Aboth: "The value of man as creature lies in the fact that he is created in the image of God; but a higher value resides in this—that he is conscious of his having been created in God's image."

The means of coming to realize this situation, namely that man should understand himself as *creatura* in contrast with the *creator*, is for Philo the fear of God; εὐσέβεια as ἀρχὴ ἀρίστη πάντων ἀρετῶν (*De Decalogo* 52). He sees as the alternative whether the man who is not living according to the will of God wishes to try to understand himself by his own resources and so bring about the θάνατος ψυχῆς (*De Posteritate Caini* 73) or whether through the τιμὴ θεοῦ he wills to receive afresh the ἀειθαλὲς εἶδος of his being (*De Agricultura* 171). By the fear of God mankind receives peace and blessedness of life (*De Posteritate Caini* 185); to live without the fear of God is to fall away from God (*De Spec. Leg.* I, 54). Arrogance or ὑπερηφανία is the defect of the soul which does not appreciate that it stands under God and is not therefore humble and God-fearing (περὶ φιλανθρωπίας 171 f.). A return to the creaturely situation is, however, always an open possibility to the arrogant, as the concluding section περὶ μετανοίας emphasizes.

These examples already suggest one trait that is throughout typical of the Alexandrian and especially the Philonic philosophy of religion; namely, the anthropological approach to religious phenomena. Here belief or the fear of God means the right understanding of being

---

[1] The Grisebach scholar Gerhardt Kuhlmann, *Theologia naturalis bei Philon und bei Paulus*, Gütersloh, 1930, has especially concerned himself with this aspect of philosophical theology—unfortunately in the not quite appropriate forms of thought of the modern philosophy of existence. Cf. my review, *MGWJ*, 1938, 272 ff.

as creaturely being, while unbelief or arrogance implies a wrong conception of being as domination.[1] The decision between self-glorying and the fear of God, between evil and good, is that work of man to which the divine commandments would lead him. Doubtless in Philo's theology of creation we find a fundamental trait of Jewish piety in general, for the demand for the fear of God is inferred from man's creaturely status, so that man can grasp it as a possibility intrinsic to the nature of his being. Philo consistently declares the first and most holy commandment to be ἕνα τὸν ἀνωτάτω νομίζειν τε καὶ τιμᾶν θεόν (De Decalogo 65).[2]

In this respect Philo is at one with the point of view of the LXX as it is reflected in the contrast of the עבדים (σεβόμενοι) and the איבים (ἀπειθοῦντες) in Is. 66: 14. Here it is no longer, as in the Massoretic text, the servants of Yahweh as a people who are contrasted with the hostile heathen, but rather the God-fearing both in Israel and among the Gentiles who are contrasted with those who are disobedient to God. G. Bertram[3] comments quite rightly: "This means that the fear of God is made the basic attitude of the Old Testament believer, on which both faith and trust rest and from which they spring as from their root." Thus in like manner a strong orientation towards a theology of creation can be proved from the LXX.

That the fear of God can be deduced from a right understanding of creation is a meaningful statement for Jewish theology only when to it we add that the revealed commandments are nothing other than ordinances implanted in creation itself. Such a view, however, will always run the risk of slipping into a naturalistic theology, to which the position of Philo has always been very akin. A more reasonable derivation of the law will start from the fact of divine revelation, which by no means coincides with creation; and this approach has been fairly consistent in Jewish philosophy of religion. Since the middle of the 12th century the latter has been moulded on essentially Aristotelian lines, and has borne a strong impress of intellectualism.

---

[1] In the latter case he is the φιλοσώματος (De Migr. Abr. 22, οἰόμενος ἐπὶ τῶν ἰδίων δογμάτων) who instead of loving God loves his own body, as Philo deduces from a tortured exegesis of Gen. 45: 1. In De Decal. 58 he defines the fear of God (εὐσέβεια) as παράγγελμα μηδὲν τῶν τοῦ κόσμου μερῶν αὐτοκρατῆ θεὸν ὑπολαμβάνειν.

[2] Cf. Kuhlmann, op. cit., 27. In De Specialibus Legibus, I, 299–314, Philo with reference to Deut. 10: 12 emphasizes the tendency to reduce the Biblical commands to one kelal, one foundation principle (fear and love towards God). Cf. I. Heinemann, Philons griechische und jüdische Bildung, Breslau, 1932, 491.

[3] "Praeparatio evangelica in der Septuaginta", VT, 1957, 237.

Human perfection was thus sought in the perfection of knowledge. The most influential of all these thinkers, Moses Maimonides, ascribed to the Biblical giving of the law the function of bringing about physical and mental perfection.[1] But human perfection springs from communion with God. And this is rooted in the fear of God for which Abraham is the prototype in the Aqedath.

> For our forefather Abraham did not hasten to sacrifice Isaac[2] because he feared that God might punish him with death or the loss of his goods, but because he wished to instruct man about what we should do for the sake of the love and reverence we bear to God, and not for the hope of reward or the fear of punishment, and this we have illustrated from many texts (M.T. Yesode Hattorah, VI, 1–3). And when the angel said to him: "Now I know that you fear God" (Gen. 22: 12)[3] he meant to say: "By this deed, on account of which you deserve to be called a perfect fearer of God, all men must realize to what extent the fear of God can go." Consider moreover that this thought is particularly emphasized in Holy Scripture and that it has been expressly stated: "The final end of the law (שתבלית התורה) in regard to both the commandments and the declarations and narratives which it contains is in truth only one thing: the fear of God" (אחר והו יראת השם— Moreh Nebukhim III, 24).

This conveys with all possible clarity that the fear of God is the final aim of the Mosaic law, and similarly Bahya ibn Paquda in the 10th chapter of the book on the duties of the heart, or Abraham ibn Ezra (Yesod Mora VII, h. 28) consider it to be the *kelal* (basic commandment) which sums up all the others. In Moreh III, 52, Maimonides defines the *yirath adonai* more precisely as a "feeling of awestruck fear" which the pious experience when they become conscious of their own unworthiness in the eternal presence of God. Maimonides here equates the fear of God with the human reaction to the confrontation by the holy (the *fascinosum et tremendum*).[4] The final step which he takes is to define the close relation of the fear of God to the legalistic statutes of scripture which have this as their ultimate aim—this he infers from Deut. 21: 5–8—while he defines the ultimate aim of the

---

[1] Cf. J. Guttmann, *Die Philosophie des Judentums*, Munich, 1933, 201 ff., and the discussion of this work in Leo Strauss, *Philosophie und Gesetz*, Berlin, 1935.

[2] Maimonides implied previously that Abraham's decision for the Aqeda was not spontaneous and impulsive, but reached only after three days of wandering (Gen. 22: 4).

[3] Cf. also Rashi's commentary on Gen. 22: 12, which makes Abraham's fear of God the ultimate ground of God's love towards him.

[4] This is also well brought out in the very solid work by Ch. Neuburger, *Das Wesen des Gesetzes in der Philosophie des Maimonides*, Breslau, 1933, 47 f.

"doctrines of faith which articulate the knowledge of the essential being of God" as that love of God with all the heart and soul demanded in Deut. 6: 5. But the fear of God and the love of God are not opposites for him, nor are they related to each other in degree; they are two aspects of one single experience of communion with God. The tension between deeds springing from the fear of God and those springing from the love of God which we find in early rabbinic writings, the debate as to which is of higher rank, seems to have been resolved in Maimonides, who—in this respect like Yehuda Halevi (Kusari II, 50)—makes use of this dualism only as a means of dividing the Torah into legalistic precepts and doctrines of the faith. The fear of God and the love of God are both the final aim of the service of God (Moreh III, 29).

The most detailed and the clearest statements about the fear of God as the final end of the law are, however, to be found in a thinker of the close of the scholastic period, a thinker whom critics usually regard as only a syncretist and compiler.[1] The *Iqqarim* of Rabbi Joseph Albo, which appeared first in 1425,[2] in fact combine thoughts of Maimonides, Hasdai Crescas, and Simon ben Zemah into a dogmatic system which reduces the thirteen doctrines of the faith enumerated by Maimonides to three fundamental dogmas, and which in method owes much to Duran.[3] But so far as I know, there is no philosopher of religion who has given so luminous a description of what Jewish theology means by the *yirath adonai*. In III, 31, Albo writes as follows:

The end which the soul during its stay in the body is capable of reaching through the fulfilment of the Torah is nothing other than laying the foundations of a stable disposition (תכונת) towards the fear of God. And when it has attained the virtue of the fear of God (literally, fear of the holy and dreadful name) the soul is exalted and prepared for eternal life. The fear of God is defined by Albo as "the

---

[1] Cf. J. Guttmann *op. cit.*, 261 ff., and G. Vajda, *Introduction à la Pensée Juive du Moyen Age*, Paris, 1947, 186: "This writer, who owes his popularity to the synthetic character, the easy style and the expository clarity of his work, is hardly more than a compiler without originality, a fairly clever dialectician who knows how to make a specious assortment of the many writers with whose expressions he adorns his work."

[2] We cite from the critically revised text of J. Husik, 5 vols., Philadelphia.

[3] Duran's three *Iqqarim* he has independently divided into nine *shorashim* (corollaries) and six *anaphim* (secondary principles) meant to comprise the full extent of the supernatural Jewish doctrines of the faith as fixed by Maimonides. Cf. H. J. Schoeps, *Geschichte der jüdischen Religionsphilosophie in der Neuzeit*, I, Berlin, 1935, 13. The question of Rambam: What faith-ideas are indispensable to the Jewish consciousness? was modified by Albo as follows: Which doctrines are fundamental as basic principles and roots of the Jewish faith?

true symmetry (השווי האמתי) to which nothing can be added and from which nothing can be taken away". It is man's right and true way of being in the presence of God, attainable only with difficulty and great struggle, but the very foundation principle comprising all the commands of the Torah (כולל כל מצוות התורה). But Albo adds that God has lightened for man the strenuous task of achieving the true fear of God by commanding him to observe the divine ordinances and statutes. Deut. 10: 12–13 is to be interpreted to mean that instead of the fear of God which is man's real responsibility God demands nothing further than "the keeping of the commandments and statutes of the Lord which I command you this day for your good". In other words, the keeping of the law inevitably leads to the fear of God which is the "beginning of wisdom". And in continuation of Ps. 111: 10—"a good understanding have all those who practise it"—he alludes to the exegesis of Berakh. 17a (adopting the reading of Rabbi Jacob ibn Habib in his עין יעקב) that it is not the study of the law but the doing of it which God has required.

In chapter 32 he gives further, on the basis of older authors, a psychological interpretation of what the fear of God is, suggesting that it can best be understood as the feeling of creatureliness. It is a mingling of awe, in the face of the loftiness of God, and fear of God's anger; and this twofold note he finds expressed with special force in the Book of Job. It is in this sense that he interprets Job 31: 23: "For I was in terror of calamity from God, and I could not have faced his majesty", and Job's question to his friends: "Will not his majesty terrify you and the dread of him fall upon you?" With the following verse: "Your maxims are proverbs of ashes, your defences are defences of clay", he links the admonition: "If you consider this, that you are comparable to ashes and are made out of clay, then you must surely fear God in the twofold way suggested. Such is the notion of the fear which man should experience before God and by reason of which he is described as God-fearing." Finally, chapter 33 deals with the question how the joy which flows from the right attitude of being before God is compatible with the fear of God: "If the soul recognizes its own lowliness and also the greatness and majesty of God, and recoils from the latter, then it delights in its fear because it has understood the divine roots of this fear and regards it as a token of its own spiritual wholeness and health. If you attain this fear your service of God will be perfect." We are taught this by the psalmist: "Serve the Lord with fear, with trembling kiss his feet" (Ps. 2: 11).

Thus I think I have furnished a certain amount of material (which can easily be enriched and widened by liturgical texts) calculated to illuminate the nature of the fear of God as the right attitude of man, and to show how this note is the sustaining ground of the Jewish faith. At the same time it should be clear that this has nothing to do with the meaning of faith for Christian theology. The Christian religion does not express an attitude of man gained from the realization of the confrontation between the *creatura* and the *creator*—like the Jewish *emuna*—nor any state that can be attained by action in obedience to divine commands, but it is an *opus operatum* made possible by Christ's revelation in man. The Christian faith can neither be defined objectively as *opus* or *virtus sub proprie merito*, nor is it neutrally a mode of being to be aimed at by *poenitentia* and *attritio*; it is always an *imputatio spiritus sancti* made possible by Christ. The gift of faith to man is divinely bestowed. Man cannot attain the mode of being proper to faith, nor even prepare for it. Christianity is the testimony to a *voluntas aliena* in man, the *testimonium internum spiritus sancti*. The creeds of all the Christian churches are at one in this, that it is the divine grace proffered in Christ which is the basis of faith, and by which alone a special quality of life arises in the Christian who is in communion with Christ. There is no such thing as Christian faith resting on man's free choice.

But it is precisely this possibility that is offered by the fear of God, which in Judaism occupies the place that the Christian church assigns to faith. It is a possibility for man which stands in the freedom of his choice.[1] If he opens his heart to God's appeal to the fathers and adheres to the law, then he attains this possibility; for all the commands lead to the disposition that is God-fearing. According to the Proverbs, this fear may be acquired from the study of the law (2: 1–4): "If you receive my words and treasure up my commandments with you . . . then you will understand the fear of the Lord and find the knowledge of God."

This is possible in the last analysis because, for the Jewish faith as contrasted with the Christian, the image of God persists in man even though obscured by sin, and gives man the possibility of understanding his original status as creature and the existence of the world as a creation. The dignity of his spiritual being consists in the fact that he can recognize his own nature in the mirror of God's word latent

---

[1] Cf. Shalom ben Horin, *Die Antwort des Jona*, Hamburg, 1956, 73: "The fear of God can be practised by man. As a thinking ego he thus becomes aware of the infinite qualitative distance between his temporal 'I' and the eternal 'thou'."

in the *tenakh* and that by affirming his creatureliness he can come to the knowledge of the truth about himself. This, however, means the consciousness of man's nothingness, the realization that in himself he is nothing but dust, that by God's power the whole meaning of his life is spiritual. In his very weakness he recognizes God's almighty power, in the realization of his creatureliness he receives the truth and dignity of his being, he is able to be the Creator's creature, and is plastic to the touch of the potter.

Hence the fact that the world is a creation makes possible the human creaturely situation. The law has the office of leading him constantly to realize this situation, as it is only from this situation that the law springs. "For a man who has the knowledge of the law without the fear of God is like a treasurer who has been given only the keys to the inner sanctuary of the treasure house, and not the keys to its outside: how shall he get in?" (Rabba bar R. Huna in Sabb. 31b.) The law does not bind the Jews to God so much as it is the means whereby God in the *berith* has bound Himself to the Jews. And the covenant rests on the *yirath adonai*. The latter is the true attitude of the creature as determined by God, an attitude in which the distant God becomes both distant *and* near, a condition of the soul in which the original creaturely mode of man's being is expressed as a correlation and as *emuna* (faithfulness). The fear of God as the attitude of man recognizing his creaturely status as the truth and thus bowing before God his Creator: this is the Jewish counterposition to all heathen self-affirmation and self-deification, as also to the Christian dogma of the Mediator between Creator and creature. The Jew believes that man can and must always return to the creaturely attitude of the fear of God.

Of course it is not equally easy to attain[1] at all times. Thus Berakh. 33b (Megilla 25a) causes Rabbi Hanina to speak thus: "Is then the fear of God a little thing? If a big thing is desired by a man and then he is granted it, when he has it it seems to him like a little thing; if he desires a little thing and has it not, then that appears to him like a big thing." And if for our present time it must be said that the fear of God is a big thing, in fact the biggest, it none the less remains according to the Jewish faith a possibility for man. If he decides to turn again, not to the law, but primarily to the covenant,

---

[1] I will merely mention here that this dependence on man's understanding of existence as determined by historical time, constitutes the Jewish idea of saving history, as distinct from the profane and evil. Cf. my study: "Theologische Motive in der Dichtung Franz Kafkas", *Neue Rundschau*, 1951, Vol. 3.

then this attitude shines like a beacon guiding him into truth. "The gates of repentance are never closed"—so runs an important sentence of rabbinic writings (Midr. Teh. 65, 4—R. Shemuel bar Nachmani, Am. of the 2nd generation).

The real nearness of God as the mystery implied in being within the covenant is a truth which has never been entirely lost by the Jews in any period of their history. The *kawwanah*, or surrender to God, has flowered even in the thickest undergrowth of juristical debates and decisions; and the Shekinah, which means the real presence of God now, has never departed from Israel, according to her faith. The law can have a history, has had one, and still has one, but the covenant not. For God's covenant with Israel which stands above the law is a covenant embracing all times and generations, as the prophet Jeremiah promised in his vivid image (31: 35–36): "Thus says the Lord, who gives the sun for light by day and the fixed order of the moon and the stars for light by night, who stirs up the sea so that its waves roar—the Lord of hosts is his name: if this fixed order departs from before me, says the Lord, then shall the descendants of Israel cease from being a nation before me for ever." And it is just this truth which Paul, with his assertion of a hardening of Israel and an election of the Gentiles, has ceased to be able to grasp in its entirety, although an affirmation such as that of Rom. 11: 29 really implies a full understanding of the fact of the covenant.

The objective historian of religion must in any case accept the *berith* as the fact in which the Jews believe and as the reality lying behind the object of his study. The correct interpretation of this situation belongs to his concern as a critic; it is not a confession of faith of any particular type. If, however, in this last section Paul's criticism of the law has been placed in the framework of the history of the Jewish religion, and has been explained as a possible means to the renewal of the classic Judaic fear of God and a new realization of the meaning of the covenant, even though this means in fact has never been adopted, this was done because the historian of religion is concerned to do justice to every aspect of a matter. The Jews might with some justice describe the venture as the rescue of the heretic.

INDEX OF MODERN AUTHORS